The Travel Chronicles of Mrs. J. Theodore Bent

Volume I: Greece and the Levantine Littoral

Mabel Virginia Anna Bent

WORLD ENOUGH, AND TIME

The Travel Chronicles of Mrs. J. Theodore Bent
Volume I: Greece and the Levantine Littoral

Mabel Bent's diaries of 1883–1898, from the archive of
the Joint Library of the Hellenic and Roman Societies,
London

Published for the first time, with additional material by
Gerald Brisch

The Travel Chronicles of Mrs. J. Theodore Bent:

Volume I.   *World Enough, and Time: Greece and the Levantine Littoral*
Volume II. *Make Our Sun Stand Still: The African Journeys*
Volume III. *Deserts of Vast Eternity: Southern Arabia and Persia*

Also available in the Archaeopress 3rdguides Series:

J. Theodore Bent, *The Cyclades, or Life Among the Insular Greeks*
Cecil Torr, *Rhodes in Ancient Times*
Cecil Torr, *Rhodes in Modern Times*
Christopher Wordsworth, *Athens and Attica*

The Travel Chronicles of Mrs. J. Theodore Bent
Volume I. World Enough, and Time: Greece and the Levantine Littoral

© Archaeopress and Gerald Brisch 2006. Unless specified, this transcription and all material © Gerald Brisch 2006.

3rdguides is an imprint of
Archaeopress
First and Second Floor
13-14 Market Square
Bicester
OX26 6AD, UK
www.archaeopress.com

All rights reserved. No part of this publication may be reproduced, stored in a retrieval system, or transmitted, in any form or by any means, electronic, mechanical, photocopying, recording or otherwise, without the prior permission of the publishers.

ISBN 978-1-90573-902-8

3rdguides series editor: Gerald Brisch

Cover photograph © Nikos Kasseris (Ólymbos, Kárpathos)

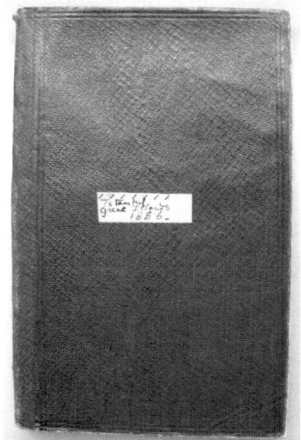

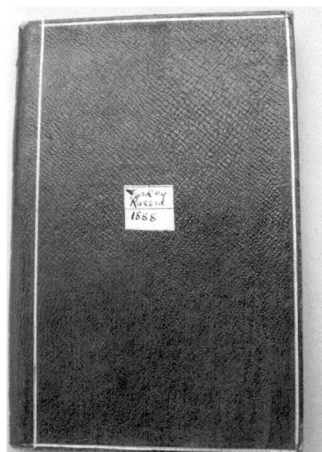

Mabel Bent's Chronicle *covers. Top left: the Dodecanese, 1885; top right: the Eastern Aegean, 1886; lower left: the Northern Aegean, 1887; lower right: the Turkish coast, 1888.*

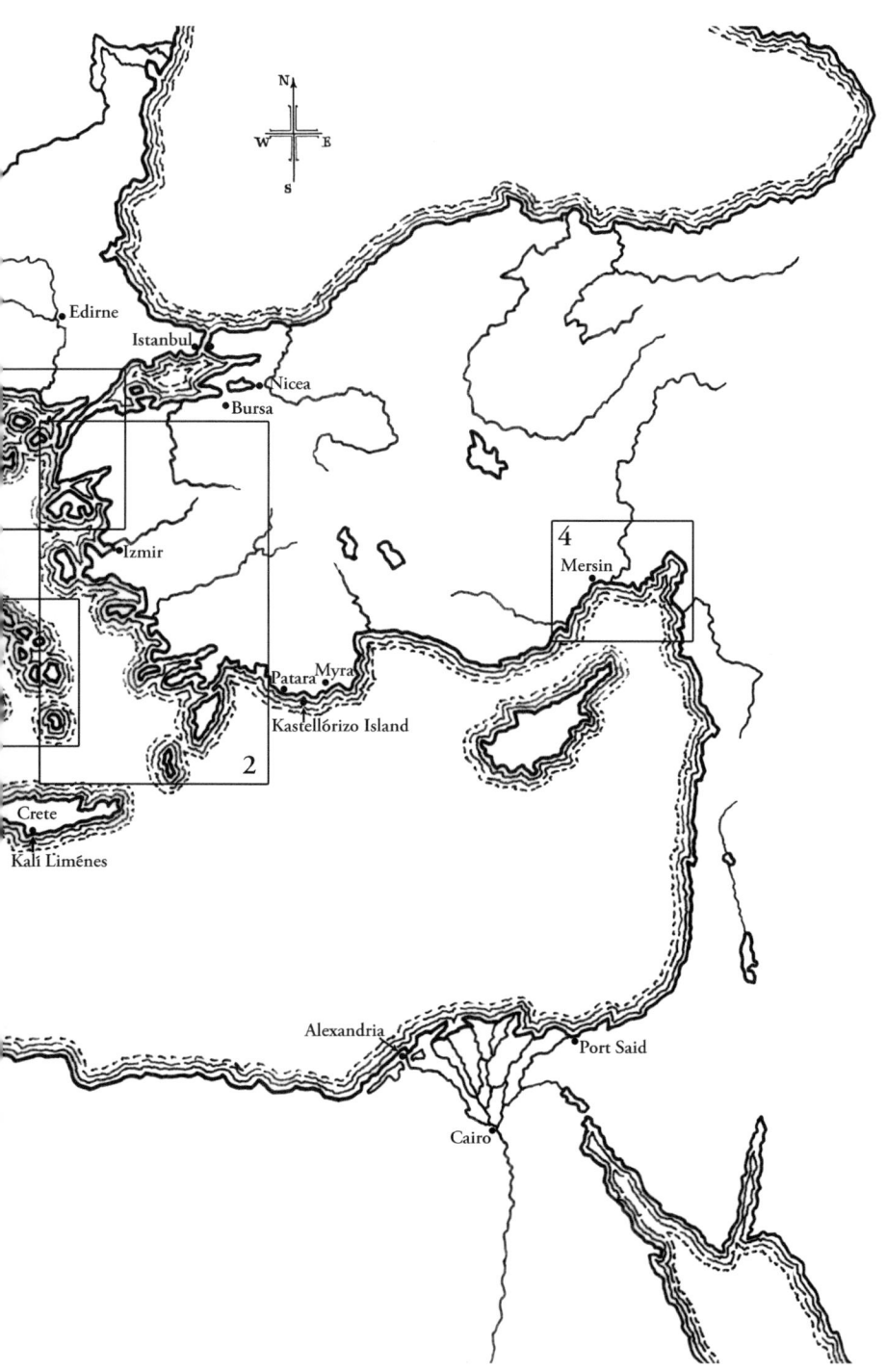

Indeed it is quite an art to arrange Aegean travel… [The] only course is to soak yourself in that most fascinating of travel literature, the sailings of Greek island boats…To me this is the most moving poetry of travel: the Neraïdha leaves daily at 8 a.m. for Aegina, Methana, Poros, Hydra and Spetsai; the Helioupolis leaves at 9 p.m. on Thursday for Andros, Córthion, Ysternia, Tinos, Syra; the Anatoli leaves on Friday at 7 p.m. for Syra, Paros, Naxos, Heracléia, Amorgòs, Anáphi, Thera, Pholégandros, Síkinos and Niòs; the Messaria leaves on Saturday at noon for Zià, Cýthnos, Syra, Sériphos, Siphnos, Milos and Címolos; and on Saturday afternoon the Aighaion leaves for Mýconos, Samos, Leros, Cálymnos, Symi and Rhodes. One would like to go everywhere…

Robert Liddell, *Aegean Greece*

The sea, autumn mildness, islands bathed in light, fine rain spreading a diaphanous veil over the immortal nakedness of Greece. Happy is the man, I thought, who, before dying, has the good fortune to sail the Aegean Sea.

Nikos Kazantzakis, *Zorba the Greek*
(translated by Carl Wildman)

Contents

List of illustrations and maps	xii
Introduction	xv
Acknowledgements	xxiii
Notes to this edition	xxv
The Chronicles	
The Cyclades, 1883–1884	1
The Dodecanese, 1885	63
The Eastern Aegean, 1886	127
The Northern Aegean, 1887	181
Cruising the Turkish Coast, 1888	225
'Rough Cilicia', 1890	263
Athens, 1896	322
Athens, 1898	327
Bibliography and sources	333
Sidetrack – A tale of two dragomans	339
Index of principal characters	345
Index of place names	359
Illustration and map credits	365

List of illustrations

Frontispiece	Mabel Virginia Anna Bent	ii
1	Mabel Bent's *Chronicle* covers.	v
2	James Theodore Bent.	xxii
3	Limestone figure from Kárpathos.	66
4	Theodore Bent's *samboúna,* acquired in the Dodecanese in 1885.	126
5	Theodore Bent's *lýra,* acquired in the Dodecanese in 1885.	128
6	The Bents' find of Fl. Vibia Sabina (2nd century AD) in 1877.	201
7	Three of Mabel's doodles.	261
8	The mandragora leaf Mabel pinned into her 1890 *Chronicle.*	272
9	'A ladder was needed…and very cleverly it was managed.' This paper print, taken in 'Rough Cilicia' by Mabel, was inserted in her 1890 *Chronicle.*	281
10	An example of Mabel's handwriting from her 1896 *Chronicle.*	324
11	Theodore and Mabel's grave and memorial (on the right) in the churchyard of St Mary's, Theydon Bois, Essex.	326
12	Mabel took this photograph in Socotra in 1897. Theodore is seated on the left. The figure	340

	standing on the right is thought to be the Bents' long-serving dragoman, Manthaios Símos from Anáfi in the Cyclades.	
13	Sir William White, H. B. M. Ambassador, and his staff in Istanbul during the Bents' travels in Turkey.	344
14	The early branches of the Hall-Dare family tree.	357
15	The Grand Hôtel D'Angleterre, Ermoúpoli (1905). Mabel's hotel of choice on Sýros.	358

List of maps

1.	The Eastern Mediterranean	vi–vii
2.	The Cyclades (from J. Theodore Bent, 1885)	4–5
3.	The Dodecanese and Eastern Aegean	62
4.	The Northern Aegean	180
5.	'Loryma' (top) and 'Lissae' and 'Lydae' (below), Theodore Bent's own details from a contemporary Admiralty Chart	224
6.	'Rough Cilicia'	262
7.	'Part of Cilicia Tracheia', Theodore Bent's own map of their routes in the area	268

Introducing Mabel Bent's *Chronicles*

'...serious doubts as to the advisability of a lady undertaking such a journey were frequently brought before us at the outset; fortified however by previous experiences in Persia, Asia Minor, and the Greek islands, we hardly gave these doubts more than a passing thought, and the event proved that they were wholly unnecessary. My wife was the only one of our party who escaped from fever, never having a day's illness during the whole year that we were away from home... She was able to take a good many photographs under circumstances of exceptional difficulty, and instead of being, as was prophesied, a burden to the expedition, she furthered its interests and contributed to the ultimate success in more ways than one.'
(J. Theodore Bent, *The Ruined Cities of Mashonaland*, 1892)

In the fifth decade of Victoria's reign, two paths brought together an indefatigable Anglo-Irishwoman of means and an Englishman of mettle; on the second of August 1877 they married. The newly-weds, she thirty-one, he twenty-five, moved to live in London, a stone's throw from Marble Arch, at 13 Great Cumberland Place, W., and within a few months the couple were off on a series of inseparable, breathless, annual trips that were to continue until, twenty years later, on the fifth of May 1897, the Englishman, an 'archaeological adventurer', died from malarial complications, and Mabel Virginia Anna Bent found herself once more on a solitary path, left with her memories and an assemblage of travel *Chronicles*, that she 'always wrote during [their] journeys'.[1] After her death, formidable and eighty-three, in 1929, these *Chronicles* in the form of two dozen small leather notebooks found their way into the archive of the Hellenic Society, out of the light and overlooked. These are the journey accounts of Mr and Mrs J. Theodore Bent. And what journeys.

---

[1] Preface to *Southern Arabia* (1900).

Sooner or later, today's tourists who venture as far east as Karachi, south as Cape Town, west as Lisbon, north as Warsaw, will undoubtedly find themselves on a route once followed by the Bents. Before the invention of flight, they were the amongst the most-travelled husband and wife teams of their generation: the coverers of goodness knows how many equivalent circuits around the globe by ship, train, carriage and cart, on horse, camel, mule or donkey, and, of course, on foot. Thousands of miles under hot sun, nights under canvas, in regions where every other European might expect to have his or her life drastically shortened by illness or injury: as was the fate of Theodore… at the age of forty-five. And the reasons for all this effort and expense? Their objectives? The modern bibliographies that have to do with archaeology, anthropology, ethnography, botany, and other fields with similar suffixes, in regions from Abyssinia to Zimbabwe, are still very likely to refer to the articles, papers and monographs of Bent, J. Theodore, and, occasionally, Bent, Mrs J. Theodore. In addition they were alert commentators and observers, they enjoyed their food and drink, music, customs and costumes. They also felt they had a duty to minister to the sick as much as they could – with a great medicine chest full of arrowroot, brandy, quinine, and demijohns of Brand's Beef Tea.[2] They were fortunate; they were comfortably off Victorians (their atlases were stamped the colour of their monarch's soldiers' jackets) and, blessed with extraordinary stamina, they had world enough, and time…before the great wars.

In pursuit of their researches, their reputations increasing with each campaign, the Bents preferred to travel abroad during winter and spring, returning to London (and from there making shorter journeys to see friends and family around Ireland and the English countryside) for long, pleasant summers, and to write up their findings, lecture, and plan next season's adventure. Mabel's *Chronicles* provided Theodore with much of the background material he was to use for his monographs and articles. A look at his long list of publications brings into focus three concentric, geographical circles – the Eastern Mediterranean (Greece and Turkey), the greater continent of Africa, and the Near and Middle East. And this is how his wife's travel *Chronicles* are presented

---

[2] The notion of 'product placement' is, of course, a few years' off, although Theodore was not averse to asking for sponsorship from bodies such as the Royal Geographical Society and the British Association for the Advancement of Science.

in this, the first, publication of her notebooks: in three volumes, chronologically, and within these regions.

This first[3] volume of the *Chronicles* includes the couple's archaeological and ethnographical findings, over a total period of some twenty years, in the Eastern Mediterranean, representing Theodore's significant finds in the Cyclades, the eastern islands, and northern Greece (then Turkey). Each of the following transcriptions of Mabel Bent's travel notebooks in this region is introduced in turn, so all that is required here is a brief introduction to the two leading characters.

Mabel was born in Ireland on the twenty-eighth of January 1846, the second of four daughters, born to Robert Westley Hall-Dare of Theydon Bois, Wennington Hall, Essex, and Newtownbarry House, Co. Wexford, by his marriage to Frances,[4] daughter of Mr Gustavus Lambart, of Beauparc, Co. Meath (a descendant of a younger son of the first Earl of Cavan. Mabel was educated at home by governesses and masters and developed a sharp intellect, a gift for languages, practical skills (she was to become a pioneer travel photographer), and a thorough grounding in what might be called 'common sense'. Five feet eight inches tall, a green-eyed, sturdy redhead – striking in her photographs – her flaming, plaited hair was often the subject of native wonder.[5] Outgoing and confident, she was as happy taking

---

[3] The second and third volumes will give Mabel's personal accounts of their other major expeditions – into Arabia (and on which much of Theodore's reputation is based today), and Africa (in particular the couple's finds in Abyssinia and Mashonaland).

[4] Frances gave birth to eight children: Robert (b. 1840), Olivia (Iva) (1843–1906), Adelaide (1844–1850), Mabel (1846–1929), Ethel (1848–1930), Fanny (b. and d. 1856), Frances (Faneen) (b. 1859), and Charles (1860–1876). Tragically, Charles accidentally shot himself in the train on the way to school, the year before Mabel married Theodore; she never refers to the incident.

[5] Keeping up appearances in the bush was obviously difficult, as a fellow traveller to Mashonaland, central Africa, confides: 'One Sunday afternoon [October 1891] some interesting visitors appeared at the door of our hut. They were Mr. and Mrs. Bent…We had hardly shaken hands, when Mrs. Bent asked us what we thought of her dress. This was most difficult to answer. Mrs. Bent's costume consisted of an ordinary print blouse, worn over obvious stays; a woollen kilt, reaching to just below her knees; knickerbockers; top boots; and a pith helmet. We gently suggested that if the fair explorer had consulted Redfern, or, better still, Martin of Dublin, either would have built her something much more workmanlike and beguiling. After this Mrs. Bent made herself very pleasant, showed us photographs which she had taken with much skill, a talent which was no doubt of great use to her husband' (*Adventures in Mashonaland* by Rose Blennerhasset,1893). Mabel is not so forward in her account of the meeting in her *Chronicle*: 'Yesterday we went up to visit the hospital nurses: Misses Blennerhasset, Welby and Slieman. Very pleasant they were and lent us some books.' (This editor is very grateful to John Theakstone for bringing Miss Blennerhasset's diverting aside to his attention.)

fences at full gallop in her native Wexford as she was dining with British ambassadors in Cairo or Constantinople.

Travellers are often obsessed with food and Mabel's accounts of meals, good and bad, and delicacies (she loved *myzíthra* cheese and hated *oúzo*) are always to be savoured. Fascinating, too, are the lists of accessories and gear the couple have to transport everywhere with them. They certainly did not believe in travelling light. Included with all the paraphernalia, especially on her later expeditions, were cases of cameras and photographic equipment (with portable darkroom); sadly, very view of her prints or plates have survived.

As for the hundreds of characters they journey with and meet along the way, rather than add to the inescapable quantities of footnotes, an Index of principal characters is provided at the end of this volume. Soon appearing in the first *Chronicle* is one Manthaios Símos, the Bents' trusted Greek dragoman. He is to remain by their side on nearly every trip over the next fifteen years, and his story is told in the Sidetrack on page 339.

However, the resources of character that enabled her to cope with the day-to-day hardships and practicalities of travel in the remote corners of Africa and the Near East are sometimes reflected in her *Chronicles* in a less than totally flattering light. Every reader will have to decide for themselves how likeable she was – bearing in mind the attitudes of the time. Certainly Gertrude Bell, another leading 'Arabist', was firm in her opinion (in a letter to her father, February 1900): 'I met Mrs. Theodore Bent, but having thrown down the Salaam, as we say in my tongue, I rapidly fled, for I do not like her. She is the sort of woman the refrain of whose conversation is: "You see, I have seen things so much more interesting" or "I have seen so many of these, only bigger and older"…I wonder if Theodore Bent liked her.'

Theodore, by all accounts, was likeable. He was born in Baildon, near Leeds, on the thirtieth of March 1852. In contrast to Mabel's large family he was an only child, the son of James Bent and Margaret Lambert. The family home was Baildon House, Theodore leaving there for preparatory school first at Malvern Wells before Repton and Wadham College, Oxford, where he graduated in 1875 with a Second in modern history. Fair-haired, blue-eyed, short and stocky, the twenty-three-year-old Bent had a predictable legal career lined up and he moved to Lincoln's Inn as a student of law; however, he was never called to the bar. Of private means he was able to make a career for himself first as an historian, and later as an 'archaeological explorer'. He was boyishly enthusiastic, resilient, and hard to dissuade from a course of action (or from some of his more eccentric theories) once his mind was made up. Suffice it to say, he was a friend of the great adventure-writer Rider Haggard (who called Theodore's death 'so great a loss'), and, as much as anything, a Rider Haggard character, once viewed as such, is not the least appropriate way of imagining Theodore Bent.

Their last journey together was to Socotra, in the Gulf of Aden, in March 1897. Theodore died on the fifth of May 1897, back in London, from pneumonia following on from malarial fever. Mabel, understandably, lost her desire to travel and her last *Chronicle* (1898) is prefaced 'A lonely useless journey'. After a few trips by herself to Egypt and Jerusalem[6] (she was an adherent of the Anglo-Israelite theory, and for a few years was a Keeper of the Garden Tomb in Jerusalem) she retired to her London town house, where she enjoyed entertaining her many nieces and nephews, feeding them, apparently, quantities of nourishing artichoke soup. The couple had no children, and Theodore no siblings, but Mabel's *Chronicles* often include references to her aunts and sisters, and they strike a pleasant, domestic chord. Bit by bit she disposed of the many souvenirs the two of them had brought back to London, finally letting the British Museum have, a few years before her death, her last remaining finds from the Cyclades, including the little jug that she acquired with Theodore on the islet of Thirassía, opposite Santoríni, The little artefact is now in Room 11 of the Museum,

---

[6] Coincidentally, a further Jerusalem reference provides an insight into how Mabel might have passed any idle hours (she always had a little sewing in her pocket too). The Bodleian Library has a copy of a tiny book of patience card games she published herself in 1903. Inside this book is a folded letter to card-game specialist and collector F. E. Jessel, who is keen to see her 'little whist markers'. She would have replied to him earlier, but having "...only just come home from Jerusalem... I wonder if you could call tomorrow afternoon after 4 as then I am sure to be at home. If not we must fix another time. Yours faithfully, Mabel V. A. Bent'. She had other admirers. There is an odd printed dedication in Thomas Fitzpatrick's *An Autumn Cruise in the Aegean: A Transatlantic Holiday* (London, 1886), 'To Mrs. Theodore Bent, distinguished among her sex for the ardent pursuit of Eastern travel and exploration, these jottings of a holiday tour in the West are, with sincere apologies, inscribed by the author.'

labelled, 'Pottery jug decorated with eye-like circles and dots, *c.* 1500 BC'. It is a characterful and assertive piece – it would have reminded Mabel of Theodore.[7]

Mabel Bent died at 13 Great Cumberland Place, W, on the fifth of July 1929 at the age of eighty-three. Her *Times* obituary (6 July 1929)[8] includes that, as an experienced photographer and accurate observer, she was of enormous assistance to her husband and 'famous for the explorations in distant lands which she undertook with [him]. This was at a time when it was much more rare than it is now for a woman to venture forth on such journeys […] During her long widowhood of more than 30 years Mrs. Bent was well known in literary and scientific London. She was a good talker, with an occasional sharpness of phrase which was much relished by her many friends.'

And would there be any 'sharpness of phrase' about seeing her *Chronicles* in print? Did Mabel intend them for publication? Apart from the fact that Theodore relied on the leather notebooks for the provision of background details in most of his publications, the chronicler has left one or two clues within her pages. From Room 2 of the Hôtel de Byzance, Constantinople, in February 1886, Mabel confides: 'I must begin my Chronicle somewhere if I am to write one at all and as in this matter I am selfish enough to consider myself of the first consideration because I write to remind myself in my old age of pleasant things (or the contrary) I will begin now.' So we know, at least, that they were for her to read later in life, and that she intended her aunts, sisters, and nieces to share her adventures. (There are several asides such as, 'We have constant patients coming to us and I am sure you would all laugh to hear T's medical lectures.' And 'You must excuse these smudges as I am sitting cross-legged on T's bed.') There is also certainly nothing in the millions of words that could be classified as terribly indiscreet, let alone anything close to libel – or nuptial intimacy

---

[7] The Bents brought back with them hundreds of items and had associations with many of the leading English societies and institutions. The *Chronicles* go into detail here and there. The largest assemblage today is housed in the British Museum, with a choice, but much smaller, collection in the Pitt Rivers Museum, Oxford. In addition, the Bents had dealings with the Royal Botanic Gardens at Kew, the Natural History Museum, and the Victoria and Albert Museum.

[8] The obituary begins: 'An explorer's wife and Companion. Mrs. Theodore Bent, who died yesterday at her home in Great Cumberland Place, at the age of 83, was famous for the explorations in distant lands which she undertook with her husband.'

for that matter, although there is a little false modesty and coquetry here and there. (Only two or three pages are missing from the entire series of notebooks.) But the most obvious hint that Mabel, at the very least, might be aware of a potential wider interest in her *Chronicles* is the letter still preserved (in the 1885 volume) from her friend, Mary Graham, complimenting her thus: 'I carried off your Chronicle…and… I never enjoyed these hours more than when reading it in the train coming down here yesterday – as soon as I have finished it I will send it you back – but why oh why don't you publish it? It simply bristles with epigrams and I am certain would be a great success! You ought to blend the 2 Chronicles into one and I am sure everyone would buy it.' (Letter, December 1885)

Well. Perhaps not everyone. Mabel's *Chronicles* are not great travel literature; even someone as fond of her as I have become over the past five years would never be able to support that. They are her on-the-spot recollections of long days spent trekking, exploring, digging, dealing with villagers, arguing with minor officials; they are snatches of gossip, snobbishness, likes and dislikes, barking dogs, vicissitudes, poverty and pain; they are delightful souvenirs of music, dancing, colourful costumes and wonderful meals. Great travel literature? No. But great travel writing – accounts of wonderful endurance and a reflection of courage, attitude, apogee of empire, and spirit – most certainly. *Chronicles* any of us, openly or secretly, might have been happy to write, had we but world enough, and time.

Gerald Brisch

Oxford – Anáfi
September 2006

James Theodore Bent

Acknowledgements

The Bents were early members of the Hellenic Society, founded in 1879, with Theodore being on the Council for several years. This project to publish, in three volumes, all the travel notebooks of Mabel Bent could not have been undertaken without the support and assistance of the Society, and I am most grateful to Russell Shone and the Officers and Council for their permission to publish transcriptions of these notebooks for the first time.

The Society helps to maintain the Joint Library, in conjunction with the Roman Society, in whose archives Mabel's *Chronicles* are preserved. I am extremely grateful to the Librarian, Colin Annis, his Deputy, Paul Jackson, and staff, for all their help over several years. In particular, I am delighted to thank my friend and Senior Library Assistant, Susan Willetts, who has been unfailingly kind, enthusiastic and diligent in all matters to do with Mabel – as we have referred to her since the project began.

Mabel and Theodore had no children, but several descendants of Mabel's siblings have been overly generous with their time in replying to my many questions and requests for family information. Among them I must thank Mrs Clody Norton, who initially opened the door for me to the remarkable Hall-Dare family, Captain Beauchamp Blackett, and Mrs Caroline Bond, who wrote that Mabel's hair was, of course and as hoped for, red.

Many specialists and institutions have supplied information and material. At the British Museum I would like to express gratitude to Thorsten Opper and the Department of Greek and Roman Studies. Jeremy Coote at the Pitt Rivers Museum, Oxford, advised on the museum's fascinating collection of objects acquired by the Bents. The Records and Archives Department of the Victoria and Albert Museum, and the Library of the Royal Geographical Society, have been most helpful. Staff at the Bodleian Library Map Room and Aberdeen Library and Information Services are also due thanks.

Of the many fellow travellers on this project, so far, and providers of serendipitous and appreciated details along the way, I would like to mention David Davison, Rajka Makjanić, Wendy Logue, Paul Naish, Martin Biddle, Birthe Kjølbye-Biddle, John Theakstone, Brenda Stones, Glyn Griffiths, Revis Cruttenden, Michael Nisiriou, Yanna Bitha, Nikos Kasseris, Andreas Michaelopoulos, and William Pryor Binney.

This first volume of Mabel Bent's *Chronicles* is for my mother, Susan Brisch.

G. E. B.

Notes to this edition

'I decided, acting on advice, just to put the whole thing into as consecutive a form as possible, only saying that the least of the writing is mine…' (Mabel Bent, *Southern Arabia*, 1900)

When faced with the long transliteration process presented by these *Chronicles*, the first decision taken by this editor was to try and speed the reader along as much as possible over Mabel's twenty-year journey.

Any journal writer, or private diarist, writing longhand, will be aware of the stylistic shortcuts, idiosyncrasies, and disregard for consistency and accuracy that develop after a while…ampersands, repetitions, one-line paragraphs, inconsistencies of spelling (particularly for place names, accents/diacritics, and the like), and much else besides. They, inevitably, tend to impede or trip up newcomers to the chronicler's work, so they have been smoothed over, as much as possible, in the pages that follow.

These, then, are not facsimile transcripts of Mabel Bent's travel notebooks – although her actual *words* are unmolested. No attempt has been made to retain Mabel's pagination. (She averages about 120 words per page.) In the whole series of notebooks, only three or four pages look to have been deliberately removed. Occasionally there are blanks left for names and dates – obviously Mabel intended to fill them in later. Her handwriting is remarkably clear (unlike Theodore's) and only a handful of words in the following thousands have proved illegible and defeated the wonders of digital enhancement. For graphologists a sample page is reproduced, alongside its transcription, later in the work (page 324). The actual size of Mabel's writing does vary – depending on her nib (almost never resorting to pencil), her location, her state of health or mind, and whether she felt she had enough pages left in her notebook for the weeks to come. Several journeys are recorded in more than one book: she travelled with only a small stock of them.

Readers should be aware of the calendar differences then in effect between Europe and the Eastern Mediterranean. Place names, too, present the usual difficulties. Phonetic variations result in frequent spelling inconsistencies. Generally, Mabel's first choice has been adopted for future references, but where there may be justification to vary them her preferences have been respected. Editorial intrusions, within the text itself, are limited and placed within square brackets. It was thought helpful to emphasize and extend dates in bold type. Other intrusions extend to short introductions before each *Chronicle*, and far too many footnotes – although people and place identifiers have been removed to separate Indices. The maps are not intended to replace the armchair-travellers' personal favourites.

Abbreviations

Theodore was a frequent contributor to the *Journal of Hellenic Studies*, which is abbreviated in the following text to *JHS*; and *Royal Geographical Society* is also abbreviated, to *RGS*.

The Chronicler's language and attitudes: an apology

So many Victorian attitudes and prejudices are unacceptable today, and Mabel Bent was very much of her time and class. There must be, however, social and historical value in these attitudes and prejudices, so the present editor has deliberately opted not to delete words and phrases that would sit very unhappily and unwelcomed in modern texts. Nevertheless this editor and the present publishers take this opportunity of apologising if any of Mabel's language should cause offence.

Chronicle I, November 1883 to May 1884:
The Bents leave Marble Arch for Mýkonos…

After their marriage on 2 August 1877, at Newtownbarry House, county Wexford, Theodore and Mabel begin their twenty-year series of regular annual travels. Having decided a barrister's life was not for him, and with a career as an historian, perhaps, ahead, Theodore guides his new wife down through to Italy, which they revisit over the next few seasons. These tours result in a sequence of short monographs and articles on, amongst other topics, Garibaldi, Genoa, and San Marino (they both henceforth proudly acknowledge the honour conferred on them of 'citizenship' of that little republic).

Meanwhile, the English journals are starting to fill with the archaeological discoveries coming to light in Greece and Turkey. This was the great period of pioneering archaeological work at Troy and Mycenae, and the curious Theodore embarks with Mabel on their first tour of the region in 1882… and they obviously enjoy what they find. They explore the Greek mainland and some of the Aegean islands, including a hasty sail around the Cyclades. What he had managed to see on this scattering of submerged limestone mountaintops and exploded volcanoes that encircle mythical Délos convinced Theodore that there was much to gain – archaeologically and ethnographically – from a lengthier and more in-depth exploration of them:

'…these islands, especially the smaller ones, offer unusual facilities for the study of the manners and customs of the Greeks as they are, with a view to comparing them with those of the Greeks as they were…' (from the Preface to Theodore's *The Cyclades, or Life Among the Insular Greeks*).

There is no *Chronicle* in this present collection of Mabel's 1882/3 travels, but there are several references to them in this, and later,

Chronicles, as well as in the many articles written by Theodore subsequently, in particular his contentious paper 'Two Turkish Islands Today' (*Macmillan's Magazine/Littell's Living Age*, September 1883), protesting conditions on Sámos and Chíos. It caused quite a stir (Arthur Evans had written on a similar theme a few years before) and questions were even raised in the House; Theodore was to regret the consequences as, understandably, the Turkish authorities were less than enthusiastic to his requests to research in their territories in future.

That first trip prepared the way for a further six years of extended voyages around Greece and Turkey, and kindled in Theodore an interest in archaeology, which, from then on, was to assume equal importance for him to his historical and anthropological enquiries into the regions he chose to explore.

November 1883, therefore, sees the couple start their second trip together to the eastern Mediterranean. What Theodore had seen in the Cyclades in the spring of 1883 convinced him that a little *ad hoc* spadework on these little islands might produce some tangible rewards. He was right; his discoveries on Andíparos led to new theories for a distinct 'Cycladic culture' sandwiched, geographically if not always chronologically, between the Minoan and the Mycenaean. He and his small team of excavators found several unopened graves, and there is a letter from Theodore, dated 30 May 1884, to the Keeper of Antiquities at the British Museum enquiring, 'Do you care to make me an offer for my figures, vases, ornaments, etc., from Antiparos? It occurs to me that a collection of this nature is rather lost in private hands.' These artefacts now form the core of the Bronze Age Cycladic collection in Great Russell Street, and were first published in the Journal of the newly established Hellenic Society shortly after the couple's return in 1884.

Mabel's *Chronicle* of these months provided her husband, in addition to his own notes, with much of the material he used to write what has remained the most entertaining of English accounts of the area, *The Cyclades, or Life Among the Insular Greeks* (London, 1885). It is clear that Theodore relied heavily on his wife's journals to help him when it came to the writing-up stages of his own material; he often quotes her verbatim, especially relying on her for colourful references to costumes, customs, board and lodgings.

Mabel's modest notebook begins at the end of November 1883, accompanying its owner from London to Calais – Naples – Athens – around the Cyclades – Athens – Corinth – Corfu – Brindisi – Ancona – Loreto – Bologna – Bellinzona – Basle – Calais, and finally returning home again to 13 Great Cumberland Place, London, by mid-April 1884.

On their 1882/3 trip the Bents employed a translator (Kostandinos Verviziotes) for the Greek mainland, and one George Phaedros of Smyrna for their tour of the islands. For 1883/4 they decided to reemploy George as their *dragomános*, or translator/factotum. His efforts, however, are less than satisfactory and he is 'let go', on Náxos, in favour of Manthaios Símos of Anáfi. They meet, casually, in a remote mountain village, but it turns out to be the beginning of a relationship that is to last until Theodore's death in 1897. With only a few exceptions, Manthaios is to rejoin the British travellers every seaon on their explorations. In their early years in Greece, before they both acquired the language, their new dragoman was invaluable in terms of helping with provisions, travel and accommodation. There were then no hotels between Sýros and Crete, and the couple had to rely on local hospitality – towards which they were usually expected to contribute – or their own tents.

They transported a large amount of luggage with them, augmented all the time, it seems, by archaeological finds, souvenirs, and, especially, embroideries and fabrics. Their possessions included a much-used medicine chest; both Mabel and Theodore considered it their duty to provide medical care when they could. On Ándros, Theodore was in need of treatment himself, and we hear of the first in a series of fevers to which he was susceptible.

A feature of her *Chronicles* is Mabel's (often gossipy) references to her fellow travellers and other characters they meet along the way – particularly in capital cities and towns, and on board various, very slow, steamers. These cast-lists include Empire servants, missionaries, archaeologists and scholars, friends, occasionally family, and casual acquaintances. Rather than footnote them in the following pages, an Index, with a line or two in the way of biographical detail if appropriate, is provided (of those men and women who could be traced) on page 345. It is pleasurable for Mabel, and us, to bump into again later, by

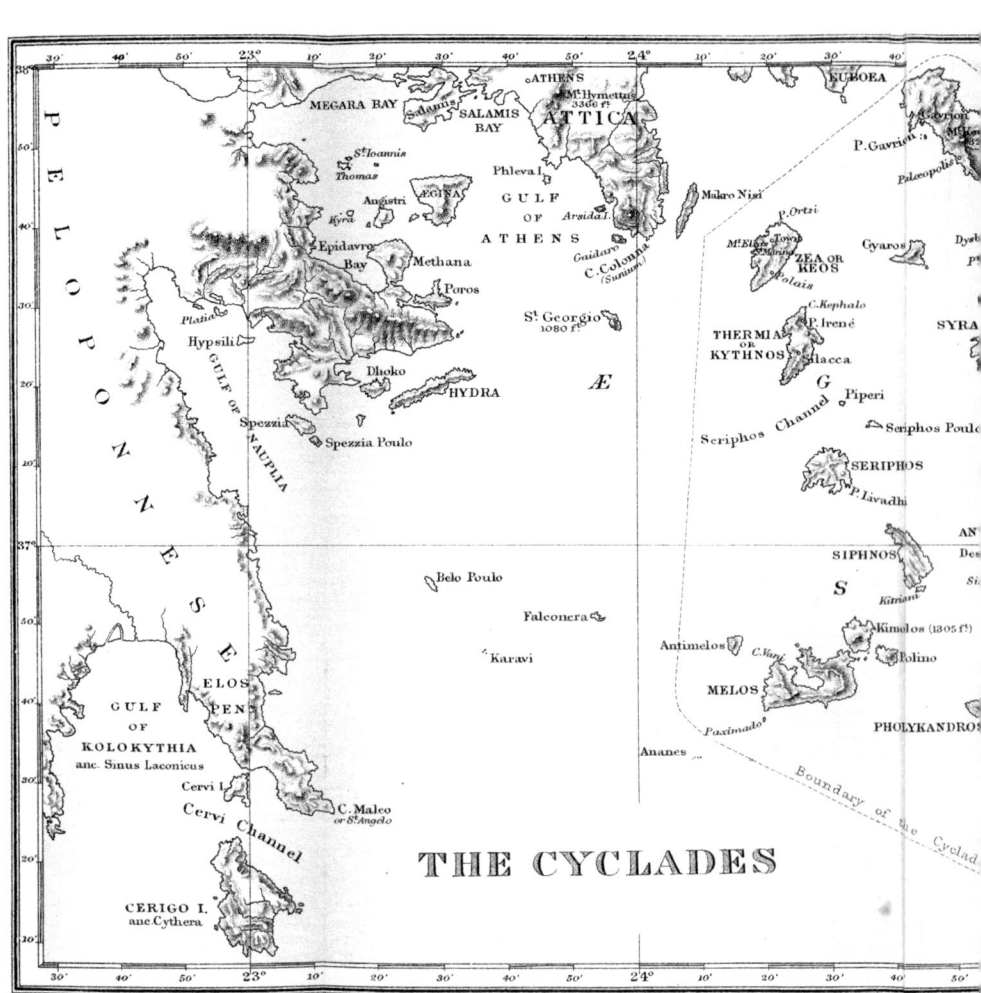

Map 2. The Cyclades (from J. Theodore Bent, 1885)

The Cyclades, 1883–1884

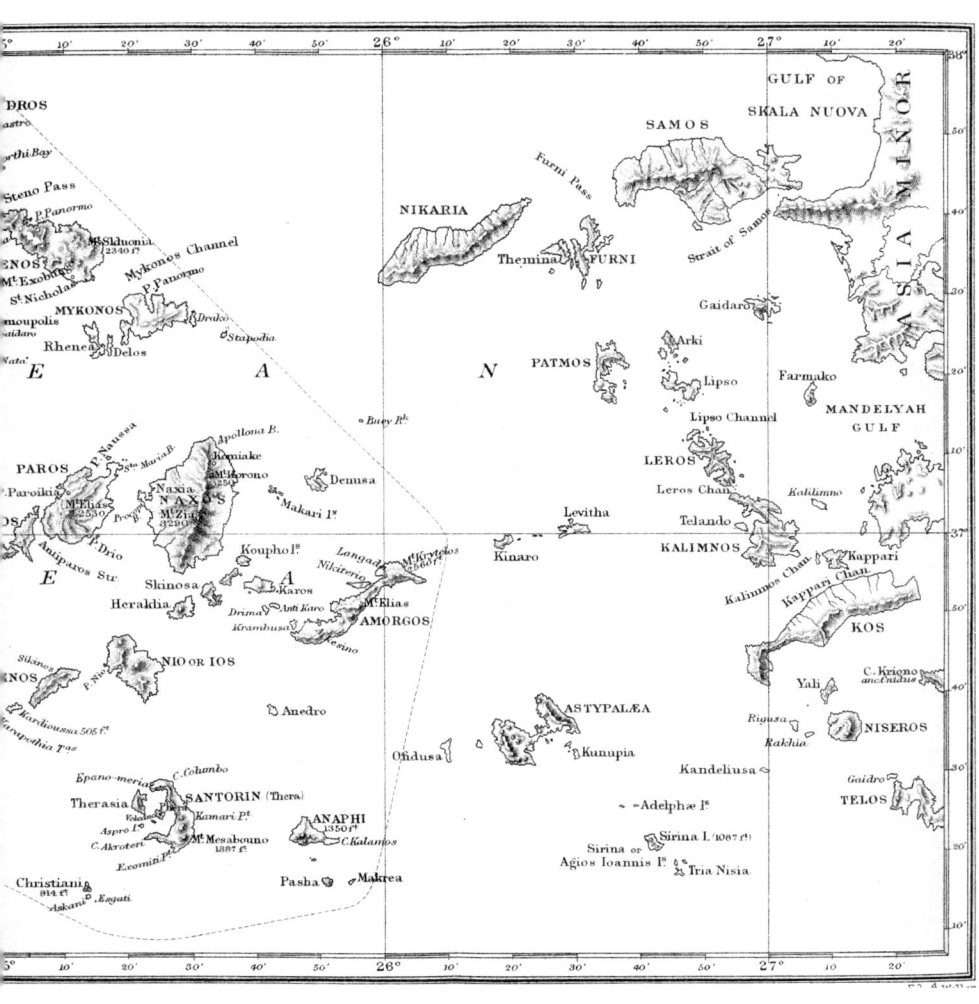

chance, characters we have met before on these remote islands. Also worthy of note from this 1883/4 *Chronicle* are the Swan brothers, John and Robert, calamine miners, living and working on Andíparos. They become firm friends and Robert, in 1891, joins the Bents as a specialist engineer on their journey to Africa.

One newsworthy event is alluded to by Mabel. As the travellers sail around the islands, the dawn and evening skies are stained by the débris from far-distant Krakatoa, which erupted so devastatingly on 27 August 1883.

Before we join Mabel in her travel *Chronicle* of the Cyclades, there are a few last-minute details to attend to. Notes on this transcription appear on page xxv. It is Mabel's practice to refer to her husband as T throughout, and their Greek assistant, Manthaios, as M. This first *Chronicle* is written in a lined and columned accounts book (£/ s/d, of course); it has marbled endpapers and edges and measures 175 x 110mm. Mabel completes 94 of its 130 leaves. The book once belonged to Theodore and he has written in the back of it 'J. T. Bent. Acct. Book. Oct. 13th 1871'. He would have been nineteen and about to enter Wadham College, Oxford. It is as if, just before they set out for their second trip to Greece in November 1883, one of the couple hits upon the idea that Mabel should keep a record of the trip, and a simple, dark-red leather notebook that has been lying around the house for twelve summers is the first thing that comes to hand. But from this inconsequential idea flows a fifteen-year stream of travel diaries unparalleled in their scope and addictive in their appeal.

We can begin, at last, Mabel's Cycladic *Chronicle*, her first, in Athens on Monday, 26 November 1883, at the Hôtel des Etrangers…

Mabel Bent, her Chronicle in
The Kyklades
1883–4

Dedicated to my Sisters and my Aunts

Υπομονή[1]

November 1883 – Athens

Monday, November [26th?]. Hôtel des Etrangers, Athens. We, that is Theodore and I, arrived here last Thursday, having come by the M.M.S.S. *Cumbadge*, the same we came by last Jan.,[2] and travelled straight from London with the exception of sleeping at Calais. We saw Miss S. Forbes there in the morning. We stopped at Naples a couple of hours and delivered Iva's wedding presents and made acquaintance with her husband. Our voyage was prosperous and uneventful. No very interesting passengers. Mr. Kennedy, Sec. B. Emb. at Constantinople, and his wife came on at Naples but they were too sea sick for us to see much of them. On our arrival here we were pleasantly welcomed here by our acquaintances of the spring. T went to see Mr. Ford – our Minister who was away all the spring – and goes tomorrow to Paris, leaving Mr. Egerton *chargé d'affaires* as before: Sir Brook Boothby, 2nd Sec. He also went to see Miss Trikoupis and next day to see her brother the prime minister by appointment.

We went to see the Schuylers yesterday, American Minister, and there tonight. Among the people in this hotel are Mrs Damales, Chiote and mother-in-law of S. Bernhardt, such a known *intriguante* that we are warned against making her acquaintance, and a lady who signs herself Elpis Malena of Crete, Baroness Schwartz, a great Garibaldina.[3] We start tomorrow night for Syra.

December 1883 – The Cyclades

Friday [actually Saturday] Dec. 1st. We had a quick but very rough passage, starting at 7 and getting here about 3.30 a.m. Wednesday. The *Pelops* was quite

---

[1] 'Patience, forbearance, endurance.'
[2] This is the Bents' second trip to the Eastern Mediterranean, and Mabel makes many references to the earlier journey, which included extensive parts of Turkey and Greece. There is no *Chronicle* of this trip in the present collection.
[3] Theodore, a student of Italian history, was also a great 'Garibaldinist'. He wrote a monograph on Garibaldi (*The Life of Giuseppe Garibaldi*, London, 1881), a short study of San Marino (*A Freak of Freedom*, London, 1877), for which he (and later Mabel) were awarded honorary citizenship, and *Genoa, how the Republic Rose and Fell* (London, 1881).

new and very clean and I should have slept well but for the fleas.[4] We landed at Ermoupolis at 6.30 and sat on the balcony overlooking the port for 2 hours as there was no bedroom vacant, nor did we get one till 5 o'clock. Mr. John Quintana, H.B.M. V. Consul on whom T called, came and fetched us and we spent 2 hours at the Consulate in Mr. Binney, the Consul's room, very large and nice and *so* tidy. Mr. B. must be a most orderly man for everything was ticketed and docketed. T called on him in Athens, says he is like a slight Greek, foreign accent and Greek wife. Then we went home to the H. d'Angleterre to breakfast and I lay in a passage room with a headache till we got a fine large one to ourselves, evidently planned as the drawing room. At dinner we were joined by Mr. Charcutsis, the Editor of a newspaper, who wished to give T details why Mr. Anamesakis, our consul of Chios who lives at Chesmé on the mainland, had been so bound to the Turks as to say when asked by Lords Granville and Aberdeen that T's statement at Chios and the taxation, though true, was exaggerated.[5] He is to have a great many particulars written out in a fortnight. Phaedros our Dragoman had been here some days but we did not meet till the afternoon. He dined with us and on the symptoms of Homer becoming aggravated we retired to our bedroom to have it sung in private. To me it sounds like a bagpipe.

Yesterday we mounted asses to ride to the other side of the island to the point called Ta Grammata – the writings – a place where the white marble sticks like the beak of a bird into the sea, almost polished, and the sailors who used the little bay as a harbour scribble and scratched little prayers to Serapis for good breezes. My donkey I had no power to turn, guide or check so I desired to be led by a string as I felt dangerous to the public safety. The way was very rough and steep up and down, for the whole island is a mass of stone and treeless hills.

[4] Fleas and bugs generally were an obsession for travellers of the time, no doubt for good reason. Ermoúpolis (Sýros) was the major 19th-century Greek *entrepôt* before the development of Pireaus, and the Bents were always coming and going there. Their new steamer made the passage in around eight hours; today's fastest ferries do it in under four. The Hôtel d'Angleterre, although abandoned, is still a fine building opposite the Town Hall in Miaoúlis Square. It is illustrated on p. 356. The reference to Homer and the bagpipe is unexplained. Perhaps Theodore, after a merry supper, recites a little in Ancient Greek and Mabel finds his chanting similar to the bagpipe? Over the next ten years, the couple get to know the island very well indeed. Theodore writes an evocative article for Macmillan's Magazine on it in 1884 – 'The Capital of the Cyclades': '…future ages will quote this little spot as the brightest specimen of activity produced by the revival of the long dormant spirit of independence in Greece…I visited it many times, and was always glad to get out of it, savouring as it did too much of this busy age.'
[5] Mabel makes a number of references to an incident that occurred on Chíos during their earlier trip to that (then) Turkish island in 1882/3. Theodore wrote complaining of Turkish oppression and it led to serious unpleasantness and questions in the House. There was a precedent that would have been certainly known to Theodore. In 1875, the young Arthur Evans wrote a book on Turkish oppression in the Balkans and Gladstone quoted from it in Parliament (*Through Bosnia and the Herzegóvina on foot during the insurrection*, August and September 1875, London, 1876).

Our muleteer had never been to the Grammata and soon was quite astray but we fortunately met with a man who knew the way, the only man we met, and he having given us figs and water accompanied us. We had to get off and climb at last. We ate, T deciphered inscriptions and the man dug up 3 bits of copper money and a little smoothed oblong bit of marble all at the same time. We took 4 hours to get there but not so long to get back and arrived just in time for the dark.

During dinner we conversed, through P, with the harbour master and Mrs. Quintana, and Mr. Tcherlendi came and spent the evening with us. Mr. Quintana is a British subject of Spanish origin on both sides from Malta and reminds us of Sir F. Turville. T has been to see the Archbishop who was very civil and said he had 'seen us returning last night like Christ entering Jerusalem'.

In the afternoon we drove on an excellent road to Della Grazia, an old harbour, stopping at Mr. Tcherlendis' villa, white and flat roofed, in a great mess as the family is away and he only goes there for the day. He poured out wine and asking me 'What do you preffer for liquer?', gave me besides a glass of anisette, a thing that I hate.[6] Then he took us through a wild little garden and gave us oranges and flowers. This south side of the island is much more fertile.

[Sunday] Dec. 2nd. Up at 6.30 and hastened on board the *Ydra*. Filthy little ship, full of people and cargo. We had to wait at least 2 hours while they finished loading. Rough passage. Landed about 1 o'clock. Very pretty island [Serífos] – full of bays. The inhabitants seemed very friendly. We had a letter to a family in the upper town, about ½ hour's climb from the sea, where there are a few *magasias*. A man took us to his house – flat roofed and whitewashed within and without, floor and all. The ceiling of canes laid on the bias on rafters. We were given coffee, rose jam and water, pomegranate, and an orange cut in slices on a plate, and were asked to spend tomorrow night there.

We then proceeded to our family, I on a red, lame mule and the luggage on another. Found another *very* clean house, scantily furnished and most welcome. Cherry jam, coffee and *mastika* liqueur were given us.[7] The Schoolmaster, a deacon, came and we proceeded to scramble up the filthy town, full of pigs in the worst sense of the word, said to be valuable scavengers and as active as goats, but horrid to meet when walking up the main sewer, sometimes not 2 feet wide and very steep and slippery as it was drizzling.

The Demarch, or Mayor, and others formed quite a procession. The church had a beautiful carved *tembelon* or screen. All the time of our first arrival in this house, when our hostess was being assisted by a friend in doing all she could,

---

[6] *Oúzo*, then as now an acquired taste.
[7] A typical selection of hospitality refreshments. The mastika liqueur is flavoured with mastic resin from Chíos.

P was running to the kitchen to fetch the woman out to tell legends, or rushing in to ask what plants grew here. How bored *we* should be if ordering dinner for unexpected guests and they came to the kitchen to ask if dandelion grew near, if we made tea of it, etc. There is some talk of T's being a Godfather tomorrow. How is he going to see that the child is well brought up to worship archangels on horseback and believe in *nereids*,[8] besides!

We heard in Syra that there is indignation that Anamesakis has been decorated for his help of the Chiotes by the Greek Government and 'T ought to have had it instead'. Also we hear the Sciotes[9] say that if any help comes, whether they are joined to Greece, made a principality like Samos, or the taxation lessened, they mean to make a statue of T! Also I think *he* will want a Godfather, for his name is now Mpénthios instead of Mpenth. The ticket was made out thus and P introduces him so. We are starving and the table is laid for 6 people. Good prospects for dinner. The kitchen range is a small earthenware pot. We beguile the time with discussions of what pills, potions and draughts will do P good before and after sea voyages.

In the town an old woman ran out with incense in a little pot to welcome us (so we were told but really because it was Saturday when they always burn incense); and he was given a large bush of myrtle and a cake 6 inches across – barley bread.

What a night we passed! First we got an excellent dinner about 8 o'clock. Macaroni and some rather too strong cheese, an excellent pair of chickens, salad dressed with oil and lemon juice. Also there were olives, capers, oranges and almonds. The wine was very good. Then coffee.[10] The friend, H Kyria Revinthaki, sat in the room and the host dined with us. He is the captain of the little ship in which we were to sail to Siphnos. Soon we went to bed in a cage 9ft by 8, with no door but a gate; solid up to 4ft and open above. The house contains 5 rooms all communicating thus. In the dining room, which is the entrance, P and his host sat up late. By ducking I managed to undress and when in bed had to console myself by remembering it was where all wished I should be.

---

[8] Any of a number of assorted sprites and spirits. An important theme of Theodore's *The Cyclades* is his interest in island folklore. He was to write up his findings in several papers for the *Journal of the Anthropological Institute of Great Britain and Ireland* and similar publications. In *Macmillan's Magazine*, 51, pp. 366–371, under the title 'Old Mythology in New Apparel', Theodore provides a compendium of many of the curious customs Mabel is to record in the following pages of her *Chronicles*, illustrating how much he depended on his wife's notebooks (as well as his own) when it came to preparing his future writings. On this occasion for Macmillan's he concludes, 'From these points it will be easily seen how much that is old lives today. In manners and customs and daily life the peasant Greeks reproduce even more that can be identified as ancient, but this is apart from my present subject.'

[9] Scios/Khios were alternative spellings for the island of Chíos.

[10] The first of Mabel's lengthy descriptions of the board, good and bad. Food, of course, is more often than not an obsession for travellers.

We kept a night light floating in a tumbler of oil alight but it went out at last and the fleas and a violent and long thunderstorm roused us up. The paraffin lamp was alight in the outer room, so I looked up to see what neighbours we had there and beheld the black beard of P in the divan. We could hear the rain as plainly on our roof as if it was a bandbox and we were bonnets. A great hailstorm and then P's lamp was put out by the rain coming in. Much movement; our host coming in. He and P walked about a good deal, arrayed in white, and opened the house door to look out.

We had a lively night and very early P appeared at the gate in the same dress to make plans for the day. Dressing wasn't easy but when over we started on mules, with our host and 2 muleteers, for the monastery of the Taxiarchos or Archangel Michael. About 1¾ hour. We had to go up the fearfully dirty town again to the other side of the island. It looks like a fortress seen from the top. A high wall with a sort of terrace inside composed of flat roofs, then steps down to another terrace and steps down again to the church in the middle. Outside a high stair against the wall leads to a door about 4 feet square and very thick and strong. When I saw those steps I feared I might be condemned to sit on them, but when we got up the only old monk we saw seemed quite pleased with me. He had on blue *bags*, bare legs, a blue cotton jacket lined with horrid looking fur and a black cap, to show he was a monk, on grizzled and shaggy hair and beard. His poor old head was all on one side.

We went into the church, which is lined with half gone frescos and saw a very nice carved *tembelon*, and the *proskenéon*, or canopied desk, where there is a picture to kiss, was beautiful – all mother of pearl and tortoise shell. The lectern was something like but very much damaged. We did not stay too long but went on to the village where we hoped to eat the food we had with us, so we promised to return afterwards. Galena, which means peace, is the name of the village. From above it looks like a lot of little precipices. We dismounted and scrambled to nearly the bottom where the Demarch lives. He is 80 and having had a presentiment that guests would come had had much bread prepared and at 'breakfast' we had 3 pieces each. We were introduced as O Kyrios Mpénthios and H Kyria Mpenthíou to many people, were given rum and water for the 3rd time that day, and as we were anxious to hear some stories of *nereids* an old woman of 100 was fetched. She was really nothing but skin and bone and had a very large and crumpled brown skin. It seemed quite impossible she had ever been a little smooth pink baby. She had a white cap very much forward over her eyes, so that sideways only nose and chin could be seen – a shawl that looked like a table cover on her head and wound round her chin – a snuff-coloured short petticoat and stockings the same, a fur jacket and over it a wide coat of brown Dutch carpet.

She seemed terrified of us, and when asked what she knew of *nereids* said 'I know nothing' over and over again, and groaned and threw up her hands and shut her eyes and mouth and after a little bit rose up to go. She required a great deal of persuasion to sit down again. She said to our host 'Oh! My boy, what are they going to do to me?' Everyone consoled and patted her and said we were good people, and not only should do her no harm but should give her a little present, so then she told her tale, but I know T is writing that so I shall not.[11]

She seemed very much pleased with her coppers, but when T asked her name she did not like it at all and said, 'Is that possible! Is my name known in England?!' After that the table was ready, our chicken included. A plate with little brown bits of pork and some lamb, which the old man cut with his knife and thumb and gave us in his hands. I got mine into the dish. Some sheep cheese and wine – then coffee. A knife was given the old man but we had great difficulty in getting away. We had to pay 4 visits before we could get to the Taxiarchos again.

One was to the brother-in-law of the Demarch and father of the Superior. He was in bed wrapped in very rough blankets, clean looking but scratchy. He had a shirt of the same and a brown carpet coat. He seemed as pleased to see us as if a circus had called on a bedridden villager at home. He said he was not ill but having walked about for 95 years his feet hurt him and he was very cold. We got jam there too. All the house seemed as neat and clean as possible. The beds were like a ship's berth – huge – the whole length of the house, or rather across the end. A curtain all across, split near one end and tied back with ribbon, to get in by. Lots of people gave us flowers, oranges, quinces, almonds, etc.

When we got to the monastery the Superior was waiting for us, dressed in a ragged and green-black gown. He showed us a magnificent silver-bound gospel and some worm-eaten manuscripts. We had a little shower after starting but it was like summer all day. We had a good deal of rain about an hour after our return. The evening and dinner were just like the night before. The man who asked us to stay near the *magasia* and his son-in-law sat by. He is our host's uncle. Kyria Revinthaki was there too. She looks like a respectable housekeeper, our hostess like a very humble servant, has been in Athens and evidently knows what 'quality' is.

[Tuesday] December 4th. Better night – bugs – heavy rain: Up very early as we wanted to go and see some inscriptions and a magnet place where you put down your knife to take it up [sic]. I gave up and P was terrified of the rain. He

---

[11] The first of Mabel's references to Theodore's note-taking. His journals of these years are not with Mabel's.

is like a cat and so are the rest afraid of water. Dressing even more public. P in and out.

A wide and dirty torrent descended the rocky way to the Chora. Two hours spent hearing of clouds 'soon coming from every point of the compass – not possible to go today to Siphnos'. 2 hours – sea looking very calm. 'Siphons' or waterspouts may come. At long last, 10 to 10 they have gone, still raining but lighter. It got quite fine. Wind very favourable for Siphnos. Told at breakfast the boat was quite ready, so we descended to the harbour. Captain Georgios Hadgi Nikolaos Ibelligeka then began telling us a series of lies and threw every difficulty he could for 3 hours. Everyone groaned about 1.30 about night coming on and we heard the words 'winter', 'night', 'dark', '*Boreas*', 'evening', 'calm', and all other bogies. Then the boat was not ready, the sailcloth bulwarks had to be nailed on, bread fetched, then oil, though when night did come on we sailed without lights. Then water and then an enormous lot of talk of the most gloomy description. P, who had never been to sea but in a steamer and always seasick, quite terrified.

Well, after constantly affirming that we were not afraid and wished to go, we started at 4.30, with a good breeze, but so mild and warm that we did not care a bit for our wraps. Had we started early we might have made the passage in 2 hours but we took 8. It rained a little but we were becalmed quite near Siphnos. We tacked about, often rowing some time, and it was just like St. Brandon's Isle, 'sometimes behind us, sometimes before,' but a little breeze carried us into the port or bay of Charónasos at 12.30.[12]

A man, we had 3 in all, went in a boat to seek admittance at a few cabins on the rocks and at last found some one to take us. We scrambled up the rocks in the dark and found an old potter and his wife just out of bed waiting for us. They were old and fearfully patched and poor and their home was one room with the potter's wheel in the middle, some built seats, a few stools, one little low table and all the pots unbaked chiefly. Their bed was made of some boards fixed to the wall on 2 sides and supported by a rough bit of tree, with a small branch left to help in climbing up 4 feet. Some hard woollen sheets and a grey hairy rug.

They implored us most kindly to sleep there and we made many civil refusals but finding they would be offended we took off our boots and climbed up all dressed. P and the old pair slept on the floor. There was such a storm of rain and wind and the door often flew open and we felt glad we had not waited till 2 a.m. when the skipper had told us we should start. In the morning we all washed in the same basin and towel: I first, no soap. Put on our boots and were ready for the day. Had to wait till 11 for mules and in the mean time breakfasted off

---

[12] A reference to the 6th-century AD Irish Saint, Brendan, and his fantastic voyage in search of the Garden of Eden.

fish broth and then the fish out of unglazed earthen cups. One glass was all the kind old people had – we gave them 5 dr. and a pair of scissors.

A great fuss with the captain about the cost of the *kaïke*.[13] He wanted 150 dr. but finally got 80.[14] He accompanied us to Apollonìa where the family of Captain Francois Tropos took us in. It was very trying sitting on the sofa with all the neighbours pouring in and screaming as the Greeks do. After dinner, which we got from a café, we went to spend the evening in the house of Mr. Gkionn,[15] which represents a French name. Our hosts accompanied us and Miss Athená, the fat daughter, took my arm.

We were glad to get into a small room with a large bed and about as much room to dress as a ship's cabin. Rather dirty, satin quilt and magnificent Greek lace valance. Bugs and fleas and a window, unglazed, to the next room where the captain and his fat wife were sleeping on a sofa, enabled every breath and snore to be heard. Greeks sleep with a light burning and talk a good deal in the night. We had 2 nights there, much the same except that the 2nd a pig got into most of the rooms and created a disturbance.

Thursday [December 6th] we went to the Kastro, or old Venetian town, and saw a great many interesting things. We went accompanied by Mr. [blank], a lawyer, into a good many houses to see those old women who still keep to the *pina* or headdress. Most of the houses had nice old cabinets and Venetian glasses, very much out of repair. In the house of the lawyer, which is very large, were lovely chests, pictures, etc. They showed us a suit of clothes such as used to be worn for best. Cloth of gold petticoat, white moiré deep waistcoat, splendidly embroidered with gold and colours and green velvet overgrown with gold trimming and hanging sleeves and beautifully embroidered *pina* with gold and tinsel flowers of various colours besides some beautiful jewellery, enamel and gold.

After breakfast we went to the Holy Chrisostom, formerly a nunnery but now only 2 women keep the church, a very poor one. Then we went to the Monastery of the Virgin or Springs, a cheerful place. In the reception room about a dozen men, women and children and quantities of children running about. In the middle of the divan, which ran the whole width of the room, was perched the very old and wrapped up mother of the Superior, with her knees to her chin and her heels on the sofa. She was a very gay old person and spoke very highly of our nation, had been in Constantinople during the Crimean War

---

[13] Caïque. A light rowing boat, often equipped with a sail/sails. The standard form of short-range sea transportation.
[14] Drachmas (and sometimes francs), then the Greek unit of currency.
[15] A Cycladic family. One Carolas Gkionn (Gion) wrote a history of Sífnos, published in 1876 in Ermoúpoli.

and said how well our soldiers behaved, quite different to the French. When asked about *nereids* and other fairies she said they had none now here and that we might travel comfortably and need not be a bit afraid. I felt ashamed she should think us so credulous.

We got home at 4 and I was left among a dozen people all making remarks on me. They said from my dress we must be very rich: my dress all embroidered in gold (some bronze bead butterflies). Our luggage was like that of monarchs. My brooch – a Scotch pebble and Cairngorm one – visible, was emeralds, sapphires and diamonds. Such little hands! – here fetched out of my muff by Miss Athená. And such a little and beautiful body. I had great work not to laugh – every virtue also. How glad I was when I said I was fearfully tired and must go to bed. So I went to bed and had my dinner there and T had an immense and noisy party. I find my crimson flannel dressing jacket an immense comfort 'to shield my arms and shoulders from those impudent beholders' and am sure the great use of a husband is in case one may ever want to travel in the East.[16] We paid the café 25 frs. for our food and gave our hosts presents. T had been given by Mr. Gkionn a thing to whistle into: white earthenware, found at Athens and very like a door handle.[17]

[Friday December 14th] On Thursday morning, which is now to me yesterday, we mounted our mules and went to the Convent of Panagía to Vounó, or Our Lady of the mountain, which mountain looks over the sea.[18] There are 6 nuns. The Superior was a handsome old woman in shabby black. Monks and nuns are generally poor and shabby old people, in any dress, but with black fez or handkerchief on their heads. After lunching in a snug little nook on the road, we got down a tremendously rough road to Vathý, where there were only 2 or 3 houses and a white monastery jutting into the sea. It was quite warm in the pretty little bay. Our green *kaïke* came in at the moment we did, and we immediately set off for Kimolos.

We had a very fair wind. 2 hours. A good deal was coasting off Kimolos. We were quite close to Polenos,[19] an island not inhabited. Our captain, who is evidently anxious to get home, put us ashore a full hour from the only town in the island. He has since handed us over to another man to take us to Milos

---

[16] Perhaps a reference from a recent edition of Dante Gabriel Rossetti (1828–1882) – 'For very surely, / Though my arms and shoulders / Dazzle beholders, / And my eyes glisten, / All's nothing purely! / What are words said for / At all about them, / If he they are made for / Can do without them?' In any event, an amusing aside.
[17] Theodore was a keen collector of musical instruments. A few have survived and are now in the Pitt Rivers Museum, Oxford.
[18] Mabel is writing from a cliff ledge on Kímolos, off Mílos. It is not clear, but the date is possibly Friday, 14 December 1883.
[19] Polinos, Polybos or Polivo (the ancient Polyaegos) lies some 2km south-east of Kimolos. It is not permanently inhabited.

tomorrow. We walked some way, then got an old woman named Limoniá to lend me her ass, and at last got one that the sailors had fetched for me. We did not get to the town till quite dark and very hard to get through the narrow, rocky, muddy streets. It is walled round by continuous houses.[20]

We got in to a house by an outside stair. It consisted of 2 rooms. The furthest and largest had a big bed in it. Both were sitting rooms. We soon had crowds of visitors, to our eyes of different classes but among themselves they all seemed equal. Very little supper. At the head of the bed was a little window in the wooden partition, glazed and curtained off, but we hear the noise of 4 Greeks sleeping, including P. Sometimes for ¼ of an hour all is peace save the snoring and then one wakes up with a loud groan or sigh. This wakes another. They talk as loudly as if they were tipsy and quarrelling, and if they wish to speak to a sleeper call him loudly till he wakes. They sleep with a lamp burning and can't make out why we don't. As I said once I was sure it was bad for their eyes; they connect it with my eyeglasses and think my eyes require the dark.

We were there two nights, the 2nd much the better for the flea powder of the night before. I was not feeling very well the morning after our arrival in Kimolos so as it was inclined to rain I was to rest and write this Chronicle while T and P went to the old Kastron. Accordingly I sat down but soon had about 9 people and finally a tall and fat young lady, Miss Afentaki, rushed in and said 'Bonjour Madame' and talked bad French for a couple of hours. Said it was only her duty to come, hearing I was alone and was really very well meaning, but grossly flattering and awfully boring.

A great many people came, to whom she translated. I was thoroughly thankful when she felt she must return to her mother and I sat down to a very nasty luncheon. Some very strong smelling pig broth, and most awfully thick hard biscuit that had to be soaked in water.[21] My horror was great when that kind girly returned saying her mother told her by no means to leave me. I should be melancholy alone and she wished I would go and see her and she wished me to stay with her 1000 years! So she ate an enormous breakfast by my side. I had to say I was ill and giddy. I was tired enough by the time they came back of being kissed and stroked on the face. We had to pay Mrs. Afentaki and the Eparchos, or Lord Lieutenant of 4 islands, visits and at last escaped into the crowd at home from the crowds abroad. The mother of our hostess, addressed as 'Kyranió', performed a charm over me.

---

[20] An architectural feature of many old Cycladic towns, the central houses arranged, for defence, in a square. Snickets at the corners allow entrance to an open square in the centre, often the location for a church. Examples of these attractive structures remain on some islands – Síkinos has a particularly memorable one.

[21] The hard, double-baked bread/biscuits, *paximádhia*.

Sat. Dec. [22nd?]. It is a long time since I wrote in my Chronicle – a whole week. Last time I was perched on a ledge halfway down a cliff in Kimolos and now we are storm-stayed on board the *Ydra* (YΔPA) in the harbour of Vathý in Siphnos, since yesterday at 11 a.m. and no chance of getting away today. The steamer has bad engines, is small and it is very stormy. No post. No telegraph. So we fear our friends will be uneasy about us, as we might as well be in the moon. I had better go back to the charm. The old woman took a good sized handkerchief, tied a slipknot in one corner, laid it on her knee, set her elbow on it and solemnly measured to the opposite corner, from her elbow to her middle finger, nipping it between the fingers till she laid the first finger of her left hand straight across the measured mark. The kerchief went 3 times and about 4 inches over. She held this piece in her left hand and waved the knot vigorously across and over the sides of my head saying some verses the while, which T has copied down. After this she again measured the kerchief in the same way exactly and it only seemed to reach twice as far as the wrist. If you are suffering from the sun it shortens itself. If you are all right it remains the same length. She then got water, dabbed my head, did the incantation over again, and it was thought that I should be quite well when the sun went down as the shrinking did not take place.

Next morning, with bag and baggage, we mounted 5 donkeys, as there are no mules in Kimolos, meaning to cross to Melos, which takes about 20 minutes. Donkey riding is horrible as the mule saddles are too large and swing about and one must hold on. When we got to the ferry place, accompanied by a very nice soldier, Costés, assigned to us. A very unnecessary guard, gun and all. The sea was not *quite* smooth, so P and the boatmen made an awful row, and the muleteer too. They said we might as well return at once to the town. It would blow for 48 hours, and we should never get across today. After an immense deal of talking and screaming about the winter, etc., we said we would not go to the town but go to a place called Elleniká, 1¼ away, and return at 5, for the breeze would die away then.

I was prophetic for once in my life for I told T perhaps we should have regretted not going to Elleniká as we might be going to find something. There is a small rocky island called Daskalió once connected with the main island by an isthmus of soft rock or very hard sand, now eaten away. It is full of graves, and quantities of things from here are in the British Museum. Consul Brest, everyone's consul, whose father found, or rather bought the Venus, did not know this; when we told him he seemed excited. The Demarch Affentaki digs by night, pretending to cultivate his field and smuggling things away. (By the bye, everyone in telling how he makes his livelihood calmly adds that he smuggles.) After having gone into a sort of catacomb 4 feet high and 30 deep, we went and sat on a ledge about 3 feet wide over the sea, glad to be by ourselves and read and wrote. P and the muleteer came to beg us to return to town, but we said no, we would go to the ferry first.

On our return to the donkeys we refused to be guided by the signs to keep to the top of the cliff and preferred to go along the bottom, dodging the waves. T looked back and exclaimed 'Look what I have found' and there was a cup sticking in the cliff about 6 feet up. We had all passed it in the morning. We rushed at it and cut it out with knives. It was burst round the lip from about 20 feet of sand, quite hard above it. We got all the pieces, tied it in a handkerchief and veil round my neck and said nothing of it. I felt it a most anxious charge on the donkey.

We had left the baggage in a little ruined church in care of the soldier and when we, on pressing in *not* taking the turn for the town, got to the ferry, the boat was seen far away near Melos. The man said he would return for us *very* early in the morning. As it was not too bad for him to have a sail up we were very angry. So was the soldier who wanted to carry a basket of eggs to Melos. So he made a fire and with his presence frightened the men and they returned and we had ½ an hour's row and got across at sunset.

It got dark immediately and the boatmen said we must stop at Appolónia the night. They took us to the best lodging they had – a filthy cabin about 7 feet by 12. One room, a very dirty bed of boards, stools 6 inches high, and table 4 inches high. Here we squatted and dined off caviare, rye bread and water. We got 5 donkeys and set out at 6.20. It was bright moonlight. The way was very steep and slippery and full of water and muddy. After an hour, away went the moon and down came torrents of rain so we turned into a large cavern, of which there are quantities all over the island, mules and all, lit a large fire and were told we should have to pass the night there. It was a most romantic scene just like the theatre. The 5 donkeys, their man and girl, the soldier and a large bit of sky high up lit by lightning. We got away in ½ an hour and reached our destination, the Kastro at the top of a conical hill, at 10.15.

We applied at the house of Mr. Photopoulos, whose name P had heard, for admittance and were at first thought to be brigands. No steamer had come in and we did not even come from that direction. But hearing we were English and 'knowing us to be a capricious and daring race capable of travelling by night,' furthermore seeing the soldier, Mr. Photopoulos gave us a kind welcome. We remained 2 nights there very comfortably. I stayed in all Sunday and wrote letters which are on this very ship **[Mabel is still storm-stayed in Váthý, off Sífnos]** and T went to see the catacombs in the valley of Klisma.[22]

---

[22] At Trypití, the cemetery of early Melian Christian community dating from the end of the 2nd century AD. The extensive complex of catacombs were first explored by the German archaeologist Ludwig Ross in 1844.

We find the Greeks great people for telling lies. Most evenings on our arrival one of our visitors tells us he means to accompany us in our next day's expedition and show us some things and he never turns up. Accordingly Mr. Photopoulos told us we were to sleep at the house of a relation at Empório, after having been to the convent of Sideroyanni, St John of Iron. It was a beautiful house, well furnished and as fine as his own, which is really very large. The key was given to the soldier. He added that the next night when we should sleep at the harbour of Adámantas (diamond) he would see that a good dinner was ready and would be there. But we saw no more of him.

We were off very early, walking down to Klima, quite close to the place where the statue of Neptune was found.[23] About ½ hour very steep, then by boat to our house. We did not go in then but after breakfast outside a cottage, set off on donkeys for Sideroyanni. It is a rough steep road to a neglected and empty monastery, quite white. As soon as one gets in sight one comes to little heaps of stones, 2 or 3, one on another on the rocks. People put them up and promise they will come back and pull them down next year if they are well.

When we got back we found the splendid house was a very damp cottage. Mud floor, no sheets, board bed, thin mattress and quilt, no window glass. The soldier had remained behind cooking 2 woodcocks, which with some caviare, eggs and mushrooms made our dinner. The cottage where we had breakfasted had a fireplace and we begged leave to eat our dinner on little low stools, with a lower table there. P also slept there fearing the damp, but we, fearing publicity, went with the soldier to our 'own house'.

We started before dawn with nothing to eat, for we did not know we could not get coffee there. We rode to Agia Maria, a suppressed convent, and in a cell there a poor family gave us a little wine and water and we ate caviare and bread and they offered us some with mastic berries but that we could none of us eat. The *tembelon* was nicely carved. Then we rode to the top of a hill where there is a little building with 2 rooms, one within another. In the innermost is a *very* narrow passage down a steep slope ending in a little round cave about 5 feet across with rough stone seats. Here they take a sort of Turkish bath. It is very hot indeed. They cool on olive twigs in the outer room. Next we went to the ruined and deserted town Zephiréa, a large town still inhabited in this century but very unhealthy. There is one church out of the many still standing, a very fine one with decaying frescos. No doors or windows, a shelter for mules.

---

[23] Mabel is referring to the imposing 2.5m marble statue of Poseidon from an eponymous temple on Mílos. His right hand is held aloft for a (missing) trident. A dolphin jumps around his right leg. It dates from the last quarter of the 2nd century BC and is displayed at the National Archaeological Museum, Athens. A section of the old mule track can be found just as the modern road gives a first view of the monastery away in the distance. Along the track there are still low cairns of stones.

We breakfasted near the church. We caught an old inhabitant come for olives who said we were on the site of a hotel. They have no hotels in the island now. And showed us a few stones where his café was, also an upright stone where they scourged criminals. The beautifully carved *tembelon* is removed to Adámantas, also a piece of board pierced by a swordfish. The sailor vowed to make an *eikon* of it if saved, and a picture of the occurrence is painted on the lower half of it.

After seeing this we went to a cave with an alum spring, warm, where baths for the itch are taken. We got to Adámantas early in the afternoon and no dinner ordered. Great trouble about food. The English squadron had eaten everything. We got a tough old hen made into soup and ate some of our own sardines. All the time the inhabitants were saving woodcocks for Syra and there are quantities on board which I am hoping to eat if we stay here much longer. (The following day we 3 had a woodcock for dinner and one for breakfast.) Tuesday morning we were told the boat might come from Crete. Start at 4; but we waited till 1 p.m. and then gave her up. We sailed across to Klima but did not dare stay long. We paid *many* visits to Consul Brest, an old gentleman with a Greek 2nd wife,[24] and had many *glyko* (jams) and cups of coffee, also wine and almonds. He gave us a pot of jam made of *kolokinthos* (vegetable marrow) and almonds.

At one time we made up our minds to go by sailboat to Folégandros and Sykinos and a man agreed to take us but when Consul Brest began to make a contract the man backed out of it. They are *such* cowards, and our P is quite the worst croaker I ever heard. It consoles us, for if they are frightened at so little, there cannot be much to be afraid of. It is a good thing we did not start though.

We waited all Thursday and in the afternoon rode up to Tris Bassella, a mountain village where we saw a woman dressed in her Sunday dress. White flowered satin skirt, silver *stomakikó*, or waistcoat, silk gauze apron, white edged with lace, just like Cluny, 150 years old. A silk scarf 10 feet long, with lace ends wound round her head, over some stuffing: gold necklaces and purple silk jacket edged with fur. We had to get fresh donkeys here and bargain was made for 1 fr. each but as P stayed behind the men stopped the donkeys and threatened not to go on unless we gave more. T upset his man by making the donkey kick and utterly refused more. The man said it was 'nykta' at 3 o'clock! At last I saw T get off his donkey and so I kicked and prodded mine to give them as good a chase as I could and get over as much ground as possible. But when T got down they gave in and we arrived at home very wet. At 3 o'clock next morning we were called and came on board in the rain. Went to bed till

---

[24] She is buried in the Catholic church in Pláka.

morning. Called in at Kamára in the island and went on to Seriphos. Fearful north wind half way so had to turn back past Kamára to get here. Constant heavy showers all day and even in this little bay we roll about. There is no ballast. P went on shore at once and we did after breakfast for a couple of hours. T sketched.[25] P on shore still. Most of the 1st passengers are Candians in their own dress. 2 *Papas* and an Italian engineer. He and we and the captain have our meals together. We have no hope of leaving before 4 tomorrow, if then. We are quite content and thankful for our clean and very small cabin, after sleeping in public so often.

T is lying up today for he blistered his heal with his boot, neglected it for a day or 2 and it is very sore. He has had to travel in his tennis shoe down at heel, and we have plenty of books. While in Melos we bought a beautiful flat cup with a chariot race round it, 2 small ones, a little jug with figures, and a little Cretan lace fastened to an embroidered towel.[26]

Christmas Day in Naxos [Tuesday December 25th]. I am fearfully in arrears with my Chronicle! We started on Sunday [16th?] at 5.30 a.m. and in due course got to Syra. (Finding that on account of this delay this same steamer was to proceed on Monday morning to Paros, we left our luggage on board and only landed for a few hours.) We saw Mr. Binney and Mr. Quintana and Mr. Tzerlendi, got letters and embarked. About 3 hours brought us to Paroikiá, the capital. An unhealthy, dirty town, full of old architectural scraps, whitewashed into the houses and with a ruined castle of which several courses are formed of columns. We had rather a comfortable room where we unpacked and rearranged our luggage and spent the afternoon walking about.

Tuesday [December 18th?]. Rode 1½ hour to the nearest point to Antiparos carrying only our night things and a card of introduction from Mr. Binney for Mr. R. Swan who has a calamine mine on this island. Crossed in about 10 minutes. Found the population all enjoying the feast of St. Nikoloas who replaces Neptune. At one house I was obliged to join in the *syrtos* holding 2 handkerchiefs. We sent a messenger to Mr. Swan and knowing he would take 3 hours to return, rode to meet him. Met Mr. Swan who more than fulfilled our warmest hopes. He took us to his house, and after resting told us that in making a road he had come upon a lot of graves and found a marble cup, broken etc. So, we manifesting a great wish to dig too, he got men and we opened 4. They were lined and paved with slabs of stone and the people must have been doubled up in them, they were so small; we only found, besides

---

[25] Theodore was a keen sketcher and water-colourist. Some have survived and appear in later publications.
[26] Some of the couple's acquisitions from Mílos are in the British Museum, including a cup, lekythos, and two terracotta heads.

bones, 2 very rough marble symbols of men and women, little flat things and some broken pottery.

Next morning we rode to the cave in the top of the highest mountain. There is first a large open cavern and in the back of it a hole 4 or 5 feet across, down which one must slide clinging to a rope fastened to a stalactite at the edge. 3 places we went down by ropes and two by a ladder, holding ropes too and at last got to an enormously large and high sort of hall with lots of stalagmites and stalactites. The former, some of them look like trees. In one corner is 'the church' where services have been held several times. One must dive under the stalactites to get in. We made a large fire which lit up the whole place. We did not feel the heat much while we were down but were glad of our cloaks when we got out.[27]

After luncheon and some very good wine made by Mr. Swan, we rode down to the town. As the weather was fine we determined to go all round to Paroikiá by boat.[28] We did not tell P we meant to do more than cross straight and he was as terrified as usual and made everyone laugh. Mr. Swan dined with us in a kitchen. I made a sweet omelette. T had the misfortune to take a stranger who had come in to stare for the son of the house and asked him 'to get another plate'. He took this for an invitation to dinner and joined us. We were obliged to grin and bear it. During the Greek Advent we never have too much dinner and have to treasure our remains for next day.

Next morning we went in a tram drawn by horses up to the quarry of marble with a Belgian and a Greek belonging to the French company who work it. The road is so steep that no horses are needed for the descent. We were received by the engineer who took us down the quarry. We all had miners' lamps, not very light to hold, and scrambled and slipped and crawled through the various passages up and down. When I saw the plan of where I had been I had no idea how many ramifications we had been through. At the entrance is a bas-relief of figures dedicated to the Nymphs. It is carefully covered with wood. The middle figures have been removed by someone. It is a bright brown colour.

P of course would not go down either, or at Antíparos. We lunched at the engineer's house. The Belgian promised me a little lamp found in the quarries but this I still look on as a bird in the bush. Then we mounted mules and rode 3 hours about to Levkés up in the mountains. The Demarch received us kindly for the sake of Mr. Swan who had helped at his election and after visiting the new and very hideous church where, however, one gets a lovely sea view. We settled

---

[27] One of the best websites on this notable cave is http://www.showcaves.com/english/gr/show-caves/Antiparos.html (summer 2006). It was used as the location for a midnight mass by the Marquis de Nointel, Christmas 1673.

[28] The Bents are taking the long way back by boat to Paroíkia, the capital of Páros.

down to dinner and after it a dance. The Demarch did this really out of *hospitality*, for next day he said the 10 frs. T gave him was far more than he had spent and really had to be pressed to take it, and not from *philoxenía* which is never satisfied with anything. Some time the host refuses loftily to take anything but leads us to understand he does not answer for his wife and she always takes it.

We parted from Mr. Swan on Thursday morning hoping to be joined by him later at Santorini and rode to Ábyssos. No road and the place did not repay us a bit. Lunched there by the sea. Then to Kepídoi, which by reason of the strange accent of the island they call Tchepídi. We stopped at the house of the Demarch della Grammatis for 2 nights. Our bedroom had no light but from the door. Bought 2 of the rough little marble people[29] and hearing of a good many graves in the neighbourhood we decided to dig next day and hired 3 men at 2 frs. each. We dug in 3 places and in one we found lots of bones and a buckle or brooch of copper and in another a rough little vase. On our return T, though they said it was nearly night at 3 o'clock, went up to the castle or acropolis above the town and said there was a magnificent carved *tembelon* rotting from neglect.

I was shut up in the dark on my bed and much kissed and covered up constantly if the thick quilt came off. I was warm enough as I had my Ulster[30] on.

Sunday [December] 23rd. Rode to Naussa, a very small poor village in an immense and very safe bay. Lunched there and embarked in a sailing *kaïke* for Naxià, the capital of this island. An excellent passage. Christmas Eve was a lovely day and we did nothing but wait to see the steamer come in with such a crowd round us on the beach, where we sat on two chairs like King Canute, that the police had to drive them away. And row to a little island, now much diminished by the waves where there are the ruins of a temple to Bacchus lie [sic], only the lintel and 2 door posts stand and have been kept white by wind and spray.[31] T was getting worse and worse with a sore throat. Mr. Tcherlendi came by the steamer. Christmas Day was a downpour and as our rooms are not watertight came in through doors and windows. The wind howled and our prospects of food were faint.

A wild duck that was found just before luncheon cheered us however so much that we ate it all but a wing, which I prudently cut off to keep. We thought something *must* turn up for dinner, but when dinner-*time* came, I can't say dinner,

---

[29] These are, of course, the famous Cycladic marble figurines – the iconic souvenir of these islands. There are three of the Bents' figurines from Páros in the British Museum. They are all around 15 cm high and date from the middle of the 3rd century BC. Interested readers may trace them by their Museum registration numbers – 1884, 1213.9–11.
[30] As worn by Sherlock Holmes, an Ulster coat is essentially a sleeveless overcoat. It maintained its popularity into the 20th century.
[31] At the time of the Bents' visit the islet of Palátia was not linked by the present-day causeway. The scant remains of Apollo's temple have been restored.

and T was in bed eating arrowroot and I was supposed to be dining *tête-à-tête* with P, I felt so dejected that I could only silently drink T's health and think 'the fewer the better fare'. They had boiled the duck's skeleton with much water and rice and the skeleton came up as a dish with the cold bit which we divided. I went and made some arrowroot for myself and fervently prayed that I might ever after be glad and thankful for a good Christmas dinner.

[Thursday] December 27th. Yesterday morning, T having gone to bed with a temperature of 102, I was in great despair at getting food with such difficulty, so I started forth with P to Mr. De Lastic, a descendant of France, to whom we had an introduction, to ask how we could procure anything as he is a 'Western Christian'.[32] He was not at home. I was so unhappy but Mr. Tcherlendi came to call as soon as I got home with my mind fixed on poaching eggs myself and making Brand's beef tea. He had a Mr. Mavrojeni with him. I explained my difficulty and they said I could get a turkey so we got a very small one for 7 frs. It was a funny conversation for Mr. Tcherlendi spoke English and Mr. Mavrojeni French. P understood enough French to join in in Greek with the two. I understood Greek enough to join in in English or French.

Mr. Mavrojeni had come to say he had some old dresses to show us, and T being really better for a good luncheon got up and we went to his house at 2 and saw 2 skirts, crimson satin with gold embroideries and yellow silk and silver. His wife is of a Venetian family. We then climbed to the highest point and saw the 2 Roman Catholic churches. As T was so feverish on Christmas night I slept on the sofa and caught 13 fleas and the following rhymes came into my head. I copied them and P was very much pleased with them.

The Lay of the Landlubber

T'is the voice of Phaedros,
Thus I heard him complain
You have got me to sea
I will never go again!
T'is a beautiful day,
There's an excellent breeze,
And both my companions
Are quite at their ease.
They are chatting and laughing
In capital cheer,
But I sit on the deck

---

[32] 'Brand's Beef Tea' was an essential restorative and the Bents never travelled without a good stock of it.

And must croak out my fear.
'The wind from the North
fights with the Wind from the South
There are Siphons!'
One bit I can't put in my mouth!
The weather is fair, but
I think it may change
From Ill-luck to Misfortune
My thoughts ever range.
As soon as the Sailors
Are ready to tack
I think there is danger
And wish to put back.
When the spray dashes over
'Pray lower the sail'
I am sure there is really
A terrible gale.
If there is not a storm
There will surely be calm,
And one way or other
We must come to harm.
The folks take to laughing
And all ridicule
Me and call me Old Woman
And Coward and Fool;
But it's all of no use
They might speak to the dead
I feel rather seasick
And cling to my driad.
For whether in East Wind
Or Wind from the West
To be safe on a Continent
'S what I like best.
Oh dear! as we pass on
From Island to Island,
I heartily wish that
Our way lay over dry land!
And sometimes a lady's voice
Strikes on my ear
'Look the sailors aren't frightened

> Then why should we fear?
> If we're born to be hanged
> We shall never be drown'd.'
> In such sentiments I think
> No comfort is found.
> Let those islanders laugh
> All my terrors to scorn
> I'm a coward at heart
> And a landlubber born.

This morning we packed and waited for mules. No mules came but heavy rain did. It is impossible to start today. We had cold turkey for [lunch?] and having got a leg of lamb we hoped to have it roasted for dinner but the baker has no dry brushwood for his oven and can't even bake bread and to heat it with charcoal is unheard of and we consented to have it cooked in a pot here by the people of the house, but now the rain is pouring in and they fear they can do nothing. They are so improvident and all the woodwork and building is of the roughest. We have a little sitting room with 3 outside walls and a bedroom with a trap door in the floor, liable to open at any minute; a glass door over which we hang a rug when we go to bed. We sit in our Ulsters and don't know when we shall get away.

I forgot that on Wednesday we went to call on the Bishop of Naxos and Paros. He is a dark, delicate looking man and looks good. He gave me his photo in Episcopal robes and most kindly fetched his mitre etc. and put them on to show us. He is not more than 45. The mantle is violet satin in a long peaked train behind, all ironed into small pleats; at the [corner ?] and shoulders square pieces of white brocade with flowers are laid on and the whole is trimmed with gold braid. 3 little silver sheep bells fasten it at the bottom. He showed us 2 pastoral staves, one ivory tortoiseshell and the other silver guilt, both the same shape. A large sort of locket of enamel representing the Resurrection and set in jewels; and the mitre was just like an emperor's crown – copied from that of Constantine, eagle etc. and lots of jewels, uncut emeralds, sapphires and rubies, lots of diamonds and all on a smooth foundation of red velvet. A diamond cross at the top – imitation but very splendid to look at.

Saturday [December] 29th. It was raining but looked like clearing up so we wanted to start to Philoti, 4 hours up the mountains and down. But no muleteers came and Messrs. de Lastic and Mavrojeni both came and assured us no man or beast could travel. P of course joined warmly in saying Winter! and rain! But at last a brave man with an umbrella and a mule was found and another man with 2 more and we got off with great difficulty. The saddles are very small here and they said I must ride straddle-wise, so when, after a mile of real wide road it turned a bridle path – otherwise a river – they should all have been ready enough to turn back if I had said I could not ride that way. I said of course I could and the 2 men standing on each side came to help me. One held my leg firmly and the other hitched the left one across the mule's neck. It was as if they were breaking a merry thought. It was not so bad after all. I dare say stirrups would be an improvement. Sometimes when I got tired I managed when the beast browsed to hitch one leg on his neck.

We found ourselves going along a mountain road, while on the opposite side of the valley we saw several villages, called Kato, Mesa, and Ano Potamiá, Lower, Middle, and Upper. We said we would go through them and would sleep there that night. They said it was impossible, no road and a wide roaring river. I saw a little twist of road and said it must join the road we were on further on, and we saw a farm and we felt sure it must have a way up and to the opposite villages. So we jumped off and T said he'd wade and carry me and we two went scrambling down on foot; where it was not rocky and thorny it was dreadfully wet. But when the *agogiates* (mulemen) saw we were determined they and P came round another way and met us at the farm, where we mounted and went down to the river.

The men were terrified and I do not know what we should have done but a man on a mule came down and plunged in and laughed at our men and I tried to make my mule follow in vain, so P took off shoes and stockings and led him across. The water was knee deep and very swift, tumbling about till the oleanders all seemed sailing round. T followed and one man on P's mule and as the other 'feared a cold', P led the mule back for him. When we got to Potamia we had to sit 3½ hours in a small room with 20 people all staring and occasionally giving us coffee, sweets, nuts, or *raki*.[33] All this seems hospitable but when they all claim to be paid next day and expect enormous sums one's opinion changes.

After waiting all this time for dinner we retired to an empty summer country house. An 'apple room' full of oranges. A bed of board and flock like walnuts. Clean sheets, no glass in the windows and dripping so that we had to cover our clothes in waterproofs for the night. We slept well though and next day, though raining again, we felt we should again have a fine afternoon, which we did but we had the same awful commotion about the rain. The man with the umbrella had lost his mule and we were left to the mercy of the Potamiotes. They wanted 25 frs. for one bed, without food but we gave 5 frs. and made out a bill of 12 frs. for the food, down to sugar and salt and 6 frs. for 2 chickens and called them thieves and laughed at them and they simply

---

[33] The ubiquitous clear spirit distilled from grape residue.

shrieked and screamed with rage. T put his hand on one man's mouth to keep him quiet.

By perseverance we got the mule and one of the worst screamers who, when cowed was quite friendly. All the road to Chalkí was downhill 1½ hour. It was a wet road, of course, for as they take the bed of a torrent for their road, they suffer for it when the torrent [comes]. We sometimes went up real waterfalls, one just coming to Potamià, so called from the rivers, had steps of rock about 1½ feet high. My mule bounded up there when well whipped for he was afraid the others were not. I wonder if Abraham had neighbouring villages of Ano Potamiá and Kato.[34]

At Chalkí the house we went to had as dirty a mud floor as I ever saw and a strange smell which never left our noses all night, explained by hearing that lambs, fowls, etc. are obliged to be kept in the house on account of the people of Apéranthos. We had hens under the bed which would have been comfortable, for it was very clean, if the upper sheet had not been made of white linsey-woolsey, and it dripped on our faces and necks like a shower bath. People do not seem ready to take in strangers or do more than *try* and cheat them. We astonish them as much as if we were red Indians, not because we are foreigners – but because we go out in the rain. Everyone gives the people of Apéranthos a bad name as thieves. It is said that when Barabbas was set free he went back home to Krete. He was a pirate, but he behaved so badly he was chased away and settled here and these descendants are all thieves, so clever that they can steal the hat off your head or the soles of your boots without your finding it out. They only marry the people of Amorgós, also 'Klephtes'.[35]

We made a very good dinner of a Potamiá hen kept from the day before so it was tender and T said he had eaten too much, when our host came in and sat down at the table with *his* supper, a large plate of rice, boiled with oil and snails.[36] T and P set to work and ate nearly all those snails, T being occasionally fed off the other man's fork. When I get home I shall buy a special saucepan and at the same time feed T cheaply and horribly and benefit England. I shall wait till a famine. Before dinner we sat nearly an hour in a general shop, were given nuts and *raki*, which I hate but gulp down this damp weather when our clothes have to remain damp on us. We bought a quart of honey for 1 shilling and some cheese.

---

[34] Mabel is referring to Abraham and his travels along the Jordan River.
[35] Thieves, brigands and other miscreants.
[36] Edible snails (there are many everyday species) are still common fare. Folk are often to be seen collecting them after rain, or they are sold from sacks in general stores. They first need to be 'purged' (usually by letting them feed exclusively on wheat bran, corn meal or rolled oats) for 2/3 days, followed by an equal period of starvation. They can then be boiled with a little vinegar or lemon and eaten from their shells.

This morning – **Sunday, December 30th** – we padded out, literally in the water, for though I had galoshes and stepped carefully they got full. We after had to climb walls where we could not get along the roads. Being Irish I don't mind walls a bit and they were astonished that 'the woman' could climb. We went to the little churches, Agia Marina of no interest, Agios Georgios ditto, and Agios Stephanos, which must be very old indeed and drips like the wettest cave. It was all frescoed round with saints but in a dreadful state of decay. On the lintel of the inner doorway is an inscription but so dripping it could not be found out.

Last night we made an agreement with the nice muleteer with the umbrella to come at 9 o'clock and to accompany us all through our time on this island as he wished. He had followed us to Chalkí, we having met him on the way with his saddle-less mule. But he never turned up and after 10 we started with one mule for me and our host and his son with our big bag. ¾ of an hour to Philoti. We found a comfortable home in a tower (*pirgos*), wooden floor and a brazier and really have had a very quiet afternoon, reading, writing, greasing our boots and drying somewhat.

The Papas Eleftérios was very kind in helping us to arrange ourselves. We are in very prosperous circumstances; no pictures on the whitewashed walls but plenty of woodcocks and partridges, for which we have paid very handsomely 6½d each! instead of 2½d. The priest threw off his gown and helped to pluck them for our dinner which we had in the middle of the day. We were brought 2 loaves of bread and sent them away because they wanted a franc a piece. When reduced by hunger we wished to buy one it was sold so the priest sent us a piece of holy bread offered in church i.e. to him. Our muleteer came here after us and we said we had now made arrangements with others so his only chance is the unpunctuality of our last night's host who is gone home to sleep. This is a very beautiful village on 2 hills and with trees and sorts of peaky mountains round. These 3 villages must be damp as there are mosses and ferns and ivy.

Naxia. **Old Christmas day.**[37] I have never had an opportunity of writing since Philote. Our host Gabalas turned up in due course and the other two, T and P, went up to the Cave of Dios (Jupiter). 3 hours they were away and I spent the whole of it tidying and mending. We started after breakfast or luncheon, 1 hour and a half to Apéranthos, quite excited at getting among the thieves. When T and P went to look for a lodging our 3 men were told to look well after our things. As I sat on my mule I saw many very civil countenances.

After a search, the brother of the Demarch took us in and all our things were put into a stall out of the sitting room that is a very small room with no

---

[37] Christmas Day in the Orthodox (Old Calendarist Style) Calendar was Sunday, 6 January 1884. Mabel is catching up with her *Chronicle*.

windows and a gate. When we were going out we said 'Here are our things' in a marked manner but the people seeing what great Lords we were said 'We will take them into the next house, it is better and safer'. So we passed through a room into the daughter's house; very grand, no sofa, only 1 dozen Austrian chairs. Our *pragmata* were put in a stall and we afterwards found it locked up, and our host called out when we got into the square 'Take care that no one gets into my house'. As we saw gratings on the windows and bars to doors we felt very adventurous.

But we have had no reason to change our opinion as far as we are concerned for when asked next day to let us pay for the expenses we had put our host to he said 'God forbid' and began to load our pockets with nuts, figs, etc. and some gin. I gave them some little presents and the wife rushed and got me a long towel with the ends worked in red and blue.[38]

January 1884 – Naxos

We started for Komiakí in fine weather, 3 hours, but on the way had hail, rain, mist and violent winds, in fact we past [sic] 'the Wind's dancing place' (Anemokhorévtros) and they were sure having a ball. All the men tried to go to Vothri but we stood firm to go on to Komiakí. We rode straight to the house of Mr. Kostantinides, the Demarch, and were already upstairs when we were greeted by his pretty little daughter Athena, about 15. We bought lamb, some hens and eggs and made ourselves at home with the fruit, wine, honey and bread of our host, who was away. The muleteers, who seemed old friends, and Gavalá, a relation, all sat in the sitting room and this is how we spent New Year's Day 1884.

We had a great deal of difficulty in the morning about starting to go and see an unfinished colossal statue said to be of Apollo, 1½ hour off near the sea. It was raining and after T had said he would walk and the muleteers could stay at home on half pay according to our agreement, and after they had agreed to go and P had rushed out of the room saying he would not expose himself to more dangers and T had told him he would not be paid at all that day, we all set out at a fine moment only to be plunged in rain very soon. Once we got below a certain level we got into fine weather. We had to leave the mules and climb with hands as well as feet to the quarry and on to the statue, which is enormous and very rough and weather worn.

---

[38] Mabel kept this cotton hood, 'with a border of blue and red cotton (birds), worn as a coal-heaver wears a sack'. In 1886 she exhibited it at the Anthropological Institute. A range of their souvenirs from Greece and Turkey illustrated a talk given by Theodore (see Mabel's Appendix to the *Journal of the Anthropological Institute of Great Britain and Ireland*, Vol. 15 (1886), pp. 391–403).

When we returned to Komiakí we were told T's brother, Mr. Swan, was come. He had followed us by double journeys and we were delighted to see him. When Mr. Konstantinides our host came home he found 10 people drying their clothes, us two and P, Mr. Swan, and a man called Mantheos,[39] a native of Anaphi who is to show Mr. Swan mines there, we were all for the 1st table, and the muleteers. The Demarch was very kind and reminded us that he had seen us on landing and invited us. We had a very merry dinner, much politics talked and many international toasts drunk.

Next morning the Demarch would not hear of any return for his kindness and we parted. I gave some little gifts to Athena and T was given a stone chisel found near the Apollo. We rode to the monastery of Phaneroméni down a fearfully steep road. We were very gay and raced our mules whenever there was room for 2 to pass and the whole 10 kept up a continual fire of jokes. At Phaneroméni women are not admitted but they let me in as I had come so far and I suppose out of curiosity. The superior was not at home and the Economos[40] took this upon himself. They gave us coffee, nuts, etc. and I said how much obliged I was and how wretched I should have been on the doorstep. I shook hands with all the monks I could see standing about and they looked at my hand and said Ugh! And made up their minds to take it.

We then went towards Engaráis, straight along the sea; first we were nearly stuck in the mud for about 180 feet and thought we should have to dismount and then we had some wide rivers to cross running into the sea, which were exciting and amusing. At Engaráis we were received by the Papa of the village. He was very polite and looked like a shabby Chinese. His clothes all green and his long wrapping gown, short overcoat and his plait of hair not done with hairpins as is usual but tucked into his hat like the handle of a teapot and sometimes down. He walked on tiptoes, smiling and when I was left alone he sat and smiled at me. I was forced to try and speak Greek.

After dinner we had a dance. From the moment we arrived the room was full of people. Such a lot of babies. The priest's eldest daughter of 16 owned one of them, not her eldest for she said gaily it was dead and was much nicer than this. Her father said when his wife died he thought he had better get her married. We saw several married women of 15 or 16 in this village. We saw a great many pretty dances and athletic performances but as I know T has taken notes of them I shall not.

[Friday] January 4th. We rode to Trípodes, crossing and going over part of the road we had taken to Potamiá. The Demarch took us in and we had a great walk over the village to find food. It was a very wretched house and full of fleas.

---

[39] The Bents' new dragoman, Manthaios Símos (1846–1935?), is hereby introduced.
[40] The priest responsible for the day-to-day business matters of the monastery.

Our host keeps a sort of public house. There was a fine dish of snails to T's delight. When we went to our bedroom and I wished to shut the door, I found it was gone so we had to do without and cats and dogs came in freely.

In the morning I rode and the others walked to the Plaka where there is the ruin of an old Hellenic tower made of large stones. We had a very severe hailstorm coming back. After luncheon we rode to the town, stopping in a shoemaker's shop to shelter and I bought a beautiful piece of embroidery. We went to the same house and found the people cleaning and putting out their smartest things for this was their Christmas Eve. We would not be allowed to sit in the sitting room, only Mr. Swan slept there. And we had to dine in the bedroom with the trapdoor.

Early on Xmas morning the family began to receive visitors and we were had in and introduced; once I was obliged to shake hands with 9 men. Really they wished to show us as curiosities. We had visits too from Mr. de Lastic and Mr. Mavrojenes. After luncheon we went and visited the Demarch, Mr. de Lastic, Mr. Mavrojenes, and the Bishop: these 2 last were out. It was so cold in the house that we were glad to go anywhere.

I went home and had not been there a minute when I was told the Despotes[41] was there, so I had to go in alone and say T was out. I was wretched till P came in. I asked permission to visit a convent, and he said he would ask the Papa who was with him to accompany us, also to prepare them for our visit. The Bishop had his enamel locket on. When T and Mr. Swan came back they said they had walked to the convent of S. Chrysostomos and got upstairs before they found some nuns, who met them going down, and when told they were Angli asked where that was, if England was near Europe, and then if they were Christians. In the evening we got an invitation from the Bishop to dinner next day and the Ephoros to luncheon. We accepted conditionally on the arrival of the steamer.

[Monday] January 7th. Breakfasted at the Ephor's, the harbourmaster, who talked German with me, being a guest. We saw the steamer so we went to say farewell to the Bishop and embarked about 2 on the ΕΠΤΑΝΗΣΟΣ for Santorini, which we reached next morning at dawn. We left Phaidros at Naxos.[42] It is such an extraordinary place. A wall of land composed of Thera, Therasia and a smaller island. The crater full of sea too deep to anchor and the cone smoking in the middle with hot water round it. The town Pherá on the top of the cliff and a winding road up the precipice. We did not go up but breakfasted below off bacon (English) sent by Mr. Binney from Syra with some butter and a piece of his own plum pudding, and embarked in a kaïke at 9.30 for Anaphe, 16 miles away.

---

[41] The 'Despotes' is the Archbishop. The 'Ephoros' mentioned later is a prominent layman appointed to assist the monastery with its community affairs.
[42] George Phaedros has been 'let go'. He later writes to Theodore asking for compensation (p. 342).

We paid the boat but they took advantage of our going to send the post for the first time for 2 months, though as the Eparch told us there were letters of importance to the government. An old man whose son-in-law had died in Anaphe also went to fetch his daughter. We had 3 sails. It was undecked except at the end. We took 16 hours on the voyage as the wind was unfavourable and at 3.00 landed, not at the nearest point to the town, and scrambled over thorns, stones, rocks and streams for an hour. We found a little whitewashed chapel with a broken door, lighted a candle we found there and with 2 rugs and 3 stones made a bed on which we 3 lay till morning dawned very cold and hard. Then we made a fire, toasted bacon and waited for the mules which M had gone on to order.

The luggage and I had 3 mules and the others walked. We and the post took 2 hours. The town is 1000 feet up, and long, in fact an hour away, we saw a crowd watching our approach. We went to the unused house of M's brother. We had a bedroom and Mr. Swan as usual the sofa in the sitting room. Everyone came to see us of course and we asked the Demarch, a little shrivelled old man, to dine. As we 3 sat on the sofa Mr. Chalaris, who is very deaf, said 'Ti anthropoi einai' 'What people are they?' He was answered 'Angli', but he thought they said 'Agri', wild, and he said 'No! I will *never* believe they are Wild Men', and then the mistake was explained to him.

The following morning we set out with the Demarch, who spoke Italian to me, all on foot but I. We went to the ruins of the old town, and saw quantities of opened graves and lots unopened, and statues lying about headless. The old woman who owned the spot gave me a little clay model of a fig found in the tombs.[43] We then went to Kalilymákia by the sea where we saw a temple ruin and then had a very gay though not luxurious luncheon. The Demarch had some abominable looking black and green bacon, all lean, which he seemed offended at our not eating. He was pleased when Mr. Swan took some but he privately hid it in the weeds. We gave the Demarch some very good chocolate which he would not eat and said he would keep it to make coffee of, but he seemed to think it horrid stuff.

After dinner a fine tall handsome niece of M's called Evtimia Chalaris, dressed in a beautiful old costume of silk, violet flowered brocade skirt, green velvet bodice, gold embroidered stomacher and a short pink satin jacket edged round the cuffs and down the front with pink fur. Her head was very prettily arranged with 2 of the little embroidered towels we use for antimacassars. There was a regular ball and the Demarch danced most actively. We looked on and Mr.

---

[43] This little clay item has survived and is in the British Museum (1884, 1213.73); it is not a fig, but rather the 'petrified clay mould of the interior of an echinus shell' and is 3.5cm high. There are also five attractive steatite beads that Mabel gave to the Museum in 1888.

Swan and I from time to time made a plum pudding for which he had brought the materials.

[Thursday] January 10th. We went to the monastery of Kalamíotissa on a promontory. We went by boat. We walked down to the sea. M had dynamite with him and he killed lots of fish. He went onto rock while we waited for the dynamite to go off. Then we came and caught the fish, some in our hands, some with bushes tied to canes and some with a harpoon. The Demarch was of the party. The monastery is a very curious place built on the site and with the stones, and using much of the old building of a temple of Apollo.

On the **11th Sat. [January, actually Friday]**, finding the wind fair we determined to be off in the boat that was waiting our pleasure, so we got the post and this time our party was much increased. The old man had his daughter who was very sick and her baby and M had a cousin Margarita who was to go to Antiparos with Mr. Swan. All the women kissed me at parting.

We landed in 4½ hours at the chapel of Agios Nikolaos [Santoríni], a little white thing under a red rock on the other side of the island. We sent M for mules and thought to walk on a little ourselves but got quite lost in a deep gully half stopped by prickly pears, but however T saw M high above us on the ridge of a hill, not at all where we meant to go. We shouted and he said he could not see us. It was getting dusk but at length he found us but told us to climb up to him. Tremendously steep and rough, but firm footing, not like the place we landed which seemed all composed of crumbling cinders which broke away if one touched them. We went to the village of Akrotiri (on a promontory) and slept in the castle. We could get nothing to eat but what we had with us, so we slept there and went on to Pherá, the capital 2¼ hours off, early.

The road lies all along the topmost edge of the cliff and I was the only rider. The walkers found the road so horrible, all powdered pumice, that they walked on the top of walls whenever they could. We passed a colony of lepers. The town is very long indeed, all on this cliff. We got a very large uninhabited house and the Eparch kindly lent us furniture, 2 beds, 6 chairs, 2 tables, 1 basin and jug and some plates. We spent a very long time in his house and saw many babies and relations of his. He is a nice man and talks French. He also gave us an old woman to cook for us, Kyria Maria.

Monday [actually Sunday, January] 13th. I rode down the steep road and we took a boat with 3 men and in very rough weather rowed to the cone. The water in and out round the volcano is quite yellow with iron and sulphur and fizzing and smoking. It is difficult walking to get to the top but my 2 companions aided me so I got over the rolling stones and ashes. All the top is very hot, smoking and covered with beautiful sulphur. At the bottom, which took great scrambling to reach, we bathed our feet in the water which was delicious and quite as hot as we could bear and then we lunched. We had a violent shower on getting into the boat but took refuge under the stern of a large ship and in due course got safely home.

[Tuesday] January 15th. Mr. Swan and the cousin went off by the steamer to our grief and T went on a walk to a part of the cliff where the Roman Catholics used to live till it began to fall away. The Eparch paid me a visit and after luncheon T and I went to see Mr. Nomikos, who has a great many old vases, and also Mr. da Corogna who wished to show us some Italian pictures of which he thought a great deal. They were not very good, though most likely the only ones in the Kyklades. We also went to the Roman Catholic convent and saw the nuns, and to the Greek church where there is a beautiful *tembelon* of carved wood, not painted. The Bishop's seat is all gilt.

Today our mules were ready but my leg, which a flea bit December 28th and which had gathered, gave me such pain that we got the Deputy Nomikos, who is a doctor, to it and I was left at home to lie on the bed doctored by Kyria Maria with linseed poultices and [illegible] water. It is pouring.

Saturday 18th [January, actually Friday]. Therasia.[44] Yesterday, I mean the day before, we left Phirá, though it was raining, for the village of Emporion. Our way lay along the same road on the cliff and T and M went to see the lepers, but I would not and am glad I did not. They live in houses cut in the pumice stone and have a chapel at the top. They walk on the cliff. T saw them all with the exception of various lacking hands, eyes, etc. and one who was in bed. We were dreadfully wet when we got to the house of the Demarch of Emporion, who took us in for nothing. We had a very public bedroom with a door into the sitting room and a large window on each end of it and the basin in one of them. A huge and very damp bed closely covered with a calico mosquito-curtain so most of the undressing was performed in it, the rest leaning against the door.

T got up at 5.30 to see the feast of Saint John the Baptist in a most curious old church made of remains of temples from Mésa Bounó. There is an old altar hollowed out, with garlands and rams' heads round, placed before Saint John the Baptist's picture and this was full of water and an orange floating in it to make it more sweet. The large cross was carved about with a large bush of basil behind it. It is said to have grown over the cross when St. Helena found it. Everyone dipped basil in the water. The priest made crosses in the water with his hands and blessed it and then everyone began to scramble for it with cups, jugs, bottles, etc. After breakfast and my kissing everyone who wished to kiss me we departed on mules, with large bits of basil in our hands, for Perissa.

---

[44] The little Cycladic jug (1800–1550 BC) used as an illustrative detail throughout this volume was acquired by Mabel on Thirasía. She gave it to the British Museum in 1926, where it may still be seen (1926, 0410.9). It is 12.5cm high and of considerable charm and humour.

I must say I object to Santorin. I am sure it does not agree with me as I have a headache nearly always from the volcano, I am sure, and it is so horrible to think that in an island with no springs water can cause such havoc as we saw yesterday. We were shown where a house in Emporion stood that had been washed away with a man and a good deal of cattle of all sizes and I could see *nothing* to show that a house had ever been there. 7 men have been washed away during these rains and many vineyards destroyed. The vines have a very funny effect as they are plaited round into hampers[45] and a field full of hampers looks most odd. A great many hampers were full of stones and earth from the rain. In other islands they straggle on the ground for fear of the wind.

We had most lovely weather till 4 o'clock. Perissa is a huge many-domed round white modern church (with flying buttresses 30 and 29 feet across), built because they found a rough iron cross in digging. Near it is a small round temple, of large smooth blocks with inscriptions on them. It stands about 10 feet high now and in a sort of pit. The Papa gave us coffee and having got to the end of the plain we went straight up the very steep Mésa Vounó, or middle mountain, between Holy Elias and Stephen, where the old town of Oea stood. I sat at the top in a little rough chapel for an hour and read. The wind was howling. The chapel was made of old temple and very badly put together. T went to look for some inscriptions. He hardly came back when he went off to a cave and I went down to the sea on the outer side of the island with the mules, a very difficult way as there was no road and the mules sunk [sic] up to their knees in the rolling pumice.[46] If there were a larger stone it rolled away at a great pace. Though the saddle was unusually safe, I had to hold on with both hands, the wind was so high, and when I got near the bottom and the animal began to tread on me it nearly made me sick.

T and M were down nearly as soon and we looked at some old scraps of marble at Kamaris[47] and then mounted in a downpour to go to Pherá. It soon got dark which was not pleasant as the road was washed away in many places, sometimes 4 feet deep and we had to take to the vineyards. Kyria Maria had dinner ready for us when we got back.

This morning we walked down to the sea and got into a small boat with 3 men in rough sea. We had to skirt nearly round the inside of Santorin and Thera before setting sail. We had a very small sail which was held by hand. It was very rough and cold, and snowing and blowing and we got well washed by the waves.

---

[45] Vines curled into nests, to protect from the teasing winds, are still very much a feature of the Santorinian landscape.
[46] One of numerous occasions the Bents walk over extraordinary sites that remain for others to uncover. Here they are within metres of the astonishing finds of Akrotíri; on Mílos they miss Phylakopí, on Kéa they are unaware of the great settlement at Ag. Iríni.
[47] Kamári, on the east coast of Santoríni.

We had a stiff climb up here, like at Thera. One can see by the many-coloured strata that this is part of the same circle. I am now sitting in the Demarch's room with him and T gone for a walk.

Monday 21st January 1884. When we wanted to start we found one of the sailors dreadfully tipsy, Marinos and T had to support him down the zigzag path. He often fell. I had to walk close behind as he would not go at all unless I came. He was bawling to me all the time. I answered him soothingly. When we got to the beach he wrapped us both up in coats. I was so afraid of being kissed that I put my mackintosh over my head. Just then M came down with the other two, one quite drunk. The two rushed at each other and rolled over and over, biting each other's cheeks and hands till they and their clothes were covered with blood. T and M separated them and as they both began to call me to come to them, when they looked away I lay down behind a rock. They next began to undress and throw their clothes about. The beach was strewn with them and our cloaks and rugs for some length. T's man having got rid of his sash, thinking his Ulster was a gown and, I suppose mistaking him for me, kissed him all over his face and petted him.

By this time the boat was got ready by Nikóla, and Manolis who was not quite so bad, but very quarrelsome, got in and now we were all perched on a small rock, both men anxious to help me in. They jumped into the water to carry me but T and M helped me, and went to fetch a load of clothes and there was great difficulty in hauling the two in. T's one with his shirt-tails fluttering round. As soon as we were all in and pushed off, these two flew at each other again. Nikóla, who had had more than enough began making Anathemas and assisting M and T to pull the men apart. Of course as the boat was small I got mixed up in the fray and nearly sat upon and stamped upon. During this time we got under the bowsprit of a larger boat and nearly broke the mast.

Next we got within a foot of a rocky cliff but T steered us off. Then the rudder got unshipped and T and M had to ship it. But at last after T's hat had been knocked off and fetched, though we begged to go on we got clear of Therasía but not before we wished ourselves back. But that was not possible. The men were not willing and the landing difficult. At last we settled down. M keeping Manolis forward, T holding Marinos tight by the tail to prevent his fighting and falling overboard, but not before when I was obliged to move he had taken me in both his arms, and made me almost sit on his knee.

It was amusing to see T when he changed places with me. Marinos had his arm round his neck and holding a coat round his head to keep off the sea and squeezing his hand and speaking affectionately and telling him not to be afraid. Nikòla said *he'd* take care of me and grinned and winked at me. I was glad both his hands were full with rudder and sail and smiled at him to keep him in peace. The wind was good though rough and the sea covered with a sort of smoke and spray which turned in 'siphons', a sort of waterspout, one of which had thrown us near the cliff. We were so glad to get here and as I could get no mule I had to walk up.

Yesterday we went at 2 o'clock to the wedding of our muleteer's daughter Marousaki, a pretty, tall girl and a little, stout man called Evstakios (Eustace), about 5 feet. As T has written all about this I shall not say more than that in church he kissed the bride and bridegroom. I could not kiss that little man so I say I have a kiss to the good for any man I like.

Today T and M are gone on mules to Apáno Merià, along the cliff and I am staying in bed for warmth and old Kyria Maria keeps me locked up for safety. It is snowing, and so it was yesterday and the sea looks black and rough and I am in great fear the steamer may not come to take us to Ios, or Nio, tomorrow. No fire and this on a volcano in the Sunny South.

[Wednesday] January 23rd. This is 2nd day we are in waiting for the steamer. It is a lovely day but still so cold that I can hardly write. Yesterday we went to see the Eparchos Markos Mavrojenes (or black beard) and wandered about. The Eparch came to see us before dinner and the family da Corogna of Italian origin after. They are pleasant people and wished us to receive the son of 18 when he comes to England in May.

Today we have been to pay a visit to the Alexakis', he very large and rich, though a tasteless house, and the Dekigallas'. Mr. Dekigallas a very learned old man with whom T has made friends. This island is very damp, or rather so dry that it does not absorb wet and everything, boots, bread, silk, etc. gets mouldy quickly. The Dekigallas' or really de Cigalas', spent the evening with us and we were called at ¼ to 6 for the steamer ΠΑΝΕΛΛΗΝΙΟΝ, the smallest and worst. (The *Panellenion* ran the blockade in Krete.) Very rough passage about 2 hours to Ios.

Breakfasted at a kafeneion and sent our letter up to the Demarch Lorenziades, who at once came down from the town and told us he had no rooms for us to sleep in but we were to feed with him. The baggage and I were put on mules and we went up to the Khora. The family consisted chiefly of the Demarch, who has a little common 2nd wife very inferior to the rest but a kind little thing. I should have thought it unnecessary to marry her when there are so many other women in the world; his elder brother and 3 very pretty jolly girls Marousa, Aikaterena and Kaleroe, all tall and fat. A 3rd brother is the schoolmaster. All were quite like gentlemen and all in black frockcoats. There were at least 6 more people.

They received us most kindly and were really the most congenial people we have met. We took a house consisting of bedroom, pantry and sitting room, where M slept, and a kitchen, and went for our meals to the Demarch's. They did everything they possibly could to please and amuse us. The dinner party consisted of the three brothers, the wife, Marousa and we 3. The first day we had chicken soup boiled, and roast chicken; 2nd ditto kid, 3rd ditto fish, and 3 times a day did we get *mesithra*[48] and honey. *Mesithra* is a sort of curd made of sheep's milk in a basket, just like *Broccio* of Corsica. After dinner some of them dressed up in old costumes, of most splendid gold brocade and gold lace and embroidery. Such is the power of dress that we did not know where they had got the wonderfully beautiful woman in green and gold, and never found out till next day it was Aikaterene.

Next morning, **Friday [January] 25th,** the Demarch came to fetch us to breakfast, and, M having evidently informed about the English customs, we had 2 eggs, a glass of milk and some *mesithra* and honey. Afterwards we and the Demarch started to Plaketos at the other side of the island: 3 hours. We saw the supposed tomb of Homer who died here on his way from Samos to Athens and then went to a little hut of an old man where we lunched in a very rough way; wine in a large wooden basin and scooped and drunk out of a little gourd. The hut was very low, door 4 feet high and a bed built of stones with twigs and straw 4 feet square. Even in better houses the doors are often too low. We had cold fish and cold soft eggs and they are hard, whether hot or cold, to eat without a spoon. The 5 muleteers got very gay and led by the Demarch played a lot of games, all of which we had seen elsewhere. We got home at 4 and retired home soon after dinner.

On Saturday we had Marousa as a companion in our ride to Palaó Kástro, a mass of Italian ruins on a white marble mountain over the sea. It was very steep and Marousa was surprised I dared not to dismount, but I don't care to walk as my leg is not well yet. At the top is a very shabby rough little chapel where Marousa incensed the pictures very gaily amid crossing and chattering and I was made to scribble my name on the wall and the *tembelon*, or screen, both in Greek and English:[49] Μάιμπελ Βιργινία 'Αννα Μπένθος, which I thought irreverent and vulgar. By the way, I go by the name of Virginia now as they cannot say Mabel, it is if they had something sticky in their mouths as they cannot say B. 'Maimpr'.

---

[48] This light, refreshing cheese is to become a favourite of Mabel's. She varies between mesithra, mesethra and mesythra, but never from her relish of it. The couple bring home a primitive cheese strainer; it is in the Pitt Rivers Museum, Oxford (2005.68.1). The Bents visited Corsica in the late 1870s; Corsica was for centuries under Genoese control until 'sold' in 1768 to the French. Theodore covers the history in his *Genoa, how the Republic Rose and Fell* (London, 1881).
[49] The walk up to this little deserted hamlet is very fine (off season). The chapel is usually locked. Inside, the stone tembelon is whitewashed. If the Bents signed their names on it, the signatures are now obliterated.

We went then down to Agia Theodote near the sea and lunched on the grass, and afterwards went to see the church, which is a very rough Byzantine building. One aisle was filled up with stone-built benches and table where they eat at the pilgrimages. In one corner was a heap of immense pots and some large wooden spoons stuck in the wall. Everyone brings a contribution of food which is thrown into the common pots and cooked. The better class play all sorts of games in the church.

We had a delightful evening, about 30 people came, including a priest, and we had a constant succession of games in which I took part, also T. We actually stayed up till ½ past 10. First 'Blind Man's Buff'. Then a 'Blind Man in the Middle' and every one dancing around singing till he stopped us and put out a stick and touched one. That one having taken up the end of the stick and put it to his lips made some little whistle or buzz. If the name was guessed by the blind man he was released. Then 3 sat on pillows on a rug, side by side with legs out straight. The middle one had string put round under his feet and kept working about pulling this up and giving unexpected bangs with the back of his hands to the legs of the others who defended themselves with each a slipper, and if they hit they got the middle place. 2 people lay down on a rug with their heads on pillows and were covered all over with a quilt. Everyone went and gave them a bang with a knotted handkerchief on the most exalted part of them. They had to guess who. A person kneels on a pillow on the rug and is covered with a quilt; one after another people come and kneel in front of him with head also under the quilt and the confessor asks questions and imposes penance and at last when one comes who has never played this before the rug is lifted by the corners, the confessor slips off and the penitent is lifted in the air. These are a few of the most amusing, but there were many more.

Next morning, **Sunday [January] 27th,** Marousa came early to bring me a magnificent piece of red silk[50] embroidered 'to remember them by', also her pocket-handkerchief with her name worked and some pine nuts. We were really sorry to leave these kind people and they pressed us to stay but 'the ship was ready and the wind blew fair and we were bound for the sea'. So after breakfast, and giving them a few of the little presents we have with us, but nothing half as valuable as they had given me, we went down to the harbour with 2 mules and the 3 brothers and 3 girls. We sat in the kafeneion and drank coffee and ate sweetmeats and were given Kaliroe's pocket-handkerchief full of sesame seed

---

[50] On Ios (and Naxos) Mabel acquired the fine bed valences she displayed in 1886 at the Anthropological Institute. A range of their souvenirs from Greece and Turkey illustrated a talk given by Theodore (*Journal of the Anthropological Institute of Great Britain and Ireland*, Vol. 15 (1886), pp. 391–403). She describes them as consisting 'of a silk embroidered border 6 feet long and a narrower border 10 inches up the sides sewn to a piece of line, tucked in to the edge of the bed'.

that we might remember Kaliroe, or Callirhoe I think is the English way of spelling the stream she is called after. After an affectionate parting we set sail and after much tacking got out of the deep and safe bay and made straight for Sikinos.

Our *kaïke* is decked all over and we have hired her to fetch us from Sikinos and take us to Pholegandros and Antiparos. It was very rough and we got very wet. This is a very precipitous island and there is no port and only one *kaïke* and she is at Ios. We landed at a tiny little bay on the east, 2 hours from the only town. After lunching off the Demarch Lorenziades' good things M walked to send mules and in 4 ½ hours 2 came, or rather a pony, its foal, and a mule. I and the baggage mounted. We had to climb some steep sharp rocks though. It was some time before we struck into a track at all and it began to get dark and was quite before we arrived, but our way was cheered by meeting Mr. Swan about half way. He had arrived the day before with a letter to the Demarch, which was lucky for us as we had no letter to this island.

He reminds us of Mr. Walter Hore and he received us very hospitably. We have a real bedroom and washing table and all. We were soon at dinner and many people came in to see us. The *mesethra* of Ios was much welcome. It was the first they had seen this year here and was handed round to all.

When we came out of our bedrooms yesterday morning, **[Monday, January] 28th**, my birthday,[51] we had a tray with a coffee pot and sheep milk and some very hard bread with sesame, all at different times, and *very* soon after eggs and wine, and then set off with a good many men on mules and foot to the Church of Episkopí, once the temple of Apollo Pythios, about 1½ hour off, of course a steep and rocky way. One could quite well see what it had been in spite of the Christian alterations.[52] We rode on about ¼ of an hour to Agia Marina where there are the foundations of a large city on a steep cliff toward the sea and sloping down on the land side. Then back to Episkopí where we lunched and home quite early, so to fill up the time we went to a wedding dance. They had been firing guns since 2 days before and were married on Sunday and go on dancing for 3 days. The bride, who was not very good looking, looked worn out. We got cakes of honey and sesame and spirits to drink and stayed half an hour. M, who had been out shooting, as he is today, brought home a brace of partridges and woodcocks.

Today it is very cold and blowing hard; our boat could not come from Ios so we have to stay here and went to a Baptism. The babe is 3 days and very small and of the deepest shade of crimson. His nurse removed first of

---

[51] Mabel is 38 today; she was born on 28 January 1846.
[52] In *The Cyclades* Theodore writes that 'there are few remains in Greece… more perfect'. It is a temple-tomb of the 3rd century AD.

all his upper clothes and gradually as the service went on he was reduced to a white cloth and a cap. The font was a large goblet-shaped lead thing and large pitchers of hot and cold water were brought in. The priest turned up his coloured silk cloak till it was quite inside out and turned up his sleeve to the elbow, as for the washtub, which of course it is. He mixed the water and read a great deal, constantly stopping and making a cross on the water and blowing on it in that shape. He also did the same to the baby. Oil was poured in 3 times in a cross, and when the godmother held full of oil [sic] the cap was taken off, the cloth opened and the poor little red object exposed to view and oiled in various parts. Then the priest took him and held him aloft like a skinned rabbit and plunged him 3 times in to the water, head and all, and took such a long time about. The godmother received him in 3 white clothes, and after a little while, when his cap and shirt had been blessed, the priest put them on him and the nurse sat on a step and quickly swaddled him up, arms and all. He was held by the calves of his legs quite upright and his cap taken off; hair cut off in a cross, that is in four places, mixed with candle wax and burnt. Then a blue pelisse was put on by the priest and a hat and a ribbon put round his waist, crossed at the back, brought round over its shoulders and tucked in in front. The priest took it to kiss all the pictures in the screen. He was laid on a bench alone and then carried round and round the font, made to kiss the gospel and finally wrapped up and taken home, whither we followed, the priest, etc. singing all the way.

Mr. Swan, T and I all were seated in a corner and we all had the usual refections. We were surprised to see the mother walking about entertaining the company and my neighbouring ladies made many remarks to me that made me wish I did not understand Greek, as T and Mr. Swan seemed so amused.

February 1884 – Folégandhros

Two days more we were storm-stayed in Sikinos and did nothing particular. The house was so damp that our clothes were quite wet and dew was on our boots in the morning. I had an awful cold and stayed shivering in the house most of the time and we also paid some visits. When our boat came, on the evening of the 3rd day, the sailors brought me a nosegay from Ios and the 3 girls had each written some verses to me of a flattering nature. We rode (or rather I and the baggage, 3 beasts) on Friday morning February 1st [1884], 1 hour to the port and embarked at 9 o'clock, and as our wind was not good and we had to tack, we took 9 hours over the voyage of 8 miles.

(At this moment I have a crowd round me looking at my European writing, the neighbouring rooms full and quantities of people at the windows.) To return to the voyage, we had nice warm weather and were very comfortable lying on the deck. M had to lie below as he did not feel well.

Pholégandros. It was most beautiful just as we arrived. There were the most precipitous and mysterious looking rocks and some white shining ones, which T said looked like witches waiting for us. The last glimmer of sunset and the wonderful red light, which is supposed to be direct from Java.[53] The crescent moon and some stars looking quite blue in it and all the rest of the stars. The water was quite transparent, and as we stood on the deck gliding in after we had dropped anchor, we thought no pantomime was ever so lovely.

Now that I have seen the place by daylight I cannot imagine how we landed in Pholégandros. The second step we tried to take we were all on our hands and knees. Fortunately a sailor said he would 'hold the woman tight or she would slip into the sea' and held my wrist and dragged me. We had to crawl for about 50 feet up a smooth rock, called the Plaka or flat, sloping 45 or 50 degrees and often slipping back and having great difficulty in finding anything to stick our nails into. As there was water streaming over it, it was very slippery. T and Mr. Swan said it was quite as much as they could do and if the barefooted sailor had not helped me I am sure I should have slid down.

We then went up a waterfall and scrambled over stones and thorns till we found a rocky road and in about an hour got to the only town and to the Demarch's house, which admitted us. He is not a very lively man but means well. He does not understand feeding us. We had fishes' heads, cold, for breakfast one day and were expected to eat their brains and eyes. But we got a good dinner. Yesterday we rode to the port, an hour, and rowed to a large cave called Kryssospilaio, the gold cave, high above the sea; immense rocks piled up below and a sheer precipice above. I did not go up as I saw it was too difficult for me, and the Demarch took 2 sailors to help him. He had never been before. I stayed in the boat and rocked violently about ½ an hour till they came down.

We got back for midday dinner. (Oh how the table and floor and my elbow are shaking with the crowd.) Our ship had gone round to the port and did not reach it till 12.20 and we got no baggage till morning. We have not got a private bedroom and have to hang up an Ulster to hide us while we dress. Neither door shuts. We have a basin, for a wonder, and Mr. Swan is able to wash there by day.

That afternoon we went up a high rock near the town to an old church. I rode. A great many people came to see us in the evening and a Mr. Mavrogene. Brother to the one (Epamisiondos) in Paros has said he wishes to 'make a table'

---

[53] Krakatoa, the infamous volcano in the Sunda Strait (Indonesia) exploded massively on 27 August 1883. It bruised skies around the globe.

for us this evening, so we sup there. He has also asked a passage on our ship to Antiparos, whither we hope to set sail tomorrow.

This afternoon we have been to the doctor Venier, of a Venetian family, a fierce political foe of our host. Party spirit runs so high here that however sick people may be the doctor is not called in by his enemies. We have been consulted about a very serious case here but we do not like to suggest anything as our directions would surely not be carried out properly. Dr. Venier showed us the hangings of a bed, in which King Otho slept when he visited Pholégandros.[54] All gold lace, silver lace and the most beautiful silk embroidery on linen. The curtains were striped silk gauze with gold lace insertion. The pillows gold edged real silk. We were also shown lace-edged sheets and gold embroidery. It was a really splendid sight and fit for a museum. We also paid another visit and had coffee, jam and water and mastic at both.

In the evening we sallied forth led by a boy and a lantern to dinner. I, who had hitherto only been seen in my Ulster, now appeared in my dress which has bronze bright bead butterflies on it and these and the make of my dress and my European figure caused a great excitement before I started. The Demarch begged me to take off my cloak and said it was a pity the women should notice the fashions, but I told him I thought he was just as interested in them. He was in Paris 17 years ago and considers himself a great authority. He speaks French.

Our guide caused some confusion by taking us to the back door, so we had to go in through the kitchen. The table was very nicely laid and we four and our host and 2 little girls were the eaters, but while we dined several masks[55] came in and walked round and out. I forgot to say that at Ios also there were masks but they just walk in and out and do not stay a minute or say anything. A great many others unmasked came filing in and shaking hands with us all and sitting round. One of the viands was cuttlefish[56] of which I ate and had indigestion for a week.

Monday morning, 4th February, we were all out and ready while our sailors were still in bed and had to wait for mules too. Also when we got to the port the boat was not ready and so though we had got up at 6 we did not start till 9. No Mavrojenis (Themistokles) made his appearance, but an old woman with a big box did and stepped on board our pink boat with no leave asked. She was put in the hold and we set out for Antiparos.

---

[54] King Otto I of Greece and his Queen, Amelie, toured the Cyclades, guided by his Director of Antiquities, Ludwig Ross. Ross published his tour in 1840 (Ross L., *Reise auf den Griechischen Inseln*, Stuttgart, 1840).

[55] A carnival custom.

[56] The cephalopods are often confused, but all welcome at the Greek table. The three common species are the cuttlefish (*soupiá*), squid (*kalamária*), and the octopus (*okhtapódhi*). All are Lenten fare.

But soon the wind changed and we spoke of Amorgós. Then we had no wind and found we could not get to Amorgós, so we would try for Ios. Mr. Swan had heard such a glowing account of the young ladies that he was dying to go. So we tacked and rowed and did all we could and it at last, about 4, got very rough and we feared we must go to Santorin. After that we nearly had to turn in to Sikinos, but we hated the thought of the long way up to the town, the damp house and probability of being weather bound and no hope of help from the steamer, and when we got near we found how difficult it was to get in so we determined to make one more try for Ios and a good wind just came and helped us in after 10 hours on the sea. M and the woman quite shut down in the hold and very sick. We went to eat in a kafeneion and sent a message to the Demarch. He did not come but Marousa and her father the Proendemarchos did and we heard that the poor little 2nd wife, Marigó, has been very ill ever since we left and that Kallirhoe had had a presentation that we should come. How they all kissed me! We had some maskers in the evening and a good deal of talking and laughing but felt very sad about poor Marigó.

We all slept in that house and left by the steamer **OMONEIA** (harmony). We had a very rough passage and there were threats of stopping for shelter at Naxos, but the *Omoneia* being a large steamer we got on to Paros. Mr. Tcherlendi came on at Naxos but we did not see much of him. Mr. Swan's brother, Kyrios John, was there to meet us. He has not been so long in Antiparos as his younger brother, about 3 years, and he had already the name of Kyrios Swan (Σουων).

We embarked in a good-sized schooner sort of boat owned by a man called Christos and tried to get from Paroichia to south of Antiparos but there was too much sea so we had to land at the town of Antiparos. Mr. Swan and I went first in a wet little tub to shore and walked to the Papa's house where we got coffee and waited for 2 mules. It seemed quite strange and very pleasant after the long cold windy ride, helped, as our night journeys have hitherto been, by the blessed moon, to find ourselves arriving again at the same place and to know beforehand what it would be like and to have no uncertainty as to having a door, or a gate, or none, or any window. I rode and was glad to have T's Ulster on by way of carrying it, it was so cold on the top of the mountain.

As I have been very lazy about my Chronicle, I will only say that there I stayed 3 weeks, during which time we did lots of fishing, sometimes with dynamite, which is against the law and very dangerous, but the fishermen here did it. We had nothing to do with throwing the cartridge but we netted up the whitebait and caught them in our hands; and also we used various kinds of lines and caught red mullet, etc., but what amused me most was catching octopus. There was a large can with a glass bottom and through this one could see the bottom of the sea quite plainly and the 'octopodi' worming about and drop the bait[57] near him and see him bounce at it. The fisherman bites him in the back of the neck to kill him, a very nasty sight, and he changes colour several times, blue and red, and moves about a good deal afterwards.

We sailed about too and went into a lot of caves. One which was very deep and dark had a seal[58] in it. We could hear him breathing and then rush past us. We were lying in the boat and the entrance is very narrow. The place he had been lying in was quite warm and there was a most awful smell. When we got out T found he had been sitting on a dynamite cartridge. We lunched in all sorts of jolly little bays and caves on the coast of Antiparos and Despotico, a very pretty island quite close. Very like Corsica in its green shrubs.

A good deal of grave digging was also done and a good many pots of earth and marble found, also knives of volcanic glass, little marble figures and a little silver one also, very rough, and some personal ornaments of brass and silver. T and Mr. Swan found the foundation of a marble temple in Despotiko.[59]

During the last week of my stay, T went to Amorgós.[60] I was not well and remained for further rest. I joined on the steamer ΕΠΤΑΝΗΣΟΣ at Paroikia on Ash Wednesday, February 27th [1884] after having waited a day and a night as the weather was stormy. We had a great tossing going to Syra. We stayed there one night and then went in a *kaïke* to Mykonos, 3 hours and very rough indeed. Here the Demarch Kalógera took us in. The family were gentry this time and very kind and pleasant, father, mother, 3 daughters. They have a large and well-furnished house and we stayed with them 3 nights. We had a real bedroom. I stayed in bed all the next day and T wanted to go for a long walk and it was a safe place to be out of the way. I worked and read and got up for dinner.

---

[57] The Pitt Rivers Museum, Oxford, has a peculiar wood and glass octopus bait brought back by the Bents from Foúrni (1888.37.1). It is designed to dangle under the water, glinting, and (with its array of barbed hooks) irresistible to cephalopods. Similar devices are still widely employed today.

[58] Rare and protected in the Aegean, this is the Mediterranean Monk Seal (Monachus monachus). At the end of the 19th century they were regularly seen around the islands and 'Phoca (seal) Bay' is still a common placename on maps.

[59] This 3–4 week interval on Andíparos and Dhespotikó was the opportunity for Theodore to carry out his major excavation work. Theodore's report of his excavations there are to be found in the *Journal of Hellenic Studies*, Vol. 5 (1884) pp. 42–59, with illustrations of some of his finds, entitled 'Researches among the Cyclades'. The Keeper at the British Museum received a letter from him, dated 30 May 1884: 'Dear Sir, Do you care to make me an offer for my figures, vases, ornaments, etc., from Antiparos? It occurs to me that a collection of this nature is rather lost in private hands. Yrs truly, J. Theodore Bent.' This 'collection' of over 60 artefacts forms the core of the museum's prehistoric Cycladic material, Mabel even relinquishing the silver bracelets and necklace. Of particular interest is a fragment of one of the strange clay objects often referred to as 'frying pans' (1884, 1213.49). Their purpose is not fully understood but, with the distinctive marble figurines, they epitomize some phases of Cycladic culture. (The volcanic glass is an assemblage of Melian obsidian blades.)

[60] Mabel had already visited Amorgós twelve months before. Theodore wrote a charming account of their Easter on the island for *Macmillan's Magazine* (Easter Week in Amorgos); it appeared in the 1884 May/October issue and Theodore expanded on it for *The Cyclades*.

March 1884 – Delos

Saturday March 1st. We went in a large *kaïke* to Delos, 1½ hour. No one lives there but a shepherd who is to see that no one bags a column or a statue. We spent 6 hours there. The whole place is a mass of ruins not half excavated. The French were excavating but they stole so much our host says they shall not dig again.[61] But T is begged to come and dig and stay in his house. On Sunday we arose early and awaited the steamer but did not start till 3 o'clock. We were given an *eikon* of St. Nikolaos in a crab shell gilt.[62] He is the saint of the sea. We embraced at parting and set out for Tenos on the large steamer *Xios*.

This was our second visit. We were at the great pilgrimage on the Greek March 29th, that is in the beginning of our April 1883.[63] It looked so quiet. We were the only passengers landing and last time we had nearly been knocked off the pier by the crowds. There were many steamers and a sheet of boats. There were booths all up the streets and 4,500 people in the different dresses of the islands, the Peloponesos, Walachia, Asia Minor, etc. We went to a new hotel, the 1st guests, the furniture not even settled yet. It is to be called Victoria in honour of us. This was the last day of carnival and one would think all the hens knew Lent was come as we had great difficulty in getting even eggs. We went off on mules, or rather I did on one, past Exóbourgo, which we had been up last year, and through several villages where they were having great fun and dancing because it was the first day of Lent. An odd reason, *Kathará Devtéra*, Clean Monday. They were dancing on the roofs and we went up to see them and bought a musical instrument,[64] also a little dug up lamp which the owner was now using.

We lunched at Kardiané. We had the luck to ask to eat in a shop kept by a very nice old woman who took us to her private room and was delighted with us as she had lived in Rome 5 years in an English family. We had the inside of

---

[61] The French School of Archaeology was the first to be established in Athens in 1846 and its premises are palatial. They began excavating on Delos in 1873 and have continued researching the island ever since. Their work and publications are, of course, regarded as exemplary. There is a hint of sniffiness in Mabel's remark. Later this year, Theodore gave the British Museum four sherds from this holy island, including a 'fragment of pottery vase; with part of the lip; stamped with two squares of pattern' that he had managed to acquire (1884, 1213.56).

[62] This shell (and another ikon from Mýkonos) were displayed by Mabel in 1886 at the Anthropological Institute. See p. 40, note 50.

[63] Mabel's notebooks do not contain a record of their first trip to Greece, but the couple had a whistle-stop tour of the Cyclades in the spring of 1883, when they also visited the islands of the eastern Aegean, as well as the Greek mainland. See p. 186.

[64] Theodore was fond of Greek musical instruments and brought a few back with him. The Pitt Rivers Museum, Oxford, has this reed and horn double-pipe from Tínos (1903.130.21), as well as one from Páros (1903.130.16).

a lamb we are carrying about cooked and thought of Ethel and the Aunts at Sutton Hall as we ate it.[65] I picked up a relic of old times on the road, a basalt thing for smoothing marble, very much worn by weather but the grooves and place for the handle still visible.

On Tuesday we set off with 3 mules for Isternia, meaning to sleep there. The road was as bad as we have been on and I had to walk sometimes. We lunched at the oddest convent I ever saw, Panagia Kekrovounon. It consisted of a village all full of nuns, 110. They had pigs and poultry running about and some seemed quite young and had bare heads. They are the only inhabitants but I saw 3 men too. We lunched in the Superior's house with our own food. The Eastern nuns dress quite differently to Western ones. They tie a black handkerchief under their chin to the top of their head, like a bib, and another on the head the ordinary way, but hanging over the forehead, and wear a black gown and shawl but these had coats just like the priests.

We then rode on to Isternia where we meant to sleep but could not find a decent house so we pushed on to Pirgos (Fort) having a letter to the Demarch. He received us most kindly. It was not a grand house. We got here about 6 and at 8 dined. We had a great many visitors. A very small room and only a public wash in the morning. We had to leave about 8 to return to Isternia to get our steamer tickets. We were very sorry to leave as Pirgos is one of the prettiest villages we have seen. A rocky river makes the street wider instead of the crowded passage full of pigs. It was very cold indeed and windy. The *Praetor* or agent of steamers gave us coffee and jam and we then rode down a fearfully steep road to the sea. There was a great crowd of 3rd class passengers all seated on the sand and one poor cabin where coffee could be had. The sea was very rough but we had the certainty of the steamer as we could see her come out of Syra harbour.

She was a very large one, the ΕΛΠΙΣ, formerly the *Truthful*. We had a great difficulty in getting on board and also in getting off on account of the sea. We had an excellent luncheon and slept below for a couple of hours, having had too much fresh air on the mountains to care to be on deck. We landed at the Khora of Andros about 3. A woman on the boat was so alarmed that she kept hold of T's hand till she seized his leg and kept that.

We had a letter to the Eparch Matzo and we were very kindly taken in and had a very comfortable room. On **Thursday [March 6th]** we set forth with 2 mules to Menetes a most lovely place, water in plenty and trees, ivy, ferns, and rocks and we even saw some primroses, the only ones we have seen in Greece. We had a letter to a Kyrios Krete who took us about and gave us coffee. We were

---

[65] Mabels' aunts had connections at Sutton Hall manor, near Macclesfield, in the north of England.

there about an hour and then went up to the Monastery of Panacrantor under the shadow of the rocks where the sun never comes. The roads in this island are all very bad and rocky.

T and M went a short cut which brought them to the Monastery 20 minutes before me as I went a long way round on account of the mules, so I had to arrive all alone. The muleteer asked several people we met if some strange men had come and always said 'no', so I really did think I was the first. When I had crossed a large court I was greeted by a madman who took my hand in both his and asked warmly after my health. I told him I was well and wished to see the Egoúmenos. I passed such long passages and through several courts and up and down inside and outside staircases and thought I should never arrive and wished I had the letter of introduction, but when I did get to the Superior I found T and M already shivering there.

We got the usual refection but were told we must eat Lenten fare and no entreaties would persuade old Gregorios to let us eat our own lamb. So when dinner came we had soup of rice boiled in water and strongly flavoured with both ingredients, a soup of lentils (which I hate) and onions, cheese, caviare, black of ours and red of theirs (I do not know what fish it was the roe of),[66] oranges, and *khalvas*, a sweetmeat made of sugar, flour, and sesame oil, and wine. One other monk besides the Superior dined with us and we had a very cheery dinner.

Our bed was in a most fearfully damp cell, no sheets and everything, even pillows, so wet that we have all had neuralgia and colds more or less since. We did not get a chance of washing next morning. All the monks were at church from 4 till 0 and only a little boy of 10 who got us some coffee but we could not find the sugar. We are shaking with cold. When the Superior came he gave *raki* but I do not like it. T said he was so glad we had no basin because if we had we should have thought it necessary to wash and it would have been unpleasantly cold. I could not help agreeing. We went to see the treasures of this very rich monastery, such a quantity of crosses and reliquaries of silver and jewels all crammed together without any care and very dirty.

We started in rain and then had some snow but finally got to a milder region, Aedonia (Nightingale) near Korthý with a letter to the Demarch who has an immense tower. All the houses used to be towers with very small holes to creep in and only approached by ladders, but within about 20 years they are not so much afraid of pirates and have put in doors and windows. Only 40 years ago they dared not live near the sea. We had a nice large room and no fleas and having arrived before luncheon we went for a very pretty walk in the afternoon.

[66] Carp (*taramá*). Greek *táramasalata* is the well-known spread made from carp roe; naturally white, it seems to be preferred dyed pink.

This island is much more fruitful and pretty than any other except Naxos, as there are plenty of streams.

Next day **Saturday [March] 8th**, we came 4 hours to Paleopolió, sometimes over rocky paths, sometimes quite pathless rocks, the worst we have seen. We had to put up in a poor mud-floored house. We had our own food and bought a new lamb 10½ pounds for 10 francs. I must say I hate the poor pretty little kids and lambs being brought alive and left running about. I never can look at them. It is an unpleasant plan.

We had a fearful night with the fleas, about 30, and left without washing and with our clothes and luggage full of fleas and went to Mpazeí, a little bay. I am sure the name means Vathý, a deep inlet into the land. There we breakfasted or rather lunched with the Demarch in an earthen-floored house. Our lamb and cuttlefish were the chief dishes. And then we came on to Gavrieon, a port where the steamer touches, and we meant to have come today for a tour in the north and returned here to go to Syra on Friday, but T was feverish and had to go to bed last night before dinner and is not up today. A doctor walked in of his own accord to see him but gave no advice and wondered I could not write English so fast.

[Tuesday] March 11th. T still in bed, temperature 103¾. M not well and the Demarch and his wife in bed all with rheumatism or some such thing. We might as well be in the palace of the 'White Cat' and served by 'invisible Hands'.[67] We see no one but a dear little servant called Orsa, aged 11. T's bed is hard and he has no top sheet, but it is not so hard as some we have had and not 4 feet high. The room is only 6 feet by 10 but it has a door and window and T can see the sea and boats.

This is not the 'lap of luxury' but we have plenty of Brand's Beef Tea, arrowroot, eggs and oranges, and certainly hard fare, if it makes one more greedy, makes one less dainty. I had to munch very dry bread, very early too for breakfast and some dry little figs that I would not eat if I weren't hungry and afterwards a little cup of black coffee. But now I can eat, or rather drink, sheep's and goats' milk thankfully and wish I had some here. A cold windy day. I must be forgiven for writing so gloomily for I feel rather forlorn.

Wednesday [March 12th]. I did not go to bed or undress last night. I had no bed to go to and T's temperature was a little over 104. I rolled myself up in my fur cloak and screwed myself up on the corner of the bed and would have been more comfortable if there had been no fleas. The doctor came last night and this morning. He says it is from cold. I don't know what it is. The noises in the house are dreadful and nothing can be done. The doctor only talks Greek

---

[67] A popular children's story of the time, anthologised by authors such as Horace Elisher Scudder (1838–1902).

and is surprised that I can write English so fast. The doctor who constantly strolled in and screamed at T is only an old man with some knowledge of herbs. He wanted to give T *kina* and was not at all satisfied that quinine was the same thing.[68] We stayed in Gavrieon till Sunday. T's temperature went up to 104½. I did not go to bed for 5 nights. We meant to go by the steamer on Friday to Syra but as it was the *Ydra* and, of course, late we had time to change our minds.

On Saturday T and I had mules and we went to the village of Phelló, inhabited by Albanians, like the rest of this neighbourhood, who all talk Albanian. We went into a house and had fruit and jam and bought a single saddlebag of native manufacture. It was quite a short ride. We also went to see an ancient abandoned quarry, not interesting.

Sunday March 17th [Sunday was March 16th]. We rode up to the monastery of Agià where we were hospitably received by the Superior, a fat and jolly old man who slaughtered fowls at once and made no objection to letting us eat them. We got there by 2 and were given luncheon and well warmed by a brazier. We had been in the snow. The wind was howling and rattling. We went to Vespers and then examined the library and plate. All the silver dirty and stacked up in a little glass cupboard and the books piled up and very damp and worm eaten in a little room with a broken window. Some of the books are extremely valuable M.S.S., one of 1156, but the illuminations sticking together from damp.

At dinner we had the Superior, the Archiserios or Archpriest, a very clever old man, and a deacon, eating octopus, etc. We had a nice room and my part of the bed was made with a bench and some chairs, not soft. Next morning we breakfasted and lunched and visited all parts of the monastery. It is very large, high up on the mountain and looks just like a fortress. It seems rather ruinous. There are 13 monks. One very old one has a little house to himself and his decrepit old sister in law to live with him. The Archpriest gave T some coins and beautiful scraps of pots found near Broussa in Bythinia or Vroussa in Vythiniá[69] as he said.

We had dreadful cold and wind riding over the mountains. First we went to see an old Hellenic tower before going to the monastery. I mean near the

---

[68] Quinine, the organic anti-malarial agent, takes its name from the Peruvian 'kina', tree bark (from the cinchona tree – genus *Cinchona*). A godsend for 19th-century travellers, quinine was first isolated in crystalline form in 1820. Synthetic quinine was developed in 1944.
[69] Broussa (today Bursa, north-western Turkey) was taken from the Byzantines in 1326 and was capital of the Ottoman Empire before the fall of Edirne (and then Constantinople itself). Mabel is to visit in 1888: see p. 230. In 1926 Mabel gave to the British Museum an actractively decorated sherd (1926, 0410.46) found in Bursa. It features a partially-clad figure seated in front of vines, and might well be the same fragment given to the Bents in this remote Cycladic monastery.

village of Agios Petros. It is quite round and 5 stories [sic] high. The door 4½ feet high and 5 feet thick, so one had to stoop and on getting in finds oneself in a round vaulted room like the Treasure House at Mykene,[70] and no communication with the upper rooms. The middle of the vault has now fallen in and one can see the wide winding stair all round. The way up is to screw yourself through a hole in the middle of the roof of the doorway, like going up a chimney, and then you get to the staircase. It is quite one of the most curious and interesting things we have seen, and very prettily situated too.

We left the monastery about 12 and in about an hour reached Katákilo, a scattered village. In the town of Andros we had met a certain Mr. Zariphonithes, a missionary he said, who had been in America, speaks English well and has an American wife. He invited us to stay so we accordingly went and were very kindly received. Mrs. Zariphonithes comes from Illinois and was a schoolteacher and is very fair and slight and nice looking, quite young and speaks without much American accent.[71] They have two very fair little children. They had a delightful fire and gave us some tea and bread and jam and butter. I stayed in all the afternoon and having begged for a bit of needlework I made the body of a cotton dress. After supper Mrs. Z. played a small organ and sang, which we enjoyed very much.

We started early next morning having 5 hours to ride. All over the mountain was snow in all the bushes; streams so frozen that they would bear the men and the 1st mule, and this was running water, for every few yards were fringes of icicles at the frozen waterfalls. I had a very shaky mule, so much so that some black pins that were in a paper in the pocket of my muff became quite golden, all the black[72] being scratched off. We saw a sheet of snow, at least 100 yards on a valley high up. I got very tired and was glad when we came to Lámira, about an hour from the town of Andros where we dismounted to lunch. We met here the Superior of Panácrantor and another monk, Pater Meletes. Everyone who has heard how we were made to fast, for M loves to tell everyone, says he is a 'Várvaros ánthropos', Barbarous man. We lunched very frugally with eggs the Zariphonitheses had given us; wine, bread and *khalvas*, and our expenses for 3 came to 8d.

A great piece of good luck befell us, for while we were sitting on boxes in that little shop, a delicate looking elderly man asked our muleteers 'if we were

---

[70] 'The Treasury of Atreus'. The Bents visited Mycenae in 1882/83. See p. 186.
[71] This family has since disappeared from upper and lower Katákilos, but, coincidentally, there are families of the same name today in the US.
[72] By way of illustration, Mabel has inserted an actual pin here on the page, between the words 'black' and 'being'; it is no longer golden, but black.

making a picnic'. They said no they are travellers so he came to us and said 'Welcome! Will you come and take a coffee at my neighbouring house?' We gladly agreed, for as we remarked, any crumb was welcome to hungry people. We went accordingly to a nice large house and were met by a pretty little faded mother Kyria Evanthea (good flower) and 3 little delicate looking daughters. The monks were already installed. There were also the host's 2 tall skinny sisters and his brother, a priest, very fat. He had a table in the window where he mends watches and jewellery. I have often remarked that it mattered little what the clergy had on so long as it was cut out rightly and they wear all sorts of trousers, but this man surpassed them all for he had magenta trousers.

We passed some time talking, waiting for the coffee. They said 'You are Europeans surely, but what country do you come from?' It seems to us so odd, for in Europe we have English written on our faces. Alas, because Greece is in the map of Europe we consider it Europe, but even Athenians speak of going to Europe and the Greeks do not think themselves Europeans.[73] I think it a very just humility on their part. We had coffee and preserves and then they insisted on our sitting down to another luncheon, and a good thing too as we got no dinner till 9.30, as an expected guest did not turn up.

They asked us where we were going to sleep. We said we did not know yet, not at the Eparch's as he had other guests. So they begged us to stay there. We went for a walk and had 15 visitors afterwards. All together the ladies nearly had all my clothes up to see how I was dressed. They questioned me a good deal and I had also to explain the mysteries of our religion to show I was a Christian. This was an awfully difficult thing but they seemed satisfied. The other day I heard some people speaking of us. One said 'Are they Christians?' the answer was 'No, Lords'.

After we had dined we were offered nightclothes and we said we had our own but they seemed unwilling we should use them and I would not even accept a handkerchief for my head. Next morning, T went out and left me to dress and the door opened and the mother and daughters all came in and kissed me. I was sitting on the bed in my nightshirt, doing my hair, with bare feet. They wanted to dress me but I declined. Of course they did not knock.

After breakfast we were taken to pay a visit to our hostess's brother. We found him in a peacock satin robe, cut like a priest's, and a dull violet satin overcoat lined with yellow fur. With a red neckerchief and fez[74] he was a picturesque object. We got preserves here and after much kissing, I mounted an ass and

---

[73] Greece joined the European Community as its 10th member in 1981. Adopting the Euro on 1 January 2001, the country jettisoned the drachma, older than any dream of Europe, without a backward glance.
[74] The Ottomans may well have gone, but the echoes of their music, food, and dress remained.

we set off to the town, our host, Joannes Parados, coming with us. It was an hour's ride. We had lovely weather. We sent our baggage to a boat and went to call on the Eparch. He asked us to lunch. Mrs. Matzo was not well and rather gave way to her misfortunes, said she was suffering terribly and suffered audibly and made a lake on each side of her chair by spitting. We went to see the library and walked about while our meal was being prepared. Our hostess of Aedonia espied us from the window of her daughter's house and up we had to go and have a sweet and water.

At luncheon, when we had soft-boiled eggs and no spoons, I could not help wishing some one had had the kindness to teach our grandmother to suck eggs and that she had handed the tradition down to us. At ¼ past 11 we went down and sat on the rocks; at 12 we were fetched into the house of one of our many acquaintances and given coffee, sweets, etc., and at 12.30 the steamer *Thesévs* came, a large one, and we embarked but did not leave till 4.30 as the captain's wife and some ladies went ashore.

Then we had instead of going straight to Syra to call at Korthý in Andros and leave the French Consul, and to the town of Tenos that the captain's daughter might say her prayers at the big pilgrimage church of Evangelistria, or Annunciation, so we did not get to Syra till 9. All the passengers were hungry but no food was to be had on the steamer. We had oranges and sweet lemons, for our friends had loaded us with quite half a stone between them. Real lemons cost 1 penny a dozen.

We fortunately got a room at the Hôtel d'Angleterre and thoroughly enjoy 'taking mine ease in mine inn'.[75] We packed a box of our spoils for England and this afternoon, 22nd [Saturday, March 1884], I rode and the others walked to Ano or Upper Syra, a hideous place with a view over this barren island. We got very tired of Syra by Friday and as we found a *kaïke* of Kythnos or Thermiá we packed and prepared to start. But the strong *Boreas* would not permit ships to leave the port so after constant expectations up to Sunday morning the 23rd we gave up and went to church, a very poor little place and very 'low' according to the wishes of Mr. Binney the Consul. Afterwards we lunched with Mr. Binney, Mr. Quinney the parson, being there also. N.B. Mr. Binney's clerk is Mr. Finney.

We left by the steamer *Thesévs* again early and got to Thermiá in 4½ hours. Rather rough. It is not outwardly a pretty island but the inner valleys are very pretty. We landed our goods at the few magazines in a little bay and then rowed round 2 headlands to another little bay where a large bathing house stands just like an old-fashioned German one over the hot springs from which the island gets its second name. It was not a very interesting sight. M had in the meantime

---

[75] 'Shall I not take mine ease at mine inn but I shall have my pocket picked?' Falstaff, *King Henry the Fourth*, Part I.

got 2 mules and we went up to the town, about ¾ of an hour. Very dirty crowded narrow lanes, as usual full of pigs and on the hillside as it is only of late years that they have ceased to fear pirates.

Our letter to the Demarch Bastas admitted us to a large new house, furnished with splendour, which we did not in any way admire, and though much more fully furnished than other houses, was bare enough. He and his wife were very nice people and we had a real bedroom for 2 nights.

On **Tuesday [March 25th]** we went with 2 mules, one for T and M between them, to the ruins of the old town, an hour off on the other side of the island near the sea. We saw nothing much except foundations and a headless sitting statue lying half covered by shingles and sand on the shore. We had a good deal of scrambling and climbing.

We returned to luncheon and set off afterwards to Sílakka, the only other village, about an hour away up the mountains. As we passed a coffee shop the muleteer called 'Kyrie Demarche!' and out came the mayor, a doctor who cast a hurried glance at us and, without a word, walked on in front of us and we, on being told by the muleteer, dismounted and marched up to an outside stair after him and then he welcomed us and made us sit down and we got coffee and jam and a great many people came to see us.

After resting some time we went to see a very large and rambling cave quite in the town. We had to slide in as best we might as earth had choked the entrance. It was not very nice as it seemed to be the dust hole of ages and old boots, dogs' skeletons and broken crockery abounded. The doctor's son, a *very*[76] smart young man, superintended us and was very kind and attentive in dragging me up and down difficult places. We had also 5 very small boys and all had candles. One part was very difficult as we were nearly sinking in the mud. The stalactites had not very beautiful names. The smart young man tried with a bashful air to alter them for my benefit, but the 5 little boys always corrected him. There were places where there were splits in the rock about 40 feet deep and we could only screw ourselves through sideways about 30 feet long. I got filthy but enjoyed it, and my clothes being like those of the Gibeonites[77] could not spoil.

We had arranged to start by *kaïke* early on Wednesday morning for Kéa, Kéos, or Zeá, but when morning came the wind was so fair that the Kaïke[78] was afraid he would not get back and though everyone called him a burnt man, a peacock, no man at all, horns, etc., he would not stir. Fortunately we came on a good-sized schooner, unloading lime at the Bath bay, so we engaged a passage

---

[76] Mabel has underlined 'very' twice. The doctor's obviously becoming son reappears on p. 58 note 85 *and* p.177.
[77] See Joshua 9: 3–15.
[78] The skipper of the caique. Common Greek insults are hurled at him a few lines on.

in her for 10 frs. less (40 frs.) and were to be ready any time in the course of the night. So first we rode to the monastery (shut up) of Holy George, about an hour and not worth going to, and then lunched in a miserable little *kafeneion* and took our luggage by boat to the Bathhouse[79] and got a bare little room there.

There is only a caretaker and when dinner time came we were told nothing could be cooked as there was no charcoal, but we got some brushwood and made a fire outside and cooked our precious bacon and warmed 2 small fish we had kept from luncheon and 2 mullet heads which M ate, and with some hard eggs did pretty well.

We were called in pitch dark but with a lantern we got through the wet sand, hot streams, and rocks to the boat with no further misadventure than a mineral hot foot bath for one of my feet, and by the time we got to the ship it was nearly light. We breakfasted of water, bacon and bread and the sailors had made a little couch on the deck where I slept, but at 9 had to be awakened as it was raining, so we went below into a little three-cornered hole and were pretty comfortable. We had a 6-hour passage instead of 2 and did not get to the place we wished, Zevs Polias,[80] on the S.E., but had to go N.W. to Holy Nikólaos, about ¾ of an hour from the town by a very good wide road, all the flat part a sandy river bed, full in winter.

We had some coffee in a grocer's shop and while M went for mules we were asked to go and wait in the customhouse. We were very much displeased but went. We thought we were to be rummaged as the ship had infuriated the authorities by dropping us and departing, paying no harbour dues. We could not tell the name of the captain, nor what part of the Peloponessos he belonged to, nor had we anything to prove we had not come from Turkey, and we had been well scolded by an old man in the white petticoat of the Albanians. We said we were English and had a letter to the Governor or Eparch, and did not understand these things. However the Customs officer, in a very smart dressing gown, took us into his neat little bedroom and asked us to rest. It was all whitewashed boards and all his trousers and coats turned inside out hanging on nails. He said he was just going to breakfast and hoped we would join.

T distressed me by declining but when I was asked I said I was hungry as it was now 12 and we had eaten at 7 and besides had not had much at the last 3 meals. We had a very good luncheon and T's appetite did not fail. It was a good thing as we never got a chance of any more to eat. The mules came and we rode up to the Eparch's. They gave us coffee and jam and told us they had no mattresses for us but we could feed there. The Demarch was fetched and finally we got into the house of our muleteer, Petro, a very long way through the piggy

---

[79] The celebrated 19th-century spa (built by King Otto) at Loutrá has a modern replacement.
[80] Poleis Bay, Ancient Karthaia, with its temple of Zeus Polieus.

streets from the Eparch's, and I went to bed till dinner. We are very glad not to be obliged to be entertained and to be able to pay.

Today T and M have gone off with an old man called Manthos[81], who knows all about the antiquities, to a place 4 hours off. They will not be back till night and I am sitting surrounded by women who are afraid I shall tire my hand or become sick by writing so much. The silk embroidery of my stocking has caught their eye and now I shall end in having most of my clothes examined. I am wanted to spend the day at the Demarchos's and the Eparchos's, but I do not mean to go. T always imagines I am going to have a day of rest but I always have so many visitors and questions. The Demarch called but I took refuge in the bedroom and my hostess, after kissing me, told him I was not well enough to see anyone.

Saturday [March] the 29th. We and Barba Manthos, or Uncle as the old men are called, rode about 2 hours to the ruined monastery of Agía Marina, where there is a ruined Hellenic tower. I remained there about 3 hours while T went on to Poiessa, where once stood an old town. M was left with me and to prepare luncheon. I wandered about for half the time and sat among the oleanders of a riverbed but at last an old man of 80 came and made me go to the tower of which he is the guardian. There is a church too.

The tower was perfect 15 years ago but is now half down. King Otho took away some stone, which ruined it. I saw them making *mesethra* by pouring fresh milk into boiling whey and had a plateful hot. We all, including Petros our handsome host and muleteer, sat down at a very low table and had a very good luncheon with limited implements, which I am sure I should not have enjoyed a year ago. We were home about 6. One thing I am sure of is that I should hate living permanently with doors too low for me. 4 feet is a common height and my head has been nearly knocked off several times by doors about 5 feet high.

Another thing about Christian names seems strange. All our names have a meaning if translated, but most of theirs like ours, Mercy, Constance, Ernest, etc., require no translation. Stone (Petros), Wisdom (Sophia), Pearl (Margarete), Goodflower (Evanthia), Goodbreeding (Evgenia), etc., etc.

Then the awful jealousy between each island and every different village is just as it was in ancient times. We are always hearing such conversation as we had this morning. M, 'You have not got good honey here!' The inhabitants, 'Yes, we have, that is very good honey'. 'No it is not; you should see the honey of Antíparos.' 'You do not know what good honey is.' And so on about wine, cheese, bread and everything. We hate M abusing the things we are very grateful to have set before us and feel very awkward when asked by our hosts, 'Is not

---

[81] Manthos Konstantinos (*c.* 1826– *c.* 1890), autodidact, local historian and collector.

this the best *mesethra* you ever tasted?', when there may be someone from the last village waiting to hear what we say. This is T's birthday but he has already celebrated the feast of the Holy Theodoros.[82]

Sunday [March 30th] we walked with Barba Manthos to a colossal statue of a lying lion, [one word illegible] and all of one bit of schist. It formerly stood at the head of a stadium but had slipped down where it is now and the government paid Barba (Uncle) Manthos to prop it up with masonry. In the afternoon we went to Barba Manthos's house and saw all the bits and scraps he had dug up and found at the sites of the ancient cities. And which he gave T next day in a large basket.[83]

Monday [March 31st] was our last day in the Cyclades. I gave my shoes a specially good blacking overnight and dressed myself in the best the saddlebags would afford and we started at 7 o'clock on a final expedition, with Barba Manthos in attendance, to some caves 2 hours off to the north where the ancients used to find an earth named *miltos*, used in red dye.[84] They were very large caves and we had some wall climbing and scrambling to do, and so many thistles I was sorry I had not my gaiters.

We came by a circuit to the port and I felt really excited at the thought of Athens. Our luncheon was stale bread, eggs, and cheese that I could not eat, with sour wine served up on a checked cloth, like dusters, not very clean and some dirty checked dusters as napkins. We decided we should eat something on the steamer. The said steamer was very late, that is 2 or 3 hours late, but we felt so excited about it and the idea of getting back to civilization again. There were many false reports and at last we all embarked and had to sit in small boats for about ¾ of an hour with great joking going on and oh! how glad we were when our old friend the *Thesévs* (ΘΗΣΕΥΣ) came.

On board were a good many old hosts of ours including the Demarch of Thermiá or Kýthnos and the kind young man who had dragged me through the caves of Sílakka.[85] When we asked for food we were told no cooking would be done on board as all the passengers would eat at the Piraeus, where we did not expect to get till past 7, so we got coffee and retired to a cabin, unpacked all our saddlebags, and cleaned ourselves up to the best of our ability that we might be fit to walk straight in to dinner in Athens if we had the luck to arrive in time.

---

[82] Theodore was 32. The first Saturday of Lent is Saint Theódoros' day.
[83] Two of these pottery fragments are now in the British Museum (1884, 1213.58 and 1884, 1213.59).
[84] Miltos, a red iron oxide valued in antiquity for its colour and wide range of uses which included pigments for pottery, cosmetics, pharmaceutical, etc. For illustrations, see http://www.gla.ac.uk/archaeology/projects/indminerals/Kea.htm.
[85] See note 76 above.

On our arrival we were invited to land in a boat belonging to one of the Men of War, with our Demarch of Thermiá. The sailors were dreadfully dirty. We sent our luggage in another boat with M, who had a carriage ready, and we arrived late for dinner. The hotel people received us enthusiastically. Mr. Graham came out to greet us with Grafton Bothamley,[86] who had joined him and Mr. and Mrs. Edward Anson at Cairo, they having been up the Nile. There were many of the same Greeks in the hotel as before.

April 1884 – Athens

Next morning, **Tuesday [April 1st]**, I walked out behind the Stadium to get some flowers for our sitting room. I crossed the Illissos near the fountain, or rather spring, Kallirhoe, and came back by the back of the King's garden.[87] In the afternoon we all 5 walked to the Stadium via the Cemetery and went into the King's Garden. On Wednesday morning Mr. R. Swan arrived and in the afternoon he and T and I went to the Museums to see if we could find out anything that would be like anything we had found, and we were very much pleased at what we did *not* see. Professor Mahaffy had called on us the day before and we had a most interesting conversation with him.

On Thursday we started at 9 o'clock to Tatoë, the King's country house.[88] In my carriage were Mr. Graham and Mr. Swan and the 4 others in the other carriage. A man who could speak English sat on the box of the Ansons' carriage, quite unnecessary, but he spoke Greek to T and me. It was 3 hours' drive. The house is a sort of chalet, not very imposing nor handsomely furnished. We lunched in a clump of cypresses and afterwards walked about the grounds. The views looked more German than Greek. When we got back we had dinner on a landing as there was a dinner given by the German ministers; we could see from our dinner the guests arriving and going down to dinner. Afterwards we packed and said farewell to Mr. Swan. On leaving, the hotelkeeper gave me a huge pot of Hymettus honey.

We started about 6 on Friday in 2 carriages to the Pireaus and went on board the *Eptanesos* (Επτανησος). I sat in the captain's deck cabin most of the time looking at charts with him and Grafton. He told Grafton that I was 'getting to be quite a captain as I knew all the harbours of the Kyklades'. He is quite an old friend, we have been on his steamer so often. We landed at Kalamaki about 11

---

[86] Mabel's cousin, son of her Aunt Emma.
[87] Now the National and Záppio Gardens, laid out originally by Queen Amalia in the 1840s.
[88] The former summer residence of the Greek Royal Family, Tatoï is some 15km north of Athens, off the main road to Évia and the north. The cemetery in the grounds contains several family members, including George I (1845–1913).

and were transferred across the isthmus[89] in carriages by the steamer company. We saw from the steamer the place where Kenchrae had been. There were a great many carriages and great confusion in finding places for the passengers. Mr. Grafton and I were in carriages with 2 Greeks and the other 4 together.

About 1 o'clock we embarked on the *Chios* (Xíos) and went below to seek for cabins. We found one of the passengers had already changed his clothes and taken possession of a cabin to himself. He was Mr. Longworth, late Consul at Volos in Thessaly. The 4 men had to sleep in one little cabin and Mrs. Anson and I had to put up in the ladies' cabin or Gynaikéion for the first night. I do not think T or Mr Anson enjoyed their taste of bachelor life. We stopped at Vostitza in the afternoon and at Patras in the night and next day at Zante, and at Cephalonia or Kephalenía, in two ports of the latter.

Saturday night we got a large cabin and the Ansons had the Gynaikèion to themselves. We landed at Corfú, or Kerkera, on Sunday morning. It is a most lovely island and the view of the mainland delighted us. We went to the Hotel St. George. We went to church, a hideous round place with 2 wide galleries, one above the other. After luncheon we drove to Benyza on the sea. On Monday we all went in various parties to curiosity shops. I bought a silver belt, some buttons and a little box. Drove to the Gun Battery and the King's Villa. On Tuesday we went to Palaiokastriz, a monastery on a hill over the sea. We lunched at the foot of it on the beach. T bought the key of the monks' cellar. Mr. Grafton bought an *eikon*.

T used to sit next to one of our fellow travellers from Athens and discovered him to be the Reverend Lionel Cole, brother in law to Olivia Cole. Mr. and Mrs. Anson and I visited the palace where our various relations had lived as Lord High Commissioners.[90] We found no one to show us round and walked in by the back door. The rooms are very fine and evidently all that we saw had been there in the English times: carpets, consoles, mirrors, and other heavy things. Afterwards we went into the fortress to the highest point. We met Mr. Cole and he came with us. In the evening Mr. and Mrs. Anson, Mr. Grafton and I went out to see the place by moonlight. It was so lovely to see the phosphorus on the sea and the fireflies fireflying about. We also made so bold as to go up the fort again. Mr. Anson would not go and was sure we should not be admitted as there was only a small hole in the gate left open, but we met no one.

On Thursday we left Corfù at one o'clock in the day on the Austrian Lloyd [name left blank].[91] I went to see Mr. and Mrs. Schuyler at the next-door hotel,

---

[89] The Corinth Canal was not completed until 1886.
[90] Corfu was a British protectorate between 1809 and 1864. Mabel's reference to the Lord High Commissioners is unexplained, but possibly there was a connection on her mother's side, from the aristocratic Lambart family, Earls of Cavan.
[91] The Austrian Lloyd steamer company, one of the two or three shipping companies with a near monopoly in the Mediterranean at the time.

Bella Venezia, in the morning. Mr. Longworth had already seconded a large cabin for 4 for himself but during dinner his heart softened and he told me he would change with us. So we gladly gave him the small cabin nearest the screw and had a very good night. We landed at Brindisi in the morning and after a walk took the train for Ancona. As the Indian mail came in we had a quicker journey. We reached Ancona at 2.30 a.m., and next day drove to Loreto in 2 carriages to visit the Holy House. We lunched at the Albergo delle Panegemelli and they charged enormously.

Saturday we started about 6 after dinner to Bologna and got to the Hotel Brun about midnight. Went to the service in the hotel in the reading-room surrounded with pictures of an unholy nature for sale and went to the picture gallery and Cathedral afterwards. Bellinzona Monday night, where I should like to stay longer. At Basle we got into the Wagon Lits and had a cabin to ourselves and a very comfortable night, just like a screw steamer I thought. The heating apparatus caught fire as we were going to start, so it was cold. This is the 2nd time in my limited experience that this has been the case. Mrs. Anson had a private cabin on the little 'Petrel' and kindly invited me in. There was a good deal of movement, they say, but I thought it just like the sleeping car. We were scrupulously examined for dynamite on account of the recent explosion at Victoria station[92] and reached Great Cumberland Place without any further adventures to chronicle, and, though we like good food and beds and ease and comfort as well as others, we think the pleasure we have had quite pays for all the pains.

I've done!
Καλή Παρίδα![93]

---

[92] A Fenian (IRA) bomb wrecked the cloakroom at Victoria Station on 27 February 1884, injuring two people. The following day searches uncovered similar devices at Paddington, Charing Cross and Ludgate Hill. These had been planted by Irish-Americans who had travelled from New York; one of their number, a Mr Burton, was arrested and convicted.

[93] 'It's good to be home!' Mabel has omitted the Greek letter 'τ' ('Καλή Πατρίδα).

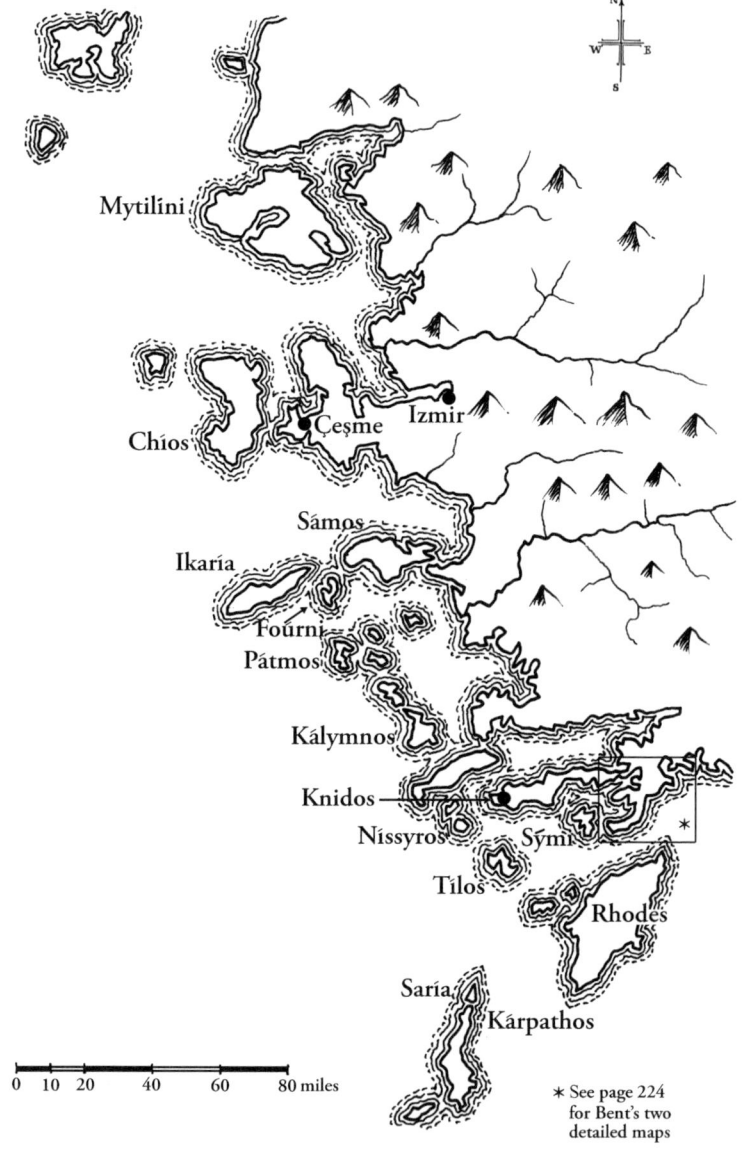

Map 3. The Dodecanese and Eastern Aegean

Chronicle II, February to May 1885:
The Bents excavate in the region known today as the Dodecanese and acquire a very curious little statue indeed…

In the new Greece, controls and restrictions on individuals wishing to excavate were making it increasing difficult for freelancers such as Theodore Bent. So where should the couple try next? In the *Journal of Hellenic Studies* for 1885, Bent hints, 'Before going to Karpathos last winter a passage in Ludwig Ross's *Inselreisen* excited my curiosity…' (*JHS* 6, 1885). His reference was to the little visited region in the north of Kárpathos, and the couple accordingly made plans to visit the islands around Rhodes, deciding to arrive there, with Turkish papers, via Egypt.

Mabel and Theodore arrive on Rhodes in February 1885, from Alexandria. They had been sightseeing in Egypt for the last few weeks. (For a birthday treat to herself, in January, she climbs one of the Pyramids at dusk, alone. The account of that trip is included in Mabel's African *Chronicles*.)

The islands we think of today as the Greek Dodecanese then formed part of the Ottoman Empire, and no Christian could reside overnight within the bastions of Rhodes' great Old Town. Theodore is rather anxious that the debate stirred up by his 1883 article criticizing Turkish rule on Chíos might hamper his chances of excavating; his choice of entry from Alexandria, rather than Istanbul, reflects this. Mabel retells the whole story in the first few pages. The couple prefer to keep a low profile and they think it best to avoid asking for permission to explore and excavate unless absolutely necessary. However, Turkey was then more amenable to parties of foreign archaeologists and the Asia Minor coast had been revealing considerable riches, especially inscriptions and architectural and sculptural remains. The Bents were to focus on the Ottoman provinces for the next five years.

Theodore wrote up his 1885 finds in a paper for the *Journal of Hellenic Studies*, in particular his productive stay on Kárpathos (disdaining anything post-Roman – to the discredit of his standing today as an archaeologist). It is on this tour that he and Mabel acquire the odd limestone statue she describes as 'the most hideous thing ever made by human hands'. The Hellenic Society (of which Mabel becomes a member in this year) are less subjective, opining that 'The objects brought by Mr. Bent from Carpathos were of great interest, and especially one rude figure, which might be regarded as the earliest specimen of an idol of any size from the Greek islands…Possibly these were the idols of the primitive Carrian race.' (*JHS* 6, 1885). Today she stands unashamedly in the British Museum's display of Early Bronze Age artefacts from Greece.

Manthaios Símos is hired once more as general assistant and he joins the couple on Rhodes after several delays. There is no reference to any remuneration for his considerable services, but for the four months he spent with the couple in Arabia in 1889 he was paid £50 (about £1000 per month in today's terms).

Importantly, this *Chronicle* contains Mabel's first reference to her role as expedition photographer, a function she fulfilled enthusiastically, but with mixed results, for all the couple's subsequent travels. Very few of her plates or negatives have survived and the technical problems she had to deal with were considerable. On her later trips she carried around with her all the darkroom materials and apparatus she needed to develop her photographs, adding not a little to the volume of luggage the couple had to transport.

This is a happy trip for the couple, with time spent on unspoiled islands that still offer much of the charm enjoyed by the Bents. Mabel is free with her likes and dislikes of the characters they meet, and her pages detail their problems with Ottoman officials – a theme that is to recur. At consular parties on Rhodes she chats to names of some note in archaeological circles, including Alfred Billiotti, career diplomat and enthusiastic excavator of the principal sites on the island, among them Kamiros and Ialysos, and Frank Calvert, the keen part-time archaeologist who first suggested that the site of Hissarlik might be Homer's Troy. A sadder reference is to General Gordon, who was killed at Khartoum in January 1885.

After their excavations on Kárpathos, the travellers have an exciting journey home, by way of Malta – a later base of the Knights of St John of Rhodes following their expulsion by the Turks in 1522. Mabel enjoys a little of the high-life there before donning her travel clothes again for the passage back to London in a grain-ship. Her 1885 *Chronicle* runs from January to May of that year. The couple leave their London townhouse for Dover – Calais – Marseilles – Naples – Cairo – Alexandria – Rhodes – Nísiros – Tílos – Kárpathos – Crete – Kýthera – Sýros – Sicily – Malta – London (Millwall Docks).

For notes on this transcription the reader is referred to page xxv. Mabel again refers throughout to her husband as T, and their Greek assistant, Manthaios, as M. This second *Chronicle* is written in a dark-blue leather notebook (185 x 120mm) with marbled endpapers and edges. There are 170 lined pages and Mabel fills 115 of them. See selected Indices of people and places mentioned.

It is early in February 1885. Our correspondent is writing her *Chronicle* on board the Austrian Lloyd S.S. *Saturn*, steaming towards the Old Town of Rhodes and the Dodecanese…

'...a very hideous statue, more than the size of a baby'
The limestone figure the Bents returned with from Kárpathos in 1885 and now in the British Museum.

Mabel V. A. Bent her
Chronicle in the
Sporades, etc.
1885

February 1885 – *en route* for the Dodecanese

Thursday February [5th]. I am writing against much rumbling of the screw of the Austrian Lloyd S.S. *Saturn*[1]. We are having as calm a voyage as needs be but not without its hopes and fears.

We left Cairo on Monday evening at 6, seen off by Major Dawson, and 'took up with' a young Mr. Tucker who left the hotel with us. We luckily had dinner enough with us to share with him, washed down with coffee at Damankoor (halfway), and reached Alexandria at [time illegible]. We were greeted with the unpleasant intelligence that the Austrian would not call at Rhodes this week, so we went to bed with the half formed intention of going to Smyrna by a Khedivieh ship and trusting to luck for a passage to Rhodes. However the belated *Saturn* came in early next morning and we left at 4 on Wednesday afternoon. We had a whole day in the very uninteresting Alexandria and took a drive.

Yesterday it looked quite black all round when we embarked and began to rain and the harbour was full of gulls – 17 sitting in a row on the rope mooring a ship near. So we felt very gloomy knowing that if it were too stormy we should not touch at Rhodes but be carried to Smyrna. But the sun came out and all became bright as we steamed off 'adagio adagio'.

You would think all our fears were at an end as we have had about 20 hours of excellent weather and hope to be at Rhodes by tomorrow morning, but no! there is 24 hours quarantine. If we could feel sure of remaining on board we should not so much mind, but if the Captain thinks it will be dangerous for the ship to remain in the roadstead he will be off, leaving us in the lazaretto, and if a sudden storm springs up we may not be able to disembark but may have to be left at Leros. There are only 3 Greek 1st Class passengers for Constantinople and the captain, who does not seem to think himself an 'unredeemed Italian' at all, and an ill tempered German Austrian Doctor. Of course Egyptian affairs have been discussed but in a much more

---

[1] The Austrian Lloyd and the Khedivieh Steam Navigation companies connected the major ports of the Eastern Mediterranean.

generous spirit than by the French. We hope to meet Manthaios, our servant, at Rhodes.[2]

We had to pay 11/6 duty[3] on some baggage that was not new and never got beyond the customs house. The official, a German, explained that it was a mistake charging more than 1 p.c. and acknowledged that T was owed the rest back, but as so many papers would have to be paid for to reclaim it that only 2/- would remain, and as the formalities would take a whole day, of course it was hopeless to do anything.

Friday [February] 6th. Day seems quite over, it is half past six, and a most anxious day we have passed with the yellow flag[4] waving us. We got to Rhodes about 3 but did not settle till 5 and the health officers did not come till 7. The Captain asked leave to go to a bay to shelter if storm came on, or the open sea, but they said no, if we wanted pratique he must remain there. But the Captain told us that sooner than lose or damage the ship he would go off with us and the two guardians to Smyrna. Great therefore was our horror at 3.30 p.m. to hear all the noises of a start, after having observed that it was getting rougher, but we only went round the corner of the island to shelter on the eastern side and hope to be returned to the capital tomorrow morning. In the mean time no one has been able to communicate in any way with the shore. It has been pouring most of the day. One of the Greeks recognises us, having seen us on Scio 2 years ago. They are most friendly and drink brandy before each meal and T to his disgust has had to accept twice as they always offer it to us.

Thursday Feb. 12th. Here we have been 5 days in Rhodes, having very bad weather in this favoured isle, 'where there is rarely a day without sunshine'. We are right glad and thankful to be here for it is not granted to everyone who arrives here to get ashore. A week or two ago the boat with the doctor

---

[2] The main ports had isolated quarantine stations (lazarettos) away from the towns. The one on Rhodes has now been demolished but the fine building outside Sýros harbour in the Cyclades still stands. The reference to 'unredeemed' is to a long dispute with Austria and Italy over disputed territories. By 'Egyptian affairs' Mabel is referring to the various efforts of the British to develop their interests in this area of the Ottoman Empire. In 1883 the powerful diplomat, Sir Evelyn Baring, was posted to Egypt. He and Theodore are later to correspond. From Anáfi in the Cyclades, Manthaios Símos, the Bents' guide and interpreter from their Greek tour of 1884, obviously proved satisfactory and was asked to help them out again in 1885. The weather delayed him this time and he was stuck at Makri (the ancient Lycian Telmessus, now the area of Fethiye).

[3] Of course, expressed in the UK currency of the time: pounds, shillings, and pence. At today's value the duty was around £30.

[4] The yellow flag indicates a vessel under quarantine. Pratigue is the permission granted to a vessel to have dealings at a port. Mabel and Theodore visited the islands of Híos (or Scio, as Mabel refers to it a few lines on) and Sámos on their journey of 1882/3, but there is no notebook chronicling such a tour in these *Chronicles*.

in it was upset in returning to shore. The said fat old Turk[5] kept us a whole hour waiting, and it would really have suited us to land a little later, but the Captain constantly feared he could not land us. However after a parade of the passengers we did get to land, though it was very rough. Of course we knew a passport would be demanded and we had lost ours, so when something was said in Turkish which we knew must be this request T solemnly handed them an old letter of credit which he held in readiness. They were quite satisfied and as I was dancing with Kyrios Aristarchis, the Government Dragoman, I explained it all to him and he said 'the trick was so good that it should be duly honoured' and he would receive it as a true passport and now we have it back.

We have actually been to a ball at Mr. Calvert's, our V. Consul's. There were Greeks and Levantines. All the ladies had handsome faces but bad figures. The dresses were very various, some good, some bad, and some in fancy dress because this is the Greek carnival. The prettiest girl in the prettiest dress was a French one dressed like a gypsy. Amongst others were Kyrios and Kyria Philemon. We had met him in Samos two years ago. He is Greek Consul and they seem to be nice people. When I went to call he sent me a nice little old terracotta jug. Mr. Aristarchis's brother had met us in Chios, so they knew all about us.

We are at a clean little inn in the separate village called Neo Marás, the Christian quarter quite close to the sandy and windmilly point Kum Burnú at the north of the isle.[6] It is quite a little walk to the town where no one but Jew or Turk may remain after sun set. The town is very interesting and full of coats of arms and bits of carving and other traces of the Knights, but see Murray.[7] There is a charming walk along the sea towards Trianda on the west coast. There are big rocks of Puddingstone tumbling about which must once have been shingle and sand and now for a second time are returning to that state. There are quantities of smooth black and white shingles which are extensively used for paving floors and court yards in all sorts of designs. The passage outside our door and the dining room too have very pretty patterns.

[5] Who the 'Turk' is is not clear. 'Where there is rarely a day without sunshine' is a little puff from Murray's *Guide to Greece* that is still much employed in today's holiday brochures. The Greek islands known today as the Dodecanese were still in Ottoman Turkish hands when the Bents visited. The islands were ceded to the Italians in 1912 and did not become part of modern Greece until 1947.
[6] One of Theodore's most appealing 'travel' articles for *Macmillan's Magazine* appears in Issue 52 (1885) pp. 297–303. Entitled simply 'Rhodian Society', he augments Mabel's following pages on the couple's brief stay on Rhodes, amusingly sketching this sleepy corner of the, then, Ottoman Empire. It is good to realize that some things remain unchanged: 'The portly hotel keeper, Nicholas, is sure to appropriate the stranger on the steamer, and carry him to his hostelry in the Greek quarter, built on the sandy promontory about half a mile from the old walled town…'
[7] A distinctive and widespread architectural feature in the Dodecanese is the use of black and white beach pebbles (hokhláki) for floors and pavements. It is an expensive, skilled and highly decorative practice, using carefully selected pebbles set (in special cement) into elaborate patterns.

All this time we are without M. First he was stormstayed at Anafi and then he arrived here on Sunday evening but could not touch so he is at Makri in Asia Minor and is due to make another attempt tomorrow.

Fancy my feelings on Monday morning when I heard 3 Turks talking in the passage. All I could make out was Theodhoros so I looked expectantly at them and they came in with a telegram addressed in Turkish and began to read 'Mylordos Theodhoros…' I said 'Bent,' and they said yes, 'Bendi,' so I put out my hand, took the document, opened it and found more Turkish so I handed it to them and said in Greek, 'Please tell me what it is, for I can't read it'. Then they handed it to each other – all read it aloud and at last one said he was afraid he could not exactly make it out but any how I made out that it was from poor M telling of his trouble. All the time we are eating we hear Turkish spoken and when any one of the dozen detached words we know turns up we are delighted.

Thursday [February 19th?]. M arrived on Monday morning; he ought to have been here on Friday. With him came the north wind and consequent fine weather. Last Sunday was quite the worst day. Thunder, lightning, hail and rain all day. We spent another evening at the Philemons and took several walks, and also on Tuesday went to Phileremo at the top of a mountain, about 12 miles. Mr. James Aristarchis, the Chios one, who talks English perfectly, came with us. I rode a mule and the others and M walked. I had a European saddle but it had no crupper. So going down hill the saddle turned and I had nearly reached the ground on the near side when Mr. Aristarchis caught me. A fortunate thing as my leg was caught in the pummels. A few steps further he could not have got between me and the precipice. So a rope was tied to the back of the saddle and M held on behind till we reached the plain. The view from the top of the hill is lovely: the coast of Caria and several islands. It was formerly the acropolis of Old Ialysos. There was a ruined church of the Knights and a subterranean Church, Greek, frescoed inside.[8]

On Monday we had been to call on the Pasha, Khamel Bey, with Mr. Calvert and Mr. Billiotti. He was not at home but his plump 18-year-old son Khem Bey was there. I went to see the Harem but was much disappointed. The rooms looked very meagrely furnished. I saw the only wife and other very old and ugly ladies. The Khanoum Pasha[9] only could talk very little Greek so Khem Bey did dragoman in French till the others wanted to come in. They were all 90 at least.

As the Government steamer is going to Karpathos we begged to go in her. But instead of saying straight out that it was impossible, as women are not

---

[8] Mabel is visiting the acropolis site of ancient Ialysos. The underground and frescoed chapel is that of St George.
[9] The senior wife of the pasha has the title 'Khanoum'.

allowed on these ships, which if such were the rule they must have known, we were kept waiting for an answer till yesterday and further told that a great row was made because some women took refuge on a man-of-war during the earthquake of Chios.[10] Furthermore the Pasha has not returned our visit yet nor sent the promised letter for the Kaïmakam of Karpathos.

The real reason for all this is that 2 years ago when we were in Chios we heard in travelling over the island dreadful stories of oppression of the Greeks by the Turks which these wretched creatures begged T to expose in England. When we reached the Chora we were on our way to ask our Consul about it but he was not at home. Mr. James Aristarchis, who speaks English perfectly, came up and asked if he could do anything for us. Theodore told him what we were about and he took us to his father (he was once Prince of Samos) who was the Pasha's secretary, in the *Konak*, or Government house. He of course being a Government official did not like to say too much, but between them all we were told to go to the Pasha. So Mr. Bent asked to see him and in walked to his amazement Mrs. Bent. T said that he had heard such bad things that it was impossible to believe them and as he did not like to go to England with a false impression he should like to hear them contradicted. But the Pasha said all was true and T said he would make things known in England.

We were given unpoisoned coffee and left. After we had gone Hashid Pasha was in a towering rage and said 'Fetch this one! Fetch that one! Fetch the other!', all high officials, and said, 'What do you think has happened? A man has been here asking questions! And a woman! What did that woman want here? They had better learn to govern Ireland properly.' And in half an hour he wished he had asked for the papers which authorised T to ask such questions. He did not get over it for a long time, Mr. Aristarchis says.

When Theodore got home he spoke to Mr. Pandeli Ralli M.P. about this affair, also Lord Edmund Fitzmaurice. Mr. P. Ralli asked a question in Parliament and Lord Granville told Lord Aberdeen to enquire about it. The Pasha was moved to Smyrna and Mr. Anamesaki, our Consul, who rather threw doubt on T, and I believe made himself out to have done most, got the Order of the Saviour, which we have often heard that T should have got instead. Besides this he wrote an article in 'Macmillan' 'Two Turkish Islands Today' i.e. Chios and Samos. This was at once translated into Greek and got about, though the Government tried to suppress it, and in Turkish, which enraged them much.

Khamel Bey was then Pasha of Mytelene and is a very clever literary man and a great poet and gets a pension to keep his pen off dangerous subjects. He

---

[10] This is an earthquake prone region and shocks, major and minor, are regular occurrences. There was substantial damage caused in April 1881 and October 1883. The Kaïmakam is the Turkish governor.

was deputed to answer T and telegraphed to Mr. James Aristarchis to come and help him. But Mr. Aristarchis said it was a whole year since the article came out and what paper did he mean to write his answer in? And who would read it? So he gave it up but Hashid Pasha did write something very rabid about T in the Villayet paper.[11]

This is the origin of Khamel Bey's rudeness, and we are assured that we should have spies set on us in Karpathos, and not be allowed to dig, and that as the steamer would get there before us and give warning we have determined to give them the slip and get them off our traces. So we never have said all day that we are giving up Karpathos, which we must get at some day from Crete. Instead of spending more than a night and a day in a *kaïke* we only say we must go by Chalki, an island half way down Rhodes on the west and more than ¼ of the way to Karpathos. We can get there by a Greek steamer, then turn north to Tilos, and together with all the letters for Karpathos we are asking for others in case we may go to the islands, and we have got a new passport for 'Karpathos and other islands'.

It is now past 5 and we do not know when the steamer will come, if we shall sleep on board or what hour we shall start. Knowing how little chance there would be of getting our letters if we wished to, we have said they are not to be forwarded. We feel very mysterious!

Nisiros **[Monday] Feb. 23rd.** We left Rhodes on the night of the 20th. We went on board the Greek steamer *Roúmeli* at 6 o'clock after waiting in expectation of its arrival all day. The evening before, just as we were going to pay an evening visit to the Philemons', they, thinking we should be busy, came to us instead and Mr. Mitso Aristarchis, who is engineer in chief to the Porte at Mytelene, joined us.

Well! The *Roúmeli* is a dirty little ship, and T and I slept in the very smelliest cabin, destined for ladies by the English builders. As it was a passage room for all the passengers a quilt was hung across, but the steward was often within our side. At 11.30, two hours after we left Rhodes, we reached Simi and in the dark and by starlight I could see that we remained in a little land-locked bay for 2 or 3 hours. It looked lovely but no doubt by day it looks bare enough and like Chalki, which we got to about 7, a most hideous island, stony like Syra and not even the picturesque town to redeem it. We did not land there; there is a revolution about the tax on sponges and the Pasha of Rhodes was just going there so we came on to Nisiros, which we reached about 12.30.[12]

---

[11] Mabel refers to this irksome incident in her *Chronicle* of 1883/4 (see p. 8 note 5). A Villayet is an Ottoman geo-political region; perhaps the reference here is to the local 'paper' of Mytilíni. The Bents visited the island in 1882/3 on their first trip to the region.

[12] The natural sponge industry along the northern Levantine littoral, and especially around islands such as Hálki, Sými and Kálymnos, was big business until synthetic products eroded the market. The islanders were granted lenient and special rights in the trade.

We passed Tilos on the way and had to come half round this island to get to the NW side, where this little town of Mandraki lies. The island is only about 8 miles across and quite round. It has been a volcano and there are no springs on it – cisterns are used. In the middle of the island is the sunken crater with a pond of sulphur.[13] One can smell it more than a mile off.

Once more, and for the first time during this journey, we found the very narrow little streets, up and down steps, and sometimes rocks a foot and a half high, and full of pigs, like on the Cyclades. We were taken to the house of the schoolmaster, Logothetis (layer-down of the law) and given coffee, *loukoumi*[14] and almonds, but he was absent as well as Kyrios Apostolides to whom we also had a letter. The Archimandrite of the monastery, situated on a projecting rock among the ruins of a medieval fortress, was soon on the spot and our baggage ordered up the hill. We followed up steep steps and rocks, winding in and out under arches, and with joy found we had a room really to ourselves, large and clean enough, and with lovely views of Kos, Ialé and Kalimnos.

As the only bed was small and dirty I have slept in my hammock very successfully these two nights. The down quilts covered with white to serve as sheets make it look as if it were full of whipped cream. I can now get in without untucking the bedclothes.

The women here wear a very pretty dress, and now we know why 'Turkey red' is called Turkey red, i.e. because all the women in this Turkish island wear an open sleeveless gown of it with a very full skirt a good deal shorter than the thick cotton shirt with handsome silk embroidery round the tail, 1½ yards round. The sleeves are splendidly embroidered. We have bought 5 of these underdresses, 1 pair of sleeves, a pillow cover, and a bed valance for £3.15.0.[15]

Yesterday **[Tuesday, February 22nd?]** we went to Emborios up in the mountains, about 1½ hours, a place exactly like this. I rode, or I may say I bestrode, a small donkey with a large mule packsaddle. The donkey's and my difficulties were increased by having to squeeze through bushes of prickly dwarf holly up to my knees. My feet and knees often got knocked on stones and rocks, and altogether it was not a very pleasant ride for me. When we started home

---

[13] Boatloads of tourists visit Níssyros daily in summer to scramble down into the small, mildly active, caldera.

[14] *Loukoumi*, better known today as 'Turkish delight'. The Archimandrite was the monastery Superior. Ialé is the islet of Yialí off Níssyros. In antiquity, after Mílos, it was the biggest source of obsidian in the Aegean. Some users preferred the Yialí product: a shiny black glass with white flecks that are generally absent from the Mílos variety.

[15] About £150 today. Between 10 and 22 June 1885, the Bents correspond with the Victoria and Albert Museum, London, about some of these, and other, items. They send three dresses for inspection. A year later, on 17 July 1886, Theodore writes to the Museum offering some dresses for £15, but it seems the Museum declines. The deal would have been a good one. At a meeting of the Anthropological Institute in 1886, Mabel exhibits manikins dressed in elaborate costumes from Níssyros and Kárpathos, as well as the valence and pillow cover she mentions. See p. 40 note 50.

with the bundle of clothes the muleteer lent his sash and the clothes were slung on to M's back. It was not a very interesting expedition.

We dine in another room very bare, but most thankful are we not to be in a family and obliged to talk when we are tired. The first evening we had to eat soft eggs without spoons as ours were not out, and we had no glass in the windows, but were tolerably comfortable for all that. On the 23rd we paid several visits, engaged a boat and wished to leave as the wind was N., but we were persuaded to put off till next day.

Tilos **[Wednesday, February] 25th.** We left Nisiros yesterday at 9 a.m. but not for 7½ hours did we step down an oar on to this island. We had calm for most of the 15 miles. We came round the E. so now we have completely circumnavigated Nisiros. We saw a good many people on the shore as we approached, but by the time we landed not one was in sight. The boatman then holloed out 'Come near, fear not! We are from Nisiros, you may come safely!' So out they came and we went to meet them and they said, 'What people are you? From *The Town?*' We said we were not from Constantinople but from England, but this did not enlighten them much. They asked if this were our first time coming to the island and after we had said 'yes', T asked something about the other port and they wanted to know how we knew there was another port. Today T said something to the superior of this monastery[16] of the vineyards near the Limena and he said 'Did you guess of yourself that we had vineyards there or have you been told?' We had passed the Limena on the steamer. There is no post here.

It was 4.30 when we arrived and we at once dispatched M to the town to see after a lodging and take our letters of introduction to the Superior or Egoúmenos of the monastery and Kyrios Kamá, and off he went bearing his coat, half a kid in one hand and a tied up bundle with his favourite scraps for his own eating. He is certainly cheap to feed. He eats all the fishes' heads and yesterday lunched of cold lights.

We left our very voluminous baggage on the beach and went off to look at a young woman we had observed from the sea, stamping like mad upon something black. This was a brown goats' hair coat, which was wet and put on a board, surrounded with stones to keep it steady, and the woman had been kneading and grinding it 4 days to get the long hairs off. She said it was cold work and her feet looked quite sodden.

At about 5 all the people began to assemble to go up to the town for no one sleeps by the sea, and they begged us to come too. We said we would wait for M

---

[16] Mabel specifies below that they are staying at the little monastery of Ay. Pantaleomonos, a short way out of Megálo Horió (not to be confused with the remote and fortified monastery of the same name behind Profítis Ilías). The site (and pretty church) still exists but it is used as a small army camp.

and we could not think why he did not come. The people seemed unwilling to leave us and frightened to stay, so we consented that they should not divide our luggage among them, and they all shouldered the heavy things quite easily. Quite an old woman took a big carpetbag. I took 3 loaves and the honey-bottle, and we were a most queer procession.

It was most fortunate we started. We were not a moment too soon, for it is a mile to the town and we might have at least sprained our ankles, for most of the way is covered with loose stones of various sizes, and then we might have lost our way over rocks and not have hit off the road again. And it was dark by the time we got to the town, besides we had to go so completely round a mountain that we did not see it till the last minute.

When we were ¼ mile off we met M and the schoolmaster Spirídonos clad in black European dress, and we went first down a great many narrow piggy streets and rocky stairs to the café, and we sat for about an hour on a balcony, homeless for one of our friends was absent and the Egoúmenos out. At last the schoolmaster asked us to come and sit in quiet at his house, which consists of one small room, half of it being according to the usual custom at 26 inches higher than the rest. He had been married 40 days he said, and had that morning returned from Kalimnos with his pretty bride, after 8 days of sea-sickness. Twice had they reached Tilos and had to return as far as Kos. So it was hardly a lucky moment to intrude on them, but they were most kind and Mrs. Kalíope unpacked her box and took out tablecloth and napkins and told us tomorrow she should tidy the house, and seemed rather disappointed that it had not been whitewashed. However when a saucepan of soup, once 'portable', was brought we felt such bores, we declared we would go and dine in the *kafeneion*, but we were told by our host that we should offend them much if we did. So we remained and ate off our own tin plates, etc., and used their pretty painted wooden spoons, which imparted a flavour of varnish to our soup.

After the Egoúmenos came and took us to the Monastery of Holy Pantaleomonos in the valley about ½ a mile from the town. We have a little house to ourselves, one room opening into a sort of court or cloister. One end is 18 inches higher and has a dusty carpet and T sleeps on the floor, his bed full of fleas but he does not mind them. We have 4 windows without glass and the door, so on 3 sides we can have air, which they tell us is charming in summer, but we like it better when we are shut up for the night as well as we may. After being homeless for a few hours very thankfully did I lay myself in my hammock.

Thursday 28th [actually February 26th]. We could not shut our door the first night and about 6 a man came in to find the 'Blessed One'[17] and left the

---

[17] The resident saint, i.e. Ay. Pantaleomonos.

door open. We did not wish to move but when hens came in I had to drive them out, indeed we had to keep constant guard against hens, dogs and cats. We had the room washed after a very slight fashion which did not kill the fleas. We paid visits in the morning with the Egoúmenos and Papa Nikolaos, both very nice men, and in the afternoon stayed in as T had a little fever.

This morning we set forth with 2 men, spades, and high hopes and dug 2 graves close by the sea shore where we landed on the North. A very strong N. wind blowing all the time. We found nothing but bones and 2 little earthen tear-bottles, one broken, and a lamp – all coarse, about 4 feet down. The opening of the tomb was 7 feet down and closed with a stone in the side of the hole that was dug. We came away disgusted. One of the men has brought in a good little black lamp.[18]

The men dress the same as all the other islanders we have seen, but the women look very like Laps. They wear a very rational dress. A shirt which comes a little below the knee, embroidered all round with red and green. Over this a light brown coat is wrapped by a scarlet belt. The shirt has a small square sailor collar of yellow and the open front of the shirt is filled with a piece of coloured embroidery, almost hidden by the great number of necklaces of different colours composed of numerous strings of glass beads, reaching nearly to the waist. On their heads they wear red pointed caps of red cloth with a bit of gold braid straight up the front and down the back. A handkerchief with the point turned up is tied across the front, and the hair, which is plaited rather high in front, is brought low over the ears and behind below the cap. Over all they tie a towel by its 2 front corners and sometimes also by the 2 back ones. Babies are carried in little cradles like the Laps' and hung over their mothers' shoulders.[19]

March 1885 – Tilos

[Monday] March 2nd. Yesterday we had not a very satisfactory day. T sent and went to the Mudir, Sapré Effendi, and asked permission to dig, but no answer came and he sent 3 *zaptichs* or policemen after the diggers and we gave up all thoughts of doing anything so sent M to the other village, Mikró Khorió (this being Megálo Khorió, and both the same size) to make a symphony[20] about a *kaïke* for Karpathos, and half a dozen women or so for our luggage. They have

---

[18] This is the area around the small northern port of Ay. Andónios, facing Níssyros.
[19] Mabel acquired a swaddling band from Kárpathos, '150 years old, cotton closely worked with black and red silk on the outer end, and with a small sprigged pattern on the rest'. She displayed it at a meeting of the Anthropological Institute in 1886, and it is now in the Pitt Rivers Museum, Oxford (1888.37.7) with another example they acquired from Évia (1888.37.8). The Bents had no children.
[20] By 'symphony' Mabel means an agreement, from the Greek verb 'I agree'. A *medjidie* was worth around £10 in today's terms.

one donkey but no saddles. I am to have the donkey. We had a visit from the schoolmaster and one from Papa Nikolaos in the evening. The latter told us the real thing was that the Mudir required *bakhsheesh* and if we gave a *medjidie* (4/-) it would be all right and he would go to the *Kanak* and hold out hopes. However last night all the Turks were too tipsy to be spoken to.

This morning it was announced that the Mudir was on his way to visit us so T hastily ordered coffee, and I got out a little plush case with a comb, looking glass, scissors, etc., and when he arrived with 3 *zaptichs*, T at once plunged into the subject and said he would give him a *bakhsheesh* and handed him 2 *medjidis* and at the same moment I gave my gift, which he joyfully took but told T to lay his money on the table and called a *zaptich* to take it, and this we hear is in order that he may be able to swear he received no money from T.

He then said he was delighted we should dig and he would go to the other village that he might see and hear nothing of it. He asked us if we had an opera glass we could give him, but we told him we had not, and he begged me to go and see his wife and asked T if I could write, for he knew that all the women of the English family knew letters, so this Chronicle was fetched and T said I had written it all and he looked through it and said it was beautiful and everyone wonders I can write so much. A great blow fell upon us when the smoking began and T fetched our old luminous match box with a cracked glass and offered a match and explained its marvels, for Sapré Effendi thanked T heartily and put it in his pocket. We trembled when he took the revolver to examine for fear he might bag that.

We parted excellent friends. Then it poured, which prevented digging today though it did not last long and we had visits from Papa Nikolaos, the Egoúmenos, and the schoolmaster, who lunched with us and he much enjoyed black caviare and lobster. Since luncheon we first went to see the bride who is very discontented, and then wandered about the town paying visits and being consulted about illnesses. There is no doctor here. One woman has erepipelas[21] in the face. Of course there is no use prescribing unobtainable medicines, so we have done what we could and hope it may be successful. M has delightedly gone off to the sick with pills, vaseline, etc. It is so cold we have to shut our windows and only keep the door open.

Tuesday [actually Wednesday] March 4th. On Sunday we walked up to the old fort above the town on a very high mountain overlooking the sea, as well as the plain, and so steep that the town looked as if it were tucked in under our feet, at least it didn't look at all for we could not see it.[22] The Egoúmenos accompanied

---

[21] Erysipelas, a skin infection resulting in large red and raised blisters on face and elsewhere.
[22] This is the acropolis above Megálo Horió. The remains of the Hospitaller castle there include masonry recycled from Archaic-Classical times.

us and we took paper, etc., to take squeezes[23] of the only 2 inscriptions known to exist but M and T each found another, so we set to work in blazing sun and in a bed of rue, but before we had finished it came on to rain so we had to spread our things to dry in the ruined church which now occupies the site of a temple of which one wall is still in place and T returned in the evening to fetch them. I in the mean time had visits the whole afternoon, wearisome but no doubt good for my Greek. In the night it poured which caused a hasty rush from our very different beds to secure our things from the water dripping through the roof. T's heap of bedding had to be dragged into safety. He has no sheets, but does not seem to mind and has his pillow dressed in a white garment of mine.

I forgot to say that a very poor old woman wished to know how much she should have to pay for our medicines. We have heard that the patients are doing well. Also I did not mention that women and little girls wear a quantity of silver wire rings in their ears. I counted 14 in one ear, each wire too thick by half for our ears and each ring too large for a bracelet. They sleep in them and, of course, the lobe of the ear is much disfigured. We saw some wedding earrings which not only had lots of beads strung on of glass and filigree, but about half a dozen pairs of good sized cheap earrings of our ordinary kind tied in.

To return to our history, we began to dig with 6 men who, though engaged to begin early, were with difficulty driven to set to work by being told they were not men at all but beasts (ζόα) and taking a leaf out of their own books, we told them it was evening and M said they were now 'half day' men, so they were got to work by 9, or 3 o'clock as they call it in Turkey. These graves were in a very pleasant place, in a field with olive trees and velanidia, a sort of oak with large acorns; the cups 2 or 3 inches across are used in dyeing.[24]

We opened 7 graves. They had to dig 8 or 10 feet and then there was a perpendicular stone mortared on to the mouth of a cave. We found nothing

---

[23] Wet paper squeezes (as opposed to dry squeezes) were used on inscriptions for taking everything from slight surface impressions to creating moulds for figure casting. No inks are initially used, just sheets of coarse paper soaked in water and then literally beaten and squeezed into the (preferably cleaned) stone using a special squeeze-brush. Deep hollows could be filled with strips of pulped paper. According to Flinders Petrie (*Methods and Aims in Archaeology*, London, 1904, pp. 60–61) the stone is given a 'severe beating to the whole, as violent as can be done without tearing the paper'. On shallow inscriptions the paper is removed when wet and hung out to dry. Mabel often complains how hard this can be in windy or damp conditions. When eventually dry, the impressions can be inked on the inner side for reproduction and the figures are reversed in the plate. Petrie is scathing about the use of wet squeezes on coloured work: on 'many kinds of tender stones wet squeezing is a crime, as it destroys the original. Fatuous tourists and brazen students have wrecked innumerable monuments by wet squeezing and it is now necessarily prohibited in Egypt [1904] unless special permission is obtained'. Mabel and Theodore probably wanted to keep the dry sheets as flat as possible when travelling, but would have had to roll them for four-legged transport; this would be quite a bundle after months of squeezing. (Petrie opines that about 50 square feet of such work is as much as can be done in a day.)

[24] The Valonia oak (*Quercus ithaburensis macrolepis*).

very fine to reward us – some very coarse plates, one containing the bone of a sepia,[25] some little 2-handled cups, a jug very coarse, and 3 immense pithoi, very large jars with pointed bottoms whole, one broken, and the round copper bottom of some vessel.

We were disappointed and decided that this had been a poor place. The big jars, as T said, we should have liked to keep if they had been dug up in the Park,[26] but not only would they have been expensive to bring home, if they had not been captured on the way, but would have caused a great fuss in Karpathos, where we did not mean to speak of excavations for a week. Hardly did the sun set when the owner of the field declared these were fine and excellent things and wished to be paid a great deal for them, so we departed, and theirs and M's screams could be heard several fields off. We had several people to beg us to take these things and pay, but we said we did not care for them and we would only pay for the crops as we agreed. The workmen also have been here for more money but vainly. A penknife has been given to the Egoúmenos this morning and perhaps in consequence all the small things have been brought us. We are in the act of packing for the Mikró Chorió.

[Thursday] March 5th. Now everything is packed for Karpathos, which we hope to reach tomorrow night, sailing this midnight. We had a very funny departure from the Megaló Chorió. Seven women came from the place and carried our luggage. We were reminded of the processions in the Tomb of Ti.[27] I had a very good donkey. Our way led for a good way along the edge of a precipice formed by what seemed to be a subsidence in the middle of the island about ½ or ¼ of a mile wide and sometimes at the bottom of it. This was evidently a volcano as this side of the island is full of pumice.

On reaching this village we were greeted by our host, a Papas who has been to Alexandria and has a bed! and keeps a café. The captain of the *kaïke* we had engaged, Alexis, who at once constituted himself a 2nd servant and shared all M's doings and became a bosom friend of his, and an old Kyrios Katré, a very cunning and talkative old merchant from Simi who, with the nice priest, clung to us continually. We were given the whole of a house about 12 feet by 9 with the bed in it. It was very tidy and clean looking. The floor had been sponged and a white quilt was got out to make a top sheet for T, as Greeks never have but one. And a great search was made for a basin, but the only one was broken, so a salad bowl was borrowed and in fact they did all they could for us.

---

[25] A cuttlefish 'bone' (this cephalopod is the *soupiá*).
[26] Presumably London's Hyde Park. The Bents lived within sight of Marble Arch.
[27] Mabel is referring to the elegant processions from the wall paintings of the 5th-Dynasty Tomb of Ti at Sakkarah, near Memphis in Egypt.

After a walk and some visits and our dinner, eaten very publicly, a band came, consisting of a drum, a bagpipe composed of a whole pigskin, and a *lýra*, a sort of mandolin, with a quantity of little bells hung along the bow – a very pretty instrument to see and hear.[28] As there were ten people in the room, we sat as if we were in the train. Yesterday we went down to the sea, ¾ of an hour's walk, very rough, and dug but vainly. One of the workmen was the priest's brother-in-law. What people would say if they knew one of my sisters is a Papadhiá I know not. All the clergy are quite common people. We passed a ragged old man on the way, I don't say *road*, building a wall, and only by his brown goatskin cap, which represents black, could one know he was a clergyman. The superior of the monastery is a shoemaker and Papa Nikólaos ploughs.

This house is haunted by 4 cats which play about all night to my terror and bump against my hammock. We can't keep them out because they have a way in that we can't stop up. We are offered a barn near the sea but it is full of rats, they say, so we shall go on board at once. The ship has a hole or hold, but we shall lie on deck I think. We are taking about 20 bottles of wine with us as it is good. The people of these villages are very jealous of each other and tell lies of each other and do not intermarry.

Before was came here we were told that all the inhabitants were lepers. Then someone else said 'in only two villages'. Each village says they are all in the other but they live among their families so we really do not know. They speak of them as 'broken people'. Before we left Megálo Chorió our erepipelas patient was so well that she tried to send us a *medjidie*, but we of course refused and are very proud of our success. All the women here are terrified at the idea of being photographed and my camera is rather a 'white elephant'. They are also afraid of T's sketching them and all run away.[29] There is one in particular, Kyriakí (Sunday) by name, one of those who carry our baggage, about 50 and very handsome, in the wildest darkest gypsy style, and when T takes his book out she skips away like a goat.

A dreadfully ragged old priest, the owner of *the* donkey and the one who was building a wall, stood for his portrait in our little house among a jammed crowd, all very much delighted when T said 'Here are his eyes, his nose; he has no mouth on account of his beard'. I espied his house key hanging at his girdle,

---

[28] This primitive bagpipe is the *samboúna*. A regional speciality is the fixing of small bells on the *lýra* bow. This originates from the times when the *lýra* (a sort of violin, placed upright on the knee) was played unaccompanied by the *laoúto* (guitar) and the bells would add interest. Theodore was a keen collector of musical instruments and brought back a *samboúna* and *lýra* and bow from Kárpathos to England. The *samboúna* was exhibited by the Bents at a meeting of the Anthropological Institute in 1886 and both instruments are now in the Pitt Rivers Museum, Oxford (1903.130.23.PR342Q and 1903.131.18.F181). He also acquired a reed 'trumpet' from the island, also at the Pitt Rivers (1888.37.5).

[29] The important first reference in these *Chronicles* to Mabel's role as expedition photographer and to Theodore's skills as sketcher and water-colourist.

very like the key we bought from the monks of Paleokastrizza in Corfu – their cellar key[30] – so we offered a knife for it, it was joyously accepted, and in order to express that I was to ride his donkey he made his 1st and 2nd fingers of his right hand ride on his left hand.

Then our host, having been given a knife, gave me half an enormous embroidered curtain. I at once took from my pocket a brooch for his wife, whereupon he flew to a trunk and gave me a little bottle with a few treasured drops of lavender water. He is going to Alexandria, so we may again see Papa Andreas Diakónoudemetríou.

Now I will recount our voyage to Karpathos. We got down to the sea about 2 p.m., as that seemed to be about the time that suited everyone, and the women were sent flying up the mountain by T, who popped out round rocks at them with his sketch book. When it became dark we took refuge in a *magazi* or shed containing anchors, planks, ropes, etc., and M cooked our dinner, which we ate off a bench sitting on a pole. The ship's company consisted of Alexis, his wife, and we suppose 2 sailors, and a young man and a little boy, who were taking the opportunity of the passage.

We had to wait for the moon at midnight, and about 7 T and I clambered down the very steep rocks and were laid by Captain Alexis side by side on the ballast with a carpet over it and our heads on the tent sack. He then proceeded to close the hold, about 2 feet deep, completely up, so we begged for mercy and only had a sail spread over us. I found the shingles awfully hard but T, after a fortnight or more on the floor, was able to sleep and it was with the greatest difficulty I shook him up, telling him he *must* go ashore for the men as the moon had been up an hour, so he went and found M very anxious to get them off but unable.

We were soon on our way. M crawled into the extreme bow of the hold where he got very wet, for the N. wind freshened and the waves were dashing over us from behind. It became so bad that before we got to Saría, an island N. of Karpathos, it was decided to give up trying to get to Pegádhi, our destination, far down on the E. coast, but to go into Tristoma, a bay on the N.W. We landed there after 9 hours and did not very much mind as we thought we could travel through the island a different way. You will hardly believe we started before the next daybreak without seeing one Karpathiote!

Tristoma has its name because 2 islands at its entrance give it Three Mouths. It is a most desolate looking place, there is a little half-ruined chapel, almost in the sea, and there we built our beds, and very damp we, and all our goods, became. A boat from Kasso was there and the men said it was 4 or 5 hours to

---

[30] On their way home in 1884, Theodore bought this cellar key. See p. 60.

Elymbo[31] and the road, or what answers to one, washed away so we settled at dawn to set off again to Pegádhi. All around were nothing but steep bare rocks so we 2 chose the softest to sleep on in the afternoon and all the Greeks slept in a heap. The day was enormously long and every one unsettled and anxious, and we heard from the men of Kasso a terrible tale of a boat kept 15 days in that bay by a W. wind and next day we wished to go W., N., E., and then S., there were many fears. We lay down in our clothes and at dawn my friend T was in a very obstinate state of comfort, warmth, sleepiness, etc., but I respectfully reminded him that I had obtained leave over night to rouse him up, and that all the others were up, no doubt unwilling to wake us, which proved to be the case.

We got out by the N. entrance, having entered by the S., got through the straits very well, and though there was not much wind, were progressing favourably when a whirling gust came down a gully in the mountains and then another and overboard went the foresail, mast and all. All hands dragged the sail in and the sailors began hacking and hewing with axe and saw, while the male passengers flew to the oars, and the sea so calm all the time. How thankful we felt that we had safely got into Tristoma bay only just in time, for only one more gust such as we had that morning might have done for us. The sail would have filled before anyone could do anything, and the big hole in the deck would have let the hold fill.

After this Pegádhi was out of the question in that boat, so we made for Dhiaphéne, where we landed and made acquaintance with some of the inhabitants of Elymbo and promised to go there for Easter. This is their landing place. We breakfasted in the open air and then got into a narrow, very deep boat with so much water in it that it had to have a hearty bailing for 5 or 10 minutes occasionally with a big basin. We had 4 men to row each on a different bench, and we 3 sat leaning against each other in the stern.

It took 7½ hours to get to Pegádhi, coasting closely and landing twice for water, once at Kyria Panagía, a very pretty little bay with a little white church of 'Mrs. All-holy' – the Virgin. All the whole time the men never ceased with every stroke to shout all sorts of verses and sayings. In spite of all the noise no one came out at our approach to help our landing, and we had to call for a lantern and got the boat on a rock. However we landed safely and that moment were asked for our *teskerreks* by a *zaptick*, or policeman. We then went into their café and enquired after various people for whom we had letters, Mr. Manolakakis, the Kaïmakam Mr. Koumpis. The Kaïmakam was the only one down at Pegádhi, and the minute the Turks heard we had a letter for him they demanded it

---

[31] Ólymbos, the northern capital of Kárpathos. A few paragraphs further on Mabel writes of 'Dhiaphéne'. This is modern-day Dhiafáni, the harbour town of Ólymbos. As is often the case, Mabel spells the names in a variety of ways.

imperiously. T said it was in the boat still but they simply clamoured for it, even a boy of 16 came to me when T was gone out and said 'Give me the Kaïmakam letter at once'. When it came it was taken to the Kaïmakam who was in the upper room of this filthy hole of a café with his Turkish secretary, a very smart young man and his Greek Dragoman, Mr. Frangisko Sakolarides.

T was put on a sofa a yard high near the Kaïmakam, and there I found him and we were given coffee and nothing civil was left unsaid. Mr. Sakolarides always translating from the Turkish into Greek, though both Turks can talk Greek. We heard T mentioned as Frank Effendi, and Lord Bent. They said they would give up the room to us and kindly departed. The room was clean looking and to get at it we passed through a small kitchen where M prepared our supper.

The woman of the house made T up a bed on the high seat, and while doing so quite calmly dropped her 6-months'-old babe into my arms. As he was good, pretty and clean I did not mind, and it seemed quite natural that I should keep him next morning, after he had been dressed only in 2 cotton shirts, quite clean, while his little brother was dressed and the room cleaned.[32] When T went to shut the door of the kitchen, where M was to lie on the floor, behold there was no door to shut but as there was no use saying anything, nothing was said, but I with my hammock quietly removed into the most secluded corner.

We were a good long time dressing as we wished to rearrange our luggage a little and leave some things down there, but about 7.30 the family was at the top of the outside stairs waiting admission, and the Turks all patiently on the beach. They all came up the moment we opened the kitchen door and we packed under great difficulties as they played with our things and unpacked some. The air pillows are a joy to all and my bed, sponge bags, etc. They said the Government steamer would be going to Rhodes and would take letters, so we all began to write, we at the table and the Turks sitting cross-legged and with the papers and a pair of scissors by them with which they cut it down after it was written.

They begged us to wait ¼ of an hour to send M and the baggage by land to Apéri, the capital, and send my mule to meet us at Vrondí across the bay, and they would take us in their boat; so we waited an hour and a half but were saved an hour of rocks by it. My mule duly met me at Vrondí, or Brontë, or 'Thunder', and a very steep ascent of about an hour chiefly up the bed of the river Chaos that led up to Apéri. We all went to the café and sat in the balcony and then went to Mr. Frangisko Sakolarides' house where we found M in possession. We had

---

[32] The Bents had no children.

many visitors including the Turks in the evening in long cotton nightgowns and grey plaid flannel dressing-jackets.

We stayed at that house 2 nights and were greatly bothered by starers and were the objects of great wonder and so we sought for a more private lodging as we wished to remain some time. We could get nothing in Apéri but eventually found a house in the village of Volátha, so close that even I could make the journey on foot. A flock of women, including Mrs. Sophrosíne Manolakakis, the daughter of a very nice man, came and shouldered our baggage; and the way leads up a torrent, hopping from stone to stone, sometimes you walk through a little water. The village is very high up and has most extensive views over sea and land. It is a very pretty island and the mountains we see from here are chiefly greenish and the huge arums in big bunches are quite lovely. No one can think why we have bouquets of them in the house.[33]

All the houses are the same here. One large room divided lengthwise, the side nearest the door has a fixed sofa near the door, very high, a panelling behind it, and a cupboard in it with a small carved door. The back half is raised, the larger part about 4 ft, and the smaller, and further from the door, is raised about 6 feet. All the wall of this is panelling and has doors by which they reach the storerooms and cellars situated inside the sleeping part. There is a railing all along and rafters and bars overhead with towels and sheets and quilts hung upon them. All the pillows and mattresses are piled in a heap and chests and trunks all round containing their clothes. Round the whole house run 2 or 3 shelves full of plates, jugs, bottles, bowls, etc. Our house is like this. Our lower floor is earth but we are pretty quiet and the people are nice and kind. We have plenty of room for our things.

The upper parts are called upper and lower sopha (*áno* and *káto*) and no one goes up there with shoes. We have many visitors and women coming to sell embroideries, also for medical advice. Every time we go out we have to go through the river and some causeway might so easily be made. There is at least a ¼ of a mile of it.

Saturday [March 7th]. On Thursday we went to the village of Spiliés (caves) passing through Othíos. I rode one and a half hours. It was very hot. At Spiliés we asked them to bring things to sell and they did bring plenty, but asked such prices that we bought little. Ten pounds here or there seemed nothing to them and as we shall pass that village again we hope they will have come to their senses. We went into many houses and a woman called Chrysánthe (goldflower) took us under her special care. T sketched a horrid old witch called Marigó and

---

[33] The white and wild arum lily, possibly *Zantedeschia Aethiopica*, although there are other regional varieties.

everyone recognises it as a good likeness. We crossed this narrow island at its widest part. It is not so pretty there, more bare.[34]

When we returned we found that a dire disaster had befallen me but which delights T. A cat had got in at the unglazed window, eaten about 6/- worth of Brand's Beef tea and then not feeling very well had taken to *my* bed, and the results were such as to cause shouts of woe from me which brought T, M, and the neighbours. Fortunately my down quilts were sewn up in sheets and everyone set to work to wash, except me. I remained in retirement. Now, however, they have been washed and are not even stained, but I have been reduced to the floor these 2 nights.

Yesterday was really a day to be marked with a white stone. We had a delightful picnic to Kyriá Panagía. The company were 3 Turks, one of whom could speak no Greek, 2 English, 4 Greeks, 3 of whom could speak Turkish. There was also an Albanian cook who could speak no language but his own and that no one understood, and 2 soldiers. We arrived first. I riding 2 hours on a bone-shaking road. The latter part was through pine woods smelling sweetly and with big single white peonies[35] and arums.

M at once set to work to cook a chicken, or rather aged cock, and was ready with brandy to offer the Turks on their arrival, and at one o'clock we all were seated round a waterproof rug of ours with 2 glasses, few plates, and a moderate amount of forks and spoons. We talked English together. The Turks talked Turkish together, but of course Greek was the general tongue. We all of course ate too much after the manner of folks at picnics; all sorts of unexpected things turned up: eggs after we had been eating boiled sheep's cream with sugar and then bowls of rice jelly and cinnamon. So happy were we and so much did we seem to enjoy overeating ourselves, that it was then and there determined to send the soldiers off for a lamb to be eaten *à la Palikári* for dinner.[36]

We 2, the 2 Sakolarides and a certain Manolakakis,[37] in whose house the Kaïmakam lodges, went on a long hot rocky walk, and I think I got a little

---

[34] Theodore retells the party's short stay around Mesohóri in a delightful article for *Macmillan's Magazine* (54, 1886, pp. 199–205). In 'A Christening in Karpathos' he reveals more of 'Papa Manoulas', 'Mrs. Chrysanthemum', and the fascinating 'Marigo': 'Marigo had lost one leg years ago, by the fall of a mast when at sea. She had supplied the missing member by what looked uncommonly like the stump of a tree...She was always dressed in rags and tatters; her nose is Wellingtonian in shape, her hair clotted and straggling.' Perhaps, one day, Theodore's sketch will turn up. Oddly, Mabel does not cover the christening described in her husband's article. She previously attended one on the Cycladic island of Síkinos (p. 41).
[35] *Paeonia lactiflora*. Wild peonies were once commonplace on Rhodes and Kárpathos.
[36] *Palikári* ('rogue', 'bandit') is much used in a familiar form to mean 'pal', buddy', etc. Lamb 'bandit-style' exists in older recipe books for a slow-cooked dish of lamb chops, oregano, onions, garlic, tomatoes, cheese and potatoes, similar to *kokinistó*. It seems, however, that Mabel and her pals devoured their lamb spit-roasted.
[37] The Manolakakis family was prominent on Kárpathos at the time. An Emmanuel Manolakakis published *Karpathiaká* (1896), a valued monograph on the history and culture of the island.

sunstroke, for I had a great pain in the back of my head which is gone today very nearly. We at length found ourselves at the source of a stream springing out of a bed of maidenhair under great big myrtle trees. It was such an enchanting spot. At 4 o'clock we sat cross-legged round a heap of mastic bushes and rosemary, and on this bed was laid the lamb who had been borne on a spit through his head and his hind feet tied to it.

We then tore him limb from limb by hand and all gnawed. I never saw a funnier scene or a merrier meal. After the lamb's bones were cleaned by the 8 sets of teeth, the Kaïmakam examined the shoulder blades and prophesied peace and quietness, then more sheep's cream and then home. We went half way together and the Kaïmakam and Co. went to Apéri, and we and Mr. Frangisko Sakolarides to Volátha. Having been taking lessons from Hassam Tachrí Effendi, the secretary, I was able to say 'Teshekür edérim', 'Thank you', to the Kaïmakam. We were led to the café by Mr. Frangisko Sakolarides and given coffee and were very glad to get home safely with only starlight to help us, and I had to walk some way.

In the little church at Kyriá Panagía, which is quite good and not ruined, there were lots of scribbled names and one of the Greeks said, 'Now we will write up your name' and I said 'Oh, not my name please', they said 'Why?' and I said it was not our custom in England to write our name in churches. So he went out and the Kaïmakam, who had put on an awestruck face, said to me very quickly 'Because it is a sin?' So I said 'Yes, for it is the house of God'. And he said, 'Yes' and I really felt glad he should see that some Christians have a little reverence.[38] The very irreverent jokes the Greeks make and their heathenishness mixed up in their religion must give them a bad idea of Christianity.

Today we are very busy preparing for a luncheon party tomorrow of 7, but are rather in a fix as the people of the house wish us to have our feast under a tree, or at Mr. Manolakakis', who is one of the guests, because their brother died 6 months ago and the neighbours will think little of them if they permit a party in the house. M and I are going to cook, but we have great difficulties; to begin at the very foundation, we must borrow a tablecloth, for we dine off oil cloth off the floor, and food is not easy to get in large quantities. The Kaïmakam gave T his beads for playing with, string on leather. T bought 14 good Rhodian plates and 4 broken ones from Manolakakis' mother, but we never got them.[39]

Sunday evening [March 8th]. Our party was over very successfully by half past 2, and surely it was the very funniest feast at which I was ever hostess. A 7 o'clock I went in my crimson dressing gown to the neighbouring mud-floored hut where M sleeps, and which is our very smoky little kitchen – to cook a

---

[38] This is somewhat at odds with Mabel's behaviour in 1884 on Íos! See p. 39.
[39] Highly-decorated Rhodian plates and ceramics still make popular souvenirs for today's tourists.

pudding. Mr. Manolakakis was already there, but we are used enough to the ways of the place not to mind that. So I set about my business. After that he stayed about an hour and we got very hungry and discovered that M thought we would not eat till the midday meal. We became very anxious about a kid which did not arrive till 10.

The people of the house then made a great row, wept, and screamed about our 'making a table' but fortunately our friend said he should be there, and if we wished to sing and dance we should come to his house. In vain we assured them we only wished to eat 7 together instead of 2 and Mr. Manolakakis had dined with us 2 nights ago. However they set about to tidy up the house, and to our amusements the sheets T has slept in nearly a week were spread over the 2 sofas. A tablecloth of calico, very small, was borrowed and knives, etc., from Mr. Frangisko Sakolarides. We put a great many Majolica jugs, of which there are 19 in this room, and a lovely nosegay on the table, and that was all we could do. They say Mrs. Virginía has a mania for flowers and that *stock* is the only one they care for.

Before we were quite ready in came a man, who, when he was asked where he came from, said 'from Apéri, you have been in my house'. T asked which house, as we have been in so many. 'The house with the bed', but we do not know his name and only remember that he keeps a shop. We only imagined him to be a casual visitor, but he remained uninvited for luncheon. The Kaïmakam brought the secretary, who can only speak Turkish, and who we also did not expect, so we were tightly crowded round our small table. The Kaïmakam and I sat on the sofa. The flowers were flanked with wine for Christians and brandy for Turks.

M is considered a first rate cook according to Greek notions. First we had a huge quantity of broth with rice. Our unknown Greek guest was fasting, so it was lucky that we next had lobster salad. Then chicken in some sauce and then lamb in another sauce. Then cheese, then each person got a soup plate *brimful* of solid milk with cinnamon strewed over, then my pudding and then the sheep's cream. Four times we all arose and clicked glasses, and as no one drank ever without drinking everyone's health, we were always saying 'Evcharistó', 'Thank you'. Everyone smoked any time he wished during the meal and we were quite as merry and talkative a party as if we had all been English. N.B. Mrs. Virghinía is the exception as far as talking goes. A tin plate with our alphabet round it and 'who killed Cock Robin?' was a delightful topic of conversation, and after coffee some views of London given to the Kaïmakam with a luminous match box, a plan of London shown, my down quilts to pinch, air pillow to blow up, and my bed to be lain in by several, and picked to pieces, were the entertainments we offered to our company.

Last night a lot of old women spent the evening with us and T drew them. One was quite terrified and all were angry at his doing it and tried to tear up his book. A little child of four whose name is Verghinía says she has the same name as the Frank lady, so she begs her mother to plait her quite short hair on the top of her head like mine.

We think of starting for Arkássa tomorrow and are already provided with a host who hopes we will remain a year if we wish. What pans and jars M will borrow to carry off the 'remains', for he could not bear to leave them behind and indeed it would be useless as everyone is fasting [sic]. We have constant patients coming to us and I am sure you would all laugh to hear T's medical lectures – we do afterwards, but at the time we are quite too busy trying to understand and advise. A child born with a twisted foot was brought to me yesterday.

I forgot to say that 2 *zaptichs* fed in the kitchen and the Kaïmakam is anxious we should have one with us but we don't want one. We should have to give him a present besides paying for a mule and feeding him.

Monday was quite too rainy and windy for us to start when we had a good roof over our heads, and we suffered very much from the cold. We shut our shutters to keep out the hurricane and had a brazier of charcoal, but the door had always to be open for light. We ached with cold, so changeable is this climate, and the damp of all our things is wonderful. We cannot imagine why we do not take cold; all our day clothes feel cold and damp in the morning and at night we are very glad of the flannel gowns we had made on purpose, but which decidedly would want airing before we put them on in England.

Tuesday March 17th. After a rainy night we set off at 8 for Arkássa. At the last moment one mule failed us, but it did not matter. Eventually all the baggage we took with us, my bed, a small portmanteau, and a bundle of cloaks, besides food were piled on all over the mule, so high that it was like a camel. I had to climb a chair and then a wall as high again to mount and sit cross-legged on the pile. We passed Othos without stopping and at Spiliés we stopped to lunch at Chrysánthe's house, and there made some bargains over embroideries.

Arkássa is on the sea 2 hours from Spiliés and the road became much easier as we got nearer the sea. I was dreadfully cold, the wind was so high. About ½ an hour before Arkássa we came to Pheníki, a little bay with very few houses. Having a letter for Kyrios Constantinos Malagarda, who keeps a combination of a café and tinker's and jeweller's shop, we turned out of our way to visit him. He gave us coffee and jam and implored us many times to remain the night, but as his bedrooms were very uninviting-looking balconies, approached by ladders, we, with hopes of better things, said Kyrios Polychrónia (many years) was awaiting us. We were lucky enough to get possession of a set of silver and gilt ornaments formerly worn by the

Karpathiote women – 3 long chains, 2 frontlets and 2 earrings. Before he left he took us into his garden, and such a garden! It was apparently a barley field in the first instance and all through it, like weeds, were various vegetables, each plant separately had to be hunted for. The only flower a bush of stock. He gave us lettuce, cardamoms, celery, tomatoes, and other things were a great joy to M as we had salads for 3 days.

Arkássa is quite a new place, about 10 years old but rapidly increasing as the masons were busy. It is built on both sides of a steep cleft containing a river and on the neck of a promontory. Mr. Manyyears's house was horrid; the floor damp, sticky and very smelly. It was a general shop with wares of the poorest kind. The 'sofa' had no railing. No window and altogether it was a nasty place but a little redeemed by a good fireplace, the first we have seen and we had a really good fire in it.

I was excessively glad of my own bed. T of course had that combination of 'Bed & Board' which is usual. Next morning we walked about and saw the remains of temples, that is a good many pillars which they are hacking up for building, but we did not think it a good place for excavation.

Next morning, **[Wednesday] 18th March**, we gladly left our cow-house and started for Menités across the mountains on the other side of the island. This part is not so pretty, it is much barer than the E. side. It was 2 hours' 'road' and Menités can be seen from a distance. It is very prettily situated; the church stands on a high and precipitous rock, jutting into the valley or plain, sloping to the sea, and the town runs up the hill behind it. Here a real mud floor seemed quite a luxury to us. There was no window and immediately about 30 people were in the room to stare, which they unremittingly did all day long.

How superior is our treatment of the wild beasts in the zoological gardens! Each one has a bedroom that he can go into when he is tired of being stared at. Yesterday morning as I wished to button on my long gaiters, I retired to the end of the room and sat down with my back turned to the multitude, but as there was a little room between me and the wall, that soon became crowded. Once M said, 'What do you want here?' and a woman said 'Only it amuses my baby to see the man write and the woman sew'.

They brought some embroideries but asked enormous prices. Every man, woman and child seems to wear on their persons all the foreign money they can find and think it very old and tell us it had been found in tombs, an English penny for instance, and such an exalted idea have they of inscriptions that they prize a new coin more highly and think it older because it has *grammatá* on it. The English idea of 'second-hand' being cheaper has no equivalent in Greek. The older, raggeder, and dirtier a thing is the dearer.

T took some pretty sketches in the afternoon.

Yesterday, **Friday [actually Thursday, March] 19th,** we returned to our home at Volathá, which seemed really quite comfortable and grand and clean, which last it really is, though very damp. We passed through Othos, where we lunched amid a crowd in the little windowless hut which serves as a café. A 3 hours' journey over the mountain, very windy and very steep on the W. side, and more sheltered and an easier road on the E., in and out of the folds of the mountains; each spur much greener on the E. side than the W. At Othos we picked up for 1f. a little Rhodian saucer and some embroidery. Mr. Manolakakis was here from 7 to 9 this morning.

We start next week for Elymbo and there we hope to get diggers to come to the uninhabited island of Saría with us. We shall use the tent but we hope to find a chapel or some ruin perhaps. M is to make the bread. It is better than the plan of making biscuits of 3 weeks' bread and soaking it in water. Our plan is to get our superfluities and purchases down to Pegádhia and leave them there, to send M for them and 'lie' at Diaphane waiting for them and to go in a sailing boat to Syra.

I have been quite interrupted in everything, and T was packing and arranging our goods when in came a crowd and now he is having Greek poetry read loudly to him and I am trying to write letters and have someone sitting tightly beside me, leaning upon and over me to see my writing. When I was at Menités we were anxious to know about a charm for fever and were just asking about it when M suddenly said the Kyria had caught cold and was suffering, so they said they would fetch a woman. Some time after M said 'Won't you have your cloak, Kyria?' Of course I accepted it and rolled myself up and made an invalid of myself. When the old woman came, she demanded my wrist and took a thread which she began to tie round it. She said 'Where do you come from?' Of course I began to say 'from England' but I was directed to say 'From the Holy Mountain (Athos). A black dog has come near me. Leave me that you may bind that'. I had to repeat this answer 3 times and when I had done so she finished tying the knot, saying I should be better in the morning. As we wanted to see another woman do it, I gave my left wrist and had to say I had come from Saloniki, but otherwise one charm was the same as the other.

On the Saturday after our return we 3 walked down to Apéri, meaning to pack the plates we had bought and which the woman very civilly said we might leave in her house till we were ready for them, but when we asked for them she would not let us have them without our paying much more, so we told her she was a liar, which is commonly done, and does not seem to enrage the person thus insulted the least. We hoped after all to have got them but we did not. [**A later footnote, October 1885**: We have them now, M having been back to Karpathos in the summer.]

We then went and had coffee with the Turks and to see Mr. Koumpis, who walked home with us. On Sunday, as I said before, Mr. Manolakakis stayed from 7 to 10 while we wrote letters, and was seeing us off to walk to Othos where we meant to lunch, but perceiving M come out with a basket and an earthen dish containing some lamb, he suddenly decided to come too, which bored us rather, and of course the luncheon for 3 had to be stretched for 4. We went to see an old man in bed, said to be a prophet. He had to tell our fortunes out of a book and what struck the crowd most was that T was nice out but unpleasant in the house, and I was disagreeable and stingy to my relations, and an old man afterwards, when I said I liked to travel, said 'yes it is better that you travel as you are not liked at home'.

On **Monday [March] 23rd** we went down to Pigádia, 3½ hours. It rained a great deal but at last we determined to be off and after 2 thirds of the way it was fine. We sewed up a sack of old dresses, etc., packed a box of pottery, and left these with a bag in the customhouse and carried up the tent and T's bed. I rode and the others walked. At 8 next day, 24th, we had many affectionate farewells and set off with 3 mules, one pack mule and 2 with plenty on them besides T and me. M walked all but about 1½ hour when he had the mule. We went through Othos and Spiliés to the W. coast and then after a little visit to Chrysánthe while M replenished our jar with the good wine of Spiliés. We turned north to Méso Chório, which we did not reach till 5.15, all very tired.

Several times we had to get down and walk half a mile or so as the way was too steep or inclined to slip from rain and once we had a great deal of trouble in getting up a rock much higher than ourselves. We had to dismount and partially unload the mules and we kicked a good deal. Much screaming took place. M told the old muleteer that his mule had no legs (ανάποδος), addressed him angrily as brother, asked him what sort of a man he was and answered himself that he was not a man at all but a beast, and at last we all arrived at the top, beasts and people. There a boy and an old man called Giorgios Barbalagónikou. He told us his surname came from his father, being very good at running after hares (*lagós*). He was called consequently Lagóniko, prefixed with Barba, or Uncle, as he evidently was an old man. Besides there was a woman who had the combined object of dragging T's mule and offering at a church here a candle for the recovery of her son a year ago.

Before noon we found ourselves lost high up on the mountainside when we ought to have been near the sea. So we had to scramble down on foot as best we might, down beds of loose sharp stones over rocks and through thorns and suffered somewhat as I had not my gaiters on. We could see the path beneath us on soft ground. It is easy enough to lose the way on stony ground, for the road is only made by the steps of men and mules. If there is earth among the stones one can trace the track by the splashing of mud on the rocks in rainy weather. When the road gets worn away, or washed away, they step aside and make a new road, even through someone's field with the corn springing up, and indeed sometimes they do this without rhyme or reason, for no one minds walking through quite tall corn.

After we had gone over a quantity of tremendous boulders, we turned up the course of a dry river and despairing of finding water we spent a very merry half hour over our luncheon, consisting of oat bread, sardines, caviare and wine out of scooped out lemon, a delicious cup which we have used before. We passed through a great deal of scraggy pine wood, very difficult to stoop and squeeze through. The sun was very burning and I broke my parasol when it was shut, and I felt it dreadfully and got a headache though I had a white thing on my head. I had the anxious charge of the brandy bottle, which M meant to carry in his hand. I had also our larder on my mule, a hare and a half, a very welcome change from boiled lamb and kids.

We went in and out of folds of the mountains, up and down and across a water-course, then up again, and were glad indeed when we sighted Méso Chório (Middle Village) seated on a jutting rock over a plain, looking as healthy as possible but exposed to fevers. We were first taken to a house of the usual shape, but gaily and wildly frescoed within, and there, to our surprise, were greeted by Hassan Effendi, arrived from Apéri half an hour ago, having left at 11 and come a shorter way over Lastos.

After sitting with him for some time we were led to our home, the schoolmasters' house. It is a poor place but has an outer staircase and that makes us feel more private than if we were on the ground. We have 5 windows so that we can close the door, and indeed have to lock it today as there is no other means of keeping it shut and there is a violent S. wind blowing at it. The bedroom, or boarded part, has no rail and is 2 or 3 inches higher than the table, so it is a good climb as there are no steps.

The bed was laid, very clean, at once, and marvellous to say we were left to ourselves so that T was able to nurse me in peace. I took to the floor immediately and could eat no dinner but arrowroot and became so comfortable, for the pillows were not straw but soft, that I would have stayed there but at 11 o'clock, long after we had gone to bed, bugs were discovered so my own bed was built and I retired to it.

There have been violent showers very often and wind all day, so we only took walks and had a long visit from the schoolmaster, a very pleasant man, and from some old women with things to sell who called us 'my boy' and 'my girl', and in the afternoon from Hussan Effendi, who found me putting the rib of my parasol together with a pencil bandaged on with rag. This is the second I have done and T is darning his umbrella. One of the shutters in this room has quite 2 inches of light round it on 2 sides. A large stone on the window ledge in churches and houses is the recognized fastening.

Friday [March 27th]. We had tremendous wind and rain all Wednesday night, which, however, very suddenly ceased and yesterday, though there were a few showers, was fine. We get up about 6 always and from the moment we were ready people came with their old embroideries to sell; some had washed them and brought them wet. We bought some things and after a good deal of exclaiming that it was now 'evening' and 'night', and 'we were losing all the day', we set off for Levkós (white), a plain near the sea 2 hours off. There are traces of an ancient city whose name is unknown and there is a little rocky island very near the land which has remains of a Byzantine fort; it is called Sókastro.

We had seen the plain below us on our way here. Though I call it a plain it is very rocky and all the fields are terraced up. My mule was led by its owner the parson, Papa Manólis. He had blue cotton bags and his long priest's robe was also blue cotton, patched and faded, but he had a very good hat. T sketched him while we ate our luncheon under the shade of a boat by the sea. It was very hot. We went in a boat to the island and had a very steep, hard, stony climb up and were not in any way rewarded by the ruins. It became quite cloudy on our way back and we saw a water-spout sailing along the sea and then run up into the mountains. We saw one in Telos too and had great rain afterwards. In the evening the schoolmaster, our host, and his father-in-law came and sat and talked.

This morning the house is dripping all over and we have spread all our waterproof rugs, etc., out to the best advantage; a rushing torrent is roaring down the street, a spout pouring off each house and T is at the door sketching with a waterproof hat on his head. I am receiving the sellers and every minute a new drip causes me to rise and move something. I have just been saving the boots. It is getting finer so we hope to be able to get to the village of Spoa where we hope to obtain provisions. This is a very poor place. We can get no milk, eggs, or bread and our kid and other things that we brought here are vanishing, also our wine and the wine here is bad.

Well! We have got back to Méso Chório safely, but not without adventure, and had a very pleasant day.

The plan in this island is to *drag* the mule until the muleteer is tired of it and then to tie up the chain which hangs under the mule's chin and drive him. Today, the minute my mule was released he rushed up a wall about a foot and a half into a field and set off at a gallop and I soon began to feel very loose, so seeing a drop of an unknown depth before me I thought it best to let myself go then as I could not stop the mule, so off I fell easily enough as I had no kind of stirrup. I fell on no stones but on a soft wet bed of vetch and was neither hurt nor dirtied. Away went the mule kicking off all our waterproofs and baggage, very properly so called, and away went the Papas, casting his stick and umbrella behind him, and were some time before they reappeared. We gathered our goods and found that the mule had gone off with the bag containing the bottle of wine, but fortunately, after a bit, I stumbled on it among the vetch.

Spoa is on the other side of the backbone of the island, and as the church is the only thing that is whitewashed it does not show at all at a distance. It has only 40 houses all clustered together. As we entered we asked the villagers to bring things to sell and a crier was sent round to summon folks to bring things to the house of Mr. Pachys (fat), for whom we had a letter of introduction. We lunched in his windowless cottage, which was at the same time a shop, and bought quite a large bundle of things.

One was a gown, whole, the embroidery not very deep but the silk ground good. Of course we only bought it because it was whole, but at the last moment the woman came and said she wished to cut off the plain silk. We refused, she screamed, and so did a number of her friends who followed us to the place where the mule was waiting and they tried to snatch the dress while dire insults were bandied. The mule was finally loaded, for we had bought raisins, sugar, a little tiny kid and 20 herrings, which we had joyfully discovered, and as I was caught by the legs just as the saddle was going over backwards, we reached home safely in time to avoid a shower.

We had a great medical consultation at Spoa, and since we came back a man came with weak knees, and then one to have an advertisement in French of Macassar oil explained.

Elymbo. **Palm Sunday. March 29.** Yesterday at 8.30 we set off to continue our northward journey. Before starting, at the last minute things were brought to sell and some camomile brought to know if that was what we had recommended for a poultice. Next, one muleteer, to whom we had agreed to pay what he asked, refused to go without more money so we had to get another mule which M drove or led with baggage. The mules were not very cleverly loaded, which caused us some trouble by the way, but the little excitement helped to pass away the 8 long hours. Everyone told us we could never pass these mountains as the roads are so very difficult, but the wind was too high for a boat and, besides, we should have had to get our baggage down to the sea and up again here from Dhreaphani.

We went so completely along the backbone of the island that had our eyes only been like those of birds, we could have seen both seas at once; as it is we had to turn our heads. Once, on the very ridge, the sumpter mule took to kicking and dancing and the string of the tent-sack becoming untied, out flew all around various sardine tins, etc. M rushed about trying to catch the mule. My muleteer helping, with his *skouphiá*, or red cap, blown off and his long hair blown over his eyes. T holding my mule which wished to get into shelter and my few clothes spread out like Prophet Elias, after whom, as usual, the highest mountain is named.

Another time at a very narrow place this mule was in front alone, then came I, and T was very angry with my man for not going in front to see if the path was broken away, for there were so many landslips from the rain, but he said 'Oh, the woman understands it all' and it was impossible to pass. But at last the first mule stopped, no one could see why and my mule overlapped him, then the first *tried* to kick but hadn't room, to my alarm, so T commanded my man to go on and he scrambled round and led the first mule over rather a bad place. T walked more than half the way and I had to walk a good deal. Once we had to build a bridge, or rather viaduct, with stones on a gully of sloping crumbly schist.

We lunched in a lovely spot among trees, in an inner angle of the road. We sat on a large flat stone with water all around it and arbutus bushes and maidenhair, and fir trees. T took a sketch. The wind was tremendous and I am sure I should have been blown off once if T had not held me, but we were so high that the sea did not look rough and we could see the rocks at the bottom for about a mile. Oh! It was a long, long way! and as for the road, there was no *trace* of any for a mile or 2 sometimes, and at other places we had to make one for ourselves as the ordinary one was washed away. We were very glad when a little cairn made us truly guess that Elymbo must be in sight from there. Soon after passing this cairn, which holds up a board with a cross in it, I had to dismount again and we had to help ourselves along with our hands, so you may fancy what a road it was.

We entered Elymbo, or Olymbo, amid startled exclamations of 'What people are these?' We went first to the house of the man for whom we had a letter. His house was locked and he was out and we have not seen him. We unloaded at his door, and soon his wife and a dirty priest asked us up. The house was so abominably dirty that T asked the way to the *kafeneion* and demanded the schoolmaster. He came forward and asked him if he could find us a comfortable house for a fortnight, as the only one we could get was too much exposed to the wind, so he very kindly placed his own at T's disposal and M was sent for me and the luggage.

I had not been very happy all this time as the people were not pleased at our deserting them. They asked me if there were Christians in my place and I said 'Naí, málista!',[40] we all were, but I do not think they understood where my place

---

[40] 'Yes, certainly'.

was. They hardly said goodbye to me and I was glad to follow the baggage to the new abode. We have a plain room, 14 ft square with a hard sofa and many rush-bottom chairs and a little very low round table, so that we keep our plates on our knees. This room is too new to be dirty, but the boarded floor streams with damp. It has a large window, one on each side of the door with glass *tacked* in.

M has the neighbouring Karpathian house where he cooks. My bed was set in one of the far corners, T's at right angles as a breakwater to keep off the crowd from rubbing on it. It is a pride and pleasure, if a trouble to M to set up these wondrous beds before a gaping multitude. We had several visitors and were glad to get to bed as all were tired, though fortunately the day had been cloudy.

We dressed in the dark, as if we had opened the shutters we should have a crowd; very soon we had a visit from Mr. F. Sakolarides, and a soldier, who is here on government business. It was Palm Sunday. We walked about; all the houses, including ours, are sunk in the rock behind. The church is the nicest we have seen as it is roughly covered with frescoed pictures; inside the walls are smooth. To reach it one goes through a room, which, though it has 4 sides, is nearly triangular in shape. Here in the afternoon we stumbled upon a parliament being presided over by Mr. F. Sakolarides. He was seated in the extreme corner on the only chair placed on a stone-built bench which ran around the room. He made me sit in this chair and more were brought for him and T.

There were about 80 men seated, some on the bench and some cross-legged upon the rough stone floor rearing and bawling, often all at once, about boundaries, taxes, etc., and often they rose up and rushed at each other with threatening gestures. Then the two soldiers stationed one at each end ran into the midst and separated them. Even when they were forced to the ground they sprang to their knees like jack-in-the-boxes to shout.

Everyone smoked and the government and the opposition, at more peaceable moments, frequently stepped across to get a light from each other's cigarettes, countless ends of which strewed the middle of the floor. The schoolmaster had a very empty inkstand on the floor before him and wrote the proceedings, and whenever he said a symphony had been come to, everyone denied it and at last they came to blows and we unobserved escaped, having long been tired of it.

You must excuse these smudges as I am sitting cross-legged on T's bed in our tent and was just interrupted by a man who came for 2 candles T had sent for that he may explore a cave.

We are encamped **([Monday] March 31st)** for 4 days at Vourgounda (Βουργούνδα). We came here yesterday with two mules and 2 workmen to make excavations on the site of an ancient city. We only took our medicines, without which we never move, necessaries of clothing, and books for 4 days, food and bedding; but I had so much to sit on that I had to hold with both hands all the way. As I did not fall off I was pronounced an excellent rider by the men.

There is a long rocky point jutting into the sea on the W. of Karpathos, far N., near Tristoma and covered with ruins. Here everyone lunched at 12 and then T set the men to work and I went to the end of the point and had the tent pitched by a high rock which shelters us from S. winds. As Sunday night was the only rainless one we have had this long time, the ground was dry and by great good luck we have a level gravelly floor. Neither M nor the other two men had ever seen a tent before, so beginning with turning right side out I had to, by example and prompt, instruct them in everything; all in Greek too.

Do not think I had only to cause the pegs to be driven into the ground and put the eyes or guys, or whatever you call the ropes, over, no, only one peg is done like that. No 2 ropes are the same, either as to length or the angle from the tent: some are under rocks, some are round rocks, some are over rocks, and one had to be strung through a hole in a rock. One of those, which support the pole, is hitched over a little cairn; it is fastened so low, while its fellow forms a right angle with the pole. They could not understand the wooden runners and wanted to *tie* the ropes in knots and were amazed at the *mechaní* when shown. I was tired enough in my tongue and limbs when after hoisting the Union Jack, I sat down to survey the tent and really the ropes all dancing have a very funny effect. The sun was hot outside but it was hotter still setting up the beds inside, 'tromeró zestë'[41] as they said.

After that I went to the workmen; who had discovered the pavement of a Byzantine church. We turn up our noses at anything 'tes Vizantines epoches', so T took them elsewhere.[42]

Soon after our arrival, a messenger came and brought us 2 letters, the first we have had for more than 5 weeks and our first news of poor General Gordon's death. As soon as we had joyfully read them we began to lament the many more that had been lost, but 2 or 3 hours later another man came with 23, and 2 newspapers, February 7 being the latest, and March 9 the latest letter.

When the sun set we scrambled home. Next to our tent is a little hut built against the wall as a kitchen for pilgrims who come to a little chapel in the cave beneath. A very steep path leads to the small round entrance and several flights of steps lead down into a large cave. The holy place is shut in by a low wall and some pillars which do not touch the roof. Holy water drips into 2 little stone

---

[41] 'Awfully hot'.
[42] The archaeology and study of all things Byzantine was not to become widely accepted as a serious field for scholarly attention until the 20th century. It remained for academic pioneers such as Robert Byron in his book *The Byzantine Achievement* (London, 1929) to overcome the prejudices that had built up against 'tes Vizantines epoches' since the time of Gibbon.

troughs and thither we hie with our sponges and towels to wash. The workmen sleep among the rocks; there are plenty of caves about. When it got dark we went to the kitchen to dine. It was T's birthday.[43]

The sacks of my bed and the tent were laid as a tablecloth on the soft wet earthen floor. We sat on 2 stones. T leaning against the middle post supporting a lambskin full of water, and I, as I found afterwards, very few inches from the lamb of the period. M built a table and seats next day. All the rocks and stones around were full of food and pots and a candle stuck by its own wax to one of them shed a dim light, except once when it tumbled down and went out.

We had a soup of lamb's head and a lot of herbs picked by the wayside, onions, and a handful of peas someone had given to T to eat raw. Then the brains and tongue boiled. Then the liver fried; a bowl of sheep's cream and sugar. Some wine from Samos and coffee. We then strolled on the rocks by moonlight and complained to each other that we did not feel at all excited at the idea of our first night in a tent – indeed, I think all we felt was satisfaction at the idea of a clean, dry shelter.

M spread his bed on brushwood in the kitchen. I undressed outside that I might bring in no fleas. As I had spread all our bedding in the sun, for once it was dry and our clothes in the morning were quite dry too. It rained in the night and T had to go out about 2 to loosen the guys and the N. wind came on in the morning, so they had to be tightened again.

It is a cold dark day and the sea wild and black. We breakfasted outside. T has gone to dig graves today and I am remaining at home enjoying great peace, nooked in where no one can stare. I am just going to have another read of the letters. In the afternoon, or rather about 10, I went and with difficulty found the diggers, as they were in catacombs whose openings were quite invisible from above. They had already begun to find things, though many of the graves had evidently been opened in the Byzantine times. Most things were broken but still there were many whole and during the whole time we became possessed of many earthen plates (20 in one grave), the remains of copper mirrors and boxes, some glass things broken, and some broken but very pretty vases, etc. But the best thing is quite perfect, a bowl shaped like a pineapple about 4 or 5 inches across. Besides this, 3 round boxes and 2 lids made of lead, we think, a sort of button with a hanging ring but we know not what metal, and some little twisted bits that seem to be gold. The prettiest lamp, quite perfect, has a word on the

---

[43] The cave-shrine is that of John the Baptist at Vrykoúnda. It is an ancient cult-site sacred to death and healing, with overtones of child sacrifice; John is said to have rescued a baby who fell into the sea here. There are still festivals on 7 January and 29 August – the red moon at the latter symbolizes the saint's severed head. As for Theodore's birthday, Mabel is inexplicably out by a few days: Theodore was born on 29 March 1852; he was 33.

bottom and T copied some inscriptions painted on the stucco of the vaults. We are altogether very much pleased with our success, and if we do not find things on Saría may return.[44]

April 1885 – Kárpathos

On Thursday morning (March 21st, I mean **April 2nd**) **[March 21st was a Saturday, April 2nd was a Thursday]**, I did not go at all to the digging. To get there one must climb up, down, or over 17 walls, and as I did this 3 times the day before, besides wandering in search of tombs, I am sure I had a good deal of climbing. I was not much use as the men preferred grouping themselves round me when T's back was turned, talking to me, looking at my eyeglass, scissors, gloves, never before seen in Karpathos I am sure, and asking innumerable questions. In vain I suggest they should work but when the *Aphentikó*, as they address T, comes it is different.

Besides there was much to do in cleaning out the earth from the pots with very little water. I had to mind the camp while M went to seek a meal in the sea. I had a visit from 5 women and girls who without any ceremony called me nothing but Verghinía. This is the first time I have not been called Kyria Verghinía, but I suppose these people really never have seen anyone superior to themselves and their only idea of a 'Kyria' must be the Blessed Virgin. They said 'come with us Verghinía and we'll give you cream', but they terrified me by playing with the pots and I gave them no encouragement to remain and was glad when they left.

I packed our personal possessions and the more delicate 'finds' and after luncheon T went off again and I broke up the camp with M, though T had sent me a man, which I told him was quite unnecessary. The man was busy all the time turning a lamb into food, which I fortunately did not find out till he was dead.

By the by, M had not slept a 2nd night in the kitchen, which was really as air tight as a nutmeg grater, but taken refuge in a cave about 30 feet above our heads.

We had 3 mules as we had 2 huge baskets of pots and seaweeds. About 4, T and his men came and everything was carried about ¾ of a mile and they and I were loaded on the mules and we reached Elymbo by dark. Sunny day.

---

[44] The Bents' 'excavations' on Kárpathos were extensive and Theodore wrote up their finds in the *Journal of Hellenic Studies*, Vol. 6 (1885) p. 235. The graves they excavated date from the first to the third centuries BC and very many of the finds are now in the British Museum. Theodore's researches at Vrykoúnda were systematically undertaken and the graves themselves numbered and recorded. These were relatively early years for archaeologists and there was little in the way of common, let alone best, practice.

Good Friday was a fine sunny day and we unpacked the panniers, for we were quite too tired to look at anything on our arrival. It is very exciting work digging, first finding something, then is it whole? Then have we all the pieces? The men grind the edges trying to fit them and any metal they cut with their knife. Fortunately they never saw the little boxes. T found and pocketed them.

We cleaned as much as our limited means would allow (a milk jug and a Russian wooden bowl such as grocers have with 2 lbs of tea). We packed the pots into 3 boxes, all except a very large earthenware jug, 2 of which were found whole and one of which T gave away. It is to be carried loose all the way home and now we empty our bowl into it. These two days before Easter are employed making bread and cakes with red eggs stuck into them and every oven is smoking. Elymbo (Ολυμβος) is rather a disappointment to us; we think Méso Chório was a quainter place. This Saturday is a rainy day.

Now here I must I think make a few remarks about the Greeks founded upon my 3 journeys amongst them and staying in the houses of high and low and seeing them in town and country.

Though they have a king, surely never were more true republicans than the Greeks. There appears to be perfect equality among them and a complete mingling of classes, neither dirt, poverty not want of education seems to make any difference.

When we were in Chios we went to see Mr. Choremi who has a very nice house in Athens, is very rich and in the best society there. Phaedros,[45] our dragoman, whose wife is quite a common woman, glad of a very old dress of mine, was treated quite as an equal. Mr. Philemon, who is the Greek Consul at Rhodes, and who is quite a gentleman and whose wife is quite a lady and very well dressed, has a most ragged and dirty old father-in-law, Dr. Klados, and no one would take Mrs. Klados for a lady. Mr. Philemon gave us a letter to various people in Rhodes, particularly to Mr. Manolakakis, evidently quite an equal. He lives with a mud floor. His daughter of 17 with bare legs carried our luggage about a mile for 6d on her head and one of his little boys I saw running about with only a tattered frock open all down the front and bare feet. He is quite one of the chief men of Karpathos and Mr. Sakolarides's children also have bare legs. But these people are not like us in keeping up a good establishment in the country,[46] for though they are as smart as possible in Athens, Syra, or Smyrna, once they get to the country they cast off their civilization with their collars and seem content with any kind of an untidy picnic for any length of time. Mr. Manolakakis has a cousin, a bricklayer, and one of our friends here is a bricklayer

---

[45] George Phaedros, the Bents' dragoman on their earlier trips.
[46] The Hall-Dares had extensive properties in Essex (Theydon Bois) and elsewhere.

that T met at Mr. Manolakakis's house. He gave us letters of introduction to all kinds of peasants, some very dirty, but they all seem quite equal and we always noticed in the Cyclades that our muleteers used to sit down in any house and help themselves to tobacco. Certainly whatever their education is, they all seem to have good manners, if not quite according to our notion.

We are expected to know any English engineer on any steamer, etc.; in fact they do not seem to recognize difference of rank at all. As to our being 'a nation of shopkeepers'[47] the Greeks cannot understand our buying anything for ourselves and think every bit of embroidery and everything else is bought for sale, and they often ask us if we have different things with us to sell. The women are quite like animals and are very much looked down on by the men (violent hail). Every man but a priest or two and a few old men leaves the island every summer for 6 months or more, chiefly as bricklayers, and every field labour, wine making, etc., is done by the women. There are no girls' schools and few of my sex can read.

Here the women's dress consists of a pair of full white trousers and a white night gown flowing open to the waist. When cold they wear a blue wadded-cotton coat, rather shorter, and then both men and women have a coat of brown goats' hair with a hood. Sometimes they wear brown leather top boots, sometimes not.

All these Greeks seem to love money dearly and always are wondering what everything is worth. They seem to like to 'go back of their bargain' too. Twice have women come demanding to cut all the plain silk off dresses we had bought. Once having bought a worked sheet because it had good lace on it, after the money was paid the seller asked to cut off the lace and once or twice after we had bought a bundle of bits they tried to remove one or two.

Easter Sunday, April 5th 1885.[48] This morning was sunny after the first two hours so we opened all our windows and the door and tried to dry our things. Though T forgot to put out the brazier for the night and though it was still burning in the morning, some *clean* clothes hung *over* it on 2 chairs in the morning. We hung out the Union Jack in honour of the day. We had a visit from the schoolmaster, who is being doctored by us and is the better for our treatment, and took a walk with him. By the bye, one of T's patients (cold tea for the eyes) brought 2 eggs as a thank offering.

A little while after our return M came to say luncheon was ready if we were, for he thought it must be noon. T looked at his watch and found it to be half past 10; however we agreed our appetites were ready, so to our amusement we found we had everything cleared away by 11.30.

---

[47] Napoleon's (after Adam Smith) famous observation on the British.
[48] 1855. A rare year, when Western and Orthodox Easters coincided.

We spoke over the difference we observed between the inhabitants of Karpathos and Tilos and the Cyclades and the other islands we have visited, i.e. Niseros, Rhodes, Chios, Samos, and Mytelene, in their not offering coffee, etc. to visitors. In the other islands we were always at once brought coffee, or jam and water, or *raki*, or almonds, oranges, or pomegranates, but here the only one who had offered us coffee was the Kaïmakan and the wicked owner of the plates who is a Greek from Syra. I agree with T in thinking it a Turkish fashion, but it is odd they never have offered us any thing till about an hour or two after this conversation when we were asked into a house, which we entered, and very soon a large dish of sheep's cream was placed before us and a *kouloúri*, that is one of the wound-up serpent-like cakes they make in great numbers for Easter, generally with coloured eggs in them. I could hardly get any down so soon and my horror was great when she said, 'now you must eat some lamb!'

Such cooking is going on these 3 days. First bread and *kouloúris*, then yesterday and today lambs, and we see the lambs come out of the oven in every imaginable shape in which they may have been flung in. Well! She fetched the family lamb and tore us off bits. She handed me a whole leg, but I cried for mercy and was let off with a smaller bit. It was very tender and I gnawed away industriously till the kind woman took my bit and rubbed salt into it with her thumbs, having been to fetch a handful of salt. I managed to continue eating inside bits till, when everyone was excited over my gloves, I squeezed up my lamb and bread into a tight ball and pocketed it.

Since this we have been to church. Only men and little boys go into the church, the women remain in the outer room where the parliament was, but as I count as a man, sitting at meals, etc., they invited me in. In I went. All the little boys stood in front, some very small and very pretty – indeed there are lots of pretty children here, though their elders are not handsome.

Everyone but we had a candle, but just before the time for lighting them came a man with two very large ones, hot and newly made so that we were glad to have them in the tray in which they lay, they were so soft. Of course, when they were so kind we lit up like the rest and I consoled myself by remembering that it was in honour of a truly Christian feast in which we could take part, in fact we recognized many parts of our own service.

There were 5 priests with such dirty rough-shock heads of uncombed hair. Their poor robes were made of printed calico. People chatted a good deal and we often heard a loud 'shsh!' It was very odd seeing the priests dressing and undressing inside the *tembelon* (τεμβλον) or screen. They walked about a good deal in a way I could not understand and 2 or 3 young men stepped about with large prayer books and repeated 'Christ is risen from the dead' (Χριστός ανέστε εκ νεκρον) and wherever they went the bystanders looked over and raised their voices.

The gospel was read on this wise: one papas read a verse or two in Greek, then each of the other 4, and then a young man read them in French! We did not discover this till the very last set of verses, as the French was very bad, but the last set but one I began to suspect. M tells us each of the priests ought to have read in a different language if he could, Turkish, Arabic, etc., that all the world might understand. A very good idea I think.

After the service was over all the papas came out and, clearing away the candlesticks, etc. which stood in the way, and holding up a silver-bound gospel, cross, and other things, they stood in a row and the men who wished passed before them kissing each object in hand once, and the papas once on each cheek and on the mouth. We did not perform this ceremony.

When we got out there was a wonderful sort of a 'guy' set up over the gateway of the church to represent a Jew. His head was an earthen jar and he had a child in his arms. This the men shot at, getting nearer and nearer till he got on fire.[49] I was sitting among the women who constantly begged me not to fear and thought I must be cold as I had on gloves, but I answered, 'Είναι συνήθεια μας', 'It is our custom', which finishes off all discussions. They are really very kind people, though more like animals. They are very un-enterprising too. We see many fields propped up by walls but uncultivated; they do not fish or build boats. At Levkos they said they had a boat 'but the captain was dead'.

I think we have got to the end of our 7 days here and are no longer great wonders, but every Sunday we always are one of the amusements of the day. We however had a great amusement of our own. The Schoolmaster during his visit asked us 'if we knew Captain Hatteras?' We said no. He told us he was a great English traveller and had been, as we thought, to Constantinople. We both imagined he said 'Eis ten Polin' 'Εἰς τών πόλεν', 'To the town' as they call it, and he thought we might know him.

I said to T I was sure I had heard the name, so T said 'we know the name but are not personally acquainted with him.' 'He has written a very interesting book' said our Host, 'Have you read it?' We had to confess we had not. After a little he said 'By the bye, I have Captain Hatteras's book, a translation, should you like to see it?' So at our request he brought forth a book of Jules Verne's – 'The English at the North Pole.'[50] We did not then take in that he really believed this book to be true, so we never undeceived the poor Pedagogue, but talked lightly of Jules Verne's other books and then of other things. Afterwards it dawned upon us that what we had taken to be 'Eis ten Pólin' was 'Eis tón Pólon' ('Εἰς τών πόλον'), to the Pole.

---

[49] A custom, complete with rifles, witnessed on a small Cycladic island by this editor at Easter, 2004.
[50] Jules Verne's *Les Aventures du Capitaine Hatteras*, later translated as *The English at the North Pole*, was published in 1864.

As an instance of the stupidity of the people, we ordered a lot of milk to be sent daily, and a lamb on a certain day, but though we have given this order at 2 *mandhras*, or shepherd's dairy, no notice is taken of us and preserved milk is our portion. Easter Monday. Dreadfully rainy, many inundations in the room. Every house is full of dairy produce, for every shepherd gives every house 3 small curd cheeses and a lot of cream and each house returns a loaf and a *kouloúri*. Each godchild of a shepherd receives a lamb and cream.

We have only one joke of our own, made by T, now an old friend. They commonly call cream here, instead of *dhrilla* or *anthógala*, by the Turkish name *kaïmak*. T's joke is to call it *kaïmakam*. We suppose the word must mean something superior, but our knowledge of Turkish is limited. Such is the force of example that I have just had the joy of hearing M ask for *kaïmakam* to be sent us. I laughed and he is dreadfully confused and says it is very hard to understand the people and that he has ordered *dhrilla*. It was a dreadful slip. He does not understand as quickly as we do, for, of course, our ears are used to so many dialects and they use such odd words.

We always get up without difficulty about ¼ to 6. It is better to do like the rest of the world and we go to bed very early. It is now about 12.30. We have short gleams of sun and try to dry up our clothes – then violent downpours. We have bought a little very pretty marble head, larger than an egg and a wee bronze cow. We have also had patients. The schoolmaster, who is 'doing nicely', brought us a bottle of very welcome ink – a suitable fee – and the news that a woman with a pain wished to be cured. So his little girl of 9, Maroukla by name, was duly despatched to say that T was ready, and soon a young woman was led in by her husband.

I really was inwardly convulsed with laughter at the very home-questions T had the courage gravely to ask her; the schoolmaster pursuing the investigations even further. It is really no use mincing matters here, for no one wishes to have matters minced and indeed the lady cared no more than if the enquiries were about a cold in the head. Well! We did our best but we must always confine our prescriptions to available remedies, such as the herbs we see on the mountainside (always avoiding poisons) – rice, oil, and hot water, the latter a difficult thing to get.

It is a sad thing to see these poor creations depending on such ignorant people as we are, but there are only 2 or 3 doctors who, they say, know nothing, besides which they must pay them 3 or 5 pounds (18f the pound), pay a mule and wait till it is convenient for him to come. Sometimes they say they have to pay more but I can hardly believe it.[51]

---

[51] Large sums of money indeed, if Mabel was correct. One pound sterling at the time was worth about fifty today.

Our next patient was a very small baby, 2 years old with a fever. These people sent us: one, 6 eggs (red) and the other 2 large pieces of *mesethra* pastry and sesame seeds and honey. After that came the schoolmaster's mother-in-law with a gift of a dish of *kaïmak* and 2 more pies.

We then went all together to a ball in the outer room of the church. We sat in a heap of people in the middle and round the edge sat mothers, each with a babe and a string of men screwed round in the narrow space left, preceded by the *sampouna*, pronounced *sabouna*, or bagpipe, and the *lyra*, a thing like a mandolin played with a bow strung with little bells.[52] Only little tiny girls danced in this string but tomorrow is the great day when the young ladies will be dressed smartly and dance. When it got too hot inside we went outside and there being more space the dance was much prettier, but we found it too cold to remain long.

I went home and when T returned from a walk he found me doing my best to entertain 6 visitors, 2 clergy and 4 laymen, giving my very humble opinion on old coins of which I know nothing, but T endorsed all I said, showing them maps, etc. They had really come to see T's sketches and were delighted at the portraits of Papas Manolis of Mesochório and Marigó of Spiliés.[53]

Tuesday April 7th. Very fine day. This is a very busy and gay day. There is to be a ball and, as it is a holiday, we have many visitors. I was going to the ball in my Ulster,[54] but a crowd of women discovered a white dressing gown of mine covered with yellow lace and blue bows. They begged me to wear it for the ball, so of course I agreed. Over this, flowing open and with the sleeves tucked up to show the lace and bows of the dressing gown, is a flannel gown made extremely plainly for sleeping in in damp places. We have each one and I call them Flood-gowns, as Noah and his family had the same for the Ark and all that wet weather. My Flood-gown has only a little bit of lace round neck and sleeves and down the front, but then it is crimson so it has a fine effect with the blue, yellow and white.

Everyone has a display of jewellery today, so have I. The trumpery bracelets and brooches brought as presents were shown and I was made to put on gold, silver and garnet bracelets. Over my hat, with blue and yellow tuft in it, is a large white lace handkerchief, which I always wear for the sun, but 3 brooches, one a blazing diamond, are under my chin. A bunch of marigolds and geranium leaves in front, and over this is *trained* by my friends my steel watch-chain. I had 3 plain gold rings on one hand and one has been removed

---

[52] Theodore's Karpathian '*samboúna*' and '*lýra*' are now in the Pitt Rivers Museum, Oxford. They are reproduced on pp. 126 and 128.
[53] See p. 85 note 34.
[54] Mabel's trusty sleeveless coat.

to the other hand, and they insist and implore that I shall not wear gloves, for it is a pity to hide such pretty white hands, which they liken to those of Maroukla, who is really only 7 years old and evidently the spoilt darling of the town.

They are quite delighted with me, and T and M are in fits of laughter. I am very smart indeed, but not a bit gayer than my neighbours with dresses of scarlet, orange, green, and blue. At the ball we sat in the middle of the court of the church with the mothers and the older men. No married ladies dance or boys, but grown up and very little girls and young men.

The circle had just room to get round sometimes at a visible pace and sometimes hardly perceptibly. The first man only danced and jumped, according to his fancy. The men *occasionally* spoke to each other but without causing any change in the expression of the girl they talked across. No one seemed in the least to care who he or she was next to, for with rare exceptions none of the dancers spoke and all the girls looked nothing short of sad. How they could keep jiggling round and round I know not. They seemed untiring. We and the sitters were merry enough. They sat on stones about the size of one's head or smaller that they brought in for the occasion.

The married women were all plainly dressed, but the very ugly girls had all sorts of brilliant colours and had their heads and necks loaded with silver gilt necklaces and ornaments. It was a great comfort to us to have secured a set. The little girls and babies were also a mass of chains, etc. I sneaked into my gloves, but on all sides I heard what a pity it was and many turned down my gloves to look at my wrists, and my sleeves were often pulled up to show off my bracelets.

I took a photo, as they said I 'telegraphised' them, which I daresay is as good a word, and returned home with the instrument, followed by some men, and as M almost immediately slipped out with a mustard leaf to bear to the sick, it was eagerly hailed as the result of my operation.

Wednesday [April] 8th. T has gone off to sketch. A very dirty and poor looking woman has just been to ask me to sell her an orange for a halfpenny. I could not do it as the four oranges had just been brought by Maroukla and her sister Eirenió as a gift and Maroukla was in the room, so I referred her to M. He was very angry and said she was to go. She begged for the orange as medicine. M loudly shouted that it was good for no illness, no medicine at all, and if she were to offer ever so much we would not sell neither an orange nor anything else. They screamed for a long time but I watched my opportunity and beckoned to her and said 'Take it quickly and say nothing about it; it is a present from Maroukla', and of course I could not give it before her, and stuffed it into her coat, the usual and only pocket. She thanked me warmly and offered the halfpenny but I said 'Típote! Típote!'[55] and refused it; so then she hugged and kissed me and begged me to come to her house when my man came home and she would give us cream.

Oranges are rare here. 3 visitors came.

On **Thursday [April] the 9th,** being tired of Elymbo and finding it very damp, we determined to go to Dhriapháne on the coast, more especially as there was to be a pilgrimage and great festivities. So at about 6.30 we opened our door and a multitude rushed in, amid which we packed under the guidance of the schoolmaster who tried to make us pack the very boots and hats we wanted to wear. However thanks to the hurrying at 8 our baggage started, a wonderful thing considering the 7 women who carried it were always laying down one thing and taking up another and requiring great screaming at by M. It is such a comfort to have him; we never could 'phonasé'[56] loud enough.

The room looked bare enough when the beds were gone but we remain there till 2, T sketching and I working, and the schoolmaster talking and people bring clothes to sell. We bought 3 dresses. When we started we had a horse, or rather pony, laden with our food and cooking things and a little donkey, which I rode. M in both his hats and holding a sort of honey-pot which he never quits, and T holding a Rhodian jug which is our tea-pot and our washing jug.

We had two boys. One about 16 for me and one about 14, Manóli, for the pony. He had never been this road before and was quite excited about it. He carried the frying pan. He gave us a great description of the road, always ending with 'etsi legé' (so he says – meaning Michaél, the big boy). It is an awful road; the worst we have been. I began by walking a good way, then I mounted the little donkey who is quite the most courageous beast I have ridden in this island and a good jumper, which was needful as the path was gone in some places. We came down a river and the donkey was very much frightened of the waterfalls and once rushed up a bank but I was easily able to get off. I do not the least know how many times we crossed the river or how many times we had to walk down the middle of it. It was not deep enough to wet one's feet except in some deep pools and the walkers had to wet their boots some times.

Once my ass seemed so frightened that I got down and what he might have done with me on his back can't be said, but the pony fell on his side and we 3 saw a sack full of our goods lying in the water while the boys were busy with the beasts and we were clinging with hands and feet to the rocky wall of the river, scrambling along. No harm was done but the pony had shed everything and took some time to reload. We were glad the women had taken the precious packing cases.

[55] 'Nothing! Nothing!'
[56] 'shout'.

Another time Michaél took off his boots and we went down the smooth bed of the river while T and M scrambled into the height above, but the donkey began to slip about and I thought I had better slip off, so I did onto a dry rock in the middle and to T's surprise my head appeared out of a thick bush of oleander which I forced my way through. We then got among pine trees and into a really pretty enjoyable part where one could spare one's eyes from one's feet for a few steps at a time, and in 2 hours reached the end of what we think to be our last land journey with beasts of burden.

We found that our luggage had been placed in the abode of the Protopapás, or first priest, and were well content with our dwelling, which offers some advantages we do not always enjoy. It is a small shop up an outside stair with a balcony on 2 sides and a door on each and from this we can get onto the roofs of 2 houses, about 10 feet from the ground. We have also a window which we can dress by as the balcony is public property. The room is small and the upper part does not do much more than hold my hammock, so T has his bed on the *pátoma*, or lower floor. A little high and very dirty counter, a fire place as high as a table, where we have a good basin, and are well lighted by the chimney; 2 chairs and some fixed boxes along the wall are the furniture of the room and we have added a pile of packing-cases by way of a table.

The boxes contain various wares for sale and we were induced to examine them by various mysterious sounds, caused we found by hundreds of live snails crawling up and falling down. T wanted to eat some but M says these large and shut up snails are not wholesome, and they add to the smells from which we suffer.

M takes his bedding and sleeps in a boat on the shore. There are very few houses here but it is a charming situation in a bay with rocky headlands and such beautiful walks up numerous branching valleys, and trees too, not very fine or close, but a great relief to the eye.

We had not sat down when a man rushed to us for advice for a very mysterious complaint that we do not understand, so we could only be guided by our natural instincts and as in a similar case in Elymbo order poultices, hot. In about 10 minutes I went out on the roofs and an old woman directed my attention to a little girl who I desired her to take to bed and I at once went and was soon cooking arrowroot in her cottage. The grandmother is called Hadji Mangaphou, as she has been to the Holy Sepulchre. (Hadji being a Turkish word with 2 letters that the Greeks cannot pronounce, *h* and *j*, they say Χᾶδσι (Chátsi). The child is Mangathoula. She soon was well and the old thing tried to give me 3 eggs but I refused them and afterwards brought a *kouloúri*, but it was also sent away. We gave her our washing to do but had to provide soap and next day they brought some of the clothes, tied up in one of T's pocket handkerchiefs, dry, and the rest to hang in our balcony.

By the time it was night the pilgrims began to arrive with mules and many bundles and after our dinner we wandered out, as there were no rocks to clamber over, to see what was going on. The master of the house was giving the feast and 8 or 9 lambs were hanging round the middle post which is in each house. Everyone was also making *kolivá*, or a sort of pudding, placed in the church all night as an offering to the departed relations and distributed after the liturgy in the morning. This is a round heap of boiled barley and sesame and sugar, with heaps of white sugar on the top, and some stock flowers stuck in.

We were asked into a house where a good fire of pine-chips was blazing. I and the men sat in a circle round it and the women on the outskirts. We stayed there for some time. About 8 they began to dance, all very smart, and continued dancing and singing till the liturgy, about 6.30. Then they sat outside the church, close under our balcony, and everybody handed round the *kolivá* and by the time everyone had taken a handful or even a few grains of every dish, they must have had a good substratum for the feast which soon began.

We in the meantime breakfasted and were summoned to visit our patient who seemed really very ill. She was a stout woman of about 50, with her shoulders, sides and back robed in a grey woollen garment. A most animated discussion over the complaint took place, with young men and maidens, old men and children all very noisy, and they got T's sketch book and really recognized people before they were told by us who they were, in a very satisfactory way with loud exclamations of 'It is himself!' I asked the patient if she did not mind the noise but she seemed to think it as inevitable as the roar of the sea.

We had the greatest possible advantage for seeing this feast, for we could see both the eating and the dancing from our roof. Inside the men squatted round and gnawed lamb in their fingers, and outside sat a man beside a huge cauldron, ladling out a sort of stew to any woman who brought a plate. We knew so many of the people that it was quite pleasant. The Protopapás and many others sat with us and we were brought a good many presents of food. Some one had told of the sketch book and they were equally able to recognize the subjects and most cried 'Panagiá' (All Holy, The Virgin) and one cried 'Dhiávolos!', and the Protopapás constantly exclaimed 'Kyrié eleïson!'.

At ½ past 10 the dancers began to tuck up their smart skirts, pull off their best shoes and stockings and put on their ordinary ones, and shouldering their bundles and saying 'Apó chróno' to their friends, set off to Elymbo.

In the afternoon we took a beautiful walk along the cliff towards the S. and returned inland into a pine wood and then we got down a watercourse and, finding we could go no farther, we determined to climb up the hillside but it was awfully difficult as there was absolutely no foot hold on the crumbly schist, all slippery with needles. As T's big boots gave him firmer hold he crawled up a bit and lay down, and I pulled myself up by his legs and then he crawled up again, and could lean on me a little as I lay. When we could gently, gently, catch a branch of a tree we never left that friendly tree till we had got above it, carefully handing each branch to each other; then another crawl to another tree, and so we reached the top, and returned home bearing a good salad of sorrel leaves.

Saturday [April] 11. At ¼ past 7, having duly made our beds, we walked up the watery way towards Elymbo. Indeed, as M said, a boat would have been useful but I got on very well with my galoshes to put on for water and take off for rocks. T took a sketch and we remained till luncheon. In the evening we saw a boat come in with the shepherds who had been to Saría and many dead lambs and kids, cheese, cream and milk, but though we have offered to pay a boy to bring milk and to buy it besides, we have to use 'preserved'. We thought to have had a variety on lambs and that we would take the opportunity of the baking day and have a fowl filled with sage, which grows wild here, and onions, also rice, but such is the manner of baking here that when dinnertime came it was not ready and we ate M's dinner, which was a great disappointment but it was excellent at luncheon today.

Sunday 12th April. This morning on looking out and seeing the people smart and idle, I remarked to T that this seemed to me to be some kind of a holiday, but he only said it was Sunday, to my surprise. We went and made our liturgy in the pinewood and after lunch T made a sketch and all day we have been anxious about the weather, as it is so stormy that we had fears of not getting to Saría tomorrow but now we are full of hopes and are expecting our dinner. In has just walked a lady who sat down and announced to T that she also is a victim to this mysterious complaint that we never came across in England and here we have been consulted by a cow and 3 women. The coolness with which she broached the subject very nearly made me laugh in her face. No one minds talking of anything here more than if they were all cows.

Monday 13th April. After being kept awake a good deal by anxiety as to the wind which howled furiously, here we sit at 7 o'clock quite ready to start and waiting for the 6 men to come down from Elymbo. They are to row the boat which we shall keep during our stay at Saría. The sea is much better though noisy still. We have to take every kind of provision we want except lambs and milk, which we hope to get, so we have laid in a good stock of bees wax candles, petroleum, lamps for the tombs, matches, bread, coffee, oil, etc., and with the tools, all our 9 beds, the tent and the necessary raiment, we have plenty to fill a boat. We leave behind an additional packing case of curios.

We have various plans for our voyage to Syra. Here at this moment we have 4 cases besides other luggage, and at Pegádhia we have 1 case, 1 sack, a 'carpet bag', and a little statue[57] still at the house of the seller. The Turks have a disagreeable habit of examining outgoing luggage and we fear that the sight of so much together, and all we *hope* for from Saría, may excite them.

One of the plans is to start from Pegádhia in the dirty little steamer *Roúmeli*, which is supposed to be going to call on May 3rd to carry off some of the male population, in this case we must go there by boat.

No 2 plan is to get the steamer to call here, and in that case M is to go and gather up the 'goods and chattels' taking coverings for the little statue, 3 or 4 ft long, and meet us here.

No 3 is that we go to Syra in a sailing boat, not yet finished, with 20 other people; 24 hours at least. M fetching the things from Pegádhia and keeping them in the boat he comes in, and changing them into the big boat, then keeping them in the new boat in Syra harbour till we can get them on board a Liverpool steamer, for fear the Greeks should wish to have a look.

No 4, which seems to me the best, is to take a private boat and go to Khalki or Simi, and let the things remain in the boat till a steamer comes and then ask Mr. Binney at Syra to protect the transfer.

Certainly we have had no difficulty as yet with the government here. They are all very kindly and the Pasha of Rhodes' letter was very civil, as we heard. He certainly did not write it till the last minute and after we had loudly expressed our surprise at such rudeness to his friend Mr. Aristarchis, but whether we have been forgotten and were never considered quite as dangerous as Mr. Aristarchis would have us believe, nothing bad had happened; still it will be nice to get our things safely to Syra. If we take a boat to ourselves, we can pick up things at Saría on the way, wind and weather permitting, for from this day out they are our masters.

About ½ past 8 we began to contemplate the fact that there was probably more wind up at Elymbo and that the men would think it too rough to come, and to look sadly at our beds and think how horrid it would be to have to unpack them again that night in that dirty room, and at last T went up the river to meet people and get news. He returned about 9 and told me he heard they were coming.

He found me having a *tête-à-tête* with the Turkish *zaptich*, or soldier, who is here as *Chorophylax*, or guard of the town. He had wandered up into the balcony and when I said 'Kal'eméra'[58] to him he came in and sat down and

---

[57] Mabel's first reference to one of their more spectacular 'finds', a limestone female figure, 66cm, thought to be Neolithic (4500–3200 BC). The Bents arranged for it to go to the British Museum and it is the Museum's earliest stone sculpture from Greece – Room 11 GR 1886.3–10.1 (Sculpture A 11). Called later by Mabel 'the most hideous thing ever made by human hands', it is a most curious object.
[58] 'Good morning!'

had been with me a quarter of an hour. He said he was from Cyprus and now English; his Greek was not of the best but we got on splendidly. This poor man appears to have nothing in this wide world to do. I pity him as I see him wandering about, now helping to pull up a boat, now digging a little, if he can find an idle spade, at the foundations of a house that is going to be built, opening on to the shingle and which will certainly often have the sea in it. But his pet amusement is to catch one of the 3 lambs, who browse in a field of quite high barley, in the ear and to nurse it walking about in the barley. There is an immense variety in the forwardness of the various crops – some barley is only just springing up.

We created great astonishment during these hours by getting out books, work, and this book to write, instead of sitting idle. They can't understand why I who am so rich should work. M shrieked at the men, of course, for being so late, and not till 12, after much more shrieking, were we 3 lifted into the boat: once there we all had our work, T to mind the honey-pot, I to steer, and M to bale incessantly. As these boats live up on the shore they are all very leaky. As for our luggage, as it lay on the shore it looked like that of gypsies. I tried to count it but gave up after 30. Cooking pots, frying pan, an immense wicker-covered bottle of wine, a huge jar for water, etc.

In 2 hours and a half we reached a place in Saría called Ta Palátia, the palaces. I felt so glad when we got past those draughty places, where our mast was broken. The coast scenery was very beautiful and the little bay here is quite invisible from the sea. It is all rocky, but a very small beach, then the land slopes very gradually back to a wall of mountains. As it is sheltered the mastic grows high and there is lots of green and actually the birds sang in the early morning, a rare sound. We thought of pitching our tent down by the sea as there is a well there but it seemed a windy spot, so we went further back near a little chapel, and, as it turns out, the digging place.

As we had built the beds and unpacked the sack which contained many things beside the tent, these were laid on the beds and carried up while we all followed laden; I with an earthen pan of *khalvas*[59]. Our floor is level but stony. Under my hammock T can contemplate mallows, poppies, yellow clover, and a white flower as he lies in his bed.

As soon as the tent was pitched, T went round to choose a digging place, M to settle himself and his pots in the chapel where he cooked the dinner and sleeps. This is not considered irreverent by the Greeks and, indeed, it is the chief use of the chapels in these isolated spots. We dined about 7, outside off a very pretty table, an old capital of a pillar, a comfortable size. We had not much meat

---

[59] Not the modern shop-bought confection, but a slow-cooked pudding of semolina, oil, sugar and spices baked in the oven.

and were to keep it for luncheon, but now there is a lamb taking his last meal tied to a bush.

[Tuesday] April 14th. We had a soup composed of onion, the only vegetable cultivated here, and wild turnip, flowers and all, and a little oil and some water – then a red herring – an omelette *aux fines herbes* and a sorrel salad from the same kitchen garden – *khalvas* and honey.

We felt quite at home in our tent; it was nice to feel it our very own and so sweet and clean. It rained heavily at sunrise and I remembered my gaiters were out, so I flew out of bed, flung my mackintosh round me and screwed out of a crack, as I could not unhook the door. I ran round to see that the pegs, etc., were all right and got very wet in the operation, but I retired to my warm bed till T dressed. He bathed in the sea, a mere tub however in the rocks for fear of dogfish (i.e. sharks 'σκυλόψαρα') and we breakfasted at 6.30, a trifle damp under foot but very jolly, and now there is a hot sun; we have the lamb, milk, cream, and M out partridge-shooting with a gun longer than himself, borrowed from the *zaptich*. It has crescents and stars and much other brass inlaying, single barrel and muzzle-loader – a picturesque weapon.

Altogether we should be very happy if we did not fear we should move tomorrow, for *Byzantine* is all we find. The little chapel is inside what must have been the apse of a Byzantine church, for the semicircular tiers of seats are behind it and we thought to find a temple among the ruins round, but as yet we have only found holy inscriptions.

Thursday April 16th. I will continue our life in its proper order, though I now write from a different camp.

All that morning they dug at what certainly was a temple but the Byzantines had destroyed everything, so after luncheon, about ½ past 11, T carried the men off to dig some tombs high up the mountain side, where, however, he found nothing but the bottom of a plate with two little raised heads kissing; he thought they were snails at first.

I did not go. First there might be no tombs, 2nd, it was excessively difficult to get through the jungle of mastic, between which were beds of nettles and thistles masking heaps of stones, and 3rd, it was not very safe to be far from the tent, as a family of shepherds had brought a family of bulls, cows and calves of all ages to have a good stare. They sat quite close and if I went into the tent, squatted at the door and I had to sit as near it as possible to prevent them and their fleas entering.

I could only take little walks, or rather climbs, as the chapel was not in sight from the tent and M busy. First I picked a salad then I went in another direction and read, but perceiving the cattle grazing among the tent pegs I had to descend and drive them out often. First I went into the tent followed to the door by a boy of 14 and a big girl called Sophilda, but I soon went out and hooked up the door and had turned my back on it when I heard the boy say 'To mandhiláki tes Kyríes!'[60], and the girl make a warning grunt. I turned round at once expecting to see my red-bordered handkerchief on the floor or to be handed it, but not seeing it I looked into the tent in vain for it and felt sure they had it, so I sat near to see what would happen.

After a long time Sophilda brought me a lump of cheese and I said 'I cannot find my handkerchief; do you know where it is?' 'Oh no!' she said she didn't. 'I thought you had seen it,' I said. 'No she had not' and here she made all the signs of negation, drew in her closed lips, threw up and closed her eyes, turned head, shoulders and hands up and remained a few seconds in this position.

I gave it up as a bad job and took the cheese to M that I might not have to eat it then and there and returned to have another try but they were gone, so I went back to M and told him my tale. He rushed up and down till he discovered their direction and with much shouting on both sides brought them to a standstill and demanded of Sophilda the Kyria's handkerchief. She utterly denied having it and M drew out his knife and said 'I shall cut your throat if you do not give it up at once'. And then she said 'Oh! There it is! There it is!' and M brought it back in triumph, but rather dirty.

M then went to fish, and about 3 minutes after the old woman of the party came to me and spoke much of 'klephtes' and 'psevtes' – thieves and liars – and I thought of course she was alluding to my handkerchief, so I told her kindly to think no more of it, to forget it, that it did not matter, but she loudly screamed that it did matter and matter very much. Then she spoke of the Elymbites that were with us, so seeing that we were at cross purposes, I told her I could not make out what she was talking, whereupon she said 'Ela'do Kyria'[61] and led me to the sacks of our men which the family had been sitting amongst and evidently examining, and drew out a blanket and told me our men had stolen it, so she carried it off and we have heard no more of it. They are certainly not very honest. As an instance, at that dance T saw one of the cheap brooches with which I was adorned fall out and be picked up by the father-in-law of the schoolmaster, a most respected man called *Diáko* Nikóla, because he 'knows letters'. I was occupied and thought he was waiting to give it to me but he never did. Both his wife and the schoolmaster remarked the loss, but we did not like to make a fuss as they were so civil.

Well, yesterday morning, **[Wednesday] 15th [April 1885]**, we had packed our personal goods, T had taken a sketch, and bathed, and we were at breakfast at 6.15, and in an hour and a half, that is at ¼ to 8, we were off, alas!, without the

[60] 'The lady's handkerchief.'
[61] 'Come here lady.'

spoons that did duty for egg and tea – *quite* irreplaceable in this island for they are not used.

At first we were in calm water with the bottom of the sea deep blue and light green and the red and coppery reflections of the rocks broken up by the ripples into feathers; I never saw the sea look so like a peacock's breast. But when we got to the strait between Saría and Karpathos it was very rough and we got a tremendous tossing. We landed at 10.30 in a little bay below the place called 'Tas Philakes', the Prisons, with 4 workmen, the others coming over and soon joining us.

We had caught several large fish on the way and M at once set up a kitchen on the rocks where we landed at one side of the bay. T walked up ½ an hour with 2 men and their tools to the Prisons. He found that there were only a few walls and a flat *kampo* and the ruins of a tower, as in many similar situations, to guard or *phylax* the crops. He did not think it a good place, which is well for he said it was hideously ugly.

In the meantime I went to bathe, having spotted from the sea a cavern to be reached bare-legged at the other end of the 50 or 60 yard long beach. I left my foot gear on the beach and ran round getting my petticoats a little wet to be sure, though I thought I held them high enough, but what was that compared to so private a dressing room? It was very large with the sea light into the mouth and so like the Lion's Den, lighted from above, that I could not help looking up to see if Nebuchadnezzar was there. As he wasn't, I had a very good time and a jolly swim, always looking for sharks though, but there was only a porpoise and some pretty diving ducks. M told us he was once stripped and just jumping into the sea at Antiparos when he saw a shark – so he dressed again.

After luncheon we sent off the boat with the 6 men, 4 to be landed at the north of Karpathos and the 2 walkers to return to row us to Vourgounda,[62] saying that if it were too rough we would stay at Tristoma, for one of the excitements of yesterday was that we knew not where we should camp. It was near sunset when we landed at the bay of Vourgounda and chose a camping ground just above the beach, near the work and with a greater water supply, though brackish, and plenty of driftwood.

We are in a square field of stones chiefly open to the sea, and 2 walls are full of tombs all cut smooth. The 4th side has low rocks and under it is our kitchen, also of tombs square cut. By the time we had pitched and furnished the tent and arranged the kitchen it was too dark to seek a dining room so we sat on sacks at the door of the tent with the lamp burning in the still air.

---

[62] Vrykoúda, on the northern tip of Kárpathos.

[Wednesday, April] 16th. This morning we rose at 5.30 and now 2 men are digging in the corner of our square – T has taken the others on the point. I soon went to bathe, having found as I thought a quiet little bay but when I reached it I found clothes being washed, so I took off my shoes and stockings, put on galoshes, and getting through a little water climbed up and then leaving my shoes and stockings I climbed down a little precipice, as T says, good footing if you are not inclined to be giddy. I reached a ledge 18 inches wide just under water. Then stuffing my mackintosh into the rock, hanging my galoshes up and throwing my hat, I was ready for the water. It was very deep and I had a good swim, no fear of sharks, and I put on my cloak afterwards and walked home with my galoshes wet, to dress in the tent.

We have been very successful in finding unopened tombs with better things than we found before. We had a baking day. Just after our first sight of the sun our dining room was almost unbearable, but we just got the shadow for luncheon.

[Wednesday] April 17th. We had such a fearful storm in the night that we could not sleep. The wind playing the drum on the tent and we were every moment thinking it would be rooted up, but morning came and found us still there and the wind still violent and a black gloomy day. We had heavy rain in the middle of the day but I was in the tent and T softly lying on a heap of fresh dug earth regardless of his clothes. We have now for some time ceased to fear that our raiment may be spoiled. We are indeed like the Gibeonites[63] now and it is funny to see T's last year's suit, hat and all getting shabbier and shabbier on M. The trousers, supported by a red sash, have a large blue check patch in them, M having sat on a sharp rock, but we hope in about a week to start home. A dog in the night broke a tumbler so it is time to refit.

More tombs and more basketsful of things. We had to place our stones in the kitchen and eat there as it was so windy. Our news from England is now a month old.

Saturday April 18th. A fine day and hot. We went to bed with great confidence last night, the tent having stood the night and day and slept well and found the wind gone down when we woke. The sun only greeted our last mouthful of breakfast! We are so glad it is Saturday and that Sunday will be tomorrow. It is very fatiguing climbing from tomb to tomb to see that the men are not sleeping or smoking. After today we dismiss 2. On Monday we mean to go to Tristoma. I do not know why this point is all terraced up and divided into fields for there is nothing but stones in them, like a newly mended road or worse.

---

[63] See Joshua 9: 3–15.

Who would think that the next place I should have an opportunity of writing my Chronicle should be Crete! and further more at Kalé Liminas or the Fair Havens! where we, like St. Paul are sheltering from the tempest.[64] We are still so surprised to find ourselves here that we can hardly understand it. All sorts of things have hurried on that we have been in quite a dizzy state. Well, that Saturday we found very little and in the afternoon had the greatest difficulty in finding work for the men and it became clear that Vourgounda was quite exhausted, so we got home more than an hour before sunset and putting our 3 heads together decided it was impossible to go to Tristoma under the nose of the man-of-war and announce ourselves as excavators to the idle crew thereof. And then we bethought ourselves that finding anything at Tristoma was problematical. In fact the Greeks at Tristoma grew sour and so we then and there determined that nothing remained for us but to return to Diaphane and if possible get on all together to Pegadhia; then it was said that Vourgounda was a most hard place to leave, and we had better leave in the morning if the wind were fair, for else we might remain a month.

The remaining daylight was therefore spent in getting the bed things into T's large handbag and the small portemanteau and others into a large 2-handled pot with a lid which we left to the workmen; about 6 big pithoi, etc., remained out and we went to bed sorry to think it might be our last night in our dear little tent, but half undecided whether we should pitch it at Pegadhia. We decided that as it was Sunday and as there was no hurry and only 4½ hours to Dhiaphane, we would take it very easy! So consequently it was not till 7.30 that we were lifted into the boat.

[Sunday] April 19th. Surely Karpathos is the island of imaginary fear! Just as we were starting the men begged us to get out our flag, that when we passed the man-of-war our boat might be taken for an English one. We said that it did not matter and in spite of their implorings we declared it was in the tent-sack, in the bottom of the boat and could not be got out. They said 'If the Turks take us, what shall we do?' We said they will only ask who we are and let us go. We laughed at their fears and could not understand them but they told us that on account of a murder just committed at Volatha they feared being taken for the murderers.[65] 'But you, *Aphentikó*,[66] will say you are our master and that we are your men and this is your boat, won't you?' They were really alarmed. I told them we would say we were all English and this comforted an auburn-haired one called Andreas. They even spoke of our being carried to Constantinople and we said it would be delightful to get there without paying our passage.

---

[64] On the southern coast of Crete, a little east of Cape Mátala.
[65] See Mabel's postscript on p. 125.
[66] 'Boss!'

It had been settled that if it were too stormy we should stay at the bay of Almiró (salt) in Saría till we could proceed, living in the tent. When we got near Tristoma, we hugged the rocks of the 2 small islets that mask its mouths and eyed the masts of the man-of-war, put in there as the engines are broken. When we got to the open S. mouth they rowed hard and greatly did they rejoice that we had been unseen, for they had been saying 'If she makes a sign to us we will row straight to the ship' but we intended merely to stop and let them send a boat.

In the strait the wind was so favourable that by hoisting a cloak and 3 umbrellas we really made way and the men were highly satisfied as we perceived some sentinels on the heights, for they said 'the umbrellas are quite as good as the flag; people with umbrellas they will know are English!' We passed these sentinels quite safely and when we came to more the men rushed for the umbrellas again and however little our enemies may be intimidated it is a fine thing to feel how safe our friends felt under the protection of the British Umbrella!

We reached Diaphane about 12, at once lunched on tinned lobster, no time for cooking, and packed all our things, for we believed the *Roúmeli* was to call at Pegadhia on Monday afternoon, but everyone said she would be late on account of the storms. When we got all done we set off with prayer books and towels, meaning to 'make our Liturgy' and bathe, but when we got to a little beach a mile off, the first place we could descend to the sea, it was 5 so we had a very cold bathe, our 5th, and found it quite too cold for an out-of-door liturgy. At one end of the beach a charming bathing-box was walled off by rocks.

Monday, April 20th. We said we would start at 5 to frighten our men, but did not get up till 10 to 5 and did not start till 8. 26 packages I counted. The schoolmaster came down and brought letters of March 4th. We had later ones. At last we started to continue our voyage home, all in the highest spirits, M quite as pleased as we were. I little thought that when they lifted me into the boat I should never touch Karpathos again!

Shortly after we started we heard great shouting after us. These were really 2 Cassiote[67] carpenters wanting a passage, but in the distance their European dress caused them to be taken by the men for *zaptichs*, so the men said they would not stop; they should not get into a scrape for the boat was T's. It was said they had something in their hands, perhaps it was ours, but we thought seriously of all our things and said it could not be and even if it were it was not worth returning for and running the risk of our things being examined. These people can shout and hear at great distance, so requests and refusals flow through the air and still we were pursued. Then a suggestion that it might be letters made us a little regretful, but still we determined to push on.

---

[67] From the island of Kássos, lying between Crete and Kárpathos.

At last it was settled that we should go under a cliff where they could not come down, not go very near but stop till we could really hear what was wanted. By this time the carpenters were recognized but still the boat was so full that we had to persist in our refusal till one of our men offered to land and give up his place. The carpenter embarked with many thanks and many polite excuses on our part. 'Had we seen who it was, etc.', but M scolded him well, called him brother, and asked why he had not told us before.

We were all regretting the half hour wasted in the 7 hours' voyage, when 'To Atmópleion!' burst from every lip. There was the steamer, steaming north and away from Pegadhia. We at once steered towards her with shouts and cries, no doubt unheard. M in the prow waved his big white hat. 'Your parasol, put up your parasol!' said the men; we said 'What good would that do?' 'Oh never mind. It will do no harm and as you have been on the steamer of course they will know it.'

We were tremendously excited as the steamer still went on and real tears came into my eyes with anxiety and I am sure if they had asked me to kneel in the bilge water I would at once. We comforted ourselves with knowing the captain and his son/mate to be civil people. At last they stopped and took us on board, leaving our whole lamb to the men and taking a large open jar of wine, as that of the steamer is bad. The captain was implored to return to Pegadhia after calling at Diaphane and was undecided, but as we saw 5 cases placed in the hold and other things, including the jugs under the saloon, besides our good-sized cabin paved, and the passage choked, we felt pretty easy, but happiest when a symphony had been come to for £13; he asked £20 for the 3 passages, and return to Pegadhia for our luggage about £5 extra.

The passengers, all deck, or in the hold, were not pleased and no wonder. '£13' was buzzed on all sides. The ship was full of acquaintances and we seemed to have to shake hands all round. A large group dragged me from the ladder to enquire all sorts of things and as for the men, T said it was sad we had so many drunken friends. The carpenter was just as pleased to be on board as ourselves, though all his luggage for a voyage to Syra was a little round basket with food on his arm, a saw in one hand and 4 feet of plank in the other.

The next excitement was getting the things at Pegadhia. I decided to remain on board and became a perfect queen-bee. I gave up moving at last for I was always followed. I eagerly watched the proceedings on shore. M set off to run to the house where was a very hideous statue, more than the size of a baby, half a mile off. T and the Turks sat down at the café.

People came to the steamer and said 'Why have you returned?' and shouts of 'Oi Angloi, oi Lordhi', 'The English, the Lords'. And 'Dekatris Lires! Lires kavalkamenes!' Or '£13 on horseback' – meaning with St. George on them

– and they could not make out why I said our luggage was in the custom house when they saw M run away. 'Where are your things? They must be at Apéri (2 hours off) for your servant is running there.' I laughed at them well and began to read, so that was a great entertainment. 'Now she has turned a leaf' they said.

At last I saw M tearing back with the burden on his shoulders and very soon they reached the ship and all was on board. We sat almost speechless in our cabin but I said 'We are not off yet. I can't stay here'. At the door I hear 'O Lordhos. Pou einai o Lordhos?' 'Where is the Lord?' For all English who appear to be independent gentlefolk are lords here. I could have been knocked down with a feather but no one tried to do it, so I asked what it was and was told – letters and newspaper. They were fetched and we were safely off.

'Oh!' I could not help exclaiming 'How thankful I am to be under the Greek flag'. And indeed with 3 umbrellas in the cabin, though all in disrepair, what now had we Britons to fear from Turks?

We sat down to luncheon at 12 in gay frame of mind and then I heard how M had run to the house and found it locked and had broken the door open, found the statue, wrapped it up in what he carried for the purpose, and ran back. T was in the meantime drinking much *raki* with the Harbourmaster and other Turks, having been to the custom house and told an old woman to take a long time carrying the three things, one by one, very slowly to the boat and thinking M would never be back; as I could see M I was luckier.

When M appeared, T could see that the statue showed behind and told him so, but he said 'No matter' and rushed on to the boat and then came back to say goodbye to the Turks. T saw them spot the statue and whisper together and shrug their shoulders, so now we are in possession of the most hideous thing ever made by human hands. We mean to deposit it in bond at the customhouse of Syra with all the cases and things we do not want. We also talked of how the delay caused by the carpenter, which annoyed us so much at the time, was really a great blessing, for had we not been delayed we should have been deep in a bay, hugging the shore and never have caught the steamer.

The longest way round is evidently the shortest way home for us. For having started 8 in our boat we went N. to Diaphane, S. to Pigadhia and on round the island; goodbye to Karpathos and N.W. to Kassos, where we remained 3 hours with all the captain's relations on board, as this is his home. He introduced us to one just as he was going ashore, and we found him to be Kyriós Nichólas Mavrís, for whom we had a letter, so T rushed and got it just in time.

Tuesday April 22nd [actually 21st]. After this we turned S.W. and sailed under Crete. We had a fearful night of storm, pitching, rolling, catching 'B flats'[68] and fears of falling on the floor. Added to which I am so spoiled by my hammock that I found the bed dreadfully hard. Much splashing took place and water flew over the ship, so about 10 o'clock, when we got close to 'a certain island called Clauda'[69] we had to turn S. then E. again and take refuge here – a very sheltered place. We went ashore with the water barrels. There is a beach and some bushes and a pretty stream in which many clothes were washed by those who subsequently landed, and all the hands and faces washed, so no doubt we came back a cleaner party than we went.

In our cabins, supposed to be the ladies cabin, there is no means of washing. We have to go to a place with 2 basins off the saloon. The seasick are offered very small shallow brass spittoons. It is about 5 and when we do leave we shall start on our way to Kythera, or Cerigo, W., then Syra, East. To have to turn our backs on the setting sun is hard, but we are in no mood to complain as this is far better than a *kaïque* and N. winds going on. To pass Cape Malea 3 times is very odd.[70]

Saucers to our cups, white bread, pepper, white salt, any vegetable but onions and any meat but lamb, are all treats to us and we are treated like princes. Not as princes usually are, but as princes would be if they travelled on the *Roúmeli*. We have our meals separately, and a dish more than is usual, and never stir without campstools being carried after us.

The annoyance at being turned back was quite overborne by the interest of coming to Kalé Liminas, and it was a great satisfaction to think that St. Paul must have drunk and washed in that very stream, and being stormstayed too was rather nice. The city of Lasea, which was nigh unto the Fair Havens, has disappeared but the place is the same. I went up the hill and found me the centre of a heap of people, not very pleasant when you reflect that several Sundays have shown me that that is the hunting day when people lay their heads in a friendly lap and the hunter is extremely successful. I saw a highly respectable woman sit down to be hunted before 25 people. One day in the street we saw an old lady in only her shirt, and that tucked above her knees into a handkerchief she had round her waist, and hunting in her other garment for fleas. I hurried by.

It is so fine and sunny and warm here but outside there will be wind and every one will nod their heads and say 'Aëras, Aëras!' (Airs, airs) or 'Thálassa!' (Sea).

---

[68] Mabel's *Chronicles* are bug infested. Her reference here is a well-known Victorian pun. 'B' is for bug and 'flat' for the shape. 'B flats': bugs, which obnoxious insects are characterized by their flatness. (Brewer) ('F sharp' specifies the flea and its sharp bite.)
[69] Crete. 'And running under a certain island which is called Clauda, we had much work to come by the boat.' (Acts 27:16. The King James's Version) The Saint landed here while travelling, as a prisoner, by ship to Rome. The ancient town of Lasea was nearby.
[70] In the millennia before steam power, any trip around Cape Malea could be your last. Ancient sailors would say, 'Round Malea and forget your native country'.

Wednesday, April [22nd]. We started at 8 in the evening and after a good deal of tossing got into calmer regions, but still were 'under Crete' in the morning. We had a lovely day. About 10 we passed Cerigotto, or as they call it Ante Kythera, and about 12 reached Kythera, or Cerigo, and found ourselves in a very pretty little double bay with a rocky promontory in the middle and a sandy shore.[71]

The 80 passengers began at once to arrive and brought the news that General Koronaios had been elected member of the parliament. This caused great pleasure and there was gun firing and shouts of 'Zeto, o Koronaios!'[72], and as we landed we left the *Roúmeli* decked with flags and a boatload of myrtle with which it was turned into a sort of bower. I had a mule and we went up to the capital, about a mile (of road) off, round, or rather near, a castle. The road was made by the English, of course, and is now much in need of repair. There is a very high bridge which once had 4 piers but now 3 are quite gone. They must also have had inserted marble tablets as the remaining ruin has a cracked one saying how the bridge was made by the first Lord High Commissioner.[73]

There was a fine view from our fortress but when you look into the island it is very bare. All the fortress is falling to bits. The town has rather an Italian look. The women dress like at Corfú and have white handkerchiefs on their heads, a contrast to the Karpathiote dark ones. We had lemonade at a *kafeneion* and saw the hero of the day and also formed the tail of the procession going to the shore till we drew up to let it get on. They threw orange flower water (*anthónero*) on him from the windows. There was such a row on land that we were glad to return to the little ship, now crowded. We went to our cabin and sorted and packed and finding our flag hung it out of our window on the deck and greatly delighted the captain.

The dinner on this great occasion was very gay and there were about 9 at it. No one could speak so they had to listen to the conversation of us and M and the captain and his friend Kyrios Kalokerinós Phýlo or Mr. *Summery* Leaf. I nearly laughed at this name and when he was addressed as Mr. Summery it was very funny because most unsuitable. All around were encamped ladies who were in very queer costume. They mostly wore petticoats of felt braided by machine with shaded braids of all colours, worn as outside skirts and red or blue flannel bodies and jackets. They all had to sleep in the saloon and in the morning when we went to have our tea we saw hats and stays even on the breakfast table. The ladies were dressing with a great disregard to beholders.

---

[71] Kapsáli, the port below the capital on the island's south coast.
[72] 'Long live Koronaios!'
[73] The stone bridge built by Scot John McPhail (1826) under this Protectorate (1814–1864) is said to be the longest stone bridge in Greece.

At Kythera a 'manifesto' was made and signed by the captain, saying he had picked us, and our cases, up in Turkey, and by the Kythera customs people to say we had not started from there. We had oily weather from there; the captain said the *Roúmeli* had put a cross on the sea to make it calm.

And now Thursday – [The date is left blank. Perhaps Thursday April 23rd]. We are at Syra, Hôtel d'Angleterre.[74] All the things are in the customhouse, the great jars tied up to the wall. We had a large boat and it was very full.

May 1885 – journeying home to England

Grand Hotel Malta. May – [The date is left blank] All the most interesting part of my Chronicle is now over but for my own edification I will write that we stayed 10 long days in Syra, a most dull place, nothing to see, nothing to buy, not even paper or books. Our only pleasures were those of the table, bathing (T rowing a boat in which we undressed), and a walk every evening along a road which suddenly fades away into the mountain with a wall across the end of the road. The smells in the town are very bad as there is no draught of air.[75]

Saturday – [The date is left blank] We started about 7 on the M.M. *Erymanthe* to go as far as Messina. She is a very steady ship. The first day was very rough and the 2nd was not smooth, but the ship did not roll or pitch at all. There was a family of 4 Armenians who could only speak Turkish, some of them. One could talk Greek a little and a Greek of Smyrna, Kyrios Aslanóglou, who spoke both these tongues, and a Belgian, M. Flagontier, who could talk Greek, so in French and Greek we talked to our companions and all got on very well together and we exchanged many regrets when at Messina we went on board the Transatlantique

---

[74] The date would coincide with Theodore's letter of 24 April 1885, written from Sýros to Charles Newton, Keeper of the Department of Greek and Roman Antiquities at the British Museum. 'We returned from Karpathos yesterday and had hoped to catch a steamer which would have brought us and our things straight to England. Unfortunately we shall have to wait a week at least, and as we have so much plunder we cannot take the Marseilles route. I had hoped to have been in time for the Hellenic meeting, but of course now we shall not reach England till the middle of May. We were fairly successful in Karpathos, finding a large number of rock cut graves unopened which have produced pottery, etc., which, if not of the highest order, offer a good deal which I believe to be of a new character. I have likewise got a good-sized statue of one of those quaint figures which I got at Antiparos last year; it is of stone and nearly a yard long. It is decidedly uglier than any which have yet come to hand. Of quaint manners and customs I have got a fine collection, also of old Karpathiote dresses and jewelry. But of epigraphs (I mean inscriptions) I have found very few unpublished, about 6 or 7 from Telos, which we unearthed from a whitewashed church. We had rather a rough time of it, Karpathos being very far behind the world in comforts, and decidedly we enjoyed ourselves best when living in our own tent. Mrs. Bent survives and is well and begs her kind regards. Yours very truly, J. Theodore Bent'

[75] This observation is at odds with Theodore's in *The Cyclades*, in which he writes 'everything is white and clean, a great contrast to a town of corresponding size in France or Italy; the drainage is excellent, and not a smell affronts the nostrils'. (Syra, Chapter VIII)

ship *Maréchal Canrobert*, which was alongside ready for us, and much waving took place as we steamed off at 5.

At Malta,[76] which we reached next morning, our first surprise was to find the inhabitants speaking an unknown tongue, and secondly to find it not so easy to find a ship for London as we had thought, most of them being crowded at this season, and lots of people waiting for passages. As to the language, I thought the language of the island was Italian, but instead it is a sort of Arabic mixed with Hebrew or Phoenician and, in fact, many words are identical almost with Hebrew, as I saw in a book. We have discovered a very kind friend, Col. Wilkie, Dip. Adj. Gen., who takes us out to drive daily and has put down our names for the Garrison Library, where we can see all the magazines and papers and T can go to the Club too, so that though we have an unsettled feeling that we may be off any hour we are enjoying this place very much.[77]

Friday, May 8th. We started at hardly an hour's notice on the *Restormel* for London and this day (13th) we hope to pass Gibraltar. Col. Wilkie came to take us out driving and found us busily packing. The *Restormel* is called after an old castle in Cornwall near Lostwithiel and is a large and steady ship with 3,000 tons of grain on board. She is not a passenger ship and we are to be smuggled into the chartroom and there concealed; when we reach London our baggage to be supposed to be travelling alone. The hiding place is only to be reached by a winding stair about 2 feet across, so I have not explored it, nor the stoke hole, though T has and we have been taken over other parts of the ship. We were to pay £16 for our passages but for £4 more we have the captain's cabin off the little saloon. It is quite a room, 12 by 10 and an alcove off it with a double bed which can be curtained off. And there is a dressing room with a large bath in it which we much enjoy. Our food, if not elegant, is good and plentiful. The captain, who began life as a cook and continued before the mast on sailing vessels, is a very nice man, not so refined as the 1st and 2nd mates. The 1st has his meals with us and hurries off to let the 2nd come.

We have breakfast at 8 with many large dishes of meat, good butter, and bread made on board. Dinner at 12.30 and 5.30 tea, a repetition of breakfast, and as the highly respectable and respectful old steward has confided to me that *he* has a cup of tea *himself* at 3, I have agreed to join him in future. We are supposed to be 11 or 12 days on the voyage and as yet have had very good weather. We saw Pantelaria, an island off Africa, where the Italians keep convicts, Cape Bon,

---

[76] Malta became part of the British Empire after the Treaty of Paris in 1814.
[77] The annual Valetta Carnival Fancy Dress Ball was thrown, on Monday 13 February 1888 (three years after Mabel and Theodore's visit), by the Governor and Lady Simmons at the Palace. Among the 900 guests was a Major-General Hales Wilkie (born 1837 and 'Commanding, Infantry Brigade, Auberge D'Aragon, Strada Vescovo, Valletta') accompanied by his wife and daughter.

and then we went out to sea and yesterday saw land again, and very pretty land too, Spain.[78]

At tea time we were all dismally disgusted at a whistle which announced that we were in a fog. One other steamer was near and we anxiously listened for her whistle. We had to go half speed and rejoiced much when in 3 hours we were out of it. Now that we can see land it is very pleasant, but otherwise porpoises are our only comfort. We saw 2 big nautiluses and lots of little flat ones and 2 turtles.

I am, of course, going to be saved first if we are wrecked, as I am the only woman on board, not the first time this has happened to me, but I never was more than 3 days without seeing another woman before. I don't miss them a bit and am rather surprised at it myself but T says I ought to be used to it. The captain tells us he was well scared at Odessa for he thought he should never get away and never see his missus any more. The place was full and getting fuller every day of soldiers and they were taking men from the offices and the captains were all afraid of being taken prisoners and their ships taken.[79] The Russians were very rude and disagreeable and a captain who was with him could understand Russian and told him all he heard.

We reached home via Millwall Dock in safety with our 24 pieces of the most varied luggage, and I am more convinced than ever that there is no place like it.

P.S. The murder at Volatha concerned 2 of the guests at our luncheon party; Mr. Manolakakis was openly said to have planned to murder Mr. F. Sakolarides from a political motive, but in the dark he changed places with a man we knew who was always drinking and he escaped and the other man was stabbed instead. A relation of Manolakakis hurriedly left the island and no arrest was made.

---

[78] Pantelleria, or Pantalaria (ancient Cossyra), 100km south-west of Sicily. Cape Bon (Ras at Tib, Ras Addar), Tunisia, the eastern terminus of the Saharan Atlas range projecting into the Mediterranean towards Sicily.
[79] Perhaps a reference to one of the frequent Jewish pogroms that occurred around this date.

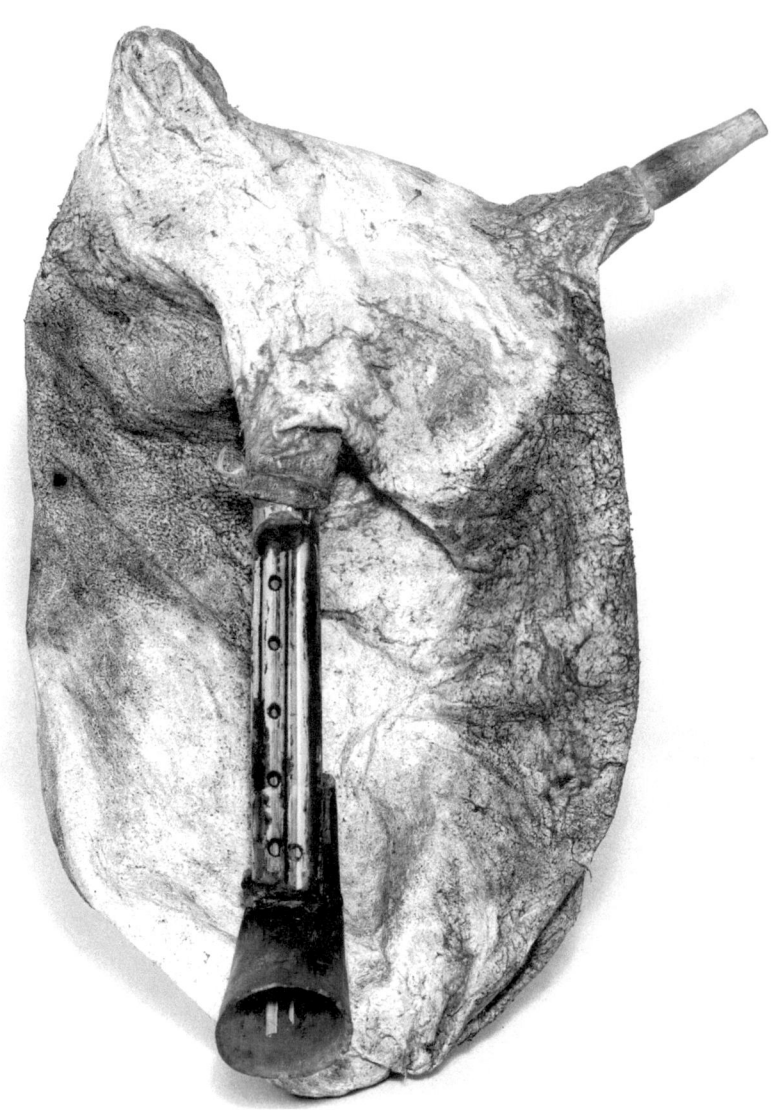

Theodore Bent's samboúna, acquired in the Dodecanese in 1885

Chronicle IV, February to May 1886: 'I hate pirates!' Adventures along the Turkish coast

Mabel styles this *Chronicle* her 'fourth', but it is actually the third of her notebooks in the Hellenic Society's archive. Mabel begins her 1886 *Chronicle* in Istanbul. She is chatty and happy and gives an insight into her motives for writing: 'to remind myself in my old age of pleasant things (or the contrary)'. She also takes the opportunity of reinforcing her insistence that she is writing notebooks not guidebooks… 'I do not, of course, intend to describe this town but only our adventures therein.'

Following the successes of their 1885 work further south, the Bents decide for this season to cruise down from the Turkish islands of Sámos and Chíos, which they had first seen in 1882/3. Theodore, now a member of the council of the Hellenic Society, had obtained a grant of £50 to equip his expedition. Once on Sámos he encountered problems with the authorities, and the Society's journal of 1886 reports that, 'owing to unexpected difficulty in obtaining permission to dig in the island, Mr. Bent has not been so successful as he had hoped. He has, however, spent only half the amount.' The £25 was returned to the Society. Mabel informs us: 'Truly the balmy days of excavators are over'.

Theodore (with Percy Gardner's help) provided a summary of his work in the region for the *Journal of Hellenic Studies* (Vol. 7, 1886, pp. 143–153), under the title 'An Archaeological Visit to Samos'. He begins his introduction: 'English enterprise in excavation has been considerably checked of late years by the impossibility of obtaining anything like fair terms from the Greek or Turkish governments…Consequently if English archaeologists wish to prosecute researches on the actual soil of Hellas, it remains for them to decide whether they are sufficiently remunerated for their trouble and outlay by the bare honour of

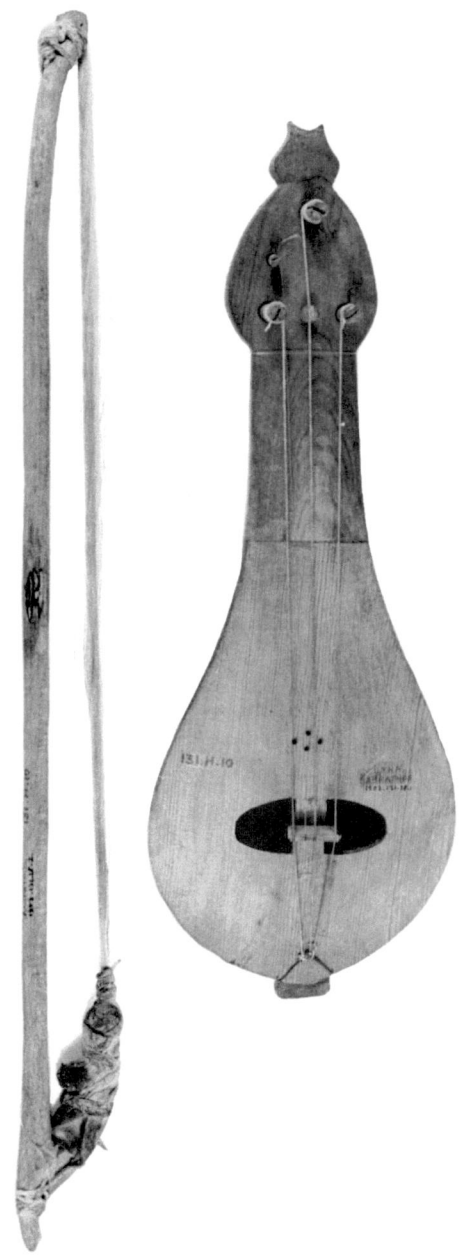

Theodore Bent's lýra, acquired in the Dodecanese in 1885

discovering statues, inscriptions, and other treasures to be placed in the museum of Athens, or, as is the case in Turkey, for the inhabitants to make chalk of, or build into their houses.' Theodore was piqued.

The British Museum has some of Theodore's Samian finds. He uncovered a terracotta mask and copied an important inscription listing victors at games held within the famous sanctuary of Hera. But the couple were disappointed and leave Sámos early to undertake preliminary researches around the neighbouring islands. Since the infamous episode of the kidnap and murder of British tourists at Dilessi on the Greek mainland in 1870, wealthy foreigners were well advised to travel armed. Mabel (and Manthaios too, in another source, see page 341) records at length their many schemes to avoid local 'pirates'. Theodore was carrying all the party's finances in gold and cash – a sum worth around £6000 today.

Another source of alarm for the travellers is the unstable political situation between Greece and Turkey. It is something the Bents have to face throughout their years spent travelling in the region. In April 1886, the European powers decreed that: 'Since the Athenian Government's answer to the common note of April 14/26 was not satisfactory to the Powers, the said Governments ordered the Commandants of the united marine squadrons to embargo the coasts of Greece for every ship under Greek flag. This embargo should be realised on the date of this communication. It should begin at Cap Maleas and finish at Cap Sounion, and from there till the border of Greece, including Euboea, as well as the entrance of the Corinthian Gulf at the west coast. Any ship under Greek flag that may try to violate this embargo, shall be captured.' The embargo lasted a few weeks until the hostile Greek forces stood down, but the Bents were prevented from moving freely in Greek waters the while. Manthaios is hampered on his return to Anáfi: 'He returned to Syra by the same *Iris* and from there he will have great difficulty getting home as, since 12 on Saturday, no ship under Greek flag may travel or move. He would have gone by steamer to Santorini and *kaïke* to Anáfi, so now he must look out for a Turkish *kaïke*.'

By now Manthaios was an indispensable member of the team and the Bents asked him to join them (with their tents he had been looking after) on Chíos. Of the other characters encountered on this tour there was the Turkish polymath and first director of the National Museum in Istanbul, Osman Hamdi Bey. Hamdi made several great discoveries in his own right, including the magnificent 'Alexander' sarcophagus. On Kálymnos Mabel is particularly keen to meet the young Greek wife of Theodore's colleague from the British Museum, William Paton, himself an antiquarian of note: as was Henry Fanshawe Tozer, who encounters the Bents on Sámos. Tozer (in *The Islands of the Aegean*, 1890, p. 302) recalls their meeting at a temple site on Sámos: 'The most important ruins are those of a temple, which have recently been brought to light by the indefatigable spade of Mr. Bent. Later, the couple's journey home is brightened by the dashing war correspondent Frederic 'Villiers of *The Graphic*' Villiers.

While Mabel is busy with her *Chronicle*, Theodore occupies himself with matters antiquarian. He wrote several letters from Constantinople to the British Museum and the Hellenic Society, most of which concern the new director of the Istanbul Museum, Hamdi Bey. From the Hôtel de Byzance on 17 February[1] he writes to Arthur Smith at the British Museum complaining about Hamdi's intractability over some casts sought by London of the famous Budrum Lion; he tries to embroil the British Ambassador, Sir William White. These are portents of similar clouds looming for Theodore himself.

The couple's itinerary this trip (see map page 62) is London – Marseilles – Sýros – Smyrna – Istanbul – Mytilíni – Smyrna – Chíos – Sámos – Pátmos (and the isles around, several times, depending on the winds) – Ikaría – Sámos – Kálymnos – Astypálea – Sámos – Ikaria – Ceşme – Chíos – Athens – Marseilles – Calais – London. They arrive home again at the end of May. Theodore has a fever he thinks he contracted in the marshes of Sámos. It is a cautionary reminder of the risks to health present in the Mediterranean and further east. That spring there was cholera and death in Brindisi, Trieste, and, of course, Venice.

For notes on this transcription the reader is referred to page xxv. Mabel, as usual, refers throughout to her husband as T, and Manthaios as M. See selected Indices of people and places mentioned. This *Chronicle* is written in a dark-red leather notebook (180 x 115mm) with marbled endpapers and edges. There are 192 lined pages and Mabel uses

---

[1] Letter to Arthur Smith, Department of Greek and Roman Antiquities, British Museum, 17 February 1886.

all but 10 of them. Included is the letter (referred to elsewhere) from a friend, Mrs Graham, who writes: 'Why oh why don't you publish it? It simply bristles with epigrams and I am certain would be a great success! You ought to blend the Chronicles into one and I am sure everyone would buy it.' A perceptive critic.

Mabel is catching up with the *Chronicle* in her room (number 2) at the fashionable Hôtel de Byzance, Constantinople. The date is Tuesday, 2 February 1886.

'Go to now ye that I say today or tomorrow we will go into this city...' St. James[2]

My Fourth Chronicle
1886

February 1886 – Istanbul

[Tuesday] February 2nd. Hôtel de Byzance (No 2) Constantinople. I must begin my Chronicle somewhere if I am to write one at all, and as in this matter I am selfish enough to consider myself of the first consideration, because I write to remind myself in my old age of pleasant things (or the contrary), I will begin now. I do not, of course, intend to describe this town but only our adventures therein.

We two and Mr. Graham have now been here since Saturday, January 23rd, having left Marseilles on the 16th by M.M. Steamer *Donaï*. We stopped at Syra and Smyrna on the way and had a passage of varying quality; from Smyrna it was quite like summer. There were not many passengers. The most remarkable was the Prince Bishop of Malattiah, in the middle of Armenia, an old gentleman wrapped in many dressing-gowns which he varied daily, not so his shirt that he had made a vow not to change. He wore red, blue, green, violet, brown, and was very cheery and talkative in Italian.

We did not land in Syra but in Smyrna, where we stayed from about 2 one day till 10 the next morning. We went to visit the Dennises and got on board in time to escape a tremendous thunderstorm which did great damage. We thought the ship had struck but it was a church near. We saw a lovely sunset off Mytilene.[3] We reached this about 3. We thought Constantinople looked as flat as Venice but really the hills seem to have grown since we came.

We are having what every traveller in every country always has: exceptional weather, but this time the exception is in our favour and it is so like spring that we are doing all the water excursions and keeping the bazaars and museum for the snow which we may have any day. We get on very well without submitting to the ignominy of being taken about by an interpreter. We have the plan and find

---

[2] Mabel is adapting James 4:13–15, 'Go to now, ye that say, today or tomorrow we will go into such a city, and continue there a year, and buy and sell, and get gain: Whereas ye know not what (shall be) on the morrow... For that ye (ought) to say, If the Lord will, we shall live and do this, or that.'
[3] This is the current Greek island of Lésvos (Mytilíni), then under Ottoman control with Sámos, Chíos and other Aegean islands. They did not become part of Greece again until 1913.

our Greek a very useful tongue in this polyglot, and I might add polychrome, place. We have learnt the numbers and the money and yet have not found any difficulty, still less danger.

We have a very nice balcony looking on the Grande Rue de Pera. Our next neighbours are a very amusing Trieste bride and bridegroom – Gargetta by name – married a fortnight. They amuse us very much in their very free and easy conduct, embracing in the reading room, and they tell us the oddest stories about each other, and as the walls are thin we can easily believe them. One evening she was going to have a party in the large saloon into which our two rooms open. We and Mr. and Mrs. Rubinstein, some Russians who we like, were bidden. The other people were Greeks or Italians. We danced and were merry but were alarmed by rather a startling incident.

The bride's mother, a rather stout dame of 58 much got up, after dancing a gallop and being left by her partner about 4 feet from her chair went on turning, we thought on purpose, then went from one leg to the other, still turning, and finally, having got into the middle of the room, fell headlong on the floor from giddiness. She was quickly picked up none the worse and begged us to laugh, which we did, but none more than her daughter, who hopped about imitating her and declaring she thought she wished to dance the cancan.

February 5th, Friday. Yesterday and today have been raining and the streets are simply awful, but really not as bad as Cairo, for here the mud will brush off, there it won't. We went to the Bazaar yesterday but we bought nothing and Mr. Gargetta only a Persian tile. We paid a long visit in the afternoon to Canon Curtis[4] and his sister Mrs. Walker and heard many interesting things. Mr. Graham went to take a bath and finding the door ajar stepped in to the great horror of about 7 female bathers, suitably attired for the occasion. The poor things naturally screeched all manner of bad names at him so he did not remain long.

At night there was a fire in the bazaars in Stamboul, awful to behold. T went over the bridge but did not dare go further as it is dangerous for Christians at

---

[4] Canon Curteis of the Memorial Chapel, Istanbul. Theodore writes of him (and of their plans to head towards Sámos) to Arthur Smith at the British Museum on 17 February: 'There is likewise a certain Canon Curteis, the clergyman at the Memorial Chapel, to whom I have spoken about the Hellenic Society. He has been here for 30 years and is well up in the archaeology of the place. He has made a large collection of inscriptions of the Hellenic and Byzantine periods, many of which he has published in the periodical of the Syllogos here. I upbraided him for his want of patriotism and I feel sure that if Mr. Gardiner wrote to him he would be glad to place some of them at the disposal of the society... We are off to Samos this afternoon, having waited here longer than we intended in the hopes that the Greek Question would settle itself, however we can wait no longer and must take our chance. Yours very truly, J. Theodore Bent'. The Greek 'Question' relates to one of the frequent territorial disputes between Greece and Turkey, often causing the Bents problems as they tried to move around the Eastern Aegean.

night. Two days ago we lunched with the American Minister, Mr. Cos and his wife, or Archaeological Angel as he calls her in some of his numerous books. He is very amusing and she full of manners and both very kind. She was arrayed in black silk, cut square and filled up with beaded lace and net sleeves. I was dressed after the barbarous manner of my island.

After luncheon Mr. Libby, an American, came in and Mr. Thornton from our Embassy. The only remarkable thing we have seen in the streets and which we could not possibly buy in England is a Turkey arranged as follows. Of course in this country this bird ought to be paid very particular attention. It is plucked of all but its tail and pen feathers. Each side feather of the tail is tied to the hindmost feather of the wing. Two feathers, loose ones, are tied together and put into the beak and the ends of them fastened to the front wing feathers. It looks altogether rather like the German Imperial Eagle.

[Wednesday] February 17th. On board the Khedivial steamer *Behéra*. 3 o'clock. I have a great deal to write up, having been quite too busy in Constantinople. We went to a little dance at the Embassy and we lunched with the Kennedys, he is 2nd Secretary. We also went one morning by appointment to Karatheodory Pasha's house at Arnaoutkuci, where we saw his father-in-law Photiades Pasha. Caratheodore Pasha took us to the house of Hamdi Bey, one of the only Turkish painters. His father was a Christian baby robbed from Chios, but he is a very fanatical Turk. His house was very pretty, all lined with embroidery and beautiful carpets and in his studio he had beautiful china, arms, tiles, etc. We had coffee and as he is head of the museums he appointed a time for us to meet him there and be shown everything. However when the appointed day arrived he was late but we saw everything very well. There are quantities of lovely things from Cyprus very much heaped together. There was a particularly fine sarcophagus, much smashed in the embarkation, the most delicately worked I have ever seen.

We went to Prinkips Island with Mr. Pears and his family one Sunday, lunched at a hotel and then up to the monastery of Agios Giorgios.[5] We also went to see the Dancing Dervishes, a much pleasanter sight than the howlers. We went to Scutari one afternoon with Lady and Miss White,[6] Fraülein Eberhard, a couple of

---

[5] These are the nine small islands below Istanbul, in the north-eastern corner of the Sea of Mamara. The Bents visit Chalki (Heybeli) to see the two celebrated educational establishments there – the Greek commercial school and the 'Theological College of the Great Church of Christ', the latter reflecting the freedom granted the Orthodox Church by the Ottomans. Theodore was much impressed and wrote a piece for *Macmillan's Magazine* in the May/October issue of 1889. 'It would seem as if the fever of education had well-nigh consumed Chalki and would turn it ere long into an insular Oxford…' ('A Scholastic Island', p. 449). Mabel enjoys the Dervishes and 'a Dervishes arm crutch of iron' is a souvenir they return with next year from Thessaloníki; it is in the Pitt Rivers Museum, Oxford (1891.4.13).

[6] Mabel's first reference to a family that will appear regularly over the following years. Sir William White was British Ambassador to Constantinople. His photograph, with consular staff, on the embassy lawn, appears on p. 344.

Turks, Conti Maurizio de Bodari and Madame de Hobe Pasha. She is a German, I mean Mme. De Hobe. Her husband is Grand Vizier to the Sultan. I went to her reception next afternoon. We went in the little launch of the Embassy and sat in the cemetery of the Crimean War and afterwards had tea with Mrs. Lyne, the wife of the Sergeant who has charge of it.

Another day we went by steamer with Mr. H. Pears to Bebek and then crossed in a *kaïke* to Kandiki on the Asiatic coast and lunched with Mr. de Branteghem, a Belgian who speaks perfect English and has some beautiful Tanagra figures[7] and other Greek antiquities in his dining room, and his whole drawing room is furnished with embroideries and old embossed velvets arranged most artistically. Even the picture frames were of old velvets or embroidered stoles. It was a most enchanting place, really *in* the Bosphoros which was glittering and twinkling and sparkling below – we returned straight by steamer. We went to Roumeli Hussar and to Bouyoukderek and got to know that part of the Bosphoros pretty well and really on the whole we had very fine weather, but the inhabitants were desiring snow.

The last day of all, that was yesterday **[Tuesday] Feb. 16th**, we went to the Treasury with a Russian, M. Serge de Jourassos and 2 Germans. M. de J. got the order from his Minister so we had no trouble and we had the *Kavass*[8] of the Russians with us. (Here I must say that through an open cabin door I can see an old Turk very busy with his carpet saying his prayers to Mecca.) We had been told it was a very difficult thing to get the order and very expensive on account of all the *baksheesh*, but we only paid £6 amongst us all.

We drove to Dolma Bagche palace and had to wait 2 hours as the *Kavass* had to go to the little palace Zildy where the Sultan lives and he was not up and he had to sign the order. We were not very much interested in D.B. except as far as the size went. There were many rooms with parquet floors and sofas and chairs round them and absolutely no works of art; cabinets, etc., to be seen – a few nice tables. The huge enormous reception hall was worth seeing from being the biggest room we had ever seen.

We went across then in a *kaïke* of the Sultan's to Bylerbey in Asia, which pleased us better and then again in the *kaïke* to Seraglio Point to see the treasury. Of course, I am not going to describe this, but certainly it seems a pity to see jewels so wasted and so ill shown off, for it was a very badly lighted place. It is a great satisfaction to have seen these things before the Turks carry them away. In

---

[7] Highly collectable terracotta figurines, known after the first finds (1874) from ancient Tanagra (Boetia). Theodore informs Arthur Smith (17 February 1886) of this little collection and its collector, 'A certain Mr. Alphonse van Branteghem, who has an exquisite collection of terracottas here, is anxious to belong to the Hellenic Society provided that he can secure the back numbers of the Journal.'

[8] An armed constable, or a government servant or courier.

the evening we parted company with Mr. Graham, and his steamer carried him towards Russia this morning.

We start at 4 for Smyrna and are to call at Mytelene tomorrow evening. We feel rooted up and both wretchedly unsettled and though not yet hungry are longing for a meal to make us feel at home. Italian is the language of the ship.

February 20th, Saturday. Hôtel d'Égypte. Smyrna. We had a very peaceable passage and arrived here yesterday morning early. We stopped and landed at the Asiatic town on the Dardanelles and were not much interested, and stayed some hours at Mytelene on Thursday night. We did not land but could recognize many places in that lovely island, where we spent some days in 1882[9], as the moon was shining brightly. This hotel has changed hands since we stayed here last and we do not like the people so well. We found we were to stay here till today at 4, so sadly put our baggage on board a most disgustingly filthy little Greek steamer, Η Αναλογη.

I continue here on this smelly boat with real tears in my eyes and laughing at the same time. It is too nasty – mosquitoes and earwigs already made acquaintance with and fleas and bugs to come, of course. We are both in turns uttering cheering things. T says that earwigs always go to sleep at night, but that is not true; perhaps it is because I begged him to invent anything I might like to hear. After all, I was last year most delighted to get back on board the companion ship, the *Roúmeli*,[10] when leaving Karpathos, and to be quite honest this is a shade better. We have been given the cabin which contains the public washing basin. There is a thin red curtain strained on nails across and all the bread is in a cupboard.

The very small deck above us is spread with Jews and even at our door there are people encamped. It is tantalizing to see the big Austrian *Niobe*, in which we went to Samos 3 years ago. We shall call at Chios tonight and get to Vathý early and there hope to meet Manthaios,[11] who is awaiting us with the tent.

I have nothing to say about Smyrna; we only wandered about the bazaars –

Sunday February 20th [actually the 21st]. Samos. Vathý. We arrived here about 2 o'clock after a very boisterous and excessively smelly passage and it was so rough that we had some difficulty in leaving the *Anatole* after she had come

---

[9] The Bents toured these islands and the Greek mainland in 1882/3, but there is no *Chronicle* for this visit in this present archive. Mabel refers to this trip, and Theodore's article complaining of Turkish treatment of the Greek population, on several occasions. Theodore's earliest training had been as an historian and he frequently returned to his interest in the fluctuations of Mediterranean power and politics. In July 1889 he published a short account of medieval Chíos for the *English Historical Review* (4, 15, pp. 467–480) under the title 'The Lords of Chios'.
[10] The steamer *Roúmeli* is an old friend from Mabel's 1885 tour.
[11] Manthaios Símos, from Anáfi in the Cyclades, joins the couple again this season as their general factotum. The 'war' here is the long-running conflict between Greece and her northern neighbours in the regions around Macedonia.

broadside on the bow of another ship. M was not there to meet us, not having got the telegram, but he soon came to us. He says the Government steamer came to Anaphi to take all the men to the war but it was so rough they could not start. He gave 7 francs to a soldier to let him slip away.

We sent him with our cards and no less than 5 letters to the Prince,[12] and since T has gone out I have had a visit from Mr. Epaminondas Stamatiades – Directeur de la Chancellerie Princière de Samos – with the Prince's compliments and offers of help, etc. I sat on the bed and he on the chair. It is lovely weather.

This room has 2 hard beds with clean bottom sheets, the top ones, sewn to the quilted cotton *paploma*, go on from traveller to traveller. Amongst those whose cards hide a small looking glass one warns us in French to beware of bugs and scrutinize our bills. A small table containing a jug of drinking water, a candle and a match box in the room, and 2 basins in the passage for general use complete our accommodation. I must add that there is a comb and a pair of slippers to each bed.

As we travelled all over the island 3 years ago and know the ways of the place, we mean to make a point of keeping our slippers handy as we must leave our walking shoes before stepping up on to the higher carpeted part to sit down cross-legged. M had a loud talk to the landlord and impressed him with the requirements of Britons so he has been and borrowed at a china shop and we now have a basin and jug. People here like to wash as at a waterfall and on the steamer our floor became very sloppy because the lurching caused the water to flow over the washer, there being no place to catch the water, only a grating, and a constant trickle had to be kept up.

As I stay in bed the captain and all the passengers came in without knocking to wash and the captain brought me some welcome narcissus. The most persistent smell came from the sour bread.

Monday February 21st [actually the 22nd]. Today we had several visits and received our guests in someone else's bedroom, ours being untenable by reason of all our baggage being open and sorted. We had the 2 Mr. Mares. One is our Consul Austrian-Levantine. We dined at the restaurant as we found our meals very cold when brought to the inn. This was a kitchen not too grand or expensive for the humblest eater. M buzzed about making known to the landlord what was suitable to be laid before us. We had a white tablecloth and napkins. Others had blue-checked towels, partly laid under the plate, partly on the lap. The food was very good.

T spent the morning with the Prince, an older and not so smart a man as his brother. After luncheon we went out for a walk and met a smiling and bowing

---

[12] Under the Turks Sámos enjoyed a degree of leniency and from 1834, until union with Greece in 1912, this large and prosperous island was a quasi-independent principality. The Sultan appointed the Prince, who was a Greek. The Turks finally withdrew from the island on 23 September 1912.

unrecognised young man. We smiled and bowed and shook hands, feeling we had evidently forgotten an old friend, but he said he had never seen us before as he was away on our last visit. He said his mother was expecting me. 'Let us go there at once!' we said, wondering where? We were still wondering when we met our Consul coming down the palace steps and he seemed sorry we were out for he said the Prince was coming to see us, so we settled to be in at ¼ to 5 and soon after to our surprise found ourselves at Mrs. Mare's. The family were greatly astonished that I could talk, as when we dined there 3 years ago I knew not a word.

Then we went to see Mrs. E. Stamatides, who preferred to air her French so we had a slow time of it. Her husband attended the Prince and this visit was also French, it being a much more *genteel* language than Greek. The Prince began to speak to me of photography, which he thought of taking up, and was very *much amazed* when he heard I could photograph,[13] but I know for a fact that Mr. Mare had told him how my processing-glass was broken and that he is going to send it to Smyrna to get a new one.

Tomorrow we are going to Tigani, leaving most of our baggage here. Mr. Mare lends us a house. T and M have gone to the café to meet our various acquaintances. I am now going to get to bed, which means clearing a path through bags to it and digging it out, as there is no place but the bed and the floor to put things.

Wednesday February 24th. Tigani,[14] which means frying-pan. Yesterday morning it was intimated to us that the Princess wished to see us, so dressed for the journey, we went at 11.30 and found a pretty, young, well-dressed and pleasant woman. We were given tea and talked French. I felt very odd, for when one is used to a crinolette one does miss it! However once we had started I found myself very suitable attired. We were accompanied by Costandino, the son of one of our former hosts, then Demarch of the Chora. It was dreadfully cold and when I dismounted after 2 hours I could hardly stand on my painful feet.

We went through very pretty country with trees, carob and olive, and streams and one river where one of the mules had to pass back and forward to fetch everyone. When we arrived we drew up at the shop of the Demarch, F. Valasiades, a charming man. The key of Mr. Mare's large house was not to be had here. It was and still is at Mytilene – a village 1½ hours away, so we were asked upstairs and given jam and water and coffee while someone was sent for the key. I sat wrapped up for 2 hours and we talked much with our kind host

---

[13] Mabel was a keen photographer and from this season on was 'expedition photographer', carrying all her equipment with her. It is a huge pity that so few of her photographs have survived.
[14] Now the popular resort of Pythagório.

and also heard from M all the particulars of his journey to Karpathos after the Rhodian plates[15] and how, to avoid opening them in Smyrna, he rowed slowly all round harbour dodging the Customs' boats and got the case safely on the English *Hilda*.

At 6.30 we were summoned to dinner and rather a nasty one – macaroni smothered in a very strong cheese and salt, our lamb cut up into shapeless blocks and violently scorched and burnt in some places and raw in others. It looked as if it had been accidentally dropped into the fire and saved. The next dish was blocks of cheese with eggs poached over them. There was very good wine and raisins also.

After dinner, Stavritza, the wife, was patronizingly called in and sat on a kind of outcast chair and the 12 year old Photinió placed her chair on the threshold. The key not coming, a bedroom was prepared. It contained a very small hard bed and 3 boxes and some pegs and was lighted by a glass door into the dining room and a window lacking some panes into the next room. It was very clean and no fleas. We hung things over the windows and did not sleep much; there was not room to.

We have not much luggage, all our wraps and my bed and a little food. This morning at 7 we were given a spoonful of hot lemon jam, some water and a little cup of coffee and at 9, after a walk, some of our bacon, some bread, wine and raisins.

We met the father of Costandino, and T's coach fortunately came up. We took a walk with him and promised to visit him. He is staying here and will come with us tomorrow. He gave T a handful of coins, 2 very good Samiote silver ones. I told him how I use the towel his wife gave me on my (dressing) table. We are going now to the aqueduct which was described by Herodotus,[16] lost till 4 years ago and disbelieved in. It was found by a priest named Kyrillos. It goes for 7 stadia through the mountains. We were in it in '83. We are going to measure it now.

Wednesday [February] 24th. I had a mule and we went to the entrance of the aqueduct about ½ a mile up the mountain. Since we were here last they have built a little house over it, but never swept it out since it was built. We took a 50-foot measure and used it. We went in for about ¼ mile beyond the place where the workers from both sides had met with wonderful accuracy, but forming an elbow, and the people from the other side had made their passage higher. We got awfully dirty squeezing against the wet walls and rubbing our

---

[15] For this adventure on Kárpathos, see p. 86 note 39 and p. 90.
[16] 'The work of a Megarian named Eupalinus', the remarkable 1km tunnel commissioned by Polykrates in the 6th century BC. http://pr.caltech.edu/periodicals/EandS/articles/LXVII1/samos.html (summer 2006) gives an excellent introduction. See Herodotus, Book 3.60.4.

heads and there was also water above our ankles in one place. The first time we only went as far as a sculptured stone, half hidden by a stalactite curtain.

When we returned we settled into Mr. Mare's house, a huge half-finished barn. We took possession of a large room with a divan all along one side of it where T sleeps. I have my hammock. He has brought his sheets and pillowcase. We had many many visits from Costandinos and his father, Demetrós. We like them both, and no one else but the Demarch Valasiades has been.

Thursday [February] 18th. [Mabel is referring back to the previous week.] We set out early with Demetrós and with 2 mules. We went into the more distant end of the aqueduct but could not get very far. The roof of schist had tumbled in and we had to climb up a mountain of stones and were glad to see an immense slab of sound stone over our heads. It would take a tremendous lot of money to put it in order again. About ½ past 11 we got to the Chora, where we were warmly welcomed and I embraced by the wife and daughter of Demetrós, Paraskevoula and Aikateriniό.

We had coffee and jam first and then a splendid luncheon: soup of rice, whipped eggs and lemon juice, really good, a chicken and some lamb out of the same, *Yaprakia*, rice and meat in little balls boiled in vine leaves, very good rissoles, yaourt (curdled milk), cheese and fruit. I have not had so good a meal for a long time.[17]

It was 2 hours to Pagounda; we got there about 3 and went to the house of the Demarch. His daughter Charíklea received us in his absence and we all went for a walk about the village. It is a very pretty place and the road was through pine trees and olives and streams, but very rough and bad and washed away by landslips. It was very cold; Kerke, the highest mountain snowy.

The Demarch and his daughter are civilized sort of people and the girl dined with us as did our hostess at the *chora*. Certainly meals are better if the mistress herself partakes of them. We passed a good night and in the morning T bought 14 pieces of *Koutaya*[18] ware, some coloured and some peacock blue, also 2 Dutch glass bottles and an Italian jug with a rhyme in Greek upon it. I was given my hostess's best shirt of fine cotton crepe and trimmed with most beautifully fine silk lace at the neck and sleeves; extremely finely done with the needle by the only old woman who now can do it.[19]

---

[17] One in a series of Mabel's memorable meals. The fare seems to have included most of the traditional Greek classics: egg and lemon soup (*avgolémono*), stuffed vine leaves (*yaprákia/dolmádes*), rissoles (*keftédhes*), cheese, fruit and yoghurt (Mabel's 'yaourt' – probably with honey!).

[18] Cotiaëum (*Koutaya*), Phrygia, on the upper Tembris, about 40km north of Appia on the north road from Acmoneia to Dorylaëum.

[19] The Bents brought back a few every-day items from Sámos and they have found their way in to the Pitt Rivers Museum, Oxford, including a pair of pigskin shoes (no accession number) and two eagle-bone pipes (1888.37.6 and 1903.130.17),

Friday [February] 19th. We went to Spathareïka, 1¼ hours off, and there we made the café our headquarters and entered many houses and T was gratified by hearing many strange charms. One very old woman, sitting cross-legged in the sun at her door at the top of an outside surface, very brown and wrinkled all over, as far as we could judge, utterly refused to tell us anything. She said it was a great sin and she would have to confess it to the priest, and now we must no longer behave like the ancients did but trust in good medicine. However after much arguing and declaring we were all quite well and did not wish to work magic but only to hear about it, and the sin would be on our heads, she said she would make a few prayers first, which she did, and then told some charms, for which see T –[20]

One hour and a half took us to Skoureïka. There are lots of villages here which end in *eïka*.[21] There the Demarch took us in. It was very cold. They brought a brazier and spread a carpet for me to sit on with 2 cushions to lean on. All these villages are prettily situated and at each one they ask us if we don't like it better than any other and cast some kind of slur on the inhabitants of the others.

T was invited to sleep in a bed in the kitchen out of which a little girl was turned, and all eyes being occupied in watching the erection of my hammock and then being occupied spreading M's bed on the floor of the passage, the poor little sleepy thing crept back and fell asleep and had to be picked out again. When we were shut in, T got out his sheets, etc., for there were none. We had many fleas and washed in a slop basin, which we found, over a sink. *The* basin is always in the passage.

Mrs. Theophanó told one there was a fearful river to cross to get to Goumeïka and I should be terrified. But of course I was not. Her brother Chrysostomos led my mule and all the men passed this great river on trees and stones and I and my mule got across all right by ourselves. We were once before at Goumeïka and lunched at the café. This time, having an introduction to Mr. Ioannis Hadgi, or Chatzi as they spell it in Greek, Theodorou. We went to his house and had some coffee and sweets. His grandfather, Theodore, had been to the Holy Grave and hence the name for all descendants.

Last time we were here we had seen in the *gynaikeion*, or women's latticed gallery, the old carved wooden *tembelon*, or screen of the church, now replaced by a hideous marble one. It was for sale and we wished to see it again, so we had it all laid out and examined every piece, but reluctantly gave up all thoughts

---

[20] Theodore presented a paper on island folklore and customs for the Anthropological Institute. Mabel 'exhibited a number of Greek Dresses and other objects of the islands'. Theodore's paper appears as 'On Insular Greek Customs', *Journal of the Anthropological Institute of Great Britain and Ireland*, Vol. 15 (1886).
[21] The suffix 'eïka' might indicate 'property of', being a form of 'eika-na' ('property'), from the IE root '-eik', 'to possess'.

of buying it as it is dry rotten and worm-eaten and would arrive home powder and crumbs.

We returned to Skoureïka to luncheon and then one hour to the sea and took a boat hoping to get there in 2 hours. We soon however were becalmed and took 5 hours to get to Tigani. It was very cold and the stars had long been looking at themselves in the water when we arrived, very hungry, in our little boat.

Having given Mr. Mare's key to Costandinos to keep and said we should be back, we were much dismayed to find when he was called out of bed that he had given the key to someone and it was gone to Vathý. All the inhabitants were drunk and here we were homeless at 9 o'clock! We of course went to the Demarch's but he was out, so we then went to the café thinking very sadly of having to go back to that little cabin instead of having Sunday to ourselves.

We asked to have some eggs cooked and presently the Demarch came, welcomed us warmly, said his house was ours – rather drunk. M said, 'Well, if it is may I have the key to put our things in?' They went and put our things in and the Demarch said he was sure it would amuse us to see the feasting and in half an hour he would return.

We ate and an hour passed and then a boy came in and called out Demosthénes the café's housekeeper and he came back and proposed to take us to a house. So we went to a large house of the rich Mr. Arés, who is away in Vathý. He gave us coffee last time we were here and gave me an alabaster tear-bottle and a little head. We had just arrived when the Demarch appeared and impressed upon us that he had said he would be here in ½ an hour and was quite too tipsy to understand it had been 1¼. He was rather offended and we feared there might be an awkwardness about getting the luggage, and Demosthénes could not make out *what* we wanted more than a bed, slippers and a comb! T and M got the things and we had a fleay night.

Sunday we sent M off to Vathý for the rest of our baggage and to lay in stores and we in the meantime moved to Mr. Mare's. We lunched at the café, Demetrós of the Chora with us, and afterwards he took possession of us and became our servant, constantly visited us, as did Costandinos, cooked our dinner, shared it with us, and finally slept on the floor in the dining room with some idea of guarding us. We were glad not to have to go out as a thunderstorm was raging.

March 1886 – Sámos

Monday, March 1st. This morning we made our beds, tidied the room and had some coffee made by Demetrós but could not go out. In these 24 hours we have had 5 thunderstorms. Demetrós had the luncheon ready when M arrived about midday, all dry, thank goodness, as how we should have dried our things I know not.

In the afternoon we went up to the church of Panagía Spilianí, so called because it is a cave. A priest of Amorgos lives there with his family and farms the place for the great monastery in Amorgos – Panagía Kosoviótissa, or Life of the World. We were refreshed in the usual manner and questioned as to our religion, manners, customs, coalmines, exports, imports, agricultural produce, salt works, population, etc., and went into the church and cave where there are many baths and cisterns; and all the pavement of pebbles done by this papas in the last few years.

We hope to go to Lipsós and Agathonisi tomorrow and to Patmos if the wind becomes good. A good big ship is engaged and Demetrós comes with us. It has been made clear that no wages are to be expected so he may not turn up. As for digging, we can do nothing till we have the leave of the council of 4, not yet elected and not to meet till the middle of April, and that will be rather late for us –

I forgot to say that at the Chora the wife of Demetrós was quite amazed that we could speak Greek and was very funny over her description of my dumbness. Even at that time I could not understand that she said to me, 'All the women in the world can speak Greek so why can't you?' And I heard her tell a woman 'She is a very nice woman but she can't speak Greek.'

I take up my pen again in a cell, up many flights of stairs in the big monastery in 'the isle that is called Patmos'[22] on March 7th **[Sunday, 1886]**. I had better continue our history in due course.

Tuesday [March] 2nd. Contrary wind and rain so we had no hope of leaving Samos, so made our beds and prepared to spend the day in the house, but at 11 a good wind came and we summoned the captain and it was agreed to start at once. M rushed to prepare food for the journey and we packed and were all ready by 12 – but the ship was not. We had been going to start that morning but they had to get oil, bread, tobacco, water, their papers, etc., so at two only did we embark. Suddenly a violent storm of rain came on and the wind went down so we had to land and sadly make our beds again. We decided to start at dawn next morning and were to be called at 3, but of course they did not come till 5.

We started at ¼ to 6. It was not very cold and the sunrise was most lovely. The very new moon was sailing about in the blue. The morning star (Αυγερινός άστρα) was shining through pink and the mountains of Anatolí (the Sunrise) were quite black. Watching the sunrise occupied us till the ship, a

---

[22] Revelations 1:91.

schooner, was all in order and then we got out our breakfast things and made some tea. In four hours we got to Agátheonisi, or Gaidáronisi, that is Good or Donkey Isle.

It is a small low, barren spot inhabited by an old man and woman with 6 sons and 7 daughters – 3 sons and 1 daughter married and some children – in all 22. They live in the most wretched huts and the greatest poverty, drink brackish water in winter and buy it from Samos in summer and pay £127 to the Turks.

They keep sheep and goats and we bought a lamb and a *mysethra*,[23] and lunched off eggs and *chloro*, a kind of junket or curd, and bread which we had carried with us. We examined the houses and a woman gave T an old knapsack of goat skin for which she of course was given a return, and at 1 we set out for Lipsi. We also had a good voyage there of about 4 hours.

We were very despondent about our lodging there and took the trouble to ascertain on the way to the little scattered village that a church was open in case we wanted to return there. The real harbour was the other side of the island but we could not get there. We all were laden. T had a basket of provisions and an earthen pan containing the lamb's fry. I clasped a large flat loaf in my arms. The path was very smooth and not very steep and we crossed the island in half an hour, getting into deep and unavoidable mud near the village.

This is the first place where the people have not been hospitable, at least in word. The man at the café said we might sleep in his shop, but there seemed no other place and no one offered anything though we said we would pay. A Kalymnos man begged for us and M took the café man out and argued with him and the result was that we got a little room at the back with a window about 6 feet from that of the café where they drank and played cards all day long. They are certainly very idle people.

We remained there 2 nights and caught fleas and did not read, for our books could not be got from the ship. From the bible to the Chronicle[24] we were utterly bookless and surely, before we knew the alphabet even, we can never have been 48 hours without seeing the outside of a book in some language. I fortunately always have a little bit of needlework in my pocket.

In getting the boat round they nearly got on a rock and then lost one anchor. We went to all the ruins and were glad to find that there was nothing of such interest as to keep us in Lipso. On Friday the wind turned N. again so we gathered up our goods in a hurry and set off for Patmos about 12. I travelled

---

[23] Mabel's Greek cheese of choice.
[24] This *Chronicle*, of course. The references to books and needlework are a pleasant reminder of the times.

away bearing a plate with some *mysethra* on it. We had 4 hours' sea again and at last had to tack a good deal to get into the bay.

I hate tacking. This bay is only separated from another by a very narrow isthmus and the island is divided in 2 nearly equal parts. The monastery, which looks like a great castle and is surrounded by the town, is about ½ an hour's climb from the sea. The cave of the Revelation is a little way down off the road. We came straight up here guided by a funny little Deacon who we met on landing. We had 2 letters, one from the Prince of Samos and the other a circular to all the abbots of Patmos and Samos from the chief Archimandrite in London, Jeronomos Myrianthos.

These were sent before us by a man but did not arrive before 2 little boys, one carrying the pan containing the heads of 2 fish and their tails, and the other a little common earthen brazier, had audaciously taken them into the Abbot's own house. We found him scolding them and he really seemed very cross with us. We begged his pardon and said they ought to have kept these things at the door while we visited him and our servant was seeking a house. We drank coffee, ate jam and were introduced to all the dignitaries, and at last the heart of the Holy Egóumenos was softened and he said it would be hard to find a house at this hour and they would manage well enough for a night and we should be put in the Cell of Gerásimos. We were delighted, and still more so when, on being led up many stairs and over and under many places, we found the cell consisted of a little house containing a hall, kitchen, bedroom for M, a sitting room 25 feet long, and a bedroom within for us.

T slept in the monkish bed. M is charmed with his kitchen and is never still. He went out yesterday morning, 6th, and shot 3 partridges and a little bird and I took 4 photographs inside the convent with one ragged old monk and a few deacons. We inspected the library and saw some beautiful old books which the awkward old *Bibliophylax* turned over very roughly. We had a visit early from the old Egóumenos and we asked to stay till Tuesday. I visited him in the evening.

We also took a walk in the town and met a little tailor called Janko who has undertaken to seek for various things we want. He took us into several large houses furnished with Dutch cabinets and chairs, a little inferior Chinese china and some of the most awful daubs of pictures ever seen: their owners or their fathers having been merchants. We also went to a nunnery. The nuns were in church in long black coats and skirts and their heads in black handkerchiefs. We went to visit the Lady Superior but she was ill in bed. Soon however we were taken to her bedroom and there the poor old thing was in all her greasy old black clothes. One nun, a fat rosy person of 55, was delighted to find we could talk French and carried me off to her cell, 3 very comfortable rooms and she told me she had been brought up in the French convent of Santorin. She spoke very well. T and Janko joined me after they had visited the other cells, some poor, some otherwise.

Sunday [March] 7th. Tremendous S. wind and rain so we did not get out till after noon. We had a most peaceful morning. We took a little stroll on the roofs before luncheon and then went down to the Cave of the Apocalypse. The highway was a roaring brawling stream with eddies and waterfalls but with galoshes quite passable.

The cave is one of a great many which we have not yet explored. It is the highest up and must have been a wide, rather shallow, cave with an overhanging roof. Of course now it is not very easy to see the shape as it has divisions to make it into a church. In fact it is a double church, one side, the right, the cave and the other a church of St. Anna. Of course no one could really know which cave St. John saw the Revelation[25] in because the island had been uninhabited for so long before the Holy Christódoulos came here with his monks to make this monastery.

This cave has in the floor some little cut channels to let water run off. Now only a little water flows when it rains and from a little cavity near the floor, where they think St. John was silly enough to put his pillow. And there are some holes high up which look as if meant for lamps, so that this cave may have been inhabited. Of course every crack in the cave has some marvel attached to it. An old ragged woman, a most kind creature, the sister of the Papas who keeps the place, bawled all these things at the top of her voice and gave us some little chips of the cave and after we left took us to her house, part of a once flourishing but now ruined school. We both agree that this is the most interesting place we have yet been in.

When we returned to the monastery we were shown the skull of St. Thomas, bound in silver, and that of 'Antipas, my witness, my faithful one',[26] who was of the Church of Pergamos, enclosed in silver. St. T's skull is in a huge silver cup. We saw the walking stick and shoes of St. Christódoulos. His real name was John, but he took this name, i.e. Christ's servant. We saw his embalmed body with a sort of box to show his head. Then we retired up to the roofs again and T and M went out and I had a visit from the Holy Pro-Egoúmenos, who was Chief last year and will be next. He remained with me about half an hour and was very happy looking with all our things. He caught sight of the legs of my bed through the door, so we hurried into the bedroom that it might be thoroughly explained.

---

[25] Theodore, too, had a minor revelation on Pátmos. He later wrote an article for *The Nineteenth Century* (1888) entitled 'What John saw on Patmos', in which he suggested that the Apostle witnessed Santoríni erupting in AD 60.

[26] Revelations 2:13. This relic survives still and is celebrated in the Monastery of St John on the first Sunday after Easter.

Monday [March] 8th. T and M are gone out again this morning and I am quite happy alone. We might really as well be in our own house as in the very top of this castle. I rather expect the Egoúmenos, but not till evening as the Greek Lent begins today, 2 days before ours, and there is much to do in Church. I shall be very sorry to leave this, but if we dig this would be too far off. By the bye, Demetrós never turned up.

In the afternoon T and I walked and scrambled and paddled to a little church called the Garden of the Saint Képos tou Osíou, i.e. Christódoulos. It was dreadfully wet and we were glad to get home, climbing up the narrow rocky lanes, in one place 10 inches wide.

Tuesday morning, [March] 9th. A new plan came into T's head in a dream! So we quite determined to go to Kalymnos and began to pack in order to be off that day, but the weather was too bad to leave the island so we settled down for another night and in the meantime changed our idea and went back to the plan of visiting Ikaria or Nikaria next. We went down to the 'Apokalypsin'[27] again and there bought a very pretty old *eikon*, much better painted than most. The first time we bought a little wooden pot, very like a Scotch quaich[28] which the old woman kept incense in.

We had a visit from the Pro-Egoúmenos, who had come to show off our things to the Ekonomos and one of the Papadhes, who photographs with wet plates. The art of photography with dry plates had to be explained to him by me. It is a thing I am ill-fitted to do in English even.

Someone in Patmos has now a good umbrella, for T left his in some respectable house where he had been visiting, but everyone denied it so we had to come away without it.

Yesterday, **Ash Wednesday, [March] 10th**, we actually did leave Patmos, with great regret on account of the comfort and quiet we had enjoyed. The floors were not washed and the rooms were bare but, as the owner had betaken himself to a hermitage, the native fleas had died. But we found digging would not repay so we said farewell and departed, I on a small ass and stirrupless and perfectly devoid of any kind of bridle. We got down to the harbour and there a fearful shower came on and we had to scramble about ¼ of a mile to our captain's house.

There we remained about an hour and a half, not at all sure of getting away at all, but at about 11 we did get off and were a very long time getting out of the many capes of Patmos. We were free of it about 1.30 and then we found the wind not very good. Nearly every island appeared to be having a shower bath but we luckily escaped. We had to pass through a group of small islands, the

---

[27] St John's famous cave, of course.
[28] A shallow drinking cup, typically with two handles.

Phourni, and as a great black storm was seen in the N., it was deemed prudent to take shelter in one of these called Chrysie, where we arrived just at dark in torrents of rain.[29]

Oh! such a night as we passed! And no hope of any amelioration for tonight. The 'Potter's Bed' of Siphnos was kindly thought of .[30] The potter *had* a bed and his floor was clean flags. Well! We scrambled up the rocks to a little house overhanging the sea on the left hand side of a little valley where the few cabins are scattered. It is the size of T's dressing room. One corner has a high fireplace, for it is the public house of the place, where, however, neither wine nor spirits were to be found. Another corner has a most filthy sort of bunk of wood across it. The other end has a raised shelf with a good many casks on it; some benches round and the floor partly uneven rock, partly damp earth. One of our old sailors is father-in-law to the old owner's son and they always address each other as fellow father-in-law (Συμπέθερε μού)

Here we sat 15 individuals all smoking but myself; a couple of dogs and some cats; the fowls who joined the party today being asleep. We could get nothing from the ship but my bed and a little food. We opened a lobster tin and ate some *mesythra* we had brought, and after a couple of hours everyone kindly left us to make the best of a very bad bargain.

The bunk was resigned to M. T made a bed on the shelf with his Ulster[31] and some rugs and I lay in my hammock in the middle. I kept my clean white bedclothes in the sack. As I was fully dressed and just had my fur cloak over one and my muff under my head: the pillows being on board, we were all devoured by fleas. No one slept and the cats careered about.

However horrid it was, and will be tonight – any port in a storm and one could but be thankful neither to be wrecked, out in the boat in the storm, or taking refuge with no roof over us, for these islands do not look nice soft snug ones to sleep on bare. At 5.30 our host arrived and banged at the door. M, who had done more undressing than most of us, opened the door and the old man came in and lit the fire. We lay still till 6 and our host changed his clothes so we thoroughly understand how Greeks dress. I have a little comb so we did our hair, put on our hats and boots, both washed by pouring from a mug, and dried ourselves on our pocket handkerchiefs, and there we were dressed.

T has been to the ship and we have a towel for tomorrow but nightclothes would be quite superfluous. We have visited every house. It is now sunny but too

---

[29] The tangled Foúrni islets lie in the triangle formed between Sámos, Ikaría and Pátmos. The party have landed at modern Khryssomiliá. On the island they acquire a fishing lure of waxed wood and mirror-glass. It is now in the Pitt Rivers Museum, Oxford (1888.37.1).
[30] Mabel is alluding to their night on Sífnos in December 1883. See p. 13.
[31] Their indispensable sleeveless coats.

stormy to start and having brought a rabbit, brought a lobster, got some milk, our first on our travels, we are not doing badly eating off our knees, or anyway we can. M is out shooting.

(About 7 p.m.) We lay on the hillside, rather damp and stony, and rested most of the afternoon. At 6 we dined, more lobster and rabbit, some fresh *mesythra* and a glass of goat's milk and a cup of coffee. So you see we had no bad dinner but we sat on a high bench, meant to sit cross-legged on, with our toes on a table about 6 inches high. Our dish between us, our plates on our laps, M waiting on us and 11 people staring. After that M went to dine on the shelf where T sleeps and divided the attention. It will be near 10 before we shut up shop, literally, and then we are all going to fill our persons with Keatrige Powder and again sleep in our clothes. I would take my hat off now but there is no place to put it. Old Panagiotis, our host, smokes perpetual *narghilehs* in the middle of the room.[32] We hope to start at dawn. Here we sit by a dim light and the horrors of night setting in.

Saturday 12th [actually March 13th]. We did start at dawn. The night was passed in the same manner but somewhat more peacefully, the cats having been chased out, and much flea-powder used. It seemed like the repetition of an evil dream to see T put on his garters, button his knees, and [blank], be dressed and the same toilette of the old man [sic].

We started at once with 2 women and a baby, and after 3 hours of a rough passage we reached Ikaría, so called because Ikaros, whose wings melted off in the sun and who fell into the Ikarian Sea is buried here. There is no harbour of any kind so no ships can remain here. I find we made a mistake in fancying ourselves to be in the Phournoi Islands. We were on one of the Korousi, (Koroussi is the ancient name, Phournoi the new) a group so close to the other that it is a wonder they have separate names.

We are now in the house of the son of the father-in-law, our sailor. It is a room up an outside stair. One end is portioned off with a very open fence about 8 feet high and has a very substantial door. Why they sometimes have a fence and a door and sometimes a wall and a gate, I know not.

We were instantaneously visited by the Doctor and soon after him by his wife and daughter. They say 'he is an old evil-doer' and he wishes to travel over the island with us – but we won't have him. T has visited the Kaïmakam[33] and I have a sleep; we are rather worn out with our late hardships. T, when unpacking, expressed himself delighted to see his dear old nightgown again.

This is a hard island to travel in as the mules are few and in some parts there are none as the ways are too bad for them and the distances are great. We had

---

[32] 'Turkish' bubble-pipes. The smoke may have acted as insect repellent: the Bents relied more on Keatrige's patented flea powder.
[33] Local governor.

another visit later from the Doctor and his daughter. T had just enjoyed himself with a kettleful of hot water and I was doing ditto, and hot water is too rare for me to hurry over the performance, so I quietly talked through the fence and continued my operations.

We had an excellent night and before we got up had a very pretty sight each on our side of the fence. A little round ray of light came through the shutter and represented the sun, and on the whitewashed wall we could see the sea glancing and dancing. The rocks and distant islands and clouds all upside down. We could hardly make up our minds to get up.

[Friday] March 12th. We have had a very fine, but cold, day – no window glass. We have been for 2 pretty walks. One was about ½ hour along the sea, or rather, high above it towards the N. to a place called the Therma. We scrambled down to a little bay and round a corner over wet rocks in a cave and under the sea bubbles a little fountain of such hot iron water that a man was once scalded to death. It is 100° Fahrenheit.[34]

The other was to a little village, scattered like an English one, called Panagia Evangelistría/Annunciation, up a hill inland. We paid several uninteresting visits there. After dinner came the Kaïmakam, an Albanian, and a Turk. The former could speak Greek well. The Kaïmakam made himself most pleasant and left saying tomorrow morning he would give leave in answer to T's written request to dig.

[Sunday March 14th] This morning we were, about 7, going to start for one place or another, according as the wind suited, by boat, as the land ways are too difficult, but in the course of 3 hours we changed our plans several times and this evening are here still, after a day of some excitement. M went for the permission to the Kaïmakam who lives next door and the Kaïmakam refused to give it so T went and offered him money; he had had presents, but this, to everyone's surprise he refused and told T he would prevent his digging or even visiting any ruins – T told him he was an Anglos and therefore could not be prevented travelling where he would, etc.

After all this it was settled that it would be useless to remain here, and, hearing from an Astypalitis, Giorgios Morphino, a favourable account of his native isle, we settled to go there and a boat is engaged to start early tomorrow morning, the ship's papers being made out for Kalymnos! to deceive the Kaïmakam. It is between 50 and 60 miles and we shall have to sleep on board *if* we go.

This horrid old Dr. Andreades is, I believe, at the bottom of it all and I believe he plans to make private diggings himself – he pays us frequent visits. The Astypalitis advised, and it was done, that T should write to his most

[34] 37.8° Celsius. August temperatures often exceed 40°.

excellent worship the Kaïmakam and say that as he had refused his written request to dig for the English archaeological societies and was told that he was not even allowed to travel through the island, T begged that he would give him this refusal in writing to show when he got home. 4 stamps were affixed to this as to the request.

The Doctor was annoyed and the Kaïmakam said he would give the answer this evening, but now he said to M, who went for it, he should give it tomorrow morning. T instantly went and found the Kaïmakam at dinner but could not extract it so he demanded the *teskerehs*, or passports, from one island to another and got them. I do not believe we shall go tomorrow as there is every chance of a calm. The inhabitants are very angry with 'that dog', for preventing them earning money. The sum began with £1000 and had got to £200,000. There have been excited little meetings. We had a visit of 7 or 8 of the judges, advocates and their families, who amused themselves with our belongings.

The Astypalitis called about dinnertime and was asked to join us – a magnificent repast of pease soup and 2 courses of kid, boiled and stewed, and walnuts and honey. He is a nice little advocate.

T saw the sunrise in his 'camera obscura'[35] this morning.

If they only knew it is almost more amusing than annoying to have such a fuss made about us.

Monday [March 15th]. We went to bed in a very doubtful frame of mind but are so accustomed to these ups and downs that we slept in peace and this morning, as a Greek calm seemed to have set in, we did not get up earlier than usual, about 6, and then made every preparation for a night at sea, with books, blankets, food, etc.; everything we could think of.

The ship was put in the water and ballasted and it was thought we would go, but then the wind changed and there was for many hours uncertainty. The ship cannot now remain here as there is no harbour and if we do not start must go to the Phournoi Isles to shelter and the question was whether we should go in her, live on the ship and wait until we could get to Astypalaia, or wait here till she returns for us. We could not leave Agíos Kyríkos as we must not waste the opportunity and we can go nowhere by boat on account of the wind, or by land because it is 6 hours on foot to the nearest place. Then we thought of going to Vathý in Samos and all were disgusted with the idea. The steamer which could take us to Kos, whence we could get to Astypalaia, is most irregular and we might be a fortnight there in great discomfort.

It feels like 2 o'clock and M has gone to make luncheon, but it really is ½ past 10. We have decided to go to Karlóvassi in Samos and shall start about 12.

---

[35] Mabel is referring to the accidental trick of the light effect they both enjoyed a few paragraphs previously.

In the meantime they are in a nice fright here. Cassim Effendi now refuses to give the written refusal and his friends are telling him T is going to prosecute him in Chios. The Doctor came here and asked T why we did not go and visit him in his house and T snubbed him rather. He has been telling M that he (M) is a civilized man and he can speak to him and asked him if the Chios notion is true. M says we have not told him anything but he can very well take in that this must be T's idea – i.e. to inquire into this new law which forbids travellers to pass through an island.[36]

M says he will make the Doctor come that T may cram him with terrors for Cassim Effendi. There is talk of shooting the Kaïmakam! We wrote some letters yesterday but find they could not go to the post for 13 days, so keep them.

Vathý, Samos. **Tuesday, [March] 16th**. We eventually left Agios Kyrikos at midday on Monday and in 8½ hours reached Karlóvassi in Samos. We got a horrid room at a café. Yesterday morning we went on foot to the 3 villages of Palaio (Old) Karlóvassi, Meseon (Middle) and Neo (New) Karlóvassi, and visited the Vorgias family with whom we had stayed in '83 in Meseonkarlóvassi.

We settled first to wait for the *Roúmeli*, which will go to Kalymnos, and then at dinnertime determined to go to Vathy, by the little *Giorgios*, and wait there for the *Roúmeli*. So we went to bed at once and slept and caught B flats till 2.30.[37] We then were hurried on board but did not start till 5.30 and got here in about 2 hours. We heard that nothing could be done about the digging till after Easter, so we got everything ready to abandon this island for this year, asking the permission for next, but T has now seen several people who tell him there is not any doubt about the permission and that nothing need be said about dividing the finds, if any, with the Government. So now we have re-arranged our luggage and are leaving things here. It is raining.

T has spoken to Mr. Mare of the rude conduct of the Kaïmakam. The Prince had sent a letter to him after us but we never got it. We got a bundle of letters.

I am most curious to see a young lady of Kalymnos, aged I hear about 16 and just married to a Mr. William Paton of Granholme in Aberdeenshire. Her father's name is Olympites, a sponge merchant and very rich. Everyone has heard of 'O Ouiliermos' in the neighbouring islands.

I took a photograph of a Samiote soldier at Karlóvassi, focusing with a bit of paper. It blew away with all its pins. I have today got my frame back with a very bad glass from Smyrna, but at all events it won't flutter about like the paper.

---

[36] Theodore was apparently seething during what was, for him, house arrest and being '…virtually prisoners for several days in Nikaria' (*Journal of Hellenic Studies* VII, 1886, p.145). He does acquire a souvenir from the island, however, a felt hat, now in the Pitt Rivers Museum, Oxford (1888.37.9).
[37] Bedbugs and fleas. See p. 121 note 68.

Kalymnos. **[Thursday] March 18th.** We were lucky enough to fall in with a clean little English steamer, *Ianthe*, where we had a most comfortable flealess night and a very calm passage here. We started about 6 and arrived about ½ past 12 yesterday. The captain, on our asking to see the charts and saying we had left ours at home, has lent us one to be left at any port here.

This is a very populous town of large houses filled with rich sponge fishers who have a reputation in these regions of being thieves, liars and cheats. We were sorry to hear that Mr. Paton had returned to England 2 days ago, leaving his wife at her father's as she does not wish to undertake the long journey till the summer of next year.

After a very public examination of our luggage by the Turks in a heavy shower, we and the crowd adjourned to the coffee house. Here M was kissed by a friend from Antiparos and we speedily made some acquaintances. I was puzzled by hearing behind my back 'Oh! Mrs. Virginia! how are you? Welcome.' 'Well have we met!' I exclaimed and wondered who on earth it was. This was the schoolmaster from Tilos.[38] We are always having these meetings.

There is no inn but a suite of rooms was given by a jolly old boy whose name I must find out and write down. It is a very cold place, for few broken panes remain to prove that many windows once were glazed, and as the doors have never had any fastening the draughts are great. We lunched off limpets and pina, a huge shellfish, and afterwards went out for a walk.

We were very much amused on landing to hear 'William has returned'. 'No, it is his brother.' 'He is exactly the same.' 'How very like he is.' 'No, it is *not* him.' And these sentences never cease to be buzzed round wherever T goes. At the British Museum they have been taken for one another and a gentleman came and shook hands with and said 'When did you come' and then 'Oh! Excuse me. I thought you were the son-in-law of Olympidis'.

A tall young man just like a Jew in the Constantinople bazaar accosted us in English and said, 'This is the father-in-law of Mr. Paton and I am the brother-in-law of Mrs. Paton'. So on invitation we entered the café and gave our history, in Greek, to the crowd. The brother asked us to come and take a walk in their garden, so we were removed to an orchard of young lemon and orange trees. Chairs were procured and we sat on ploughed beds, damp, so that one had never to forget to be always trying to sit on the highest leg of the chair for fear of overturning. He would talk English which we had constantly to help out with Greek so we sat silently for a long time till I shivered loudly and we were led silently home.

---

[38] From the Bents' 1885 tour of the Dodecanese, this was Kýrios Spirídonos. See p. 75.

We announced that in an hour we would call on Mrs. Paton. Accordingly they prepared themselves. We entered a mud-floored hall littered with broken machinery, up dirty marble stairs with a rusty banister and reached a drawing room where some matting had been thrown down, but rolled up where it could not pass under the chest of drawers. A quantity of pieces of embroidery bought during the honeymoon to Simi and Rhodes were plastered round in an absurd way. The chest of drawers had a green table cover falling over the front of it, over that a large cotton antimacassar and on top a large pier glass smashed in 4 bits, some hanging out.

Mrs. Paton is a fine big girl who might pass for 20 but some say 14. She had a pretty new dress, quite out of keeping with the place, her wedding ring and a splendid diamond one on her middle finger and a pink coral one on the other middle finger. Her face is good looking but not very pretty. She was very quiet and very much more ladylike than her sister, a coarse rough girl with a dirty snuff-coloured handkerchief on her head, a loose black jacket and a green skirt, much too long in the front. She brought us coffee and jam and seemed very respectful to Mrs. Paton. We could see some dirty little brethren in the general living room. It is very sad to see such relations for an English gentleman.

We have been warned not to go to Rhodes as there is a Pasha there who is well aware of our digging in Karpathos and angry that the packing cases were not opened.[39]

There is little doubt that the big pot the workmen stole from us and buried is here. T and M hearing the description went to see it but some lies were told so they did not succeed. The Kaïmakam sent for T this morning and pitched into him well and asked him many questions as to his intentions. Truly the balmy days of excavators are over.

A certain Mr. Logothetis, who is the richest man in Astypalaia and who has a daughter who he hoped I will love like a dear sister, and who has been obliged by M's fawning [?], begs us to dig on his property and is most polite but it is evident he does not wish us to dig without him. We are to send for him if we think the place looks likely. Well! we shall see how it all turns out. It is midday; we are just going to lunch and embark for Astypalaia.

[Sunday] **March 21st** Astypalaia. We did not start till 3, though we were ready at 12 but, of course, the papers were not. We had a very rough but good passage on a large schooner, 5 sailors, us, a *zaptick* (a Turkish policeman) and a man who keeps a café. We reached this at ¼ to 2. 50 miles across open sea, and as usual first went to the café. We only took 20 minutes climbing to the town – fortunately there was a bright moon.

---

[39] See Mabel's previous *Chronicle*, p. 120.

After a meal of our own food, with some coffee, we were conveyed to a small room up an outer ladder and most awfully dirty. A dusty desk or writing table and the usual divan made of trestles and boards with a dirty mattress on it was the only furniture. My hammock was set up and we lay down amid the mingled smells of petroleum lamp and earthen water jar – T had his own bedding.

We went to the café to eat our breakfast, not yet having a fire of our own and hoped for a better lodging, but finally found out this was the best to be got. A woman called Virgó scrubbed under my directions, used much water and got off an immense deal of mud, having previously removed a great deal of loose dirt in her petticoat as a dustpan. Then she left it very wet and was considered done, but I asked the son-in-law of Mr. Logothetis if she might have a cloth to dry it a little and much more mud departed. Now it is raised to the rank of a very dirty English floor – and the fleas did not die.

This book is so full of fleas that it must make people want to scratch themselves, but they are a matter of such awful importance to me that I hope for forgiveness.

We were lent a table, some chairs, a covering for the sofa and some very grand bedclothes for T, so we are pretty well off. M has a kitchen underneath. We live in the greatest publicity. A good view can be had through the open door and we have constant visits.

The women here wear a beautiful dress. Their heads have a long yellow scarf wound round and hanging in loops below the waist, behind and in front, over a little cap covered with beads and spangles and very large earrings of silver; a shirt with embroidery round the tail and very large sleeves like those of Nisiros. These they tie up to their shoulders when at work.

Their dress is made of a fine cherry-coloured cloth; a full skirt, echoing the embroidery of the skirt, down the front is let in about half a yard of blue cotton. Round the tail of the skirt is turned up about 8 inches of course white flannel and above that about 8 inches of the blue, so really there is not so very much red. The jacket is of the same red, square backed to the waist, where it branches out to 2 points which are left open and above the slit 3 big silver buttons all tight together. A sort of bib is worn in front, 5 or 6 inches wide, and down to the waist, embroidered and spangled and sometimes covered with gilt coins and a bit of white calico sewn to the end, which looks as if meant to tuck in but is not.

I photographed a bride. Her head was covered with a sort of mitre of gold and seed pearls and gauze scarf; dress velvet, silk shirt, jacket fringed with immense silver buttons and big blobs of glass which looked crystal, and on the back there was a quantity of silver. 3 pairs of silver gilt and pearl earrings larger than bracelets. She had 2 holes in her ears. I took 6 photographs. I have now a wretched glass but it is an improvement on paper.

The inner part of the town is walled in, a mass of narrow, crooked dirty passages, some about 16 inches wide. Altogether there are here in and out 400 houses. The people are friendly and pay many, many, long, long visits, very good for our tongues, but tiring.

On **Monday [March 22nd]** T and M left me, T to examine Mr. Logothetis's property and M to shoot. I poached some eggs for lunch and had many other good things to eat. And Mr. Logothetis's only sister, Maria, who lives opposite, came with her daughters, Smaragda and Marigo, to do their work with me. I am sure they meant to be kind but I became very weary of them. After luncheon we went for a long walk together to the Livadhi and they were constantly calling 'Virdzinia! Sit down you go too fast; we cannot cut along like you'. I was so much amused at hearing them use that very expression.

T did not think Mr. Logothetis's field a good place. He is quite a prince here.[40] A quarter of the island belongs to him and *all* the cattle. And all the inhabitants are his relations but even his sister speaks of him as 'Kyr. Ianní', Mr. John.

His only daughter is a very nice woman indeed – Eirenakí, or Renatzí as they pronounce it here. He and his daughter adore each other and she says her husband is a soft man (in island dress) and the only consideration he obtains is being father to the little prince and princess. The sister of Kyr Ianní lives in a small mud-floored windowless hovel with poultry and cats and wears patched, ragged dirty clothes, and her daughter goes bare legged. His brother, Kostí, is a rough but pleasant man who looks like the mate of a ship, and his dirty babes go bare legged too. They have a brother, a doctor in Adalia and no doubt a very smart man.

Kyr. Ianní has more property than money. He has £1000 in a church and his son-in-law told T he had heard of banks, but T quite failed to make him understand the banking system.

Yesterday we paid several visits here preparatory to our intended departure this morning. We went to see Eirenaki, and as her house is on the same pattern as the others here I will describe it. About 6 feet from the end of the room is a high wooden settle with a step. On this at one end is a trunk or chest. When you have gone up the step, up the settles and on to the chest, you have only about 3 feet to climb to get into the bed. Care must be taken not to fall through the valance into the kitchen part of the room.

---

[40] On nearby Sámos the Logothetis name was a prominent one. Lykourgos Logothetis (1772–1850) led an uprising against the Turks in 1821. The remains of his 'tower' are still to be seen in Pythagório.

When you are in the bed there is a sort of closet at the end of it, the outer side of which is a kind of dresser for plates and under which is the entrance to the kitchen. No man's house is his castle here, or in other islands, because all the tag rag and bobtail rush in wherever we go and the mistress says 'Go out! Go out! Children!' But they always stay. They screech at their children a good deal but they never obey.

The old Bishop of Malatyeh, having travelled as far as Lyons, has come to the conclusion that the children of Europe do not cry so much as the children of Asia, but they seem much the same.

We were all ready to start when the wind changed and became contrary and very violent indeed, so here we are, the house rocking and no hope of departing tomorrow.

Friday, March 26th. Here we are still. The wind has been banging and rattling night and day and these 2 days we have to keep our shutters shut. The house quakes fearfully and wind comes in at all sorts of cracks. It is not very lively; we are now hearing a good deal of gossip. People seem very jealous of Kyr. Iannί and say he is a most mean man to his relations, but I heard from one woman that they never lend anything without taking a pledge. Another funny thing that they wear their skirts wrong side out every day and right side out for great feasts. The white flannel border that I have described is the lining.

We are rather under a cloud here with one family for the supposed embezzlement of seven Turkish pounds. Giorgios Morphinos, who we met in Nikaria,[41] gave us letters to his wife and then asked T to carry Turkish pounds, for which T gave him a receipt. He then wrote another letter to his wife and gave it to Theodore. At the last minute Theodore said 'Now we cannot go straight to Astypalaia but must go round by Kalymnos and Samos and we might not get to Astypalaia before you do, so what shall be done about the money?' He said he would have it back, so requested the last letter and opened it, took out the receipt, returned it, put the letter in another cover and off went we. On getting here we delivered the letters and had numerous visits from Mrs. Virginia Morphino's mother and at last she asked for the money. We explained but in the letter Giorgios said he wasn't sending 7 Turkish *lires* and no explanations would satisfy her. And Mrs. Virginia has never been near us. Her husband was to be here in a week from now so we shall be cleared.

Sunday, March 28th. Two days more of this wind have gone by and we are now at the end of the 5th day. There is an idea that we may get away tomorrow but they say there will be a difficulty about collecting passengers and we may not start till late. I do not much relish a night on board. There

---

[41] The island of Ikaría.

is a little cabin with 2 bunks and about a foot and a half in height and 2 cats and 2 dogs on board. On our way here a cat got into the cabin and finding there was some fish in one of our baskets, tore the Turkey-red mouth of it and devoured most of the fish. M threw away all the remains he could find at once, but on arriving here some fragments tumbled out. He surveyed them then with satisfaction, murmuring 'They can be cleaned', but I am glad to say they were not presented to us.

I do not believe we shall start tomorrow.

It was a very evanescent satisfaction to me next day to have been the only person who thought we should remain, but we never got away till Wednesday, March 31st, when we reached Kalymnos in 9 hours and remained the night with no adventures but that I was given a very nice sponge.[42]

April 1886 – Sámos

[Thursday] April 1st. We started again at once in the same schooner finding no steamer was expected for a week or so for Tigani in Samos. As the wind was not favourable we could not go direct but had to get over to the coast of Asia Minor first. We set up my hammock in the hold and M and T made beds on the ballast with sail, etc., and there we made a spirit fire to heat our food.

We had a very rough time and next morning at dawn were near Agáthonisi and were a very long time in getting away from it. We nearly lost our captain more than once. First he was loosening sail and the sail was blown over the water and he had fortunately the sheet in his hand and did not get more than his feet wet with dancing in the sea.

The second time was more serious. The bowsprit had been ducking under water and so perhaps was weakened and the captain went out on it and it broke and he went under the sea twice before he was dragged in. We had the bowsprit shortened by 10 feet: everybody was terrified. I did not see it I am thankful to say.

At last we could get no further as a regular hurricane was blowing from the north, so we went near enough to land to cast anchor, somewhere south of Cape Kanapitza (Willow) at 10 o'clock a.m. The wind banged down the mountains at us all day and we tossed about as waves bounced under us. I lay on deck with my head in a big shawl to prevent its being blown off and the only variety all day was meals.

We had all the exertions of a voyage and none of the advantages. At dinner we were not extravagant enough to open some sardines as we began to wonder

---

[42] Kálymnos was the centre of the thriving natural sponge industry.

how long our food must be made to last. We remained at anchor 16 hours and at 2 a.m. we started again and had a tremendous sea. When we awoke we found the hold shut down and were at first indignant, but when it was opened and we found how wet things had become before we were fastened down. I made a very good awning over my hammock with my waterproof cloak which quite saved me from wind and wet. I felt just as if I were at sea all alone in a tiny boat. Sometimes I was on my head and sometimes on my heels and my air cushions enabled me to roll up and down the hammock as if I were on rollers.

On waking I soon clamoured for my breakfast, but T having peeped out announced we should have it on shore, for we were just in port. We called at once for Kostandinós, who lives next door to Mr. Mare's, for the key, but for the 3rd time the key was away!, gone to the Chora, so we prepared to go to the *kafeneion* to eat, but Kostandinós, who had come out fully dressed but washing, took us into his aunt's house.

She was arrayed in black and wept bitterly on seeing us led into a sitting room with furniture, pictures, looking glass and table covered in black cotton. She told us 'the house was used to receiving guests, but now she was in mourning'. We felt most awkward and thought it must be the day after the funeral, but soon found the funeral had taken place in '67.

We sat for more than 2 hours on a sofa and were given coffee, but finally got Kostandinós to fill up the teapot of the previous morning with water, so we had tea, eggs and bread and were very glad when M, who had taken a mule, came with the key. We thought the house most clean, comfortable and everything that was nice and we wondered how we could have called it a barn.

The pleasures of the toilet were much revelled in and we after luncheon went to Vathý. I rode sideways on a man's saddle and was neither safe nor comfortable going down steep rocks in a high wind with the horse stopping and shaking his head. I was nearly blown off, so I made T walk beside me to catch me.

We went to the 'Kerketeos' inn, better than the 'Samos', and got a lot of letters. T at once asked if the leave to dig was ready and there was much prevarication for 3 days. All sorts of reasons, which did not agree with each other, were given for refusal, and at last T threatened to leave and not spend the money in the island, and then leave was given for one month, and 3 times T has been made to write that he will not have any right to anything found.

On Tuesday we came back to Tigani and occupied ourselves settling and trying to get in stores. We had come the longer road through Mytelene and the Chora, where Demetros had been 2 days expecting us. We went to his house, drank coffee and appointed him to be at a certain point with 12 men at 6 o'clock next morning, he being superintendent. This road has fallen into ruins after having a great deal of money wasted on it under the Prince Mousouros.[43] It is very wide and was planned to be 12 metres. There is not a wheel in the island.

On Tuesday we set to work at some graves without much success. M brought us our luncheon as we were too far off to return. In the evening arrived from Vathý Professor Tozer and Mr. Crowder, also of Oxford. Dr. Tozer had told us we might possibly see him. These are very veteran travellers compared to us, for they began travelling in the East in '53. Mr. Mare had directed them to come to this house and luckily for them the key was not absent. M always gave them their meals at their hours and ours did not ever agree. They have a man with them known to M, also beds, basins, pots and pans. They remained till Friday morning when they went to Patmos.

Thursday we still dug among the graves but that day we literally found nothing but serpents, petrified snails, and scorpions, which last caused a great commotion among the men. We dug in another place too without success.

Friday we began digging a trench and Saturday T went off in the afternoon with a man to finish out a grave forbidden by the owner of the neighbouring field. He came back with 2 glass bottles to find me proudly sitting over an immense inscription,[44] of which I had taken a squeeze. We were much delighted at this. Mr. Mare came over to see how we were getting on. We always have a policeman to watch us.

On Sunday we allowed ourselves to lie in bed late but did not care to remain beyond 10 past 6. I washed my hair and had it hanging about and had just got a couple of my buttons of my Ulster fastened when, about 8, the door opened and in stepped Mr. Mare and a Captain Averino from Genoa, who is loading his ship with wine. Fortunately the beds were made and the room pretty tidy though not dusted yet. This is the result of having no bedrooms but sleeping in the sitting rooms.

---

[43] http://www.samosin.gr/photosoldpolitikoiuk.htm (summer 2006) has an interesting photo album of Samian worthies, including a Stefanos Mousouros who was '10th Prince of Samos' between 1896 and 1899 (but Mabel is writing now in 1886).

[44] For 'squeezing', see p. 78 note 23. See Percy Gardner's contribution (*JHS* 7, 1886, pp. 143–153) for a complete account and transcription of this find. In a few pages, the non-specialist can glimpse the level of scholarship, detail, and arcane science that underpinned classical studies and epigraphy at the time. It is a bravura performance, and, of course, no English translation is provided – only a modern Greek transliteration. The reader's knowledge of the language is taken for granted. Gardner begins: 'The chief fruit of Mr. Theodore Bent's recent visit to Samos is the discovery of an important agonistic inscription, which gives a list of victors in some games at Samos, probably the Heraea. The limits of date are given on the one hand by the mention of Apameia, founded by Seleucus Nicator, on the other hand by the absence of all Roman names. The forms of the letters with their squareness and strongly marked extremities seem to indicate the second century B.C.' Mabel does not indicate the find-spot of the splendid terracotta Satyr mask (*c*. 500 BC) that they brought home and gave to the British Museum.

After an hour T took them out and I dressed and then they came back to luncheon and Mr. Mare would talk French to us though he could quite well speak Italian and we all were obliged to speak it to the Genoese. We thought it more civil to stick to that language but Mr. Mare ever returned to French, just because it is a much smarter one to talk. It would be positively vulgar to talk Greek to the Prince. All this time we had to be talking Greek too, for Paraskevoula (Little Friday) the wife of Demetros had come by invitation to see us and had bought her little girl of 10, a walk of an hour, who had never seen the sea before.

This morning, Monday, I came home at 8 for it was so hot and I am not wanted as all the men are in one place, but this afternoon T is to take a gang off so I shall be on duty. A Christian little inscription has been found and Mr. Epaminindas Stamatiadis has hurried over to see the big one.

Tuesday we dug in another place but to no effect so we decided to leave and on **Wednesday 13th [April 13th was a Tuesday]** early we started with 4 well-laden mules in the direction of Karlóvassi on the N.W. of the island. We had a lovely ride up a gorge full of vegetation and heather 8 feet high in bloom but when we were near Pyrgos, four hours, we were overtaken by a heavy shower and arrived wet through as far as my arms and T's legs were concerned.

The man who had been Demarch 3 years ago rushed out to greet us and took us into his house; we had stayed at his stepdaughter's before, the schoolmaster's wife. As it was 6 hours on to Karlóvassi and there was neither a hope of a good lodging in either of the intermediate villages, nor a certainty of where we could stay at Karlóvassi, we yielded to the entreaties that we should stay the night (for which they got 7/6,[45] we eating our own food). It is such a pretty old-fashioned little town. All the houses have overhanging storeys and balconies jutting sideways and a little carving. The situation is charming, quite among mountains, but flat enough not to have rocks in the streets.

We went to see the big new church, Sleep of the Blessed Virgin, to which we had formerly contributed.[46] We were asked to do so and for the sake of the people who had been so kind to us we gave £1, and Phaidros was very angry with us and said it was not nearly enough. We assured him that in England if we gave £1 to a church we had no connection with, it would be quite enough. He said 'they think you very rich and now they won't'. We told him to tell them we were not very rich but he said that would be very mean and did not understand at all when we told him we should consider it mean to pretend to be rich when we are not. He assured us it would be far

---

[45] Mabel is indignant at the cost, about £25 today, without meals.
[46] From their trip of 1882/3. The Church of the Dormition in Pýrgos was obviously partly funded by the Bents. It can still be seen. George Phaedros was the couple's former dragoman; he was, of course, replaced by Manthaios Símos in 1884.

better not to give them the £1, but to promise to send £300 from England and not do it. We felt glad we had not taken his advice on the subject.

The place where the women get water is most beautiful, a stream jutting into the rocky river.

We started early the following morning and got to Karlóvassi about 1.30. We passed through Platanos without stopping but halted at Kondeïka, at a cottage where we once had to stay. The old woman flew out as she saw us pass, pulled me off my mule and kissed and hugged me and gave excellent wine to us and our whole following. I sat in the house with many women on the floor round me while my hostess, between much embracing, told us anecdotes of my speechlessness on the former visit. As I did not write any chronicle in those days I must here write my remembrances of those times.

We passed Kondeïka late in the afternoon and the master of this house poured wine on the ground to Zeus of Strangers and gave us to drink and begged us to remain the night, but we refused as we intended to go to the Monastery of Prophet Elias, about an hour on. When we got there at about sunset we found the abbot away with the keys of the guest rooms and so we had to retrace our rough way through a wood in the dark and ask for admittance in this cottage.

We were kindly made welcome and entering through a room almost entirely taken up by a loom, we went up a ladder to a little room containing a trunk. A sheet was spread on the floor and removing our shoes we squatted on it and then dined off a 4-inch high table. All the world came to see us, including the priest who remained after a mattress had been spread, and when everyone had gone the priest stayed on till we had unfastened our clothes. The following morning people were walking over us as we slept and the priest walked in to witness our toilette.

Well, when we got to Meseonkarlóvassi, we went to Vouria's house and hoped to find a comfortable dwelling but eventually had to sleep in his house, which is unfurnished and undivided into rooms and has holes in the roof and walls. M slept in a corner shut off by some open laths and we had a wretched night, the family coming in before we were up, but they were invited out while I rushed into my raiment. As T was undressing he was just putting down his coat on the cat and removing her found he was just in time to welcome a kitten –

I spent the afternoon on the bed with my work and book, as they seemed to wish me to while T and Vourias went an hour and a half to inspect a place for digging at Panagia tou Potámous, or 'of the river'. He decided it was such a lovely place that we must try there, so on the morning of April 16th we embarked in a boat and in half an hour reached the mouth of a river and soon pitched the tent on a flat place under some olive trees by a rushing river in a most lovely gorge.

We were all quite delighted at the change from the ugly 'frying pan',[47] where indeed we were being fried. It has a pretty view of the mountains of Asia Minor but in itself has no beauty and was very hot the last two days. We should have been ill if we had remained.

Just above our tent is the old church with some old pillars in it; not fine work. Here M made a little stone table and it was our dining room and pantry, but not a very good pantry as the church mice, having plenty of candles to eat, are a thriving race. The cooking was done outside but at pilgrimages people cook in the dirty church. We were a little embarrassed when seating ourselves to breakfast on 2 iron tripods, meant to put saucepans on, when the workmen came in to kiss the pictures but no one else minded. There is a water mill near, shut up at night.

The digging was, I grieve to say, not successful. T thought he had got among some Hellenic cottages; temples, palaces and statues were not to be found, only a large smashed marble pan of unknown use, so after 2 most delightful days in every way but the archaeological, we struck our tent and departed.

We had had awful rain the afternoon before, that is yesterday, and everything was and is still damp, though we had no actual wet in the tent. As soon as the rain began the men were told to dig a trench round us and I found they had cast up earth a foot high on the tent, so it had to be well cleaned at once with the scrubbing brush kept for cleaning inscriptions. It was a horrid sight. When night came we put all our day clothes under the mattresses to keep dry and the tent presented the neat appearance of a sickroom when the patient is not likely to want his clothes for some time.

We came to Kastaniá, passing Tzourlei and Lekka in 2½ hours, I being obliged to ride in manly fashion. When we arrived we found Vourias had prepared his cousin, the Papas, for us so we were kindly received in a very clean house and after luncheon T and Vourias went off to see the supposed digging place. We don't care for Vourias but he is a man of influence and an old acquaintance, so he is our foreman here.

Finding the place hopeless, at ½ past 3 T and Vourias set out afoot for Marathrókambo, to the house of the doctor where we slept long ago. No mules could be had here so M and I remain and T is to send mules early. I shall not hear English till I see him again.

At the river M built himself a bedroom of cypress boughs and all the waterproofs of every kind, just high enough to sit up in and even after the rain

---

[47] Tigáni/Pythagório.

found it dry enough. He travelled here with a large earthen stew pan as a hat and another in his hand.

[Thursday April 15th?] Camp at Kastri, Thursday. I got on pretty well all the afternoon and went for a walk with some women and sat in the open space near the *kafeneion* and addressed a crowd of all ages who asked me divers puzzling questions. I dined alone and at 7 was asked if I wished to go to bed; of course I said yes. So the Papadhiá came and carried out the mattresses, which were folded in heaps, first enquiring which corner of the floor M should sleep, to which I answered '*Exo*'. A coloured quilt and a rather uninviting silk *paploma* were laid out for me and no sheets and I felt rather sad at heart, but I perceived 2 clean sheets kept to lay over the bedding and now thrown aside, so when I had tied the door up a string I bagged them and made a very comfortable bed, though it was eventually visited by diverse insects.

I was all ready to start at 6 as I had begged T to send me mules by then but they did not come till 7 and we left at 8, I being perched on luggage and sitting as on a camel. It began to rain in time to have all the things and us thoroughly waterproofed.

The men brought me a note from T telling me to come straight to Kastri, to encamp and not by any means to allow myself to be detained by the doctor. Something delayed M at the outset and he did not get to Marathrókambo till 20 minutes after me. I was there in an hour, having a good mule. I thought there was no use waiting for him as it was raining and I knew I must visit at the doctor's and thought to get it over by the time he came and go on straight. So I had my journey alone over an awfully steep road.

T was fortunately still at Marathrókambo as it was too rainy for him to go to Kastri, where 16 men were at work, causing great envy to the poor folks of Kastaniá! He was out when I arrived. I was embraced by my kind and gentle German-looking hostess. Last time the doctor was not at home. He is a most good-natured, short, fat man with bushes of black hair.

We had to remain the night as it poured all day. They have a drawing room and all the place is carpeted with drugget.[48] The furniture quite Germanic.

One of our visitors was a photographer who came to see my camera and went into ecstasies over my lens, so much so that he begged to borrow it and I have left it with him. We developed 3 or 4 of my plates which seem to be very successful.

The bedroom was so small that we had to dress with the hammock on the bed and had bugs and fleas to fight with, also an awful smell in the house

---

[48] A floor covering made of coarse woven fabric.

which gave me a headache and I am sure is killing the two dear little children, Evdhochía and Iannis. Evdhochía is 6 and stays up till 12 regularly.

It rained hard about 4 next morning, but as it became fine we determined to go to Kastri and so we did. It is near the sea. We went through lovely flowering shrubs and among big old olive trees. We found the whole place very wet, so we spread the tent and all our things to dry and did not pitch it till evening. The day was very sultry without much sunshine and there were 2 tiny showers. There were a good many starers and it was a lively scene. We have a pretty girl to cook for the men and carry water for them to drink, and more to basket away earth, one called Argyró, or Silver. M sleeps and we dine in a cow-house; he cooks outside. There is also the usual chapel, but no dwelling near.

Yesterday was a blazing day and we put out *all* our goods to roast, and bathed in the sea. The men worked splendidly, much better than the Tigani ones, and unlike them are utterly ignorant about ancient architecture. By the bye, one of our diggers at the Potamos was father to a young Greek sailor who was lately hung at Cardiff for mutiny on board an English ship.[49]

Everyone is firmly convinced that the books we read will tell us exactly what is going to be found. Alas! T has just come up, about 10, to say work is stopped, bad signs having shown themselves in the building; it is useless to go on. I am so sorry for the men. We shall have a half-holiday and T is going to Panagía Kakoperata, or 'bad steps', as you cannot pass in a N. wind, and tomorrow we go to Kalambaktres. After that we have only one more chance, the village of Phournoi.

An entomologist would be quite delighted with our tent. There are spiders, daddy-longlegs, different grasshoppers of various sizes and hues, and large winged ants.

We sent M off to Marathrókambo, or 'fennel field' for clean clothes, etc., and I kept guard over the tent while a soldier slept near the pots and pans. I once stepped over his feet and stole a pail of water. We have to have a soldier with us for the night as there is a very wicked man just out of 7 years' prison. He was going on a *kaïke* journey, which he mysteriously deferred, and it is thought he is going to visit us. We always have one to watch us dig. While M and T were away the doctor came on his way from Kalambaktes and sat in the tent whither he was followed by others, consequently instead of no fleas I had 29 to catch in the night. T went first to Panagia Saranda Skaliótissa or '40 Steps' and then pathlessly to the 'Bad Passage'. He says his way was so bad that he never noticed the bad passage.

On Good Friday I took a photograph of a very large olive tree, one of many as large and said to be 500 years old. M, T, the soldier and the muleteers stood

---

[49] A probable reference by Mabel to the infamous *Caswell* mutiny that occurred in the mid 1870s.

under it and Kerketeos in the background. Then we struck the tent and started about 8 for Kalampaktes, about 4 hours via Agia Kyriake. The way was awfully difficult but the scenery lovely. We are now again on the northern side of Samos. We went entirely round Kerke, a most solid mountain more than 4800 feet and with woods on the spurs. The paths were not more than a foot wide in many places and overgrown with bushes and it was very hard to squeeze through with laden mules; we had 3. The views over the Phournoi Isles and Ikaria were quite beautiful. We had great extremes of heat and cold on the way.

We had heard of a cave with gigantic bones in it, and as the muleteers said they knew the way T and I diverge a good deal and had to leave our mules and walk a good way. There are a good many large caverns which we entered but the one we were specially to visit was an old tomb with some very ordinary bones.[50]

When we got to Kalampaktes we found M settled in a nice clean little house where we enjoyed the most profound peace for the rest of the day. On enquiry it turns out that these big bones are at Panagía Makriné, or 'Distant', in a cave which has a chapel in it. T is gone thither now with a guide for whom he had to wait till 8 as he was busy killing his lamb. Everyone is in a busy and excited state, hungry and preparing cakes and killing lambs. The place has a very sanguinary look as the killing takes place at the doors.

M is gone at 7 to Karlóvassi to fetch luggage left there; it is 5½ hours off and a very bad road. We are now determined to leave this island and give up the village of Phournoi and go to the Phournoi Islands, taking a couple of workmen from here and then waiting for a good wind to sail to Syra. When we arrived at Marathrókambos the Demarch asked to see the leave to dig. T said the Prince had sent it to Tigani but he had never sent it to us as he promised. The Demarch said rather threateningly 'I shall write to the Prince'. T, nothing dismayed, said 'Do by all means'. M heard that the leave to dig was only at Tigani which is quite false.

However this island seems to have been reinhabited by Byzantines, Romans, and moderns till there is nothing left untouched. We are very anxious to remove these bones to England, so T is going to mark the way well and he and M are going tomorrow to get them if they can.

One thing I cannot get used to is being disbelieved. Often when we give a reason for not doing a thing we are cross-questioned and afterwards asked again

---

[50] Mytilini on Sámos has a small palaeontology museum containing fossilised remains of a large prehistoric giraffe-like creature believed to have died out around 10m years ago. Other exhibits include the skulls and teeth of other prehistoric creatures. There are other interesting caves around Pýrgos. Further south in the Dodecanese, on Tílos, there have been remarkable cave finds of pigmy hippo. In 1853, French archaeologist Honoré Victor Guérin de Vaux (1821–1890) excavated on Sámos (*Description de l'île de Patmos et de l'île de Samos*, Paris, 1856).

and we find we are thought to be telling lies. I get very angry when it occurs to me and give them a good scolding, but as yet I have not been on the look out for being doubted.

T started with his food, a 50-foot measure, and a bag nearly a yard long, meaning to carry off the bones if he could, but when he got to the cave he found the aforesaid bones were not those of a Prehistoric giant at all but of a man a good deal smaller than himself. He brought away a bit of a petrified skull and was so angry with his guide that he said he knew of another cave with bones a great distance off. Thither T hurried and found the bones even smaller. We have not yet done laughing at this great Anthropological disappointment. No doubt of their size ever crossed us for not only had we the personal assurance of eyewitnesses but in the book of the French archaeologist Guérin, he mentions having seen 'des ossements veritablement gigantesques'. As to the fear that they might be cow bones there were the skulls of enormous size to be seen.

It is supposed we carry a magnet to show us where to find things in the earth and every book I read is also supposed to tell exactly what we shall find.

[Sunday, April 25th] It is Easter Sunday and great feasting is going on. I have taken 2 photographs, with great danger to self and camera by reason of the steep rocks slippery with needles. We had great difficulty in not slipping down. One was over Patmos and the Phournoi and the other of Korketeos, showing as a dot the never to be forgotten giants' bone cave. An old man called Kyriáko passing by was photographed –

The clean clothes which had been delivered to a girl with a bit of soap to wash in stream were brought home in all the shapes that the wind had blown them and were thus counted on to the floor and left. Of course towels, dusters and garments mattered little but the tablecloth was not a cheering sight and some things had been tied to the bushes by knots which were still there.

Little shy children are invariably told that every stranger is their uncle or their aunt, either Theos or Thea, or Barbas and Tchatcha, so this fiction can be no comfort to the poor things from its universality.

I am writing again from the tent, or rather in it.

[Tuesday] April 27th. We actually got away yesterday after much waiting with a man called Anagnostis or 'Reader', and another workman. We had a lovely ride, continuing our way round Kerke through the sweet-smelling forest for 1½ hours. Finally we descended to the sea at a pretty little bay called Agios Isidoros,[51] where there are a few sheds. We lunched there and embarked in a crowded boat, 11 people including a family of 6 – women and children. All these were seasick for we had a heavy sea.

[51] The party is taking a boat to the Foúrnoi Islands from the tiny (and barely changed) harbour of Ag. Isidóros/Vársamo, below Kalithéa, western Sámos.

I do not think this place has a name. There is a ruin up a very steep hill, now being dug up. This is a bay. The tent is in a river, or rather torrent-bed, which I hope may not be wanted by its lawful owner while we are here. We are delighted to be in the tent once more, though the last 3 days we had spoken much of the superiority of houses and the folly of being so pleased with the tent, arguing that no one lives in a tent unless obliged. But really is has a great feeling of 'Home Sweet Home' about it and all our possessions are most handily arranged and we are so completely out own masters.

A little sheep stall with a door 3 feet high and 2½ wide is where we cook and dine and once we are in it it is quite comfortable. And M very much pleased at having found some straw to make his bed on. The family had to await a boat from the town and lived on boiled weeds of various kinds. Vine shoots peeled are very good and no one hesitated to pick as many beans and peas as they walk in other people's fields as they like. Also the treading down of corn in the ear is thought nothing of here and our path to meals is through a barley field.

I have just been shown a blue and white solitaire-ball, a great talisman called γαγαπόυανδρα[52] by our travelling companion, the daughter-in-law of old Panagiotis, in whose shop we dwelt 2 days in such wretchedness.

As for the digging in that place, it was not promising and the 10 workmen that Anagnostis was to bring did not turn up as it as a great feast day. Furthermore, the two Samiotes declared about 10 that they should prefer to go home, so we wished them a prosperous voyage and in about a quarter of an hour they set sail and we were left boatless. We were glad they had gone when after midday it began to pour and we should only have been wasting money on doing nothing.

We spent the afternoon pretty contentedly in the tent; T painted while he listened to me reading English, and I embroidering while he read Greek to me, and from time to time we tried to cheer each other up by saying how good it was for the crops. The walk to dinner, all among the barley up to our waists was not nice and when we got to our canvas home we found it had begun to drip, so we thought it wiser to cover the beds and M and T with great difficulty got them into the kitchen, which is really a barn. The floor was clean earth with sticks lying about. There were no doors, only a doorway at each end and holes between the stones, and I had great difficulty in not sweeping away the tea-things, etc., all laid in apple-pie order on stones along the wall.

This is the very humblest bedroom we have yet had, but far, far to be preferred to many. We had all our arms in readiness and slept safely in great

---

[52] Mabel has been shown a talisman against the 'evil eye', one of the most prevalent superstitions of the Eastern Mediterranean and Asia Minor. This odd word does not appear in any modern dictionary.

danger of pirates,[53] but we did not know it. Next morning at half past 6, having dressed and breakfasted, we went down to the tent and found we should have been little the worst had we stayed. We had sent a letter to Anagnostis to tell him there was no work here and to fetch us away in his new schooner, the *Agios Menás*, by a little boy who never took it.

We packed and struck the tent and waited till 8, then a little row-boat came with 2 workmen, sons-in-law of Panagiotis, saying Anagnostis was coming with the *Agios Menás* full of workmen. We two embarked in this with our most immediate necessities, my bed, a bag of books, and our luncheon. We met the other ship, took off Anagnostis, and sent it on for M and the baggage. We reached the village[54] in 2½ and M was a couple of hours after us.

We did not have to go to the café this time, for a room was prepared which we have made pretty comfortable with our own furniture. It has 4 windows, no glass, and a door opening on to an outer staircase. M lives in a very dirty place below, and we can talk through the holes in the floor. We dine down there because the dinner is hotter and many plates have to be washed during meals, at least I should say few plates often.

I must say that it is midnight, as we are afraid to go to sleep and are dressed on our beds and armed awaiting the pirates and there is one particularly horrid one that I can't get out of my head. He was standing quite close to me today and looking so wicked.

In the port when we arrived was a large chocolate-coloured schooner and we agreed we should like to have her to go to Syra in, as she is 3 times the size of the *Agios Menás*, but M recognized the ship as a pirate that had done something bad at Anáphe.[55] He enquired and found the inhabitants pretty well aware of the character of it. There are 22 men on board and never more than 9 come ashore at the same time. They have plenty of money and are free handed with it and I saw that they are very well dressed. They have been here nearly a week and I do not see how they could know we were coming as people say, and don't believe it.

We determined to take the best care we could and the people of the house showed us carefully how to barricade the window with stones and the door we put luggage against, and our arms all where we can clutch them. The pirates know we are armed. We wished them to and as it happened, T had to fetch his revolver upstairs and M his gun down and I sat at the window loading mine as some of the

---

[53] This is Mabel's first reference here to 'pirates' and she becomes obsessed with them. (In 1870, at Dilessi in Attica, a party of English tourists were kidnapped and murdered after a huge ransom demand.) In his book on the Aegean, Vincent Scott O'Connor is lucky enough to meet Manthaios Símos and hear his account of Mabel and the pirates. See p. 341.
[54] Mabel has returned to Sámos (perhaps to Karlóvassi on a rowing boat) from their few days in a tent somewhere on the Foúrni islets.
[55] Anáfi in the Cyclades and the home of Manthaios.

pirates passed. I wonder with the Mudir[56] and 2 Turkish soldiers and 50 men they could not force them to show their colours or their papers –

Well! nothing happened last night and this morning, after a very rainy night, we were about to start to dig, having put the revolvers carefully away but the people seemed so perturbed about the pirates that we attached them to ourselves again. The Government [sic] came to interview us as we stood attended by M and surrounded by Anagnostis and 10 men (diggers) and the pirates came too, a villainous looking set they are.

We had to go to the top of a very steep hill and a lonely way, so I quite decided as long as the pirates stayed not to go up alone. Before we started we were dragged most privately into a house and a secret plan was confided to us, i.e. the pirates were to be falsely told that a steamer was expected from Chios and then it was thought that if they were good men and true they would show their flag and papers and if not go, which last they speedily did; we could see them from the mountain tacking. They had enquired where we were going and M had said, 'If we had more money for excavations probably to Patmos, if we had no more money to Chios or Syra'. We were delighted to see them go, for it was feared they might catch us on the sea.

We had our food brought up and these members of the Hellenic Society[57] sat at a Hellenic block of marble while Hellenic Studies were being made on the foundations of a tower. To put the history of this day's digging shortly, we had no luck at all.

Tomorrow is the feast of the Life-giving Spring, i.e. the Blessed Virgin, and there is to be dancing, so the men began tonight dancing at our steps and a very pretty sight it was. They seem a well-disposed family.

We were all in bed and asleep at 10 when we were aroused by their coming to say that wicked boat is only gone round the corner and that it was probable they mean to return tonight. We had not relaxed our precautions. M is gone out with one Savas and locked his door and we can hear the cats enjoying themselves. Aganostis remains outside. I heard at first a lot about 'the woman', that means me, but I was not awake enough to know what. Someone was sent up the mountain to look down and see where the ship went. This is a long winding island and all the group full of bays.

No one pretends to doubt that we are good objects for pirates. How are we to get away? We are dressed to receive the pirates with decency.

---

[56] A provincial governor.

[57] The Society for the Promotion of Hellenic Studies, generally known as the Hellenic Society, founded in 1879 to advance the study of Greek language, literature, history, art and archaeology in the Ancient, Byzantine and Modern periods. Theodore and Mabel were early members of the Hellenic Society, Theodore being on the Council.

May 1886 – Sámos

[Saturday] May 1st. M and Savas stayed down at the sea and climbing on rocks, 4 hours on the watch and then at 2 came to say it was dead calm and now the pirates could not come. So we fell asleep and at about 3 all the dogs barked furiously and we and everyone else flew up and thought they had come this time. There was a great hubbub and finally we settled down again. How thankful we were to see daylight!

I hate pirates. It is only what was to be expected when the Turks withdrew their guard steamers from Samos, Rhodes, etc. We are horribly tired and everyone had had a great fright.

T was to have gone an hour's distance off to examine a spot with the men but does not like to leave me for the whole day if the pirates are here still. I meant to have bathed in a most quiet nook and concealed myself from my numerous friends. T generally when he gets in finds from 11 to 17 seated on the floor round me.

We can never think of camping out again while the sea is so unsafe. We held a council as to how we shall get away and mean to fly by night, for of course the pirates have a lookout on the mountains as well as we. Anagnostis is gone to the island of Themina[58] and divers men have been sent up to look down into the bays and we are anxiously awaiting news.

At breakfast a woman asked me 'Had you really your weapon on yesterday when you went out?' I said I had and she asked 'How did the pirates know?' I told her I had lifted my waterproof with one hand to show them while I fumbled long in my pocket for my handkerchief and turned quite round for the pirates to see. She said 'You did very well! The pirates said 'Did you see that the woman is armed?' and someone said 'Of course. When she comes so far from home she must have the means of protecting herself'.

I was dreadfully tired, and having barricaded as before when night came, I forgot the pirates and slept soundly, hoping they had taken, for one of the spies said he had seen a steamer in chase. Another man said he saw them in the night trying to land men in the little boat, but he fired in the air and they went back to the *goeletta*.[59]

Once more we rose up and packed for one island and found ourselves sleeping in another, and perhaps just as well as the pirate ship is still at liberty. We were going in the *Agios Menas* to a place in Ikaría and another boat with 10 men, and we were to keep the boats and it was quite settled overnight but in the morning they said the people of Ikaría were very barbarous men and

---

[58] In the Foúrni group, south-west of Sámos, close to Ikaría.
[59] One of a number of spellings for the traditional Turkish sailing vessel, the Gulet.

would take their boats and they were afraid, so off we set, fully armed, for Samos.[60]

When we got about an hour from Karlóvassi we met with Vouriás, or Vorgias as it is spelt, fishing so we picked up him and his boat. It is most unpleasant the way they all know that the pirates are after us. The pirates think T has £100[61] and are about right. There are Smyrna people, Samiotes, Chiotes, etc., and their pilot in these waters is Karavás, a Samiote, of Marathrokambo. 3 weeks ago they killed a Samiote near Syra. They have plenty of arms and canons.

Sunday, May [2nd?]. We have found a refuge in a very tumbledown, worm-eaten little old house, but empty and clean. There are 2 rooms, one a kitchen, with no window and divided by a cracked wooden partition, over which we have hung things from the very small room where we sleep. There is a landing with a little sink and there we dine off trunks. On arrival it was thought we ought to make our 'martyrdom' of what we knew of the pirates, so the Demarch was fetched and we were all martyrs. These wretches cost us £1 to the watchmen.

T is gone off to Phournoi village with Vourias, M to Platanos, and I am going to cook my own luncheon. I have had a lovely blue soldier to ask for T, as the *Astynómos*, or town councillor, wishes to see him and also a woman called Kalesperiné, who says she fancies, or has dreamt, that money is concealed in her house and she thinks T, who has so many books, will be able to find it. She asked me if I thought he could, so I said 'Maybe –'

I got into a great fright when she found I could read and write and she said 'Can you find treasure too?' 'No' I hastily answered. 'I don't know how to. If anyone can find them it is only Theodore.' I have promised not to name it to a soul and that T will do his best. I have promised Mrs. Vouriás' mother to go to their house in the afternoon. It is raining again –

Three days has Kalesperiné had signs of this money and she has just brought me 3 hot fresh eggs as a sort of a fee. Imagine what I felt like when accepting them! However next morning she was told by M when he came, when she had dreamt about the money herself, not to get a strange man to find it for her. She went away looking very sad.

I am writing this under a bush near the digging. This is the last cast of the dice and, as usual, we are very hopeful! We are in a large square Hellenistic building

---

[60] The party are leaving the port of Karlóvassi for Vathý again, the main port Sámos.

[61] A large sum to be carrying around. Presumably sterling not Turkish pounds. Coincidentally, in November 1890, the Royal Geographical Society agreed to 'sponsor' Theodore's next Turkish trip to an identical amount. The RGS archive has a letter from the explorer indicating that 'the £100 will I am sure be a great assistance to us in exploring Asia Minor. Yours very truly, J. Theodore Bent'. Was Theodore hoping for a little more? In today's terms the donation would be worth around £6000. (As it turned out, the couple went to South Africa instead.)

and our great difficulty is to find workmen: all are engaged in the vineyards and we have but 4 instead of 15 or more.

Yesterday, Mrs. Vourias' mother lunched with me. It is perfectly true as T says that I entertain my washerwoman most Sundays because our greatest female friend usually begs for that post. Then after sitting some time in the Vourias' house and thinking how thankful I was for our little worm-eaten cottage. I was taken by a party to sit in the large orange and lemon orchard of one of our first muleteers. It was delicious sitting on orange blossom and under orange blossom, with my lap full of big branches of the same, which I longed to bring home for Ella's wedding.[62]

When I thanked for the flowers the man said 'Ah! thank you! *Evcharistó* was the only word you could say when you were here last!' Then he told the assembled company that 'I had understood nothing, thanked whenever they gave me anything, and was never afraid of anything'. I spent an hour or 2 not unpleasantly, for they are very nice people and then I said I must make letters, a mysterious sort of thing which needs great peace. So I returned home and did not get peace till 4 people had examined our beds.

We heard the Prince had come by steamer from Vathý, so went to call. He was out but we overtook the Princess. She said when she heard a few of the places we had been at, 'Vous êtes admirable, madame. Vous êtes admirable', and cast up her eyes. Then said she was sorry not to have seen more of us and proposed that we should return to Vathý at once in the steamer and spend a few days, at that wretched inn I suppose, and would no doubt have been a good deal bored had I said 'If your Highness will kindly wait while we pack, etc.'.

This morning our greatest excitement and a very unpleasant and sickening one has been that a most miserable leper has come from the neighbouring cabins where they live to look on. I will not describe a sight, the like of which I hope I may never more behold. He told us in a very husky voice that he is from Pyrgos, 67, and has suffered 20 years, and says he caught it at Port Said. There are altogether 42 on this island.

Tuesday 4th May. Everything seems to be come to an end, the digging, because after letting us dig a whole day with the consent of the tenant, all of whose barley we bought, said he would let us dig no more. Well! it was more actuated by perseverance than hope that we were going to dig today. The tea was finished yesterday and the candles and the soap of Europe, so this day has been spent very busily sorting what we shall leave in Syra from what we shall take home, cleaning the pots and getting our modest supply of house linen as clean as possible consistently with having to use everything till the last

---

[62] Mabel's niece Elizabeth (Ella) Frances lived into the 1940s. She married J.O. Adair in 1886. Some of Mabel's Hall-Dare relatives are listed on p. 348. See family tree p. 357.

moment, for the house is quite unfurnished. We expect a steamer tomorrow some time to take us to Chios and there was hope to find another to take us homeward.

I now find from description that it was the very pirate captain that was standing so close to me. He belongs to this place and his family are here and *one* wife. They are still at large and were quite close to us on the sea when we were passing hither. Also they have been near our camp at Kastri tou Agiou Gianou.

We saw a man today who has been a sailor and has a limited amount of English and would talk it. He wished to introduce his wife so he did by saying 'This is Mrs. Me'.

I think we are all longing to get home now. That night I had a great escape of a broken leg. I fell through the floor and my leg went as far as a leg could go but as there is no ceiling and I met with no beams, I was pulled out scatheless. It was a great surprise to me. We thought it right to lunch at 11.30 that the plates, tablecloth, etc. might be ready and at 12 we departed for the harbour, leaving the house very wretched, mouldy, damp and smelly. We were accompanied by kind people who never could be persuaded to leave us though we did not start till 6.30.

We got first to Nikaría at 10 and then went down to bed. We had looked around the saloon everywhere for any door that might lead to a ladies' cabin but there was none. The steamer *Dhikitá* has just been built in England expressly 'for the Eastern Market' and with a profound knowledge of the fitness of things. It was not comfortable to the British Female First Class Passenger, but I could not help feeling how very suitable the arrangements were.

The one enclosure in the stern filled the offices of captain's, ladies', gentlemen's cabin, saloon, smoking room and washing place. There was only quite a small table as the passengers usually bring their own food and it is quite hard to obtain any unless you mention that you wish it to the agent when taking your ticket.

The 14 berths were furnished with slippery black American cloth mattresses and bolsters to match, covered with ticking and a very coarse and very dark grey blanket and a coarse black curtain. The seats round instead of velvet were comfortably scooped wood with holes pierced like garden seats. There is no medium between deck passage and 1st class and the deck above the saloon is like a tent.

We called at Tchesméh[63] (or Fountain) just opposite Chios at 4 and got to Chios at 7 o'clock. While we were at Tchesméh it was pouring there and here

---

[63] The Turkish resort of Çeşme, opposite Chíos.

they were being much alarmed by a violent earthquake which did no damage. They must be very much used to them as never a week passes without one. We thought when awakened by a thunderclap last night that we were in for one as it was just the sort of weather and there was a S. wind, as there always is.

Saturday May 8th. We are waiting for the Austrian[64] tonight to go to Athens, the Italian that we hoped to get on by the day before yesterday having broken down.

Yesterday we went to a ruined monastery called Nea Moní, though more than 1000 years old. It was all frescoed and covered with mosaic and had a very good library but is now a complete wreck. T went soon after the earthquake and I thought it had been because of rain that I had not gone but when I got there I found it must have been because I was again 'the Forbidden Thing', as the reviewers of 'the Cyclades'[65] call me. They shouted out that the woman must not enter and they were loudly assured that I would not. We lunched outside and I said I would cover up my face and the monks need not look, but a respectable old gentleman who came out said in French 'tout à fait!' and shrugged his shoulders and said 'no how' must I go in, in Greek. Near the town it is not very pretty but near the monastery, which takes 2 hours to reach, it is very grand; wild rocks and pine woods and streams. Of course I rode.

We returned by the village of Ikariés. We have visited all the northern villages but not the S. or the Mastich[66] villages. A great many houses have sprung up since our last visit, wisely flimsy and with much wood in them and iron girders. The old houses must have been very handsome with well cut stone and arched windows and pretty balconies and pillared courts and fine staircases and all with vaulted ceilings filled up, to support the next floor, with earth which has all fallen

---

[64] The Austrian Lloyd Steamer Company, the French Compagnie des Messageries Maritimes, and the Ottoman Khedivial lines all plied the Eastern Mediterranean; the Bents were frequent passengers.

[65] Neá Moní is one of the great surviving monasteries, founded in the 11th century by the Emperor Constantine IX Monomachos. It was badly damaged by a series of earthquakes in the early 1880s and is still receiving attention to its wonderful frescoes and ornamentation. The reference to the reviewers of Bent's *The Cyclades* is untraced but obviously it relates to Mabel, as a woman, being unwelcome within certain Orthodox church precincts. She would, and pleasant to note, have given short shrift. Relief aid is not new: the British government provided funds to house the victims of the worst of the shocks after 1881.

[66] The series of so-called 'mastic' villages, from the surrounding cover of *Pistacia lentisca* and the highly-valued crop of resin produced by these bushes. There are no *Chronicles* of Mabel's 1882/3 trip to Chíos (and Mytilíni and Sámos), but some of Theodore's later articles describe, in part, some of the couple's experiences on these islands. These include 'Two Turkish Islands Today' (*Macmillan's Magazine*, 1883) and 'In a Greek Family Today' (also for *Macmillan's Magazine*, 1884). 'Some Games played by modern Greeks' is a short piece Theodore wrote for *The Athenaeum* (29 December 1883). In it he describes the games enjoyed on Sámos; one such is a version of cricket: 'Was it only a base imitation of our noble game, or was ours but an improvement on it?'

in and was very dangerous. In the villages and in the town here we rode over many houses at the height of the 1st floor and I saw all the inner structure and furniture sticking in the earth. A good part of the town is in this state now and people are still living in the shanties built immediately by the English and now rather ruinous-looking.

[Monday] May 10th. Hôtel des Etrangers, No 8, Athens. Here we are once more in civilization and very much we enjoy being in our normal state again.

The Austrian Lloyd *Iris* started about 6 and we at ½ past 5 on going on board begged for some dinner. 'We are clearing away now, you must ask the cook' was rudely answered. The cook said 'You must ask the steward. He can give you dinner if he will'. So with the usual difficulty on this line we got some dinner, closely followed by tea where we could review the passengers. They chiefly consisted of a large troop of Stangen's the German 'Cook': an awful lot.[67] They are at this hotel and drink beer between meals in the reading-room and immediately after dinner with their coffee.

The ship was very crowded and I was one of 6 in a full little cabin. I found that by the time I got up in the morning I had been speaking 5 languages in the night – English, French, German, Greek and Italian. I did not get much sleep as I was decidedly 'the neighbour' who had to be always getting up to attend to a young Greek in the next berth who suffered much and literally *groaned* all night and moaned 'O Thée moú!' and had to have the steward fetched often. The only other lower-berther being hugely fat and unable to speak Greek. We did not seem to me to have much storm and all the European ladies were all right, but our table fell over.

It is another fault of the Austrian Lloyd that they have no stewardesses so dressing is a fearful process to the modest female.

Though our luggage was not opened there was the usual scramble for boats, then a scarcity of carriages for the 4 mile drive so we had to come by train and another scramble for carriages but we got here before the Germans after all and rushed to our balcony to make them jealous.

We had great handshaking with Kyrios Ianni and all the waiters and after luncheon took leave of our good M, who certainly 'polemises' (fights) to do all he can to serve us in every way and save our money, and as he says certainly get killed before we did. He returned to Syra by the same *Iris* and from there he will have great difficulty getting home as, since 12 on Saturday, no ship under Greek

---

[67] Mabel is here being fashionably scathing about the patrons of Carl (1833–1911) and Louis (1828–1876) Stangen, who were regarded as the 'deutschen Thomas Cook' of their time. Cook (1808–1892) had started out in the 1840s as an anti-drink campaigner promoting foreign tours. His business ('Thos. Cook & Son, Ludgate Circus, London, E.C.; and branches throughout the world') swiftly expanded into the world 'brand' it has remained ever since.

flag may travel or move.⁶⁸ He would have gone by steamer to Santorini and *kaïke* to Anaphi, so now he must look out for a Turkish *kaïke*.

This 'apokleismos' has prevented us getting our letters from Syra. The ministers have all left but the consuls are still here. It is well we gave up our Brindisi plan as there is cholera there and now a later plan for Trieste is given up because the cholera is at Venice, so we hope to go on Friday to Marseilles.

There is snow on the mountains and it was very cold yesterday but better today. We went to walk in the King's garden, or rather shrubbery, a delightful wild place with all sorts of sweet smells and roses trained high up the trees, and to church at 6.

Cook's agent with a very long face on Monday said he feared a general blockade and thought we should do well to get away on Wednesday via Constantinople. No one could go before Wednesday but we wait till Friday and in the mean time walk in peace about the place we are blockading. There is an Australian here who is perfectly delighted at being blockaded. We think it will be all over soon as the government is changed, but in the mean time silly Greeks have lost a good deal of money over their folly, besides the injury to their commerce.

They have altered the face of the acropolis much by digging and have found quantities of things. We went to see the new statues, very archaic smirking Artemises all with long curls and clad in what I am sure is a representation of the very short crepe skirts worn now today.

We went to the other museums the next day and also to visit Miss Trikoupis. She told us that the kind and smart young man who had so kindly helped me through a cave in Zea 2 years ago is her brother's valet who recognized us as having been at the house in Athens. When he came in with a message we shook hands with him and asked him why he had said nothing but he had no good reason to give. Miss Trikoupis very kindly gave me about a dozen volumes of Tauchnitz.⁶⁹

When we returned we had visits from Lady Valaoritis, her daughter Kyria Kourkomele and Kyria Kyriakoulis Mavromichaelis. We soon found ourselves talking Greek with them. We both felt quite nervous but they were very

---

[68] This *apokleismos*, or blockade, followed the threat issued by Germany, Austria and Hungary, Great Britain, Italy, and Russia to Athens (on 26 April 1886) in the light of continued Greek hostilities towards Turkey. The powers decreed that: 'Since the Athenian Government's answer to the common note of April 14/26 was not satisfactory to the Powers, the said Governments ordered the Commandants of the united marine squadrons to embargo the coasts of Greece for every ship under Greek flag. This embargo should be realised on the date of this communication. It should begin at Cap Maleas and finish at Cap Sounion, and from there till the border of Greece, including Euboea, as well as the entrance of the Corinthian Gulf at the west coast. Any ship under Greek flag that may try to violate this embargo, shall be captured.' The embargo lasted a few weeks until the hostile Greek forces stood down. (http://www.fhw.gr/chronos/12/en/1833_1897/foreign_policy/sources/03.html [summer 2006] is helpful here.)

[69] See p. 55 for the 'smart young man' who helped Mabel on Kýthnos (not Zea/Kéa as she recalls here).

complimentary. Mrs. Mavromichaelis asked us to go to tea at 2.30 next day and I went and after sitting a long time and being given a huge sponge growing on a stone I was taken on a drive and to walk in several nursery and other gardens and was given a huge bunch of roses. Then she took me to her house and gave me some sherbet pistachio nuts and finally left me at my hotel at 7. Later she sent some strawberries and a pot of this sherbet.

At about 10 the steamer agent came to say that there was such a crowd that, though we had 1st class tickets, we should have to go 2nd, but we clung to our tickets and came down to the Piraeus at 6.30 and after some entreaties got a cabin. One great difficulty arose from T's only having asked for 2 beds and the discovery that his friend was a lady caused great amazement to the captain and the Piraeus agent. However when on enquiry I affirmed that I was T's wife they were very civil. When we were fairly installed I could not help shaking hands with T and congratulating him on his marriage, for had he been a bachelor assuredly he would have been in the 2nd class.

There are far more passengers than beds so the ship can't roll and we are having a lovely passage. Yesterday there were few at dinner but today all are up and as we are not to touch at Naples for fear of quarantine we hope to be at Marseilles early on Tuesday.

Our very greatest excitement is chasing our chairs. T says it is a farce having them but I think it causes us emotions which vary the monotony of the voyage. It is about 2 and we have not had a chance of either of them today. The first day one of them was never in our possession at all. I do not mind their being used in our absence but I think it is odd to carry them up and down stairs. We thought we should not want our chairs going home by Brindisi so sent them off long ago, but when I mentioned this to a kind young man on the Austrian steamer who was the last remaining breakfaster when I appeared, he said he and his friend were just going to give theirs to their guide so they were given to us instead.

We had on the whole a very pleasant voyage. I used to demand tea at ½ past 2 and consume it with 2 very pleasant Miss Edwardses, aunt and niece, and Mr. Villiers, war correspondent of 'The Graphic', who used to draw us little Burmese people and fetch curiosities from his cabin.

When we landed on Tuesday and started at 7, or thereabouts, we found the Calais carriage much crowded and when we had passed Avignon, T had forgotten a bag with this book in it and other treasures – to their owner only – so he had to go on to Valence, get out, and return to Marseilles, and eventually got home on Thursday; I having gone on and got there on Wednesday and found Iva[70] and her husband in possession, and now on the 26th of May I am

---

[70] Mabel's sister Olivia (Iva) Johnstone. See p. 348 for the Hall-Dare family.

finishing this with the unpleasant knowledge that T brought home typhoid fever from Meséon Karlóvassi, so we are rejoicing that he is not on his own bed named the *Creaker*.

Now goodbye Chronicle
    don't get lost[71] –

    Mabel V. A. Bent

1886

---

[71] Perhaps a reference to a previous 'lost' *Chronicle*, possibly the 1882/3 trip to these same islands, the Greek mainland and the Cyclades. This could explain why the 1886 notebook is called *Chronicle* IV, but it is actually only the third one in the Archive's sequence.

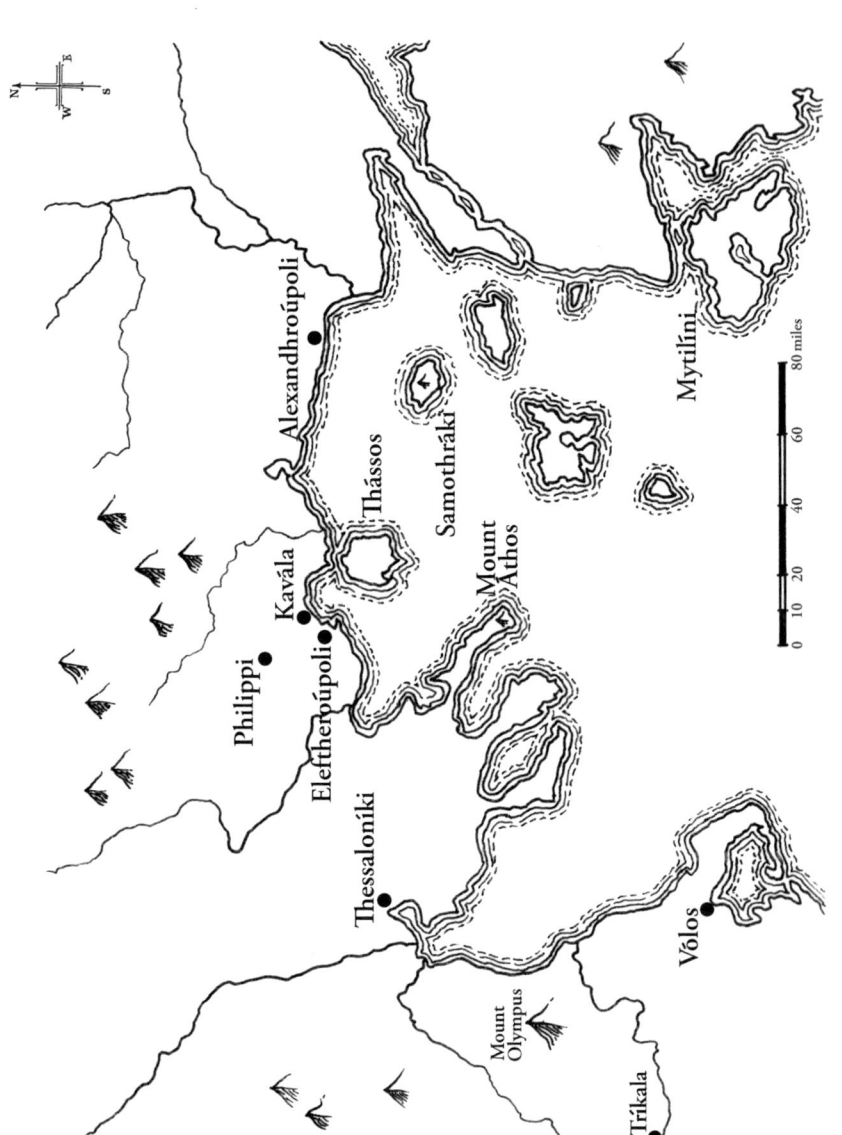

Map 4. The Northern Aegean

Chronicle [unnumbered], February to May 1887:

'Beautiful Floueivia looked lovely… The grey statue on the yellow and orange sledge, and the whole scene was one of the prettiest triumphal processions any archaeologist ever beheld.'

The Bents enjoy their summer of 1886, having cruised along the Turkish coast that spring, visiting Mabel's relatives in Ireland, including their connections in the County Carlow countryside at Bennekerry. The couple were seldom still. Theodore writes from Bennekerry to A. S. Murray at the British Museum, making first mention of a trip he has in mind up to the Thracian littoral.[1]

Frustrated in his attempts to excavate for the moment along the coast of Asia Minor, and Greece, too, being off limits, Theodore's 1887 plans are for an expedition to the northern Aegean. Spectacularly, Mabel begins this *Chronicle*, which she does not number, atop a monastery in Metéora, central Greece. She is nursing Theodore who, again, is ill with a fever. The party of travellers, including Manthaios Símos, is on its way to the Turkish island of Thássos to dig, Theodore having received a grant of £50 from the Hellenic Society, and the backing of the British Museum so to do. In the end, Murray at the Museum needed prompting and Theodore resorted to some name-dropping. In October 1886, he wrote again to Russell Square asking for a reference he could forward to the diplomat Sir Villiers Lister, who, in turn, would take up his case with Sir Evelyn Baring in Egypt. His request to Murray also contained a douceur: 'At the council of the Hellenic Society I spoke about the mask which was without hesitation said to belong to me. Consequently I shall have pleasure in placing it at the discretion of

---

[1] Letter to Alexander Stuart Murray, Keeper of the Department of Greek and Roman Antiquities, British Museum, dated 30 August 1886.

the British Museum. Believe me, yours very truly, J. Theodore Bent'.[2] The mask in question is the excavator's Samian find from earlier in the year; its Museum inventory number is 1886.1204.2. Theodore does manage to secure papers, of sorts, from the Turkish authorities. He hopes he will be allowed to remove his finds. He is mistaken.

Rich in classical references, Thássos was colonized by the Parians (8th century BC), who were the first to exploit the island's gold resources. Theodore was keen to see for himself if there were similar treasures, if not precious minerals then at least beautiful marble sculptures to rival those found on nearby Samothráki – its famous 'Winged Victory' had already been stunning visitors to the Louvre for twenty-five years. Mabel and Theodore take a two-week detour to see the great site she was removed from in 1863. Another attraction for Theodore was the region's Genoese associations. He was a student of the Italian state, whose fortifications can still be seen on Thássos.

Before they arrive in Thrace, however, the Bents make a detour to the fantastic cluster of monasteries known as the 'rocks in the air' (Metéora), reaching the region by rail from Vólos. In these pages we also have Mabel's only record of the couple's earlier trip, in 1882/3, to the great archaeological sites of Tiryns, Mycenae, and Delphi. It was these and other locations, which were in the process of continual excavation (Mycenae so famously by Schliemann in the 1870s), which inspired Theodore to focus his energies on archaeological exploration thereafter.

From Vólos, the party cruises up the wonderful (then Turkish) coastline, with Mts Ossa and Olympus on their left (west), and Mt Áthos in view on their right (east), to Thessaloníki – one of the great, commercial Mediterranean cities. To reach their destination, Thássos, they follow the route of St Paul towards Kavála.

Immediately after their arrival on Thássos, Bent's workmen start to uncover remarkable finds; they concentrate on three sites, two around the island's capital and the other at Alykí on the south-east coast. The couple also make a two-week excursion to Samothráki, but the famous monuments there have already been surveyed by other

[2] Letter to Alexander Stuart Murray, Keeper of the Department of Greek and Roman Antiquities, British Museum, dated 12 October 1886.

European archaeologists. Back on Thássos Theodore finds over forty inscriptions, including an important decree. Several publications cover his important work on the island. E. L. Hicks commented extensively on the inscriptions for the *Journal of Hellenic Studies* (Vol. 8, 1887, pp. 409–438), as did E. A. Gardner in the same volume. The *American Journal of Archaeology and of the History of the Fine Arts* (Vol. 3, 1887, pp. 408 – 506) summarizes Theodore's own reports for *The Athenaeum* of June 25 and July 23 1887, and for the July 1887 edition of *Classical Review*.

Mabel's favourite find, apart from her pet tortoise, 'Thraki', is a statue of Floueivia Vibia Sabina (died around AD 137), Empress and wife to Hadrian. She, like Mabel, was a striking and independent-minded woman. Theodore finds a memorable inscription to her: 'To their mother Phloueibia Sabina, the most worthy archpriestess of incomparable ancestors, the first and only lady who had ever received equal honours to those who were in the senate.' The statute is of some artistic merit, executed around AD 215, but perhaps not quite as beautiful as Mabel would have us believe; her nose and hands are damaged; experts can distinguish her type by her sandals – which are apparently 'tyrrhénienne'. She featured as one of a group of figures adorning an impressive Roman arch. Theodore's strategy is to use dynamite to help clear the site (Mabel reports that he is 'busy overlooking blasting at the arch'), an approach he is to repeat elsewhere and which has damaged his own reputation ever since as an archaeologist. The whole assemblage of the arch is first reported in a letter he wrote to the British Museum (in an undated letter from Kavála), and then in several accounts, including *The Athenaeum* of June 1887 (p. 839).

Despite all of Theodore's efforts to retain these marbles (including a request that the Foreign Office should send in a steamer to remove them from Thássos), the canny Hamdi Bey quietly had them shipped off to his museum in Istanbul. Theodore was enraged, resorting even to badger Sir Evelyn Baring, in effect the British 'viceroy' of Egypt. He similarly petitioned the British Ambassador at Istanbul, Sir William White. Other personalities featuring in these pages include eminent British archaeologists Francis Cranmer Penrose and Ernest Arthur Gardner.

The couple's itinerary for their 1887 season is: London – Paris – Marseilles – Sýros – Athens – Évia – Vólos – Tríkala – Metéora

– Vólos – Skiáthos – Thessaloníki – Kavála – Philippi – Thássos – Alexandhroúpoli – Samothráki – Thássos – Kavála – Thessaloníki – Üsküb/Skopje – Vranya/Vrange – Belgrade – Paris – London. This return journey, overland, inspires Theodore to write an article – 'A New Overland Route to India' – for *Macmillan's Magazine*.

For notes on this transcription the reader is referred to page xxv. Mabel again refers throughout to her husband as T, and their Greek assistant, Manthaios, as M. See the selected Indices of people and places mentioned. This unnumbered *Chronicle* (it is the fourth volume in the Archive, but the couple's fifth expedition in the region) is written in a dark-red leather notebook (180 x 115mm) with marbled endpapers and edges. The front and back covers are tooled. There are 85 lined pages and Mabel has covered 75 of them. Included in the little volume is a letter from the unhappy wife of a minor functionary in Skopje. She implores Mabel to visit: 'Monday morning. My dear Madam, You would really do me a great favour if you would spend an hour or two with me today. Ours is rather a rough kind of home, but I can offer you a cup of tea. I think if you only knew how hard it is for an educated woman to be in exile at such a place as Üsküb, without either congenial society or habitual surroundings, you would come out of charity. May I fetch you about 4? With compliments to your husband, Faithfully yours, Florence K. Berger.' Very much a theme of all Mabel's *Chronicles* is her reporting of the humdrum lives of minor civil servants and ordinary people required to oil the wheels of some empire or another.

This isolation can be imagined as Mabel sits, ministering to 'the prostrate Theodore, who is on the floor with a fever…' perched in a draughty monastery in Metéora. It is February 1887.

[There is no introductory heading or *Chronicle* reference to this volume. Mabel may have written something on the opposite page, but it has been torn out – a very rare occurrence in the long series of her *Chronicles*.]

February 1887 – Thessaly

Thursday February 9th 1887 [Thursday was the 10th]. I have certainly a strange enough place to begin this Chronicle in! and one I never hoped to reach. No less than one of the convents situated on finger-like rocks in Thessaly and therefore called *Ta Meteóra*, or the Meteors i.e. the Airy. This is Agios Stephanos. Most of them you can only reach by being hauled up in a net, but this has a bridge over a deep chasm, 12 feet wide.[3]

Well, here I sit by the prostrate Theodore, who is on the floor with a fever, while Manthaios[4] and I have only colds – mine a very awful one in the head.

But I think I will go back and write that we left England on January 26th, Wednesday, and stayed 2 days in Paris, leaving Friday 28th at night and embarking at Marseilles for our 4th voyage on the *Cambadge* next day.[5]

We had an extremely calm voyage to Syra. There was a poor Bulgarian on board with his brother. He was going home to Philippolis to die of consumption, but, eventually, his death having been announced to us the afternoon before we reached Syra, it was decided, when he revived, to land him there and he died just as he was going to be put in the boat. Even when well, the arrival at a foreign port is always a wretched time, but I think he can hardly have known what was going on around.

We invited two French people, M. and Mme de Villiers, who were going to Athens like ourselves, to be personally conducted thither. They were delighted of course. They were surprised to see many boatmen coming and saying 'Oh! my dear little Mr. Theodore! Welcome! I am come for you!' and to see the greetings of sailors in the streets from various islands and the shaking of hands

---

[3] The Bents are visiting the remarkable group of Orthodox monasteries known collectively as 'Metéora'. Of the many books on them, Patrick Leigh Fermor's account in *Roumeli* (London, 1966) is the one to have.
[4] We closed Mabel's previous *Chronicle* (May 1886) with Theodore ill of a fever and we open this one to find him similarly unwell: he was obviously susceptible to infections of this kind. These are worrying indications and in just eleven years now he will be dead. Manthaios Símos has rejoined the Bents for this expedition from Anáfi in the Cyclades.
[5] In November 1883 (and the year before), the Bents arrived in Greece on the M.M.S.S. *Cumbadge*.

with the hotel keeper, Kyrios Matses and the waiters and the conversations in the Customhouse; and when, after a day at Syra, we went aboard the *Pelops* for the Pireaus, the embracing with the Lorenziadis family from Ios, and the great welcome at the Hôtel des Etrangers at Athens.[6]

We were there 2 days and one night, and among other visits paid one to Mr. Penrose, head of the new English School. In the hotel we met Mr. Ernest Gardner and Miss Venning, both great at 'Hellenic Studies'.

On Saturday **[February 12th]** night we went down to the Pireaus, where we dined and embarked on the little steamer *Ellás*, of the Goudi company, for Volo. The day before was a great dinner on the great training ship *Ellás* in honour of the Heir Apparent.[7] It had been beautifully decorated and lit by Electric light and this evening it was permitted for anyone who liked to inspect all this splendour, so as it was close to our *Ellás* we did so too. We had a poor but clean cabin and a very rough night, and about 2.30 on Sunday reached Chalkis and there we had to wait till the current turns.

We had been here four years ago with Mr. Graham. We had gone to sea to Nauplia and then by carriage to Corinth, stopping at Tyrins, Argos, and Mykene on the way. We had an interpreter, Kostandinos Verviziotes, and a cook with us, and all our furniture, and we could not speak a word of Greek. We had great danger and difficulty in getting to the steamer *Kreta* about one o'clock and when we got there the storm was so bad they could not bring the mails or other passengers, and there we tossed till next morning when we started for Scala di Salona on the N. side of the Gulf of Corinth. Thence we rode mules to Delphi, where we slept in a miserable ruin. We could see light through the roof and the only light in Mr. Graham's part of the building came through cracks in the wooden partition that separated him from us: no window glass and ice on the puddles. We continued our ride, sleeping at Aráchova, Levádhia, Eremókastri, and then Chalkis. When we got there we found that the steamer which would take us to the Pireaus had first to go to Volo, we, after a night in Chalkis, went the round in the steamer, touching at many places.[8]

It is a picturesque town with 4 or 5 mosques and minarets, and the great snowy cone of Mt. Delphi as a background. It was very amusing landing in a

---

[6] See p.38 for this Ios family – great friends to Mabel. The Bents favoured the Hôtel des Etrangers when in Athens.

[7] George I (1845–1913), from the Germano-Danish House of Oldenburg), King of the Hellenes (1863–1913), had eight children with his consort, Olga Konstantinova of Russia. Their eldest son and Heir Apparent was Constantine (1868–1923), who succeeded his father as king. See http://www.glintofgold.org/romanovs/photos/grphoto.html (summer 2006) for photographs of the Greek royal family at the time the Bents were travelling in Greece. They were friends of various courtiers.

[8] These few paragraphs of their trip in 1883 are important for being the only account Mabel has left of their first tour around the great sites of Greece: 'Corinth', 'Tyrins', 'Argos', 'Mykene', 'Delphi'...

little boat, the current racing against us. We crawled up one side of it nearly to the castle which is built in the middle of the stream, then swirled round at a great rate towards our ship again, and then another twist on the back water landed us on Euboea. We watched all the boats go through the same roundabout little voyage.

We had to wait till 7 for the Evripos to turn, when the drawbridge connecting Euboea to Boetia is opened. It was really exciting going so swiftly through such a narrow passage. The moon was bright and the scene most lovely. Sometimes the current turns every 10 minutes, sometimes 20, in fact at every kind of interval and no one knows when it will be or what causes it to flow first one way and then another.

About 8 on Monday 7th February we reached Volo, much enlarged since our day, and went to the Hôtel de France, pretty good for such a place. We visited our consul (de Bri, I think), who has a very pleasant foreign wife and 2 pretty young daughters. They seemed very pleasant people, but he did not seem to have much to tell us about these parts.

M, who met us at Syra, was greatly excited at the thought of so long a railway journey, for we were to start for Trikkala on Tuesday and though the train did not start till ¼ to 9, he wished to leave the hotel, ¼ of an hour's walk, at 7. The railway is only just hardly finished; the carriages very draughty and thus we caught our colds. We had a very windy and not at all pretty journey and were thankful not to be on mules. All the officials of the train are Belgians.[9]

At 3 we reached Trikkala, situated on the Péneios in the very swampy plain of Thessaly, a pretty and large town, but poor and very feverish, particularly at this time of the year. We were surprised at this, so took quinine. We were at a wretched little inn 'of America' – All these inns have as many beds (with each slippers and a comb) put into the rooms as possible, and no one seems to expect a whole room more than a whole railway carriage.

I cannot make out what decides them to say, 'Now we will wash the sheets, towels, etc.'. We left the greater part of our luggage at Volo as we shall return in about a week. For so short a time M has of course brought *nothing* but his coats. One of the bye-laws for passengers is that we must not come on the platform till we have unloaded our firearms.

We left Trikkala without regret at the same hour yesterday, **Wednesday 8th [Wednesday was February 9th],** morning for Kalambaka, at the edge of

---

[9] The region of Thessaly became part of Greece in 1881 and the rail link between Athens and Kalambaka was completed in 1886, the Bents riding on it now in 1887. (They were lucky: on 17 November 1887, the first rail strike occurred.) Salonika was still in Turkish hands at the time and the rail link with the Greek capital was not constructed until early in the 20th century.

the plain. It was snowing and all the country covered about 4 inches, but not freezing – so we had wet walks to and from the stations. At Kalambaka there was a much dirtier inn, so after luncheon we mounted mules and rode hither, 1½ hour. The secretary of the *nomarch* of Volo, to whom we had a letter, visited us, a lovely man in clean white petticoats.

It would not stop snowing and it was so cloudy we could but dimly descry this strange valley with thorns and fingers and pillars of pudding stone standing up in the air hundreds of feet high. Once there were 24 monasteries, now only 7 inhabited, and holes high and low *full* of hermits, now there are none. They began these monasteries in the first centuries of our era. Some have ladders hung on pegs driven into the rocks and easily removable, and the bridge to this has only been fixed a year or two ago. In the time of the Turks it was not safe to venture beyond the drawbridge.

We had to stand outside for some time shouting in the snow till a monk examined us and asked who we were. At length the iron door was unbarred and we found ourselves in a kind of vault with an uneven rocky floor, from which we emerged into an equally uneven courtyard and after some waiting were led to the reception room where our eyes were gladdened by a huge wood fire blazing on a hearth at the level of our knees.

The Egoumenos, or Abbot,[10] was away, but the Antigoúmenos, Sophronios, received us very kindly. There is a wide divan all round the room with mattresses and carpets over them and pillows against the wall and the fireplace in the middle of one side with a projecting chimney and a stone hearth bound with brass on the divan. We were soon lying on each side of the fire drying up deliciously – When warm we were taken over the establishment, as usual, an irregular pile of buildings with precipice all round.

We saw the common dining room and sat on the Antigoúmenos' bed in his cell, and warmed ourselves at his brazier while he made coffee and gave us grapes which had hung since August. Of course, his bed was on the floor. Then we returned to the fire after having chosen one of the spare rooms, just like the reception room but carpeted all over, and as no one walks in shoes on the carpets, very clean. We have our own bedding and use it as in that respect the monks do not shine. The Antigoúmenos and we 3 dined in the drawing room, I sitting cross-legged on the divan. A small table was first brought in and put upside down, and on the upturned legs was placed a large round copper tray and then a blue checked duster over that and we had a pretty good dinner off very nice old copper tinned plates.

---

[10] The head of a monastery is an 'Egoúmenos' or (female) 'Egouméne', often called abbot (and abbess). An 'Antigoúmenos' is the deputy.

Today there is thaw, rain and mist so T is as well in bed as anywhere. I should not be badly off up if I had not such a cold and headache, but, of course, we could not both stay in bed and at all events we have quiet, cleanliness, a good brazier, and not bad food. I am looking forward with great pleasure to going up in a net but I believe going down is rather nasty.

The Antigoúmenos has been up to see us but otherwise we have been left to ourselves. This rocky tower is actually exposed to fevers when the S. wind blows from the plain. We saw many troops of horses and other cattle, but till the plain is cultivated it can never be healthy. There are about 15 monks and servants here, and only one monk in the Agios Nikólaos one. *He* was here last night and told us he has 2 rooms and a staircase zigzag up the rock and had come here for company. Five policemen who were roving about to seek brigands were kept 2 hours in the snow yesterday afternoon before they were let in.

Saturday [actually Friday] February 11th. Yesterday my patient was better, so I got up, dressed, gave him his breakfast and boiled water for him to wash, and he rose, but not till we had had our visit from the Holy Antigoúmenos. I attended to my patient's toilette and as soon as he was on his legs got off my own and into my blankets, and he received speedy degradation from an honoured and respected convalescent to a nurse. He confessed to a nose-out-of-joint feeling, but after all when you dine in your drawing room and your patient takes to bed there it simplifies things. My head ached so and I was so shivery that in spite of retiring to the interior of my bed and having blankets, down quilts, and everything warm we possessed, including all the petticoats in the family, nothing would warm me till I drank two tumblers of tea.

T donned his Ulster[11] and hat from time to time and took walks in the passages, and M brought us food and fire, but otherwise we had a very quiet day seeing nothing and cheerfully assuring each we were distinctly killing 3 birds with one stone – the bad weather and the 2 illnesses.

This morning I was much better and had my breakfast in bed. Holy Antigoúmenos didn't pay his accustomed visit. I think he was afraid of seeing me in bed as I heard him the first morning being *assured* that I was dressed. He was not so bold as a wicked Dhókimos, or novice, who T said had been hovering at our threshold, longing for a chance of getting in and at last in he came with the lamp. But alas! poor novice, all he saw of the very interesting me was the edge of my book sticking up as I read on my back. I was sorry for him –

---

[11] The essential travel item for both Mabel and Theodore – the sleeveless coat – and much referred to throughout.

I was horrified when M told me that to the Great Meteora and Agios Varlaam I could not go as women are forbidden.

Today we started off after luncheon to Agiá Triada, or Holy Trinity. It took us about a quarter of an hour. Holy Antigoúmenos Sophronios accompanied us. He certainly has no objection to me. The Holy Nicholas, who is still here, and another monk stared at me while I put on my mackintosh with the same kind of silly expression of wonder and delight with which very little children would gaze at a Christmas tree. Away went Holy Antigoúmenos, dancing down the rocks and over streams and I skipped and sprang closely behind him like a little dog, feeling very hollow from having only fed on soup and tea 2 days, and wondering how I should get back again.

The mist was such that we were all very much taken aback when Holy Antigoúmenos 'let a screech' and looking up we saw one of these strange towers looming over us and found ourselves under a shower bath from its summit. There is another peak quite near. Great shouting took place. 'Oh! Gerásime! Gerásime!', and at last shouts of 'Who are you' from the top. 'Let down the rope!' But no rope came down, so M said he would go up the ladders and explain. Holy Antigoúmenos told me I should be terrified in the net from the twisting but after much colloquy I had to take the ladders, though it had been proposed that I alone should be hauled up.

The monks were afraid their feet might slip at the capstan on the wet rock and the rope might go down with a run. After all I am glad I went up the ladders. First there was a rocky stair then a wooden one, easy enough, then a horrid ledge in the rock, about 50 feet, with a wooden railing and bits of wood on which we must put our feet on account of the narrowness of the ledge, though we were warned *not* to *trust* to the wood. We had to stoop all the way.

Then a very steep ladder in a sort of cleft like a chimney and then a squeeze through a little iron trap door, which I nearly pulled down on myself, then another turn up a real chimney in the rock with a perpendicular ladder hung from the top. The rungs, far apart, were slipped through quite loosely and we had to hold them quite in the middle and use both hands. When a joint came they passed the rung – a very large one – through both, almost too large for my hands. Sometimes the ladder swung out to meet one and sometimes was so close to the rock one could hardly get ones toes on.

My arms ached but there was no going back and I was delighted and quivering when I reached the top. Gerásimos, a most gay old man, received us with a mingling of welcome and fears at our having had to climb the ladders. He is much more like a Jew than a Greek, and had his shirt open and his collar stuck up in a Gladstonian fashion.

He flew at my eyeglass and wanted to know why I had had only one: he has two. He looked through it as we stood near the capstan and said 'How do you keep it in your eye? Have you a magnet in it?' He examined my eyes closely and many a time did he try to stick it in his eye while he called out to M and T, 'Oh! Brother, how does she manage it?'

We examined the little frescoed old church and our St. Stephen said 'it was a wretched one'. Then we retired to a nice little guest chamber with a Dutch carpet – 'A poor place this', said our friend. 'How different to ours. We have such good furniture'.

Wine was brought and I said 'This is very good wine.' 'Miserable stuff' said our St. Stephen. T said 'It is like the French wine we drink at home'. 'Not like *our* wine' said M 'It suits our taste better than that of the islands' said T 'This!' said M, who had put down his glass with great contempt and disgust, now taking another sip that he might make a worse face, 'We would not drink such stuff, colour and water!' Gerásimos and co. may not have liked it but it is the very way they would receive hospitality elsewhere.

By the bye, at Volo there is some honey M has brought us from Anaphi which will be the cause of very crushing insults as long as it lasts.

Having asked whether we had come from the interior of the United Kingdom and whether we had a king, and M having told them, when I said 'No, a queen', that the king was dead, and we having given all statistics of our royal family, we left and this time I took the 3rd place on the ladder and of course we got down quicker than we came up. Very funny M looked as his hind-legs emerged from the chimney and glad was I to pass that nasty shelf and get to the ground in safety.

To my surprise I managed to follow my leader closely and we again had the same surprise of the Antigoúmenos' screech announcing our return home and the door was swiftly opened and we retired to our abode.

Our washing arrangements are more comfortable now than at first, for yesterday we had a soup plate and today a very nice large blue slop-bowl. The first day I had only a copper basin with a grating over it and inside the slime of ages and a coffee pot with a slender spout and very hard it is to wash single handed with this apparatus. I filled my sponge with water, and also a tumbler, so I managed, but the trickler and drip-catcher are not suited to Britons, and I wish we had not left our basin at Volo.

On **Sunday [February] 13th,** M and T, after breakfast, set off, guided by a novice, on foot and went to visit the convents, or rather monasteries of Varlaam and Meteora and I remained at Agios Stephanos. M utterly declined to go up at Varlaam by either the rope or the terrible ladders, so T went up in the net alone. It swings round and round like a bottle-jack. At Meteora he went up telling M he *must* follow, and was made by the monk to take a bar at the capstan to haul him up. They went down both together and now M is filled with delight at having been up by the rope.

When they came in I dressed quickly, and T and I rushed out to Agía Triada again and saluted our acquaintances there with our whistles. They invited us up, but as they were using the rope to haul up wood we declined the ladders; we set off home again climbing about to view our airy home with ideas of photography.

On Monday we took 3 mules and made the complete round of all the Meteors. All the community came to see us off and choose 'the very tamest mule' for me. I think there was not much to choose between them; they were all excellent or we should never have got over the ground we did. I took my camera and a good many photos.[12]

We whistled at Varlaam, but though all came to see me, they would not have me up at any price. The ladders are just fearful, the joints take place every 4 feet or so, and they hang and swing and the upper part is loose from the lower, which hangs on a peg, that it may be drawn up by a chain.

We went to Agía Moní by a very rough road round and over impossible rocks clinging to little nubbles[13] of pudding stone and at last struck into the path and reached the foot of their ladders, but all our screaming brought no one out for there was no one there. At Agíos Nikólaos they said their rope was broken and the ladders were too awful to attempt. The rocks are all green with moss and ferns. We saw one smooth sheet of 'common Polypody' about 30 feet square. It was a really exciting day from the extreme strangeness of the scenery.

Yesterday, **[Tuesday, February] 15th,** we bade farewell to Agíos Stephanos and all its kind inmates, except the Antigoúmenos who saw us off at Kalambaka. I, only, rode and the others and the mules came on foot, a lovely way down into that marvellous valley. We passed quantities of vultures sitting in a pack, and went at Kalambaka to the house at which the Egoúmenos of St. Stephanos, Meletios by name, had arrived the night before. We were given coffee and the Egoúmenos gave me a pretty thing of plaited barley, which hung from the ceiling, something of the same kind as our harvest dolls in Ireland.[14]

---

[12] Mabel is now very much the expedition photographer, but so few of her plates and films have survived.

[13] Nubble = an infrequently used word for small lumps of rock. 'Common Polypody' = *Polypodium vulgare* [and related species], a fern with creeping rhizomes which typically grows on trees, walls and stones.

[14] It is hard to believe that such a fragile souvenir (480 x 200mm) could have survived. But this very item was presented to the Pitt Rivers Museum in Oxford in 1888 (1888.37.2). It is described as a 'harvest trophy of stalks (and ears) of wheat (sporran shaped) which hung in the house of the Bishop of Kalabaka in Thessaly'.

We then went to a very interesting old church built by the Emperor Andronikos,[15] and I tried to take a photo of an old bishop's throne; very dark – 20 minutes. And then Papa Sophronios, the Antigoúmenos, came and fetched me to the bishop's, where T was – a very clean neat place. Coffee again and several introductions, including some female relatives of the bishop, who 'if they had only known would not have failed to come up and be my companions'. What an escape!

Of course I was very uneasy in my mind till I could conjure up a return gift to the Egoúmenos for the barley, but fortunately in my camera-box I came on 3 candles, paraffin ones, so I presented 'these candles of England, thinking he might like to use them at Easter'. They were eagerly accepted. We had already known them to be handsome and welcome offerings.

At length we put ourselves into the train for 7 hours.[16] There is only one 1st and one 2nd class carriage. These communicate by a sliding door, constantly open to facilitate continuous visits, passing of bottles, cigarettes, jokes, etc. People spend rather the larger part of their journey in the carriages for which they have a ticket, but that is all that can be said – During the stops we were invaded with 3rds or ragamuffins from the station to visit or sightsee –

We are now the only 1sts on the steamer *Vyzantion* or *Byzantine* and thankful for such quiet. We had only time at Volo to dine and come on board, T having a bundle of clean clothes, neatly twined in his jersey drawers. But no one here would think this very odd. As we have the ship to ourselves we are allowed to choose our meal hours. This is the ship in which we first came to Volo, and where we and Mr. Graham had all to sleep in the ladies' cabin together.

We were to call at Skiathos and Skopelos (islands) and get to Thessalonika tonight, but having duly called at these islands we have found it too stormy, so here we are back at Skiathos to shelter till midnight, when it is hoped we may proceed to Salonika and be there in the morning. We are having great rain. We went on shore with the purser and roved about the tidy town (600 inhab.), spent a good deal of time in a pot house, bought a prettily made whip[17] of plated brass for 4f.: it cost 3 originally –

Here we are back very cold but in a clean ship. These people look very superior to the *animals* in Thessaly.

---

[15] Apparently the Byzantine emperor Andronikos Palaiologos (1328–1341) visited the monastery in 1333. The Church of the Dormition of the Virgin at Kalambaka is a spacious basilica with nave. Part of the floor mosaics survive and much earlier material has been recycled. The twenty minutes referred to by Mabel is, of course, the extremely long exposure time required for her camera in the dark confines of the old church.
[16] The party is returning south to Vólos.
[17] This whip is now in the Pitt Rivers Museum, Oxford (1888.37.3), as is one ('...with chain rattle and hide thong lash') they brought back from an earlier trip to Mytilíni (1888.37.4). Like a character from Rider Haggard, Theodore sports a whip and solar topee in his photograph on p. xxii.

Evening, **Wednesday 15th [actually February 14th].** Eventually we spent 48 hours there and reached Thessalonika[18] a little before sunset on Friday last, after a very thorough and lengthy examination of our baggage on the quay, during which I conversed in the Gallic tongue with a Turkish officer, to which I attribute that a bundle of 1 doz. knives and all our books were not confiscated. The latter were carried into a house and there remained some time. There were novels in divers languages, a Turkish grammar and dictionary, also some Greek books, and we heard of some children's lessons and story books never being returned. We put ourselves into the Hotel Trikále; we have a room for ourselves, one for M and a sitting room, and excellent food and pay a Turkish pound or 18/- a day.[19] The rooms are poor but quite the best to be had.

We sent numerous letters to our Consul, Mr. Blunt, and he called on us the following morning. He is quite an English gentleman though his mother was a Teniote and Mrs. Blunt's mother was an Armenian, but these facts they do not mention. There was a traveller in these regions, Blunt, in 1634 and I fancy this family may descend from him. We visited Mrs. B. in the afternoon – a much got-up dame but clever and kind and pleasant. She has written a very interesting book about Turkey, etc.[20]

We asked as to church-services and were told we must either go to hear Mr. Crosbie, Scotch missionary to Jews in several languages, or Mr. Sampson, American missionary to Greeks in Greek. She invited us to the latter with her and lunch after, which we accordingly did. There were not many at the service, one converted *papas*, Mrs. Sampson played harmonium and Mr. S. preached very well in Greek. We had met him before in Athens.

On Monday we called on both the Crosbies and Sampsons and Mrs. C. promised to take us on a walk in the town which duly came off the following day. We went into all the mosques with our shoes on.

We have a most splendid view of Mt. Olympos and also Ossa straight across the bay and covered with snow. How I pity those poor gods who seem to have had only one suit of clothes between them so that one had but a girdle, another shoes, and others had to be content to dress themselves in thunderbolts and bows and arrows. It was awfully cold the 3 first days here; the puddles, or rather ponds, in the streets covered with thick ice. We try to keep warm with a brazier and our own stove. The town is not very large but as the streets are narrow and

---

[18] The vibrant city of Salonika (Selánik) had been in Turkish hands since 1430 and was not a Greek city until 1913. For a modern history of the city, see Mazower, *Salonika: City of Ghosts* (2004).
[19] Making a Turkish pound for Mabel in the region of 50 English pounds today.
[20] The traveller mentioned is Sir Henry Blunt (Blount), 1602–1682. His celebrated work is *A voyage into the Levant* (London, 1636).

winding there is a good deal of walking to be done and as in some parts the paving is awful, it is trying alike to head and feet.

There are a good many very interesting mosques, all old churches or temples, one a S. Sophia built 1/3 smaller than the great one by Justinian with splendid mosaics tumbling to bits. Mrs. Crosbie very kindly took us a walk and is an admirable showman. We saw the room where the vice consuls were massacred.[21] There is also a splendid Arch of Constantine spanning the Egnatian Way, which is the main street here. I can go alone about the town quite safely but outside, though the people are not actually robbers, the ransom for our precious persons would be too great a temptation, so no one goes out without a guard.

I am sure if S. Paul were preaching again to the Thessalonians he would pitch into them well for they want it. This is a very picturesque place as far as the population goes, few Europeans in proportion and quantities of Jews and Jewesses in their various dresses.

We went into the house yesterday of a Jew of the sect called Dünmek. The house was extremely clean. I sat in the harem in a heap on the floor. My Turkish did not go far and when I enquired if they spoke Spanish, only a little girl of 10 said 'Sí', but her Spanish was not much better than my Turkish. However I said 'Gügül Koodchook' to the baby and this compliment pleased them as far as I could judge. As T is going to write about these people I won't.[22]

Austrian Lloyd *Medea*, **[Monday] February 28th.** Left Salonika at noon yesterday, very calm voyage.

We found our acquaintances very hospitable. We were invited to meals by all. On Friday and Saturday we dined with the Blunts and Sampsons. At the Blunts we met Mrs. Rongotti, adopted niece of Mrs. Blunt. Mrs. B. is half Armenian and her sister, Mrs. Longworth, adopted a family of Sohrabs. One is Sohrab Bey who has some post with the Khedive [23] and one the 'Consul Longworth' who was on 3 steamers with us 3 years ago on our way home via Corfu.[24] Also we met M. Ponce, secretary of the French Consul. On Saturday Mrs. Crosbie came to see me and said I was asked to tea at the house of Mr. Breitwieser, agent of the Austrian Lloyd, so thither she conducted me; kind homely people they were, who gave me an excellent tea.

---

[21] The Dilessi murders of 1870 would also have been fresh in the Bents' minds. It could still be dangerous to travel in the region.

[22] Thessaloníki was home to important and long-established Jewish communities. The principal sects were Sephardic and Ashkenazi. It is not clear to whom Mabel is referring here. Dünmek (çırpınmak) in Turkish has several meanings including 'dancing', 'hardship', and 'travails'. 'Gügül Koodchook' is akin to 'good little baby-boy'. Theodore's article on Thessaloníki's Jewish community has not been traced.

[23] Khedive was initially the title granted by the Turkish sultan to his Egyptian governor.

[24] In 1884, Mabel and Theodore were returning to England, via Corfu, after their tour of the Cyclades. See p. 60.

We reached Kavalla about noon. This was the Neapolis where S. Paul first landed in Europe when he came to 'help the Macedonians'. It is a very pretty town seen from the sea, on a headland, and so sloping that one can distinguish the 2 walls and all the towers. Nothing is left from S. Paul's time.[25]

He could not have found it so difficult to land for there was probably no jetty sticking like a little thorn into the sea. Though it was not rough we managed to lose our rudder and as there were no steps all I could do was to put a knee as high as I could at a wall and walk with my knees while hauled by the arms and thus I landed at Kavalla. Great examinations till *baksheesh* stopped it. Our prayer books were carried off but restored. We got a fearful pothouse where we were terrified by an awful smell, and hastily locking up our baggage, we rushed out with a letter to Signor Sponti, agent of the Austrian Lloyd, and our acting consular agent – an evil moment for 2 steamers pass today but we got a recommendation to go to the house of Charálambos and here we are within the edge of the inner wall overlooking the sea and with our goal Thasos straight before us. Charálambos is a kind and nimble and very friendly man and his house is as clean as a new pin. Our sitting place is a landing distempered pink and decorated with creeping, or rather dropping, plants on brackets, or trailed and festooned round the room. The bedrooms have windows into this and require things pinned to secure privacy. We provide our own food and M has succeeded today, March 1st, in securing possession of the kitchen.

March 1887 – Kavála and Thássos

We have paid numerous visits today and have not yet had time to count up how many cups of coffee, sweets, etc. we have had. We carried the Khedive's letter to Mustapha Bey, Governor of Thasos. He is a highly educated gentleman and was very polite and is very anxious for us to take one of his *zaptichs* or policemen with us. We don't want to. We should have to pay and feed him. He sent a *kavass*[26] in then to take us over the *medresse*, or college, founded by Mehmet Ali, viceroy of Egypt and native of Kavála.[27] Thasos was given to him and tithes from thence keep up his college, where free education, food and lodging are provided. It appeared very comfortably arranged. There are about 80 scholars. We also went to the imaret founded

---

[25] Neapolis (Acts 16: 11; 20: 6), a city in Macedonia. Kavála, in Thrace, where Paul first landed in Europe. It was the sea-port of the inland town of Philippi, about 16km away, and the site of the great battle in 42 BC. Kavála, then as now, is the easiest embarkation point for Thássos.
[26] An armed constable, also a government servant or courier.
[27] Mehmet Ali, 1769–1849. The school and his house are still preserved in Kavála, elegant examples of provincial Ottoman architecture.

by him too, where the poor feed gratis. All was prepared for the next cookings and bread-making, roughly but cleanly; the flour in a huge clean trough covered with a coarse flannel, the coppers (looking like sections of locomotive engines with all their rivets) full of water, logs laid under, rice, covered up, ready for pilaff, etc.

We called on the secretary or manager of this in a rambling *konak*, or palace, and Charálambos had to translate from Greek to Turkish. We understand *very* little but I said thank you when told a bouquet was to be prepared and T said goodbye… It never came.

The *Agorá* as they call it is very pretty: narrow streets with low booths and vines trained across the streets. It seems more healthy than Salonika. Mrs Blunt came to see us off when we left that place. We are going to Philippi tomorrow with 2 *kavasses* and others, all of us armed, in a carriage.

We visited the Voulgarides and Mrs. V. gave me a pretty old spoon of bone and horn which she said belonged to the Bey of Drama. We also paid a dull visit to the female Spontis and to the Moscopolides, the last a banker.[28] He sent a man called Athanasios with us to Philippi.

We started at 2 of the Turkish clock, our 8, and walking some distance, found a very ramshackle looking, but is proved *very* strong, carriage. Charálambos came too and we were told that M. Charneau, who is a rich tobacco merchant and a relation of the Blunts, had made all the arrangements for a good luncheon at our destination, so we need take nothing. However we thought it imprudent to leave without a basket and a bottle of our own.

It was awfully cold, violent north wind and many and strange were the various scarves, hoods and handkerchiefs, tied onto heads, gaily striped and gold embroidered. We had to go over a kind of pass by a most fearfully rough road of stones, about the size of flowerpots – large ones, and coal scuttles. I alone was bumped up and when we reached the top the walkers got in and we were all bumped down to the plain.

---

[28] Theodore makes good use of Mr Moscopolides' postal address to write Arthur Smith at the British Museum a breathless letter (undated), quickly informing him of their successes on Thássos and asking for help: 'Close to the arch we found a column with the inscription on it which I send for your perusal. By the side of the column lay the statue of lady in question, uninjured except the right hand and the tip of the nose. She is a most gracefully draped figure with lovely face, and I think would be a great addition to the museum if she could be conveyed home, base and all, though she is late. Now my permission to dig does not include permission to carry away, but Sir Evelyn Baring wrote privately to say that if there was anything worth removal he had no doubt permission could be obtained. I wonder if you, Mr. Murray and Mr. Newton could badger the Foreign Office to send a steamer round here and to ensure the permission to remove the things…By the way, I have found my own tomb, a tidy little sarcophagus with rams' heads at the corners and the legend ΕΡΜΗΣ ΘΕΟΔΟΡΟΝ ΠΡΟΣ ΦΙΛΗΣ ΧΑΙΡΕ, which Mrs. Bent is determined to keep for our own museum! She joins me in very kind regards. Yours Sincerely, J Theodore Bent'

Once there we abandoned the road and drove much more comfortably in the fields, only charging up on to the road with a good rush when a little ravine made it necessary and then perhaps down on the other side. It was funny to see this big road empty and men and beasts in the field. While I write all is packed and gone and I am awaiting M to go myself. A little steamer has been kept for us by Sig. Sponti so we are in great luck…No it wasn't.

The hill on which the fortress of Philippi stands puts out into the plain. There is a ruined castle on the top, the remains of walls, inscriptions on the rocks, a theatre with no visible seats, and a few columns in the plain, but otherwise little to see.

We lunched in the theatre, off our own food for no trace of Mrs. Charneau's saw we, and then in frying heat continued our pilgrimage to the ruin which was probably St. Paul's gaol – I took a couple of photos. We walked then to the Turkish village of Rachsha where everyone cultivates tobacco. We went into 2 houses and drank coffee and started home at *10*, i.e. 4.[29]

We were very sorry to leave the nice soft plain and even I walked and we found that the parapet was the only comfortable place for men and mules. The plain, which was once a lake, is now about half a swamp, which no one can pass through, full of wild boars, etc. It looked like Sodom and Gomorrah, or a prairie fire, for they had fired the reeds and other things and there were miles of fire and smoke and flames leap 10 feet high. I never saw such a sight.

And now I hope next to write something pleasant and prosperous about Thasos, our goal.

Sunday, March 6th. We arrived here [Thássos] on Thursday [March 3rd] by boat after all, for the steamer did not wait and one cannot feel sure it was true that it was told to do so. We took 5 hours not having a good wind and about sunset we landed with a sack and various baskets, bags and pans of food, besides our other luggage, at the Limenas, or port, a small new village with a *konak* for the Bey and an old ruined Genoese tower.

We were instantly made acquaintance with by several gentlemen who took us to a dirty old monastery, inhabited by one papas, who had one room, very dirty, to place at our disposal, and we were told that was our only chance. We were not much pleased, so told M to search and we were led to the *konak*, a rough, bare, dirty place and given jam and coffee.

Finally we discovered a more suitable home and as it was quite unfurnished and it was now late, we put ourselves into a family for the night. They were kind, clean folks and have a babe born the same day as my youngest niece and with the strange name of 'the newly enlightened', Neophótiste. I was as usual assured

---

[29] The time calculation in the Ottoman Empire in the Bents' day was based on the Islamic calendar. There is no space here to go into its intricacies.

that it would cry if its legs were not bound tight together and that it would not sleep unless its arms are tied straight down its sides. It is held generally by the ankles, upright.

Next morning our house was whitewashed and scrubbed and about 3 we took possession. We borrowed 3 chairs and a table and busily set to work to produce the rest of the furniture ourselves. We have a sitting room which though small has 4 windows, and a glass door to a balcony, which fill up 2 sides and a window beside the door to light the passage. There are 8 oleographs of a foxhunt that I brought to give away, our flags, revolvers, and anything else we can hang; a little packing case covered by my apron is the bookcase; a mattress in the corner covered with a rug, and everything else laid in neat rows on the floor. A little bedroom with our beds and a table of boxes, and many nails and gimlets to hang our belongings. The kitchen has no window, and there M has a room. This residence is reached by a ladder. For curtains all sorts of things are pinned up.

Friday morning we had walking about with many guides, including Dr. Christides, who is said to be very anxious to make use of our leave to re-discover the old gold mines mentioned by Herodotus[30] and which he cannot get leave to do. We always have a *zaptich* sent with us as a spy, always under pretence that it was an honour.

Yesterday, Saturday, we took 2 men and dug about at a few places, but found nothing that tempted us to continue. This place seems full of remains.

Sunday [March] 13th. Have had a most dreadfully busy and hard-worked week. Even T was tired out each evening and we went to bed about 7.30. We had about 1½ mile to walk over fields to a place near the sea W. of this called the Phournoi. We had 10 men and found after digging in a mound covered with trees and bramble trees 20 feet high, the foundations of a mausoleum. We found an oblong platform on 4 steps, but in the Roman times all the Doric fluted marble pillars (bits left) must have been carried off. We found some inscriptions too.

On Saturday we dug in the field of Kyrios Sponti and soon came to the bed of a buried stream and found what we think to be the remains of a market place situated higher up and washed down. The Bey, Mustapha Bey, came on Thursday and we are pleased. We always have besides our *zaptich* an old man called Theologos who does odd jobs and walks about with T to seek likely spots. Amongst the inscriptions, two mention 'Theodore' and one is about 'a wise matron' and goes on 'and Theodore having come'.

A man has just been here with a long story about buried church treasure including 7 gold candlesticks and also a prophecy that at this very time a strange

---

[30] Herodotus, who visited Thássos, says that the best mines on the island were those which had been opened by the Phoenicians on the east side of the island facing Samothráki (Book 6.46).

man should find it. We thought of the 'giant's bones' last year[31] and have promised to go secretly by boat, the tools being put on board at night!!

Most of our men are Bulgarians, such a ragged set that they give me grave fears as to whether they will take leave of their clothes ere long. **Wednesday 16th [March].** These who are Moslems (no, they are Christians) worked all Friday and Sunday too (at timber) and certainly if they undressed did not put on clean clothes; the Greeks are much cleaner and more intelligent but more idle. As this time I am sitting on the old and fine town wall with 3 Greeks and 5 Bulgarians in my charge. T is a quarter of a mile off at a Roman triumphal arch. We have just actually lunched at home, M having been busy overlooking blasting at the arch, where we have dug since Monday, to cook and bring food out. We also had a crowd of men, Greeks, Bulgarians, Turks and a Negro and ropes and blocks from a ship, and paid about a pound to have a huge stone, over 9 ft. by over 4, dragged up into an upright position that we may find the rest of an inscription ΚΟΝ ΜΕΓ ΒΡΕΤΤΑΝΝΙΚΟΝ ΜΕΓ ΓΕΡΜΑΝΙΚΟΝ ΠΕΡΤΙΝΑΚΑ ΘΑΣΙΩΝ ΠΟΛΙΣ about the 'great Britanikos, great Germanikos and Pertinax'. We have found some pretty capitals too.[32]

I am having a dull time as this is only the beginning here and T is, I am sure, enjoying himself grubbing beneath that stone. One army of gentlemen, buttoned into fur coats and with shawls this warm day have just left and another party come, and I am called on to propound my opinions on the place and our plans from my lofty perch.

Sunday [March] 20th. We have had a delightful, though dull and windy and cold day of rest and rejoicing after a hard but successful week's work.

On Thursday evening we found another length of the aforesaid inscription mentioning 'Kaisara M. Aurelios Antoneinos' and finally yesterday morning turned over a pedestal and found this inscription: 'Good Luck. The Elders to the most excellent Archpriestess Floueivia Savia of unblemished ancestry their own mother, the first who ever enjoyed equal honours with the Elders'.

We then became aware that the lady was lying underneath and then of course great and careful cleaning of the earth took place, a road cut in the great bank we had thrown up, and finally she was revealed; she had fallen headlong on her face, fortunately on sand and was very little broken. Her right hand and the tip of her nose were broken 'then', as the workmen say, and are missing. A ship's captain was called to our aid and with great yells and screams and counter advice, she was hauled safely out. People were addressed as 'infant', 'baby dear', 'beloved', and 'brother', including T and the Bey.

[31] See Sámos, p. 166.
[32] For literature on Theodore's extensive finds, see the introduction to this *Chronicle* above.

Poor little man, I have talked so sensibly to him about not letting the holes be filled up and he is so well-meaning that I feel sure he would like to begin a museum with Floueivia. But we want her home.[33] Scrubbing and photography now took place. In digging her out we have come upon a part of a colossal Hercules and the Lion and are collecting the bits. We have the feet of 3 men; altogether we are well pleased with our place and have decided to gather all our forces there.

Today we found that children had scribbled crosses with sharp stones on Floueivia so that I sat by her while T fetched the Bey and he desired a *zaptich*, Vasillikos, to live and sleep by her; it being piercingly cold he was not pleased but at last it was decided to remove her at once to the *konak* – the Bey's palace. Accordingly, no wheeled vehicle existing here, a forked tree was formed into a sledge with logs across and the lady tied on and then 3 yokes of oxen attached and away went Floueivia across a stream first, under the olive trees with a gaily dressed and very picturesque crowd of various nationalities, and the Chief Rejoicers following behind. The grey statue on the yellow and orange sledge, and the whole scene was one of the prettiest triumphal processions any archaeologist ever beheld.

It was so strange and mysterious to know her name and a scrap of her history and not yet to know what her face was like, and she was lying in such a helpless way with her head a little lower than her feet, one wondered why she did not help herself up and she looked so pretty

'We then became aware that the lady was lying underneath...' The Bents' find of Fl. Vibia Sabina (2nd century AD) in 1877.

---

[33] This statue was one of their more spectacular finds but they never did get her 'home'. The shrewd director of the Istanbul Archaeological Museum, Osman Hamdi Bey, acquired her from the Bents for his new museum. Fl. Vibia Sabina has been published by Gustave Mendel in *Catalogue des Sculptures Grecques, Romaines et Byzantines I*, pp.347–348, no.137 (Constantinople, 1912). The Museum inventory number for her is 375.

and young and as I sat cross legged on her inscription imploring care for her head, I wonder *why* she had ever been so honoured and thought how glad she must be to come out after being trodden on and ploughed over for 2000 years – I should have liked to have a good comfortable cry –

Monday was the fearfully cold feast of the '40 Martyrs' so we stayed at home a good deal by our *own fire-side* and feel glad we brought it with us. The only work we did was to drag up the broken lion and gladiator. He is not Hercules for he now has found armour. I think we must have most of him now, but his head not yet. The poor *zaptich* had spent the night by him and was very glad when the 3 yokes of oxen made their appearance. They did very well; it was too stormy to get the pulleys from the ship.

It is now about 11 on **Tuesday [March] 22nd** and having been out since 7.30 we came in at 10 while the men ate and T has gone back and I will remain till after my luncheon and then go to relieve him. We have only Bulgarians today (10), the Greeks find it too cold to work, but I think some will come in the afternoon as the sun begins to shine.

I was interrupted by luncheon, none too soon for me, and then went to relieve T and he was back by 12. The Greeks did not come and we had a busy and calm day of 'plain work' finding only fragments of the lion and making our place very neat and 3 times the size. I am decidedly the engineer who plans the roads. We had a fearfully cold day. We have now an Overseer called Andóni, an elderly man in blue bags who came and squatted on the edge of the embankment silently and was at length introduced to T as an aspirant for the post. T had scrambled to the top of a pedestal and sat high above people's heads and thence publicly he was engaged and we mean to complain of everybody to him till we make him very sharp.

Wednesday. We have 17 men, only one Greek, and it is a nice sunny day but very cold at early morning. M, T and I seem always dripping and having archaeological nightmares. I am writing on the scene of action. We greatly lack a good supply of tools and have only 5 spades of our own and other things we have to hire.

Friday. A most lovely morning with white frost: the very cold day there with ice on the puddles. Some new men I could not have recognized till next day all heads were so rolled up and muffled that even noses were sometimes not visible.

April 7th. Good Friday [Good Friday was April 8th]. I am now writing in the theatre[34] where we have been about a week. For about a fortnight we dug unsuccessfully in many promising and highly recommended places quite vainly.

---

[34] The Bents are investigating the Roman theatre in Thássos town.

This place is very pretty and interesting and quite overgrown with trees and bushes. There are names and letters on all the seats and we have found a couple of small bas-reliefs. We have 20 men at work and like Andóni very much. We have only today and tomorrow to work as time, money, and Bulgarians all fail simultaneously. The latter return home and only by begging stay these 2 days, and we go on Monday to Samothraki and commence our life of perpetual motion again. We mean to stay in S. a fortnight, then return and go over this island.

The Bulgarians all wish to work for us next year and 3 desire to travel with us that we may dig at any moment. They come here every October till Easter. They have to mend their own clothes and do so by putting any patch they can find with a raw edge on the hole and cobbling it down with white cotton. Two only in these 5 weeks have put on clean shirts. They evidently don't like the feel of clean linen to their skin for they wear both shirts together for 10 days and then extract the blackest. Some look as if they had really been black-leaded. We did see one wash his head and hands and put on his fez and walk off all wet. We should sorely miss towel and soap and they say truly they have no time to wash their clothes while abroad.

One day when T was away with a few men and I had 10 digging in these tempting but fruitless places I had a most fearful battle with a certain papas. I had 7 men digging for 3 hours in a field belonging to the monastery and had just left them and arrived to inspect my other hole about a quarter of a mile away, when Andónis came and said '*Kokóna*,[35] they have stopped digging'. 'Stopped!' I said 'Why?' 'They are prevented' 'No one can prevent us. Who by?' 'The Papas.' 'Go back', I said, 'tell them to dig and that I say no one can stop us'. I, of course, hastened after him and found quite a crowd. The papas and a monk and Andónis and 4 men already climbed out of the field, but I told Papa Diomedes we would not stop and he went away. I said to the policeman 'go at once, Vasiliki, to the *konak* and tell Hassan Bey or Hadji Bey, or whoever is there', and then I drove the men back to work. But the papas came back and roared at them to stop or he would throw their pickaxes at them. They stopped again and said to me '*Kokóna*, how can we go on when he prevents us?' I looked at him and said 'He can't throw pickaxes at the heads of 7 at once. Work or you won't be paid.' 'Old man we wish to work' they said. 'Stop', thundered he. In the meantime I had climbed into the field over a high and rather difficult wall, for I thought it might look cowardly on my part not to advance on to the field of battle. 'Mr. Priest!' I said, 'You need not shout so loud. You cannot prevent us. The Minister of Foreign Affairs of England has asked leave for us to dig from your *Antiking* and it has been granted. What good would it do if we were to be

---

[35] A deferential style of address – 'Lady, Madam'.

prevented by anyone who chose?' Someone said 'Can you not dig elsewhere?' 'Nowhere but here. I have nothing to do with men who will not do what I tell them. You can go home if you like and be paid a half day.'

Then came a secretary who parlayed privately with both the belligerents and left asking me to wait. As I was shaking with anger and anxiety to defend my cause well I walked to the priest's side of the field and sat on a wall reading a book which I knew would be considered an astonishing thing for a woman to do. I was all in red with a red face and a red parasol in the sun and the papas went and sat at the opposite wall in the shade all in black and with a face like a thundercloud. I occasionally laughed in my parasol but I never looked up when 2 more secretaries came. Papa Diomedes rushed to them and they at once said in a low confidential tone 'Andóni!' He hurried off and they murmured 'Work!' and away climbed my foes over the wall and I felt *so* glad it was not I for it would have been terribly ignominious to have bungled and had to be helped.

We stopped work on Saturday 16th, early in the afternoon and subsequently parted excellent friends with the Bulgarians. We occupied ourselves in preparing our baggage as far as we could as the steamer might come in the night. Of course the beds and kitchen could not be touched till the last but their yawning sacks were laid ready.

On **Easter Sunday, April 10th,** we took various short walks and hearing that there was an inscription in a garden close by, T and M climbed in and T felt the inscription but could not get at it as the wall of loose stones had fallen in and was propped on the marble, so for fear of spoiling the garlic in the garden, our Thasiote workman Nikólas, who lives near, was called to take down the wall from the outside and we took a 'squeeze'[36] of it. About 3 we saw the steamer, so we rushed home and toiled like slaves to cram in our beds and in half an hour were on board, M carrying his kitchen range and emptying the fire into the sea.

---

[36] For 'squeezing', see p. 78 note 23. Theodore took time off on Easter Sunday to write again to Arthur Smith at the British Museum (10 April 1887). There is a sense that he may be resigning himself to the loss of their acquisitions: 'We finished our work here yesterday and have got a good many marble things together, things impossible for us to remove unless a steamer comes, and therefore partaking very much of the nature of white elephants. The female statue about which I wrote you I think would be well worth having. She is very well executed and I suspect her of being an old one adapted to the purpose of representing that most excellent though late lady whose inscription I sent you in my last…And there is a lot more work to be done, so we are leaving many things and propose returning next year. I have quite exhausted Hellenic Soc[iety] money. A letter from Sir E. Baring says "The Egyptian government cannot give any formal permission to take away the things you have found but I am informed that orders will be sent to the governor, from which I anticipate that in practice you will not find any difficulty in exporting them." Such being the case, we rather think of storing them here [for] this winter [and] arranging for a steamer to call… [I] fear they might be in danger of the Turkish government hearing of them and [taking] a fancy to them… We have found 2 great toes of a colossal statue and Mrs. Bent feels sure you will be able to read a most interesting paper on these to [the] Hellenic Society. Yours sincerely, J Theodore Bent.' Mabel does not mention these toes.

It was great luck for us that the *Bellona* came, because the last 4 of our meals had consisted mainly of eggs, and eggs was all we were to have for dinner. We had the ladies' cabin of the little ship. The company at table consisted of us three, the captain, mate and 2 engineers, who all appeared to be good sort of men. We spent the night at Kara (black)-gatch and at noon we reached Dedéaghatch. What *does ghatch* mean? A railway starts from here to Adrianople.[37] We went ashore ducked by the waves and T had his hair cut while I wandered about with M. It was so cold. It is a new little town with tiny houses and very wide streets and will be nice some day; a good little harbour for sailing vessels.

Samothraki looked only like a darker, more solid, cloud and it was very rough and rainy and we had most gloomy prospects for a night's refuge and much we wished the steamer would remain the night. The captain had never been there and T had to show him on the chart were to land us in at Kamariotissa on the N.W. of the island. There is no kind of harbour only a little open jetty and the sea was racing along westward.

There are a few storehouses here and the ships drawn up on the land and in spite of all signals no boat came for us, and we did not know if we should be able to land at all. At last the captain kindly gave orders for the ship's boat and M and the bags went first with 5 men, and then we followed. It was *so* difficult and when we climbed on to the broken little jetty we had to jump several feet on to seaweed at the land's end.

We soon were led into a large dark shop, mud floor, a high bench all round, and about 14 men on it, and 3 stoves. We had some coffee and though wet were not *wretched* for we had just partaken of a 'high tea', delighted at the butter and white bread and jam. Passing through a muddy little roomful of sacks, and taking off our boots, we stepped up a ladder to a little low room with bright carpets on the floor where we spread our bedclothes and lay down most thankfully, thinking ourselves very lucky and feeling convinced that our friends would pity us immensely.

Next morning M came to the ladder and laid our breakfast out picnic fashion on the floor and soon I was *bestriding* a mule behind 2 other well-laden ones for the hour's journey to the *chora*.[38] A horrid hour it was. My saddle swung and the wind was cold and violent. The sheep we passed looked very queer with their long hair blowing about. The lambs have woolly fleeces like our sheep and the pigs here have skins more like goats. The only village is very hideous earth-coloured houses with flat roofs, one above the other, round a cleft, where a wide stream rushes down. In the middle is a large new church like a factory.

---

[37] Alexandroúpolis, known to the Turks as Dedéaghgatch ('Tree of the Holy Man').
[38] Main village/town.

We were taken to a house where it was supposed we could lodge, but as we must dwell on a landing with a kitchen beyond it and no door, we sent M to search while we drank coffee on the floor, welcomed and stared at by a quantity of lovely women and girls. We found that our home was in the house of Anagnostes. We enter at the back of the house and there is a wide passage, combining scullery and a sitting room. We sit in a small room, carpeted and with divans round 2 sides and our beds stand to the wonder of every one, one over the other by day. Mine is so long and T's so low that this is easy.

We were immediately visited by Mr. Frangomichaél, to whom we had a letter and by the Mudir's[39] dragoman, a smiling bowing mangy little Turk, and others including Kyrios Christos Rigópoulos, a former schoolmaster and a most kind and charming man who has accompanied us everywhere. In the afternoon we paid visits.

Next day we went to Palaeópolis, 1½ hours, the old spot where the temple ruins are, hoping that the Austrians had left a little digging for us.[40] I rode and on foot were T, M, Mr. Rigópoulos, the Mudir and his Turks and one or two others. This is the first time that all who promised their company have come.

We picked out a little spot where we said we wished to dig but the Mudir absolutely refused.[41] The inhabitants had besieged us with requests to dig that they might earn some money. Some days after, the Mudir visited us in state for the purpose of giving us this leave but T refused it. We had decided that as M. Deville and Coquart (French) and afterwards Profs. Conze, von Löher, Benndorf and Hauser, with a professional photographer, 12 workmen and an overseer of their own, a man-of-war and over 100 natives had been there before us there could be little that was not at least very deep, so we would return the sooner to Thasos.

We lunched under the some huge plane trees by a lovely spring. We of course ate lamb, but we had brought caviare and bloater paste for the fasters.

---

[39] The Ottoman provincial governor; Mabel obviously takes a dislike to his translator, but seems to enjoy the company of Mr Rigópoulos.

[40] The story of archaeological research on Samothráki befits its status as an island steeped in legend. Very briefly, the famous cult-site (of the 'Sanctuary of the Great Gods') that Mabel and Theodore went to see was explored in 1874 by an Austrian archaeological expedition. This study was prompted, of course, by the discovery of the iconic 'Winged Victory of Samothrace', in 1863, by the French consul and amateur archaeologist Charles Champoiseau. G. Deville and E. Coquart conducted further excavations in 1866, followed by the Austrians Conze and Hauser in 1873 and Niemann and Benndorf in 1875 (partly written up in *Archaeologische Untersuchungen auf Samothrake*, Vienna, 1875.) The French acquired further rights to dig (under Salac and Chapouthier) in 1923, and since then various teams from New York University (chief among these under the direction of K. Lehmann until his death in 1960) have carried on the work. (The original of the 'Victory' is in the Louvre; a plaster copy may be seen in the site museum.)

[41] Nevertheless, the Bents left the island with a collection of things they gave, in 1888, to the British Museum. These include four heads (1888, 1003.28–31), a loom-weight (1888, 1003.27), some amphorae fragments, and 'the leg and hoof of marble animal figure' (7.5 cm max.) (1888, 1003.33).

The former they might innocently eat, herrings have blood and therefore were a sin. But the grown up Greeks succumbed to this temptation. 'Go Geórgie' said Mr. Rigópoulos to his ragged, weather-beaten, hatless little brother-in-law, my muleteer, 'take your bread to a distance, for it is a sin for you to see the Ottomans eat, and us also'. They returned our civilities with olives and garlic, the latter of which we unwisely passed on to M.[42]

The people here have such beautiful faces, particularly the women – refined and intelligent though they, the women, have no school and cannot read – and look so good they might be saints.

The following day the schoolmaster, 'O Dhidhaskolos', as he *once* was, and we went to Xeropotamos, or 'dry river', on the S. of the isle, 3 hours. Here were orchards lovely to behold – olive, apples, peach, cherry, apricot, all in flower and among them huts, the country houses, where they come from the *chora*. After luncheon under a tree, I went and sat in one on a rolled up rug and conversed with a lot of women, giving what medical advice I could.

On Friday, their 'Great Friday', we had 3 mules and went 3 hours, beyond Palaeópolis along the beach to the sulphur spring. We passed quantities of trees, big plantations and springs and marshy uncultivated lands easy to clear.

We meant to bathe but it was cold and over-clouded and we were afraid of a chill. There are 2 springs, one a bath enclosed in ruined walls (Psaró loutró as there is a small fish) and one on the top of an out-jutting mound where a man was boiled to death. He was 110. His now old son told us of it.

Saturday was far too busy a day for anyone to attend to us. The streets ran red with the blood of about 600 lambs; eggs were being dyed and much bread baked and festive raiment hung at doors and spread on roofs to air. We wandered off alone to the monastery of Agios Athanasios, a little church attached to a farm of the monastery of Iveron at Mt. Athos. We were told that the monk was asleep after being up all night.

I forgot to say that the evening before we had gone to call at the schoolmaster's and then to church. I was particularly desired to go, as being very *grammatisomene*, or lettered, to advise the young 2nd wife to learn and to give advice on babies. As we set out with our sixpenny lantern I felt like a Zenana Mission.[43] She is a sweetly pretty little creature and a pretty and gaily swaddled baby of 4 months.

To return to Saturday, a bony old woman, who for some reason had a pair of man's bags on outside her petticoats, exclaimed when T said 'What is the name

---

[42] During Lent a good Orthodox Greek is heavily restricted in his diet and it is quicker to list permitted fare: shellfish, vegetables, grains, and fruit.
[43] 'Zenana', the part of a house in certain Asian countries reserved for women. The Zenana Mission was an evangelical movement conceived and organized in Britain with the objective of proselytising. The mission was first formed in 1852 by the missionary Mary Jane Kinnaird, with the support of the Indian government.

of the monastery?' 'Do you know letters?' 'Yes', said he. 'Then how is it that you don't know?'

We sat half an hour in the church to be cool and as we were leaving the old dame told us Papa Agathangelos (or 'good-messenger') was awake and begged us to step in. He is a very handsome and cheery old person and has 2 years yet to stay of 15 before he returns to Iveron. He loaded us with nuts from his home on the mainland and explained to us that he had only been a monk because he had no money; his sisters had it all.

Greek Easter Sunday, April 17th. Went to the noon service in church, called 2nd Resurrection and all had candles. I was up in the *gynaikeion*, or women's gallery, closed in with a wooden lattice, which was set fire to several times. It is a very large place and little children played and ran about with candles. I saved one for burning. We dropped wax on each other and the priest when he came up flung fat lumps of incense about and at length I became quite faint with the great heat and was thankful to sit on the stairs. While there a lighted candle fell over my head and the dame, on whose light blue silk dress with gold flowers printed on it it landed, pitched it indignantly, still lighted, to the bottom of the stairs.

The women wear no 'costume' but dress as they consider in the European style. A very short bodice open in front and a full skirt with plenty of petticoats, a yellow handkerchief bound across the brow, like a turban, and another cornerwise over that. It is very becoming and a little short open jacket, hardly reaching the short waist of various coloured cloth and fur down each side in front. On this high day they wore scarlet silk and other brilliant colours, pink and yellow checks, 3 inches square, and one pink and green striped, very wide and huge bouquets all over it; very large silver waist-clasps and necklaces of gold Turkish coins and earrings. These dresses were bound with quite a different coloured braid to anything in the dress and out of 8 or 9 buttons they would have 2 or 3 different colours. As for the cotton dresses they wear such stuffs as are only associated in our mind with niggers[44] – immense patterns too. It is very pretty. They are very clean people.

We paid visits, many, and, besides the usual coffee and jam, had to drink wine and eat red eggs wherever we went: very hard it was. They have a game with the eggs. You fly at your neighbour's egg, merrily crying 'Christós anéste!' (Christ is risen). He knocks at yours answering 'Alithós anéste' (Truly he is risen). Whose ever egg remains whole conquers the other, but if they like they try the other ends too.

Monday we had too violent winds, though favourable to leave, so we continued visiting and receiving presents and returning them with 'anti-gifts'.

---

[44] Please refer to this editor's apology on p. xxvi.

We got 53 eggs in many gifts, 2 legs of lambs, bowls of milk foods, a huge loaf of barley bread full of eggs and sesame; but the thing we like best and which was given us to keep our sponges on, as quite valueless, is a very good Persian tile that our host Anagnostes' father-in-law, *Papa* Giorgios, found. I got a little brass bracelet too and some terracotta heads.

On **Tuesday [March] 19th** at noon we left Samothraki with much embracing and were seen off at Kamariótissa by our kind friend Rigópoulos and his little boy Xenophon. He has another, Alexis, who, according to the pronunciation of the place, is called Raxi for short.[45]

We had a small but very clean Turkish boat out of Lemnos, smelling only of oranges, which we were invited to make free with. We spread blankets on clean new reed mats and were there till 8 on Wednesday evening, when we gladly reached the Limena of Thasos again. We had contrary winds and calm.

We soon built our beds, re-borrowed the low table and chairs and felt quite at home. We spent a very pleasant day, having ordered a case for Floueivia *on chance*, wondering at having no answer to four announcements of her arrival above ground. We walked about the lovely woods and plain and sat and picked salad of convolvulus shoots and saw large serpents and turtles in the streams and tortoises on land and thoroughly enjoyed a beautiful day. We announced our willingness to set off the following day to seek 'the treasure' and accordingly yesterday set out at 1, and in 3 hours reached a spot between Voulgaro and Hasaviti on the N.W. All round the island is lovely; there are so many inner valleys that one gets different distances, once 4, which is rare in islands.

We and all our beds, 5, and the frying pan, lanterns, lamb and everything had to be borne ashore, and a ridiculous scene it was. M took off his outer trousers and bore them aloft by the waistband. T and I had to sit, as they said, 'soldier fashion' on a man's left shoulder with our right hand on his right shoulder and our left holding his right hand. The way to land seemed long to me! We walked inland all the way through huge olive trees, about ¼ of an hour, and pitched our bedroom among them. T says it is all like one big drawing room. The kitchen is all round a tree, with the bread and lamb in the branches and the big jars of wine and water and all the pots and plates laid round, and we dine about a basket.

We had 2 little showers in the night, even M, Vasilikós the *zaptich* and 'Captain Dhemetráki', one of our former workmen who is with us, minded it. At 8 a party of 6 workmen came from Voulgaro. We had found the place from description and now all are digging at the ruin of a little church under the guidance of Anastasios, brother of the steamer agent Andronikos, who told us. It is a dull day.

---

[45] The islanders still retain a distinctive dialect that reflects the many waves of its settlers, especially Thracian/Balkan and Anatolian.

A man came by with his 17-year-old son and said 'Who are you? Where do you come from and why do you not go to the village?' We said 'We are English, who came by sea last night and cannot go up to the village without mules.' He said 'We were naturally amazed to see you, but the boy was frightened. He said 'What village is this! They must be fairies!' 'Fairies' said I, 'there are none now, they must be men'.

We soon began to think the treasure was a myth and ceased to give much attention to the digging, allowing ourselves frequent holidays to our pretty camp and enjoyed ourselves very much till 5, when it began to pour and poured all night. We of course had to dine in our mackintoshes and afterwards went a long walk, enticed along by the lovely and splendid olive trees. T had to stretch his arms nearly 3 times round many of these towers, which must be about 600 years old at least. They had great spreading boughs like forest trees and were not hollow, turned inside out, split up, crooked, sloping or pollard like others we have seen, and the mountains looked lovely through the rain.

We all had a pretty dry night and next morning 3 mules came for us. We had 6 hours journey, first for miles through olive-forest, along the sea and then we turned up a valley to Kakerachi (Bad ridge), a steep slopey village where we stayed 2 hours and lunched in a dirty little house and paid some visits, led by the 'Secretary Theodhoros' of the Limena, whose home is here. We were shown some dresses of thick-twilled silk, white, crimson and green, woven here of the shape usually worn, i.e. a tight-gored sleeveless dress with an opening in the front to put the head through. First they put on a shirt which shows below and which is seldom fastened, then a short jacket with red and white stripes going round the sleeves, then this sleeveless garment bound round with a handkerchief so that a few folds hang in front and *none* behind and a short jacket over this. The end of the sleeve is cut thus and sometimes the upper one is smartly lined and turned up. The head is like in Samothraki.

We went on to Mariaís, up a very steep fir-clad slope, good smooth path and down another equally steep. At Mariaís we were very kindly received by people who had seen us at 'the Port', particularly 3 brothers. Nikétes Anastasios, a large prosperous-looking gentleman in European clothes, is Demarch, and his brothers Kostandinos and Dhemetrios are peasants in blue bags. We visited the Demarch and found his wife and daughter in Thasos costumes, but the daughter in canary-coloured silk, a gold embroidered jacket and handsome gilt brass belt, and orange kerchief on her head.

We slept in the former schoolhouse, a bedroom for us, and a 'grill-room' where M slept. Grill-room means dining in the kitchen. I took a few photos next morning of an old lady, Afiendra by name, who having put on her best clothes, would be done by a very bad light in the house.

After luncheon we descended a valley with woods and a stream, 3 hours, to their Skala or landing place – Agios Iannis. Very hot. We had been told there was a nice house for us. This was a dirty little hut with no window and holes all over the roof. We refused this and after a parley with the Demarch, who had ridden down, while his brothers led our mules, it was settled to send back for the key of a rather better house. There are only a few, 6 or so, huts round a little bay and a little cottage of a church on a little head between it and another bay.

Whereas we had been pursued by crowds at Mariaís wherever we went, here they hardly looked at us. Having no home we went and bathed, finding a splendid bathing box in the further rocks of the uninhabited bay, while M cooked in the hut. Having neither chairs nor table, we dined on the doorstep and about 7 I set up my hammock outside the door, got a blanket and slept till 10.30.

We then despaired of the key, which did not arrive till the following noon, so M took his bedding to a ship, a very favourite sleeping place of his when homeless, and T determined that we should sleep in the cabin. I refused being too snug and sleepy to move but he made himself very disagreeable and I was obliged to suggest that if he bereaved me of my blanket I should have to move, so he acted on this hint and soon our beds were made, a mackintosh rug spread between them as a carpet and we slept very well in our cage and breakfasted on the doorstep.

Our new home was humble indeed but pretty comfortable according to our present ideas – there we spent 2 nights, Tuesday and Wednesday, and dug fruitlessly both those days. We believe we were deceived by the inhabitants to get us to spend money there, which they certainly contrived to make us do; quite different to the people of the Port, who left all to the Bulgarians, these, when T ordered '10 or 15' to come, appeared 31, and more later, the 1st day. They were paid and told to come only 10 but the man who was to engage them had written down 13 names so T admitted them but he had real war; they said they would work for 10 grossia[46] instead of 18. They said they would work for amusement and all their finds they would have. T said 'I mean to dig *here*. You dig *there*'. (We bathed in a bay E. of the hamlet the 2nd day.)

Then one of our spades was lost. We had lost one in the same way at the Limena and only by withholding a mule-hire was this found and then the finder asked to be paid for doing so in vain. They were very grasping and asked about 18 dr. a night for the hut, but did not get it.

---

[46] Under Sultan Abdul Medgid I the piastre was worth 1% of one Ottoman *lira*. Elsewhere Mabel equates the Turkish pound to about 18 English shillings. The Ottoman silver *medgidie*, worth 20 *piaştri* and issued during Abdul's reign in 1844.

We left early on **Thursday morning, April 29th [Thursday was April 28th]**, in a queer out-rigged boat with 2 men and a little boy. This boat was to go to Astris and Alkí and one man dig and the other fish for us and fetch water. We called in at the Limenari, the Skala of the Kastro, filled our great amphora with wine, lunched and went to Astris, the wind not being good for Alki. The Limenari is a wide bay with comfortable sheltering rocks at the East and some attempt at a breakwater and more houses and better than the other Skalas.

At Astris we had not a very pretty place to dwell in the tents or dig, and the only thing that gives us satisfaction for wasting time there is that we know all about it. 11 men had come down from Theologos and at noon we and they set out by land for Alkí. T rode this time and each of the men had a food bag, a blanket, a gourd bottle and a pick axe, the spades being on the mules.

We had a difficult journey of 3 hours over steep slippery marble slabs and fir needles, having to go down hill with one's nose on the mule's neck, by reason of fir trees, but have reached a lovely place at last. It is a little peninsula, long and thin, with a neck about 300 yards wide or less and 2 rocky bays and the whole place covered with stones of old buildings and old fir trees. Our tent is about 100 feet from the Eastern bay, and twice as far in the sea is a building of huge marble blocks where we are digging, but our kitchen and dining room are near and M is building a house of stones today; last night he had only branches. Vasilikos the *zaptich* also dwells apart and the workmen have their camp and those industrious Mariotises of the boat have theirs, so this lonely little isthmus is a lively place now. We have 2 dogs, 4 mules and a baby one. We paid the boat all the 4 *medgidie* they were to have had for coming here as they evidently thought our money bags must be followed.

I must now go all the way back to Samothraki because I forgot something. Be it known that M and we have each our country's passport *visés* to travel in Turkey but the Turks make us take a *yol-teskereh*, i.e. a road-passport and show it on arriving and departing. We got these at Salonika for one year. We gave these up on arriving at Samothraki – we have not a notion which is which – and on demanding them before leaving we heard that T was described as a merchant, and M as a husbandman and that more than a year had elapsed and a tremendous lot was written to this effect by the Mudir saying 'Be cautious. It is not known why they have visited the island'.

We were heartily amused and felt safe enough having shown them 3 or 4 times already. We were all packed and actually talking and laughing over this when in flew the little cringing secretary and begged to see the *teskerehs*. T produced them. 'Oh! We have made a great mistake; we know it now; it is entirely our own mistake.' T said 'Never mind, it does not the least matter!' very calmly. 'Let us rectify it!' 'Oh! Pray don't take the trouble!' 'I will be back in a minute!' with one of his stocking feet in the air. Here T quietly removed the passports from the Turk's hand to his pocket and said 'We are going and we do not wish to be delayed. It matters nothing what is written. We have our English passports and English do not need *yol-teskereh*!' 'Oh!' he said, 'We mistook the date and thought they had been taken out in the year 1302 and now it is as we know perfectly well 1303[47] or 1886.' At last he said, 'May the Mudir Effendi come here and correct it?' 'Let the Mudir do what he please so that we be not delayed', said T with great indifference.

Off he skipped and away over the stream and up and down the hills of the town and in an astonishingly short time in rushed the Mudir panting and perspiring and pouring out a Turkish volley eagerly into T's face of which all we could make out was that it began with 'A mistake! A great mistake!' The secretary eagerly translated, always finishing '1886'. The room was crowded. We had respectfully risen and advanced to the door. T laid the *teskerehs* on the table and he produced his ink, pen and a sponge and asked for water and sponged and sponged, all leaving only a dull grey. Then as there was neither sun nor fire, the two breathed on their handkerchiefs and mopped it and breathed on the paper and patted them with their hands and the secretary assured us, 'It is all right on the inside' and I said 'Yes we know and we don't care *what* is on the back'.

The Greeks said the Mudir was in an awful fright about it and it would have got him into great trouble.

May 1887 – Thássos

Sunday May 1st. We had a satisfactory day of work and a very enjoyable one in this delightful place.[48] We must be making a pine cure; the air is so sweet and we have sea bathing, mountain air and ever-ready appetites. We have had a *great* difficulty about meat. We have had none for more than a week, but fish, bacon and eggs, a hare and a partridge. There is, it appears, a butcher in Theológos, who has the monopoly and the shepherd is afraid to give us any. T heard our foreman Giorgios saying 'These royal people *must* have a kid (*avtoí basilikoí ánthropoi*)', and T said 'we may shoot and eat as many of your kids as we like if we pay for them'. Now we have one.

Last night we sent off the man at 5.30 to go up to Theológos and return this evening and bring five others and some supplies. Of course they were aware

---

[47] In the Ottoman calendar.
[48] The Bents are still excavating around the important site of Alykí, on the island's south-east coast. Under the watchful eye of the Mudir, the Bents could only remove the smallest of casual finds. The British Museum (1926, 0410.57) has a Roman 'bronze fibula with remains of heavy gilding', 5.5cm long, from Alykí. Mabel donated it in 1926, when, as an elderly woman, she was putting her affairs in order.

what the pay is, but they chose to ask and were told 18 *grossia* or *piastres*. They screamed and shouted and all gave different ideas, from 30 to 40, what they would not work without in the awful noise they made. They were told we would send to Mariaís and we did not care. They were angry at this but said we might. In about 10 minutes first one said he'd work and then another and now only 2 are rebels and we fully expect them tonight. The isthmus is very quiet with only the Marioti of the boat and Giorgios. M is now sitting in his hut. Vasiliko in bed under his tree, in fact every one at home and no one is uttering a sound but the nightingales. There is a little ruin called the Franks' Church, so there we held our service today.

We were rather disturbed by the mules who came alarmingly near the tent and we feared they would get entangled in the guys but luckily we heard them among the pots in the kitchen and M drove them away. I think having one's own tent always furnished the same takes away from any homeless feeling one might have in camping once you are in it. Our two little bays look one at Mt. Athos, the other at Samothraki.

On **Monday [May] 2nd** there came 20 men; some civilly said they would go if not wanted but were all engaged at least for one day and afterwards we found the place so good we were glad to keep them. We think the place must be a Pantheon as we found inscriptions mentioning 9 gods or goddesses and Pegasus. We had a delightfully satisfactory week and found a headless, armless and below the knees legless colossal archaic statue and several other bits and many inscriptions. T and I used each to slip off in turn each afternoon to bathe in the 'Athos' bay and on the day of St. George, Thursday, when a holiday was forced upon us we spent it busily in measurements, photography and 'squeezing'.[49]

On Saturday morning a ship came for us but the inhabitants of Theológos did not wish the statues removed and a good many of the principal ones had come down with 2 *zaptichs*. We assured them we *would* take them to the Limena but the ship was afraid and left so we sent one of our men to Hassan Bey to ask him to be kind enough to send us one.

We dug till about 2.30, when all the men took off their shoes and gaiters and the big statue was lowered down an earthy slope and into the sea. The ancients had a sort of quay of concrete and stones. This is now washed away but forms a ledge under water to the edge of which the schooner could come. One marble sat on a rock on a handbarrow, surrounded by water. A handbarrow is called a wooden donkey (ξυλογάϊδορο). We had to do this as the men were departing except one from Mariais, always addressed as 'Iannis Mariótis' (the Mariote) by the Theológos people.

---

[49] Reproducing inscriptions.

I heard some funny conversations between these Christians. One said, 'It is odd that they should have worshipped those images then'. 'Well' said the other, 'we have pictures now and surely those statues were much handsomer'. Another, 'And so it appears that God did not exist in those days. How strange!' 'Yes He did but the people did not believe in Him until Adam and Eve were born and then at once everybody believed.' Another, 'Poseidon is the god of the sea'. 'Yes, of course, you see there is a god of heaven so there must also be gods of the sea and the land.'

The ship came at 7, having travelled 12 hours with a kind note from Hassan Bey, one from Sir Evelyn Baring saying leave had been sent to take the marbles, and a welcoming one from the British Museum to the statue of Flouevia Savina saying they think it must be the Empress Sabina,[50] and many others and newspapers.

These we only glance at for we had to rush to our packing work and the marbles being safely in we were off about 8 and got to the Limena about ½ past 5, having had a good deal of calm but enjoying the rest and the letters and the lovely views of this lovely isle. Hassan Bey came down to meet us and we soon were settled again in 'our own house' after 12 days' tent.

There is a great increase of vegetation. We laid our things outside the *konak* and ordered cases for the new one in spite of hearing that the Turks would prevent us taking them. The Turks and the Egyptians pulling for the mastery. We said that we would pay any duty necessary and that have them we would, and 'Foreign-Officed' them well, and hearing more threatening this morning T stepped into a boat after breakfast and sailed off to Kavalla, leaving me to pack and see after the marbles. It is about 3 and I see the steamer in the distance and hope he may be in her, if not arrive by midnight, the wind being good.

I went to the *konak* and saw 5 cases packed. Limnios made 2, beautifully and well measured but Thasios made 3 abominable ones and had nearly to remake them they misfitted so. Beautiful Floueivia looked lovely, and I felt pleased that my duty caused me to see more of her than I ever shall again. Certainly Patience must have been a great characteristic of hers –

Now I have packed for home by land, home by sea and to be left here and am now again going to look after 3 of our Bulgarians who have returned and are filling up holes made by us. Our steamer may come any time after tomorrow and the sooner the better, for misery will be our portion because our beds must be packed and taken to the *konak*.

I was very much amused yesterday by a tiny little girl. Some women said 'Here comes the lady (*Kyría*)' and she shouted out, 'Oh! No! That is *not* a lady, that is the *Franka*; don't you see it is the *Franka* and not a lady at all'.

---

[50] Sabina Augusta, Trajan's grand-niece. She married Hadrian (AD 100) and died in 136 or 137.

T did not arrive that day and that evening I, like the rest of the world, had an illumination for the Sultan's birthday. 8 candles stuck in the window and I was a good deal disturbed by some miserable fireworks and shouts of '*zeto o Sultanos!*'[51]

I was kept in all next day by rain and thunderstorms and not till Thursday morning did T arrive, having been travelling with Hassan Bey 18 hours. When T got to Kavalla the Bey was furious about the question at issue and T lunched with him and they both telegraphed Egypt.

We prepared for the steamer but thinking it might be uncertain we decided to sail and started about 9 and reached Kavalla in 7 hours. We are now in the house of one Domenico, a barber who fled from Bari at the time of the eruption in 1872[52] and consequently now is called 'di Bari'. He has a large wildly arranged but clean house and we have a large room. It is quite close to the port and more convenient for us than having the long walk to Charálambos' – besides C's house is full.

Before leaving the customs man wished to open a packing case we had packed with books, etc., but we said he should have spoken before we shut it so we put them (2 packages) *in* the *konak* to come with the marbles.

As it happens, no steamer has been to Thasos and here *we* must wait till Thursday – longer we won't. The Bey is *very* anxious for us to remain till all is settled and a telegram from Sir E. Baring says *stop* out. As we cannot carry the things we think our duty fully done, and T having deposited £5 with the Bey to pay any demands, will, if no news comes, leave the affair with great confidence in his hands.

The afternoon after we got to Kavalla we set off in the same boat and went to the very comfortable bay of Lefteré,[53] where the Russians have settled themselves in under pretence of a monastery. We were kindly received at the house near the sea and given large cups of excellent tea and then walked about 1½ mile to the monastery. The road was good and flat and led through a fertile and well-cultivated valley. The monastery is like a big barrack, far too large for the 15 monks who keep up a great farm there. Though they are from Mt. Athos there are plenty of women there, workmen's families and one nun lives in a little cottage in the farmyard, Sister Evgénia. She is tremendously fat and very active. She once was rich and came from Russia with her husband on a pilgrimage to the Holy Mountain. She waited here while he proceeded to Mt. Athos, where he was so pleased that they each agreed to remain where they were. He is now dead.

---

[51] 'Long live the Sultan!'
[52] Presumably the eruption of Vesuvius in 1872.
[53] Today's Elevtheroúpolis. Russian Orthodox influence was significant on Mount Áthos where the monastery of Ayíou Pandelímonos (Roussikó) was developed in the mid-1800s.

The superior, to whom we had a letter, was absent and did not return till next morning. When he did we could only smile at each other, as he could talk nothing but Russian. But his place was well supplied by the novice Jósif, 18 years old, who, having been brought at 5 years of age by his father to Mt. Athos, spoke Greek perfectly. He came with a goitre which at once was removed by a miracle. His father is at Mt. Athos.

We had 2 more large cups of tea and walked in the gardens and had a very good dinner. Jósif sat by and drank a glass of wine and we had an interesting conversation on various subjects. He and M discussed religion and M maintained that the Emperor Constantine was the first Greek Christian. We slept in 2 beds in the very large drawing room beneath many picture of devils of many shapes and hues of which the Russians are so fond. I pictured to myself when a Russian army was in possession, two Field Marshals on the beds, three Generals on the divan, and Colonels and Majors on the floor.

When I was settled in bed reading with a rose 'convenient to my nose'[54] on the pillow, Jósif came in to bring a lamp and say goodnight in Russian; he seemed no more abashed than a servant monk who came in while I was dressing in the morning. I suppose that is the effect of Mt. Athos training. Though they won't let women or any female animals land at Mt. Athos, the monks seem to make expeditions everywhere and see plenty of them. 3 came to Thasos on a pleasure party.

At breakfast in the morning we had 2 English, M (Greek), Russians and a Turk, the customs house officer who travelled to Kavalla with us in the monks' boat. T found 2 newly hatched tortoises and we have brought them with us. I have also one about a year old of a different kind from Thasos.[55]

We went to a party at Mr. Picchiolis' country shanty close to Kavalla; a pleasant simple-minded affair. The barber Domenico escorted us; his wife had gone before. An organ was played and there was dancing on earth under a shed where we sat and a lamb cut up on a dish; some cheese, salt fish and bread were put on a table and all helped themselves. The invitation had been to 'come and drink a beer' and accordingly much beer flowed and though we had laughed over the invitation, we were glad of the beer after our walk.

A pilgrimage of St. Athanasios was taking place close by with much feasting. Dr. Picchioli is our consul and was very kind and we dined with them one night. He prefers talking French to Italian and does not speak English, which might be awkward for shipwrecked mariners.

---

[54] The poetic reference here is not traced. Perhaps another of Mabel's Irish ballads.
[55] This is 'Thraki', (Mabel is in Thrace) which she keeps as a pet. The little creature seems to have travelled widely with its owner. Did Mabel bring it back and forth from Marble Arch? It is eventually 'lost' in Scutari in 1888.

One evening we managed to talk French, Italian, Greek and German, but Greek is not considered an elegant language to speak here. One afternoon we heard 'Bent! Bent!' from a window and looking round saw Mr. Sampson, who was returning from a missionary tour to Drama. We invited him to have his meals with us at a restaurant where we dined and lunched. As he was not well we made him a bottle of Brands' beef tea[56] and took the spirit lamp and M heated it, as there was no food there fit for an invalid. He came home with us and we gave him a large bowl of tea and our hosts beneath the window gave us quite a treat of pretty Neapolitan songs.

On **Thursday May 19th,** we heard with joy the whistle of a steamer and hastened on board the *Bellona*, and Mr. Sampson too. We had to get our *teskerehs* signed before leaving and had a good customhouse examination.

We left about 10 and by being on the sea escaped a pretty strong earthquake. There was one short sharp shock when we were at Elevthéri. It was very dark as we skirted round Mt. Athos and so rough that 4 pilgrims having been taken as near land as that they could throw the post into a violently tossing empty boat, were quite unable to reach the shore and carried off and are of course still on the *Bellona*, not being allowed to land at Salonika without passports made out for that place.

We arrived about 6 o'clock on Friday 20th and again had our passports examined and *every* package *unpacked* at the customhouse. M had his *teskereh* all right to *land* here and we wished him to do so for some hours – but it was Friday and the Turkish Sunday, the offices shut and therefore he could not get his passport to *leave* and so had to go straight to his steamer and remain 11 hours. T had to go on board to pay and take him various things afterwards. A family remained on board lately 4 days! Not allowed to come ashore on their way to Kavalla, to which port their passport was made out. This is a new law as the Turks have become very suspicious.

Now on **Sunday [May] the 22nd** I sit on the train *2* hours before it starts, setting out on a most difficult journey home. We arrived in Salonika 3 hours before the train started on Friday, but *nearly* time enough for all the preparations, so as the train does not go every day we had to wait till now.

A passport to leave with, our own *visé* for Servia, a letter from the Pasha to all Pashas 'that the honourable British subject is travelling with his family and is to be given a guard of *zaptichs* from Üsküb to Vranya and every help is to be given to him and the Pashas are to be prodigal of exertions to that effect'. A letter of introduction to the manager of the train at Üsküb, in case he may give us a train – all these have been procured.[57]

---

[56] Along with arrowroot, Mabel's stock panacea.
[57] The Bents are on their way homeward, overland by train. Üsküb is present-day Skopje, capital of modern Macedonia, F.Y.R.O.M. Vranya is the modern Sophia, capital of Bulgaria.

Well, at 8 we are to start and get to Üsküb at ½ past 4. The station is heaped with people and bales of beds and bundles. We had the *kavass* of the Consulate, who only speaks Turkish and the Commissionaire of the hotel to translate and really T could hardly have managed the bodily gymnastics necessary to book the luggage. We saw one of these men climbing over people and things and standing high above people's heads, bending in at the pigeon hole –

At Üsküb we sleep and get the soldiers and a carriage ready for 16 hours' drive, 5 miles, over the mountains into Servia. The first night to the only halting place, the little village of Koumanova, much nearer Üsküb than Vranya.

Üsküb, **[Tuesday] May 24th.** We got over our journey very well yesterday, a cloudy day and absence of dust helped us. It is a very serious thing to take one's seat in the train at 8 o'clock on a Sunday morning and feel you have to travel till 'the middle of next week'.

The scene at the station was very funny. The 3rd-class waiting room through which we entered was paved and strewn and piled with people in all sorts of costumes and rags, with their bundles. We had the *kavass* from the Consulate, who only speaks Turkish, and we were put in the train first. When the doors were opened, half an hour before the start, we saw the 3rd class packing themselves, their rolled up bed on their back, a sack or two over the shoulders, a bag or two on the wrists, a bundle or two over the arm, a black iron pot in one hand, a gun or shepherd's crook in the other, a water gourd dangling somewhere, weapons everywhere and over all a huge sheepskin cloak. Having collected themselves, they put down their heads and made a run from the waiting room to the train and then with great difficulty tried to insinuate themselves *whole* into the carriage.

At some of the stations I looked into these carriages and it appeared as if they must be china figures, carefully packed with all these beds and bales to prevent their knocking together and breaking; under the seats and between them and among their legs and the nettings, all was chockfull.

First we went across a great plain with strange cattle with horns lying back on their shoulders, and lots of storks, and a splendid view of Mt. Olympos and the R. Vardár running sluggishly through it, and then after the valley got narrower and we had passed 2 or 3 stations, we went through a *very* narrow gorge with iron-marked rocks to the station of Demír Kapon – Iron Gate, like on the Danube, I suppose. After this the scenery was very fine indeed, mountains all around and the Balkans in the distance. The place that pleased us most was Keuprülü; *most* lovely with mosques and towers and minarets and a charming wooden bridge, but alas! the train swept through and we stopped in a hideous place.

We reached this about ½ past 4 and found a rough, clean hotel kept by an Italian Austrian Levantine: the man speaks Italian, the woman only German, one man Greek. Our housemaid is something like this, with a bucket made of a paraffin can and bare legs.[58] The place is very clean and our bed very comfortable once you get there; it is on a level with the chest of drawers.

M. Lerpoux at the station says there is a train going tomorrow at 4 a.m., which would take us to Vranya in 3 hours, much cheaper, safer and easier than a carriage and such a carriage over these rocks and we hope we are not foolish in trusting to it and that it *may* go. The hotel is full of Europeans, railway and tobacco *regie* people.[59] A lady very like Mrs. Ker, Mme. Berger, English, sent her French and English Levantine son, who is in the railway, to ask us to speak to her if we were English.

We were entertained with beer in the garden and sat half an hour with them, took a walk and admired the town and dined with the French *regie* family, Privelegio, and the Servian Consul Petchatch. *He* is to give us a letter to help us out of High Macedonia into Servia and Mr. Privilegio, who knows the Pasha well, has offered to take T and his letter. At the same time M. Berger is seeking a Bey to do the same; rather awkward!

Next morning, **Monday [May 23rd?]**, I received this letter.[60] Of course I sent an affirmative answer. T went off with Mr. Privilegio to see the fat Pasha and returned to luncheon and then came M. Berger with Nouri Bey, a very nice looking man who spoke French well and T had to get out of his difficulty as best he could with many polite speeches and then off we went to the bazaars, where we bought some Servian stockings and Turkish shot-boxes.

At 4 came Mme. Berger and took me to a pretty house, quite Turkish in style but bare enough. She really is, I think, 'an educated woman' and I spent 1½ hour with her altogether. I found my way home in great safety and peace. At dinner appeared Mr. Albert Mayer, an Austrian Subject, Jew, of the *regie* at Salonika. He also was prepared for the long drive but we told him of the train next morning –

Next morning came very soon indeed, for at 3 we rose and very differently indeed did we spend the day from what we had expected and I may add most unpleasantly. But I should not complain, as we were very lucky all through. It was the last train of ballast going and when the French Consul asked for a train for the Bishop Bonetti he was told that positively the engines were only for making the line and he could not have one.

---

[58] Mabel's doodle is reproduced on p. 261 (top left).
[59] The Turkish tobacco duty authority.
[60] 'Monday morning. My dear Madam, You would really do me a great favour if you would spend an hour or two with me today. Ours is rather a rough kind of home, but I can offer you a cup of tea. I think if you only knew how hard it is for an educated woman to be in exile at such a place as UsKub, without either congenial society or habitual surroundings, you would come out of charity. May I fetch you about 4? With compliments to your husband, Faithfully yours, Florence K. Berger'

A carriage had been ordered for us, also a *teléga* for the luggage – a sort of wagon lined with basket. Only the bundle of rugs was put in this and all the rest in the carriage, so there was little room for us, but we perched and drove off in the dark, about ¾ of a mile, through a pretty deep river and got out at a railway embankment, up and over which we climbed, loaded, for there were no porters and T and the coachman had to carry everything. We crossed a field and another embankment and found the train of trucks and climbed on and hauled up the luggage and sat amongst gravel. There were about ½ a dozen Bulgarian and Servians and Mr. Mayer and ourselves. It was rather dizzy work, flying through the cold air with the wind whistling in our ears, on a board, so to say with no protection either side. It was bitterly cold and filthy we became, grits of coal hailing on us, but how thankful not to be in a carriage.

Thus we journeyed 6½ hours instead of 3 and got out *nowhere* but at a 'box' some distance from some future station. Here T came and told me with a long face that the telegram M. Patchich had sent for us had not produced a carriage and we were 20 kilometres from the town of Vrania, but after great anxiety it did arrive. Mr. Mayer had fortunately a letter to M. Hazelaire, French engineer of the line, a most kind and polite man who asked us into his little cottage, which was tastefully decorated with 2 carpets on the wall and floor, a little divan of boards, boxes of Servian aprons, 3 chairs and a table.

He gave us a very good luncheon but before it came we were by no means lively, but almost speechless with fatigue and hunger. We could get nothing before starting and on the way only a little cup of coffee and a small scrap of dry bread.

We set off in a little Victoria, sharing a *teléga* for our luggage with Mr. Mayer. The road at first had a fine, handsome look, being *very* wide and bordered with high willows, but on closer examination it seems like a river full of rocks and shallows and with only one channel passable winding about. The horses galloped and we banged and bounced along. It was not like a carriage-driving at all but some different exercise not before tried. At 8 kilometres we swing to the left into a yard with a palisade round it and then rapidly turned to the *right* and were at the door of the customhouse.

M. Hazelaire had told us such awful customhouse stories that we trembled, but the *bouyourou*[61] was produced and Mr. Mayer flattered the head and said he spoke French like a Parisian and that the train was put on specially and that we would pay *baksheesh* and so we left untouched and in a few yards crossed a ditch into Servia. Here we were more frightened still for they are capable of taking

---

[61] Presumably official documentation of some kind.

all your family photographs in case they may be aspirants to the throne and everything printed also.

So we showed the letter which was open and here we also passed unopened. The roads seemed a little better and the house spread about in a safe looking way. 12 kilometres to Vranya (БРАЦА) and another customhouse, but M. Patchich's letter availed again and permitted us to gallop on into the hotel yard. Hôtel d'Europe, a better but untidy sort of place. Vrania is a long village, all the houses, including the hotel, one-storeyed.

At 5 we got up and drove a good long way with Mr. Mayer to the station and reached Belgrad, or Beograd as it is called (БИОГРАА), about 7. We had no time for a meal but somewhere we caught up some bread and wine and, having other things, invited Mr. Mayer to luncheon. We wished to stay at Nish (НИШ) but were told a train would leave at 2 on Friday morning, so came on here.

When we got here we were told there was no train till Saturday morning, so we have had, or are having, 2 days here. It is not a picturesque place and very German in the new parts, but there are pretty walks round and the place looks very prosperous. On Thursday we went in the afternoon, in a carriage, to Topchider, a little house and garden where King Milan IV's grandfather lived in a very simple, not to say shabby manner. We saw the room where he died and several of his garments all neatly marked M. O. – Milan Obrenovich.[62] We saw the King too, driving a phaeton. We had a great thunderstorm and heard alarming news of floods. Tonight at 9 we go and ensconce ourselves in a wagon-lit and abide there till Paris.

Nothing further of any interest happened to us and the only thing very amusing was this. In Paris we got into the train with Cook's interpreter and Gaze's[63] going to England for Whitsuntide. We were speaking French to the porters and they both at different times asked me in French if I minded smoking, and if I was quite sure I did not mind and though T and I said a few words in English, they quite made up their minds we were foreigners. We settled down to

---

[62] Milan Obrenović (1854–1901) was the Serbian king from 1882 to 1889. His grandfather was Jevrem Teodorović Obrenović. Theodore writes about this rail journey in a typically unrestrained article for *Macmillan's Magazine* in 1887 (56, pp. 290–295). In 'A New Overland Route to India' he writes, 'French enterprise in these Balkan provinces is truly remarkable…One could not but ask one's self, what are we English doing to allow ourselves to be entirely driven out of a market which a few years back was all our own.' *Plus ça change.*

[63] Thomas Cook's competitor in the early days of package tours was H. Gaze and Son, established 1844. They published regular travel pamphlets for their customers. One such was 'How to Travel: Information concerning Gaze's Independent Travel Tickets, Circular Tours and Conducted Parties' (London, c.1889). It covered such trips as tours of United Kingdom, Europe and the East, as well as 'Conducted tours to Paris and Back' for the International Exposition of 1889 (inclusive charge £4-2-0). For £12-12-0 one could go to 'Holland, The Rhine & Belgium'. But the more adventurous were offered 'Egypt and the Holy Land, 30 days in Palestine, visit Jerusalem, Wilderness of Judea, Samaria, Galilee, Baalbek and Damascus…'

rest and they talked. Gaze was French and spoke English with the most perfect accent of Ludgate Hill. Cook was English and equally familiar with French. They spoke most confidentially in French with their heads close together, but, when their secrets became too deep and dark they, for greater security, spoke English about hotel failings and tricks of the trade. Gaze said ''ope we shan't be understood'.

[Monday] May 30th 1887. When we roused ourselves to prepare for landing we thought it cruel to let them know they had been understood, so we spoke Greek. They asked us in French if they could help us to get to the steamer, which of course we declined and on Whitmonday morning we safely and joyfully reached Home.

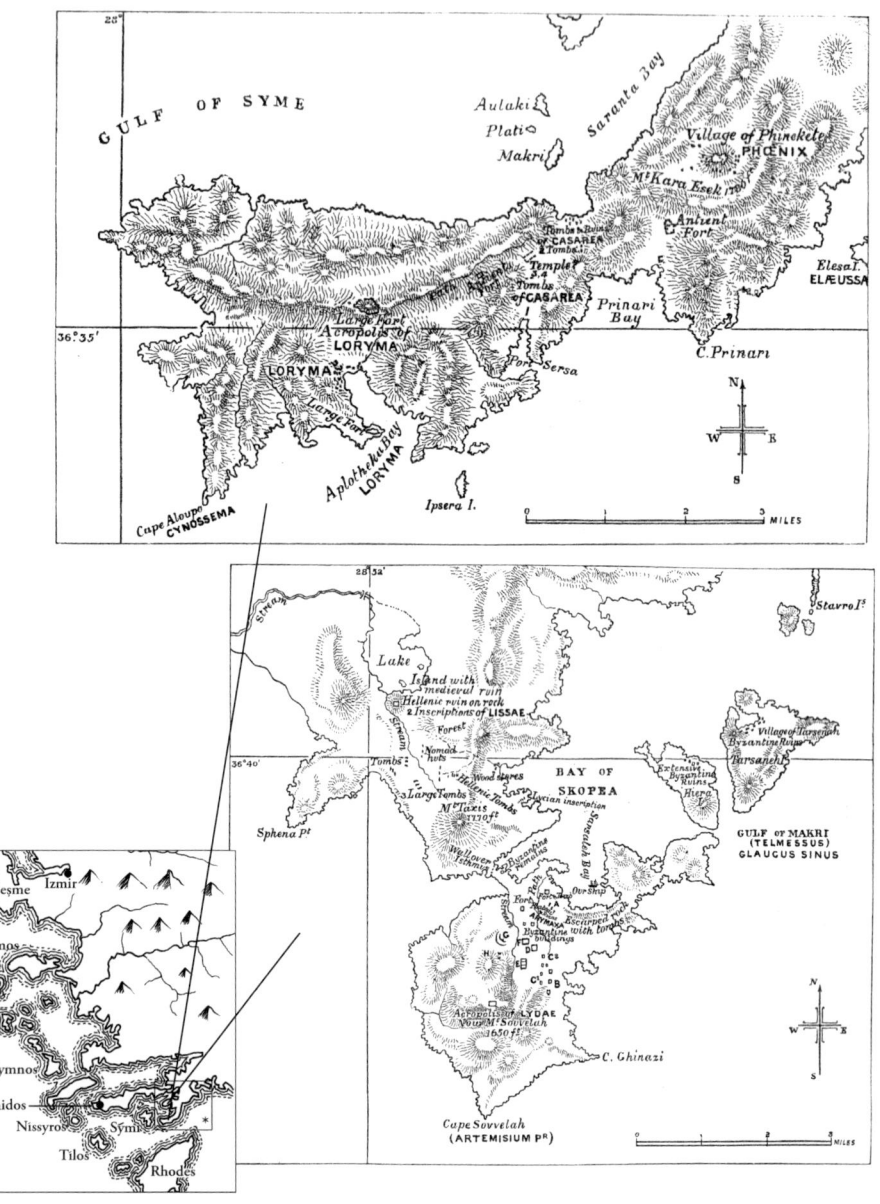

Map 5. 'Loryma' (top) and 'Lissae' and 'Lydae' (below),
Theodore Bent's own details from a contemporary Admiralty Chart.

Chronicle V, January to May 1888:
'…a paradise for archaeologists and tortoises…'

Not a couple to give in easily, Mabel and Theodore spend a good deal of their summer and autumn of 1887 trying to drum up enough support to have the marbles from Thássos saved for London. Letters exist from a series of addresses in Herefordshire (mostly vicarages), and the comfortable seat of Sutton Hall, near Macclesfield, to Smith and Murray at the British Museum: 'We have indeed been unfortunate about our treasure trove but I have hopes still. I sent to Mr. Murray a copy of two letters which recognize the fact that I had permission in Thasos both to dig and to remove. These I fancy had not reached Sir W[illiam] White when you passed through Constantinople. Seriously, the great point to me is prospective. Thasos is wonderfully rich and I have some excellent points for future work and if we could by not being over grasping get the Turkish govt. to recognize the Egyptian leave for next winter, I am confident we could produce some excellent results.'[1]

In January 1888, Theodore did receive a further grant of £50 from the Hellenic Society to return to Thássos to excavate, and the couple duly left for Istanbul. Unsurprisingly, the implacable Hamdi Bey refused him leave to carry out further investigations on the island. Despite various appeals to the Ambassador, Sir William White, he and Mabel were forced to change their plans.

Theodore may well have been expecting this. In the *Classical Review* of May 1889, he revealed that while he was first digging on Thássos in 1887 he had employed a local man to 'to make some excavations in the neighbourhood of Syme' (way down the Turkish coast, north of Rhodes) on his behalf. Obviously satisfied with the results, the couple,

---

[1] Letter to Arthur Smith, British Museum, dated 4 September 1887.

after an excursion to Bursa to see the fabled Green Mosque, decided to return to Sýros (where they chartered the yacht *Evangelistria* under Greek papers) and embark on this fallback plan.

At Sýros, in Mabel's words, 'Theodore at once took to visiting ships to put into practice our plan of chartering a ship and becoming pirates and taking workmen to "ravage the coasts of Asia Minor". Everyone says it is better to dig first and let them say *Kismet* after, than to ask leave of the Turks and have them spying there.' The couple also meet up here with Manthaios Símos, who has sailed up from his home on Anáfi, close to Santoríni.

The couple's investigations along the Asia Minor littoral (in particular the coastline opposite the island of Rhodes) were extremely fruitful and some of Theodore's marbles from this expedition are now in London. He briefly wrote up his discoveries of ancient Loryma, Lydae, and Myra for the *Journal of Hellenic Studies* (Vol. 9, 1888), but a lengthier account was provided by E. L. Hicks (Vol. 10, 1889), including transcriptions of over forty inscriptions and passages of text from Theodore's own notebooks.

The two detailed maps reproduced on page 224 are also Theodore's, adapted, later, from admiralty charts. He wrote from Sýros to his friend Smith at the British Museum asking for the charts to be sent to him urgently, but they arrived too late, a subsequent letter confides. Whatever charts he used on location, the long cruise, which took the party as far south as the present-day Greek island of Kastellórizo, enabled the couple to enjoy a subsidized sail around some of most attractive coastline in the whole of the Mediterranean.

As well as Osman Hamdi Bey and Sir William White, other characters appearing in Mabel's *Chronicle* for 1888 include Henry Mitchell Jones, winner of the Victoria Cross for his actions at Sebastopol in 1855. By way of complete contrast, there was also a supper party with the young and dazzling Maude Gonne ('a tall and handsome damsel dressed in white Broussa gauze'). The future lover of W. B. Yeats is escorted on this occasion by some of Sir William's staff. The photograph on page 344 illustrates what must have been a typical ambassadorial group of the day, the length and breadth of the Empire.

There is, unfortunately, no portrait of the Bents' helpful friend from Sýros, William Binney. Mabel records that they arrive on the island to find him seriously ill. He dies within a few weeks and is buried in a small cemetery on the cobbled route up to Áno Sýros. He, too, was a travelled man: his elegant memorial (and, with respect, this reference here), are 'To the memory of William Pryor Binney H. B. M Consul. Divisional Manager Eastern Telegraph Company. Born in Halifax Nova Scotia Canada the 21th [sic] July 1839. Died at Syra the 12th March 1888. The Lord gave and the Lord hath taken away. Blessed be the name of the Lord. Job I 21.'

Mabel's itinerary for 1888 (see map on page 62) is: London – Marseilles – Sýros – Smyrna – Istanbul – Broussa – Istanbul – Sýros – along the Asia Minor coast as far as Kastellórizo – Pátmos – Sýros – Smyrna – Istanbul – Scutari – Adrianople – Plovdiv – Istanbul – Nicea – Istanbul – Odessa – Berlin – London. The couple obviously found their journey home last year by train more satisfactory. This year they opted for a more northerly rail route, via Russia and Poland and down into Germany. Their marbles from Turkey went incognito, and under Turkish documentation, via ship to the British Museum.

For notes on the transcription the reader is referred to page xxv. Mabel again refers throughout to her husband as T, and their Greek assistant, Manthaios, as M. *Chronicle* V (the numerical sequence is restored) is written in a dark-red leather book (180 x 115mm), with gold lines on the spine and covers. The endpapers and edges are marbled. The paper is lined; there are 192 pages, of which Mabel has used 182. See selected Indices of people and places mentioned. Some doodles are reproduced on page 261.

It is January 1888, Mabel, in her Istanbul hotel, is concerned about her friend William Binney…

My Fifth Chronicle
1888

January 1888 – Istanbul

We left England on **January 19th Thursday,** travelling from Sutton Hall[2] to Marseilles, which we reached at 12.10 pm on Saturday morning and went to bed at the Station Hotel. We varied our journey by going for our meals to the Waggon Lits [sic] dining car. We embarked in the afternoon on board the Messageries[3] steamer *Labourdonnais*,[4] with only one passenger besides ourselves and a captain's wife going to join her husband. We had dreadfully stormy weather after Cape Matapan and had to shelter 20 hours in the island of Seriphos, always eating with fiddles on the table. We only got to Syra on Thursday. We landed and found to our sorrow that our kind consul Mr. Binney was dreadfully ill. At Smyrna we visited Mr. Disinnis and he seemed nearly worn out from nursing his wife.

We reached Constantinople on **Saturday [January] 21st** and after an odious landing in a downpour of rain, our goods being as usual opened in a passage roofed over only, we found ourselves again[5] in the Hôtel de Byzance. There is not much to tell of our stay there. Our great object was to obtain a *firman*,[6] permitting us to dig in Thasos and have a share of the finds.[7] With this object we went to visit Hamdi Bey, the head of the museum, accompanied by Mr. Wrench, our Consul. We drove to Arnaout Koi, up the Bosphorus.

---

[2] Sutton Hall, a few miles south-east of Chesterfield. Dating back to Norman times, the current house (now a hotel) was built in the 17th century, and when the Bents knew it the lord of the manor was William Arkwright.
[3] The French shipping line, Compagnie des Messageries Maritimes, founded in 1835 to sail between Marseilles and the country's interests in the Levant.
[4] Mabel is referring to *La Bourdonnais*. There is an image of her (summer 2006) at http://www.es-conseil.fr/pramona/labourd.htm.
[5] See p. 132 for this stay in the Ottoman capital in 1886.
[6] An authorising letter from the local Turkish governor.
[7] The Bents had great archaeological success on Thássos the previous year and were hoping to return this season.

Hamdi is a very agreeable foe.[8] He is a painter and has been educated in Paris and has married 2 French wives in succession. We were at his house 2 years ago. He was extremely polite and most willing that we should dig 'for the love of science' and the benefit of his museum. His wife is a pretty, bright little woman, who, though she receives everyone at home, has to go out in a *yashmak*.

We went twice, our second visit was to say we had given up wishing for a *firman*, as we were not justified in digging for nothing. Hamdi seemed annoyed at this but was none the less civil. Mrs. Hamdi took me upstairs to see her 2 children, Leila aged 10 and Edhem 4, called after his grandfather, His Highness Edhem Pasha, who was himself, or was the son of a slave. I also saw her mother, an untidy old woman in a dressing gown, and I had coffee.

This time we had come by steamer and had an awful walk amid snow and mud and water and slippery hard snow. The snow began on Sunday the 5th and went on for a week, a metre deep and more where it drifted. On Monday the steamers and trains stopped and all carriage traffic, and the government offices were shut and the bazaars, and we could not see out of our windows; they were drifted up with snow.

When we did get out it was dangerous work. I measured my length in the Grand Rue de Pera,[9] but as the thaw had not begun I was not dirtied and neither hurt nor ashamed as others fell too. As in the finest weather many of the streets never dry up and are eternally almost impassable: what the thaw was like may be imagined.

---

[8] Theodore writes from the Hôtel de Byzance on 4 February 1888 to his friend Arthur Smith at the British Museum: 'Just a line to say we have interviewed Hamdi. Concerning the past he is inexorable but promises for the future a fair share. Of course there is nothing to be done but to trust to his promises, and as I put it before him that if he had let us take the things last year we should have lots of money to dig with and that he has spoilt his own game by robbing us I have hopes. If you are writing to him and could suggest the same thing I am sure it would do a great deal of good, stating that to get money out of English societies there must be some results. I think he sees this point somewhat dimly. He his wild about his sarcophagus, as well he may be, and he is starting for Sidon again in March. He insists on sending a man from the museum with us, who may perhaps be amenable to baksheesh. I hope we may see you in Thasos in about 3 weeks from now. At the moment the weather here is too cold for anything in the shape of roughing it. I must say Sir W[illiam] White has been excessively unsympathetic in this business, evidently thinking it an awful bore and very much beneath diplomacy. Mr. Wrench, on the contrary, has done everything he could. I hope we may see you in April. English Post Office Constantinople will always find us. Yours very sincerely, J. Theodore Bent'. Theodore's diplomatic skills are in evidence here. Hamdi Bey is the eminent director of the Istanbul Museum and the finder of its prize exhibit, the 'Alexander Sarcophagus' from Sidon. Sir William White is the British Ambassador.

[9] The celebrated Galata district boulevard (now Istiklal/Independence) on which Mabel's hotel, the Hôtel de Byzance, is situated.

We also went to the museum and saw our statues[10] exposed to the weather, planted in the mud and really we carefully looked and saw nothing so good of their kind. No wonder Hamdi won't give them up. He would like a few things out of our own little museum for he has some rubbish in his. How angry he'd be if he knew of our digging at Vourgounda in Karpathos! Well we hope to be even with him yet for robbing us.

February 1888 – Istanbul and Bursa

On **Friday 17th February** we went to Broussa.[11] We started about 9 o'clock in a Turkish steamer, 5 hours across the Sea of Marmara to Modaniá. We were taken possession of by a driver called Pavlos, a Greek, a capital man as we found out and bargained with him to do the drives to Broussa and back for 40 franks. We were not 5 minutes in Modaniá and set off in a landau with 3 horses. The road was very pretty at first through trees and past a building containing engines and carriages which have never run on a railway which we frequently crossed, and of which the rails are slipping down the embankments.

Soon we got amongst the snow and after that into the deepest mud. It was quite a foot deep and so tenacious that one heard a peculiar crackling sound as wheels and hoofs unstuck themselves. It was night before we reached the comfortable old Hôtel d'Anatolie kept by Mme. Brotte, a French woman.[12] In the morning we sallied out in the rain and visited all the mosques, including the Green Mosque, a wonder of tiles and beautiful glazed penditives, and we saw also several tombs of the first Sultans, before the Turks came to Europe. The tombs are large domed rooms, tiled round and the tomb of some sultan or prince with inferior relations lying round. They are mostly covered with green baize and have a silk square laid over this, and a post at the top for the turban.

---

[10] Compare Mabel's indignation and response to that of her husband. For the *Classical Review* (II, 1888, p. 329), Theodore wrote this short piece (there is the whiff of sour grapes): 'The conditions of the Imperial museum at Constantinople is rather deplorable just now, for every other interest has of late been sacrificed to the construction of the new hall, which is being prepared for the sarcophagi from Sidon. The vestibule of the museum is crowded to excess with bas-reliefs and other works of art which are constantly pouring in and the provenance of which is hopelessly forgotten. The objects found recently in Thasos, consisting of an archaic torso of Apollo, a fine Roman statue and other things, were left to rot all last winter in the garden, a fatal thing for objects of Thasiote marble which is peculiarly soft.' The couple's extensive and rewarding excavations on Kárpathos are recorded in Mabel's 1885 *Chronicle*.

[11] Mabel returns to her *Chronicle* after a lacuna of three weeks. The early Ottoman capital at Bursa (Broussa or Prusa), some 100km south of Istanbul, inland from the Sea of Marmara. Trajan rebuilt areas of it and Pliny (the Younger) founded a library there when he was regional governor. Its greatest prosperity occurred in the 15th century, and traces of its many monuments and architecture were still in evidence when Mabel visited, despite ravages of fires and earthquakes.

[12] The *Baedeker* for the period has this: 'Hotels: Hotel d'Anatolie (Proprietess, Madam Brotte), with garden and good wine. Rate: 15 francs (reduction for long-term guests)'.

In Mahomet II's we saw the best turbans of gold lace and white muslin, kept in bandboxes for Bairam and other feasts.[13]

In the afternoon we went to the bazaars, which are of course inferior to Constantinople, though large, but they have this advantage that no Jews run after you plaguing you to buy. Everyone speaks Turkish so we had to live on our own limited supply.

On Sunday morning, Mr. Scholer, a German and the consul of many besides ourselves, came to take us a walk. I think he must be the brother of the 'Old Man of the Sea', he is so tiresome.[14] He is a German but will not talk that language. Turkish, I think, he knows best he has been here so many years, but he would talk English with us though he understood no remarks we made and we often had recourse to German or French and we could never get him to leave us. He took us to the Mouradish, tombs of Murad II and his relations, including Prince Zizim or Djem, with such lovely flowered tiles, and there are splendid planes and cypresses growing between the tombs.

When we could prevail on him to leave us we walked, it being then fine, to the village where the sulphur and the iron baths are situated, once visited by the Empress Theodora with a train of 4,000 persons. We went through awful mud to the village first and had some very pale tea at the hotel, a fine large one, and then took a carriage which conveyed us to the baths. On dismounting I was directed to open a door while T was taken in another direction. I entered and found myself among some very slightly draped women, each on a railed-off portion of the high matted platform going round the stone floor, being rubbed and dried, dressed and undressed. There was a stove to warm towels. I followed a girl with hardly anything on from room to room till I was nearly stifled by getting to the bath itself, steamy with natural heat.

Before I left I saw a baby with the shell of a little tortoise smaller than my little Thraki[15] now is, hanging round its neck to save it from the evil eye. The little soft shell was battered out of shape.

On getting out our driver took me and led me to another door and I thought he said it was a mosque so in I went and saw no T but many men nearly dressed. I must have looked woefully dismayed for exclamations of encouragement came from all sides, and I felt the best thing was to follow my leader. As last I met T

---

[13] The Green Mosque, east of the city centre, is a gem of Ottoman religious architecture. It was built by Sultan Mehmet I (around 1420) over an earlier Byzantine church. Mehmet II was the conqueror of Constantinople on 29 May 1453. He was Sultan from1451 to 1481. *Bairam* is Persian/Turkish for festival – particularly the two principal festivals of Islam: the *Lesser Bairam* and the *Greater Bairam*.

[14] In Mabel's day the term 'old man of the sea' referred to a nuisance or bore. It derives from the fifth voyage of Sinbad the Sailor in the *Arabian Nights*: a character called the Old Man of the Sea gets Sinbad to carry him across a stream and then refuses to dismount.

[15] The diarist's little pet tortoise.

in a puff of steam and he said, 'You're in great luck! There's only one bather in the bath'. 'Oh! Is he naked?' I eagerly asked. 'Oh no. He's got something on.' 'But *must* I go in?' 'Of *course* you must.' So into the bath I went. 'There he is' said T, so I looked about for I wished to keep away. If he had been entirely dressed I should not have seen much of his clothes, he might as well have been in a pot being boiled, it was so dark and steamy. The others were all dressed when we passed and I must say I was glad to get out.

Then we went to the other bath. Here I found I was being again taken to the men's place, so I said, 'I'm *not* going in here'. But a great outcry was raised and loud exclamations of invitation and constant assurances that there was nobody naked, so when T said fiercely, 'Come in and don't make a fuss. They all wish it', I entered a large hall with the raised divans peopled by gentry in cloaks and turbans of towels. There was fortunately no one in the hot bath as it deserved a careful examination. The wide platform round the tanks was inlaid with beautiful marbles and there were recesses with pumps, etc., also inlaid.

When we came out of this, I perceived a flutter of towels, as of wrapping up, so with heartfelt modesty I kept my eyes on my own toes and was really glad to have got to the end of a 'sight' I never had expected to see.

The following afternoon we set out and enquired for the 'Bit Bazaar', but this being the old clothes bazaar and named after the very worst insect by which one may be bit, no one would believe we wanted such a place and led us by different lanes to the other one, but at length we descried the welcome festoons of rags which showed that we had reached our goal. We had been given £10 to spend by an acquaintance at Constantinople, Captain Garrett, so with spending £7 of his and some of our own we amassed a mighty bundle and had to buy a large cotton handkerchief for T to carry it in, in a flood of rain, till we could get a carriage.

At one time T and I were both 'in pawn' at different stalls waiting for change to pay so we sat down and they gave us tea. We were within calling distance. All the time at Broussa, except in the hotel, we had to depend on our own Turkish and we wished very much we had our books with us.

On **Tuesday February 22 [Tuesday was February 21st]** we set out before dawn in Pavlos's carriage to return to 'the Town'. The river Niloufer had burst over its banks for ½ of a mile or more; before we reached the bridge the road was under a deep swirling foaming eddying torrent. The mud was worse from the rain and in the midst of it we broke a trace. Pavlos was in a nice mess before it was mended. We just reached the steamer in time and had our 3rd very odious arrival at Constantinople about 3.

We found that the man we had sent to Thasos for the goods we left there had returned with them, after being away a fortnight detained by storms. The

Egyptians were very kind and none of our things were opened. The man's name is Harrison and he is an English subject though he can speak but little English and spoke French to us. His father was doctor to the late Sultan. He himself is very poor.

We were rather unhappy when we discovered that a packing case which contained one or 2 bits of marble had been accidentally disembarked at the Dardanelles in place of another, but the Austrian agent telegraphed to have it put on board the Messagerian steamer as we passed, which was accordingly done. The other things were transshipped.

Captain Garrett was highly pleased with our purchases and they were duly exhibited in the sitting room and much admired and always a higher price put on them than we had given, but he never let us reveal the real prices.

On **Thursday February 24th [Thursday was February 23rd]** about 4 we left 'The Town' in the *Alphée* for Syra, picking up letters at the post on the way. We had no remarkable fellow passengers and reached Syra on Saturday morning about 4. As we passed the Dardanelles we got our case and opened it in a spare cabin, got out some things, put in others, and consigned it to the ship for England.

At Syra we met Matthaios and he had all our goods from the hold in Andoni's boat by the time we appeared. We did not go to Matzis' Hôtel d'Angleterre in the Platea,[16] I am sorry to say, as M had taken beds at his old hotel, now the Aigyptos, thinking well to be near the port. They were very civil and clean but the cooking not nearly so good.

Theodore at once took to visiting ships to put into practice our plan of chartering a ship and becoming pirates and taking workmen to 'ravage the coasts

---

[16] Mabel's favoured residence on Sýros. There is an illustration of it on p. 356. By 14 February, Theodore had admitted defeat as regards returning to Thássos to dig. He writes as much to Arthur Smith at the British Museum: 'Our negotiations with Hamdi have entirely broken down; he is quite inexorable about the knotty point of allowing anything of value to go out of the kingdom... Consequently we have with much regret abandoned Thasos for this year. We stay here until the 23rd and after that go to Syra with the intention of "going on a cruise" for a couple of months... Seriously though I am thinking of Capo Krio and the Doric Chersonese, and if you could manage to get me an admiralty chart of that district and send it to me c/o W. Binney Esq., H.B.M. Consul, Syra, Greece I should be greatly obliged... Hamdi is off in March for Sidon to continue his researches in the necropolis he has hit upon. I half think he has an idea that one of his sarcophagi contained the remains of Alexander the Great, but I begged him not to become a second Schliemann. We have had dreadful weather here; snow over a mètre deep, but that was nothing to the thaw that made the streets rivulets. We have seen all our things we found in Thasos; they are passing the winter in the open frost and snow, planted in the mud. The Roman lady, archpriestess, or whatever she may be, is, I think, their best statue. Hamdi evidently appreciates her as he is sending to Thasos for the pedestal on which she stood. He has kindly permitted my wife to make a photo of her, but I expect when we arrive at the museum we shall find he has given strict orders to the contrary. With best wishes... Believe me, Yours sincerely, J. Theodore Bent'. Theodore and Mabel have resigned themselves to the loss of their statue from Thássos.

of Asia Minor'. Everyone says it is better to dig first and let them say *Kismet* after, than to ask leave of the Turks and have them spying there.

In the afternoon the nicest captain they saw, and of the best vessel, came and sat in our bedroom and signed a 'symphony'[17] and now all we had to do was to prepare to set sail in the *Evangelistria* schooner with Kapitan Nikólaos Lambros, whose countenance speaks volumes for his excellent character. We had a large room, but none too large for our baggage, that part of it which we opened I mean.

Who now more busy than M victualing for 2 months and engaging workmen! We got 11, of whom one Vasilis is the chief, who are all from Antiparos and worked for Mr. Swan at his mines, and some have already dug for Theodore in that island 4 years ago.[18]

We have sacks and sacks of biscuit flour and other provisions and we also have plenty of arms, bills of health from England and the Greeks, and I think all we can require – except our beautiful hydraulic winch and 6 yards of chain, etc., which by someone's stupidity, not ours, has not reached our hands. We went to church on Sunday to a tidy little chapel, which they say will be closed if Mr. Binney[19] is no longer there to keep it up.

It was not till the afternoon of **Wednesday February 28 [Wednesday was 29th February 1888]** that we started, having previously got all our beds and big baggage on board, so we had only a few trifles, which looked sufficient for a 'tour on the Continent' to take with us.[20] We had a fair wind and all sails set till evening, when some were reefed up and it rained and we retired downstairs.

I ought now to describe the ship. She is blue and has high bulwarks and a queer little stumpy figurehead. In the stern the cabin is situated where we abide. We go down a ladder and can stand up in the middle. There are 2 wide bunks; 7 feet of floor between. T sleeps in the one facing the stairs and the other is full of luggage. There is a high seat round the stern end full of things and some little cupboards above; one, a glass one, contains the holy pictures and a little lamp hangs there at night.

At the opposite end is my hammock. In the middle our 2 chairs and table which can stretch half on to my hammock and all are easily folded by in stormy weather. Next comes the hold, a very roomy place filled with sand. Here M and the 11 have their beds and also cook. In the middle stands our little cooking stove and M can sit and cook in his folding chair with great dignity.

---

[17] Agreement or contract.
[18] In 1884 Theodore 'excavated' with the Swan brothers on Andíparos.
[19] Poor Binney will be dead in a matter of days.
[20] Reference untraced, but possibly from one of Mabel's guidebooks, or possibly a reference to Wordsworth's *Memorials of a Tour on the Continent* (1822).

The four shipmen, Kaptan Nikólaos, Andreas the *Devtero Ploiarchos*, or Mate, Gregorios and the large stout 'boy' Stavros (which means cross) sleep in the fo'c'sle. There are 2 large boats, one within the other in the middle over the hold, and a little galley on deck. There is a dog called Zouroukos, who was at first terrified, and us and the little tortoise, Thraki.

Now to return to that miserable evening [Wednesday 29 February?]. M, as usual, was incapacitated and the excellent sailors did not understand cooking for us or waiting at table, so we began by a soup which tasted as if it were made of the sea and rice. After a few mouthfuls I said I had no appetite and would sooner lie down. T was furious. He only got some very nasty mush and no coffee and found himself some walnuts.

He wished the chairs and table at the bottom of the sea and complained bitterly of his size and wished he were no bigger than me, 'and now', he said, 'I shall be *most wretched* if you take to being seasick! And you *know* you *needn't*. You are going to do it on purpose! *Eat*!! And I'm so beastly hungry and can't get enough to eat!' Poor thing I pitied him very much and myself worse for I thought it a dreadful beginning for a Pirate Bold, but my seasickness ended by this refusal of a very horrid dinner.

T spent the night saving himself from falling out of his bunk, for the little ledge which holds in a sheepskin is of little use for his luxurious bedding. I like my hammock better on dry land than at sea for it waggles and shakes and jumps and trembles at every ripple, so of course in the storm I had a fine tossing.

We continued our journey all night but when morning came the captain said we had better make for Myndos[21] on the coast and shelter there. We consequently were at anchor till the following morning but in just as rough water. We were like in a lovely lake between Kos, Kalymnos and the mainland with many islets round but it was too windy to stay on deck. M had recovered and we had a more comfortable dinner. In the morning breakfast was a great struggle as we could not get at the things we wanted.

We were off again on Friday morning and had a really delightful sail, turning to our right round Kos where we could plainly see the square fortified town with the newer one spreading round and even distinguish the top of the plane tree which was there B.C. and was supported by marble columns now grown into it.[22]

The strait is very narrow. Then round Kavo Kryos to our left and we cast anchor outside the little bay which at night we got into. The extreme end is

---

[21] The ancient city of Mydos/Myndus, modern Gumusluk, some 25km north-west of Bodrum. A fair sail from Sýros.
[22] Mabel does not seem to have disembarked at the Knights' city of Kós. She is probably reading of the famous tree from Murray's guide. It would have told her that Hippocrates' plane tree is 12m around and that it was said to have been planted by the great doctor, who used to teach under its shade. Hippocrates is also reported as having lived for a while on Thássos.

hanging on by a narrow isthmus with a bay on each side. We are in the southern one, the largest, protected by the remains of an old breakwater. All around, the rocks have been carved into quays and sloped and as far as the eye can reach up the mountainside are remains of polygonal and Hellenic walls and temples and tombs. The northern bay is very small and quite round and has been protected by a castle. Knydos must have been a magnificent city.

We landed and took a scramble and chose a digging place. We had a rainy night and the rain made us late in the morning. There was a regular gale outside and a Symi smuggler which left about midnight returned the following evening for shelter. We did not find either of the places we dug in satisfactory but it was not till evening that we returned to our blue home for another rainy night.

March 1888 – The Turkish coast

Sunday it rained so that I never left the cabin till evening, when T and I went for a wet scramble on this head. T had been a walk with a Turk called Mustapha and seen some large polygonal tombs, so on Monday we all went in the boat part of the way and set to work with the addition of 12 inhabitants. But presently we were told by some of the crowd, black and brown, that we must shew papers, so it ended in our striking work and deciding on sending M on a donkey with Mustapha 7 hours to the village for leave – with a golden bribe – and at the present time of writing, namely on the afternoon of **Wednesday, March 7th**, he has not returned.

Yesterday we went out with some of our men and dug for 3 hours unmolested. The only person who came to us was a poor old Turk, Mehmet Aga (captain), who had been a prisoner and slave in Russia 21 years. He told us of another set of these great tombs, so this morning we went still further in the boat and dug there till 10 when we were warned off quite civilly by a black *mudir*, who threatened, however, in the end to capture our tools. T told him he would have his head broken if he did and he sat down trembling and we walked towards the bay. We have onboard 2 circular altars, one with a serpent twined round it, and one with bulls' heads and garlands and a drapery round the bulls' faces.[23]

Wolves and porcupines live here and the former howl at night. T crept far into a cave where he saw a great many bones and was just going to strike a match when he bethought him it was very like a wolf's den, so he hastened out and they say 2 have been killed just here and there is still another.

---

[23] The British Museum has these. Item 1888, 1003.1 is the 'marble altar decorated with a snake', the other (1888, 1003.2) is a 'marble funerary altar decorated with bulls' heads and hanging garlands. It is inscribed "The People".'

It is the first rainless day but very cold and windy. The captain cooks for us while M is absent. 6 o'clock after dinner the same evening. We were right to be anxious about M. About 4 came a man with a note from him saying he is a prisoner 2½ hours off. He had gone to Dacha, the large village 7½ hours away, and there the *mudir* said he could not possibly give us leave to dig, and he had got back to the little hamlet (2½) when they took him prisoner, saying we must pay 5½ Turkish pounds, something less than £5, for damages and also pay a whole day's wages to the 12 inhabitants for 3 hours' work. We had offered them half. T wrote back and said we had done no damage, unless in a path which an hour's work would mend, and if they wished their wages to come to the ship with M for he would send no money. M has the gold but no change. He has 9 Turkish pounds.

First 6 men armed were going up, but then it came out that the messenger, in whose house he is, would release him and bring him half way for a pound (18/-), so he was brought on board and told to bring M to the ship and he should have his pound. So all is now activity here: preparing the ship to sail away the minute he is on board. There is a strong *boreas*[24] blowing and I dare say we shall put in somewhere. We want to go to Agios Jannis,[25] south of Astypalaia, a small island inhabited only by shepherds.

Thursday [March] 8th. M never turned up that night and no one slept very well and when morning came the *paidhiá* (boys), as they call themselves, were ready to start but T said as the road was very bad indeed, of course only a footpath among rocks, it was better to wait till he had sufficient light to travel by day and duly, to our joy and thankfulness, he appeared alone, having escaped at 5 this morning by the window.

He had been civilly treated by the *mudir* of Dacha, who said he would be reported by the neighbours and would lose his place if he gave leave, so when he returned to the little village the inhabitants took him and put 50 armed men to watch him. He did not dare write his project of escape in his letter and was most thankful T sent no money. Kostandinos did not get his pound but only 2 *medjicks* (6/8) for his message and for being civil to M.

On his way as he passed the 2 houses of Mehmet Aga and another they shouted to each other to catch him, but when one laid hands on him he gave him a couple of blows that sent him down the slope. We then set off at once, leaving the ½ day's pay and all other dues with a man called Vassili, who lives in a little hut in the bay and keeps a 'café' as he calls it.

Now we are sailing coldly but well to Dacha where we mean to have a try at digging before we are discovered. It is *rather* calm.

---

[24] In mythology, the Greek god of the North Wind who lived in Thrace.
[25] Ag. Ioannis or Sírina, the uninhabited islet due west of Tílos and south of Astypálea.

Every evening we economise our books by listening to the most marvellous stories told by one of our boys, Giorgios Nomikós, in which dragons and dragonesses, telegrams, witches, Arabs, old women, seances, kings, who 'take in their own milk every morning', and giants mingle pleasingly. Drakos and drakóntissa mean ogre and ogress. Arápis is a black man. He goes on in a most monotonous voice, like a mill, not as if he were telling but reading. Among the worst people mentioned are Russians.

On Thursday 8th at 5 o'clock we arrive in Dacha Bay. Here the cape is so low and narrow that Kos appears over it. Seeing the village full in sight but about an hour off we decided that nothing could be done there and that it was not even safe to land, so, as it was also very tiresome having to seek places for ourselves, we settled to go to the island of Symi and pick up a guide.

Accordingly on the ~~26th~~ 9th (I am always writing the Old Style dates)[26] we started before sunrise and reached the bay called Panormos, or shelter for all, which is landlocked and where a large white monastery is situated on the shore. This contains very few monks but all the labourers and their families abide there, and as it is the only house of call for any who enter the bay, the great pile of buildings is a lively place.

M was at once dispatched to the town to see what antiquities he could pick up 3 hours off; so he was to stay the night. We went ashore and landed on the quay and went up some steps and in at a great door into a court with 2 storeys of cloisters and one other row of rooms above round it, and the church standing in the middle as usual. We ascended a staircase and were received at the corner of the cloister and seated on a divan and given coffee and jam by the Ekonomos or Holy Housekeeper, the old Egoúmenos being asleep.

Presently he came out and seated himself in a passage which runs away from the cloister to the garden. A fireplace was there and cupboards and there were 4 or 5 steps from the cloister and there sat down the Holy Egoúmenos Macharios, with a brazier before him and our chairs were put round and we talked a long time, and after refusing to sleep and eat in the monastery we said we would return to our ship after vespers or *Esperinó*, which we did.

Saturday March 10th. Great bustle on board. The ship was to be blessed. The *eikons* were brought up and dusted, lanterns lit and a clean towel spread above the companion, and they upon it, with a bowl of water.

Presently Kapitan Nikólaos came on board with a priest and a deacon and a red bundle, out of which came the stoles, books, a bunch of basil and a splendid large, silver dyptich: the Holy Virgin and Child and the Lord Michael, the Archangel, the Judge, and Archgeneral, to whom the place is dedicated, also

---

[26] The 'Old' Orthodox calendar was 18 days ahead.

a lantern. Then we all took our places, bareheaded all but me. The crew stood first and 'the boys' one side and we on the other, amidships.

It was a beautiful, interesting and solemn sight. There were many prayers to many saints, but also many in which we could join, 'for the safety of the ship and the living therein'. Nikólaos and all his companions, from every kind of misfortune at sea, and that our souls and our bodies might be blessed and that we might all abide peacefully together.

All this time Gregorios had been standing with a silver censer and the deacon came round and incensed us all, and then the priest who had been reading the Gospel about the Angel, troubling the water and blessing it and stirring it with his hands, came and sprinkled us and all parts of the ship with the basil and when that was done the priests turned round to chat and drink some wine, while the bundle was re-packed and Kapitan Nikólaos divided the remains of the water between our two largest water casks.

About 10 o'clock we went ashore and were gaily greeted by the Holy Macharios, who exclaimed, 'I'm looking a bit to pass the time and amuse myself'. He had had a pot brought him from the kitchen and put on his brazier, and there he was peeking and stirring and skimming, and I am sure I think it was a very nice occupation for an old gentleman, don't you?

I forgot to say that the day we landed was Friday of the Souls, so after the service a small table was put in the middle of the church with a white cloth on it and a high dish of *kollyva*, boiled wheat with sugar and raisins in patterns on it, and a candle stuck in the midst. This was blessed and afterwards handed round. Everyone had to take a handful and it was supposed to benefit the souls in Purgatory.[27]

The church is frescoed all over inside and the carving is very fine. There is a huge 6 feet high silver Archon (Lord) Michael with only his face painted, a sword in one hand, a good little swaddled soul in the other, and some wicked person under his feet. On the other side is a curious representation of the Entombment of our Lord, made in Russia. All the figures are on wood, in very low relief and painted. They have clothes of cloth of gold with embroidered borders. The sheet is cloth of silver, also embroidered and it is all very well executed.

Well, to return to our muttons, or really lambs, we were invited to luncheon and accepted and a most tremendous meal it was. The table was round, covered with a blue-checked cotton cloth and drawn up to a sofa. There were plates for 8 and scattered round were 19 lumps of torn bread. In the middle a large round bowl of soup, with rice and egg in it. T sat in the middle of the sofa, I on his

---

[27] Still regularly dispensed after services. The rite is extremely ancient and predates Christ by centuries. The ingredients can vary but normally include wheat, chopped nuts, raisins, spices, fresh parsley or mint.

left, and the jolly old Egoúmenos on his right, perched on a bolster, with his left stockinged foot on the sofa and his right on the ground.

He was not very near the table, but with a loud sigh of 'Ahhh! Good luck to us all!' he set to work to give us brimming plates of soup. Next we saw a large iron pie-dish with a very young roast lamb lying in it. This was brought to the table and dished by a Papas, taking it by the legs and putting it in a dish, the Egoúmenos crying out, 'take care that the little thing don't cry!'

Now he set himself to work with a knife and fork and cut off the legs. These he deposited with his fingers at the other end of the dish and began to cut the sides, revealing a stuffing of rice, chopped liver and raisins. He helped us liberally you may be sure and very delicious it was.

He constantly added to our supply some tasty mouthful torn off with his fingers and while helping us, helped himself to a spoonful of stuffing and when the 4 other eaters began to help themselves, 'Stop!' he said to one, 'I want to steal a bit of that' and tore off 2 mouthfuls for me. T being next to him he could thrust bits into his mouth.

Then 4 heads on a baking dish were presented; the old gentleman seized the jaws of one and tore out the tongue and offered it but we assured him we could eat no more. 'You'll eat some *mesythra* and honey?' said he. 'Willingly' said we.

But fancy our horror at seeing the attendant youth bearing in the roast leg of a larger lamb on a long spit. This the Egoúmenos seized and cutting off bits with his knife delivered them to us in his fingers, having first been made to eat some peculiar pickle to keep up our appetites. We had to eat a little, also some salad.

Finally we had *mesythra* and honey, of which there were dishes out of the comb, and then *yaourt*, a sour milk, with honey. 'You must take some Kyriá Verghiniá, it will make all you have eaten sit down comfortably.'[28]

Just as this excellent meal was ended, in came M and he took his place and dined while he told us he had heard of lovely antiquities at Symi but could not even see them. The Turks have made such strict laws and one is afraid of the other telling of him if he sells them.

We thought there was no use remaining and anyhow it was better to be out of that port, hard to leave, so having engaged a man called Joannis, as a sort of pilot or guide and picked up the loaves of bread made with our flour, and borrowing a ship's chart (English) we bade adieu to our kind entertainers and with much tacking sailed away.

As the anchor was coming up we looked at each other and said 'Whither?' So we looked then at the chart and chose a bay called Aplotheka (or simple

---

[28] Mabel is always happy to mention her favourite cheese, *mesythra/mesithra*. One eats it with honey – as with yoghurt.

receptacle) on a large promontory south of Cape Krios and where are the ruins of ancient Loryma. We arrived there in the middle of the night.[29]

Sunday, March 11th. A hot and lovely day. The shores of this bay, which is very deep, slope to the water in most places, but there are several little beaches of sand where landing is easy. On one there is the remains of some large building and another a *mandhra*, or sheep fold. The wall of the yard runs along the shore and the family live in a little hut of rough stones, that one can see through, about 12ft. x 10ft. No window or chimney, fire on the earth in one corner, a few sticks stuck between the stones to hang things on and a shelf made with a pole across the end of the room and some branches on it. It is about 3 feet 6 inches wide and may be the bedroom, but we saw very few bedclothes or possessions of any kind, and yet the people seemed clean in their persons and certainly provide us with excellent cream and milk.

T went a walk in the morning with Vassilis, our headman, and Joannis. I remained on board. The 'boys' went to burn charcoal, which we urgently needed, varying their occupation by dancing to a *sabouna* (bagpipe)[30] played by one of them. M went out and shot a partridge and the sailors caught quantities of pinnas, which we like very much, and an octopus, which we don't.[31] After luncheon we took a long scramble and chose a digging place for the morrow. The ship rolled all night and towards morning it began to pour.

Monday, March 12th. We dug quite unmolested at large tombs, all with altars on them, but vainly. Tuesday we set off in the large boat with Gregorios, Vassilis and 5 others, Christos, Nikolaos, Spiro, and 2 Kostandionoses. There was no wind but a tremendous sea. We also took a shepherd, who promised to point out a statue of a pig (this usually means a lion). We went east to a little harbour called Sigás and then walked to the sea on the other side of the promontory called Sikies (fig tree); however, again we had a disappointing day and were very glad to put into Aplotheka again out of the rough sea. We rolled all night and set off about 7.30 for the mouth of Makri bay.

Wednesday, March 14th. We had a fair wind till 4.30, not much, but a tremendous swell and we rolled about all day. Then came a squall of wind and rain, which caused great activity to the sailors for an hour or more and we had to wish for fiddles for our dinner, soup overflowing, etc.

About 6 the wind fell and we could not get into our bay or round the island and so we continued the whole night and here we are now.

---

[29] Aplotheka Bay (below 'Kavo Kryos', on the Turkish coast, north-east of Rhodes, and an access to the ancient cities of Loryma and Sigas).
[30] For this and other musical instruments, see pp. 4 and 5.
[31] The pinna is a large bivalve. Its shells are often to be seen decorating restaurants, but they seldom appear these days on their menus.

Thursday, March 15th. We are in the bay but can't get on, so some 'boys' have been put in the boat to row us. It is a lovely day. Yesterday the Symi man was dismissed, being utterly useless and the chart returned, we being now out if it. We have now been more than a fortnight on board the *Evangelistria* so we feel quite at home. There is fortunately room for us all to move about when sailing. All my companions' beards are growing and all, including myself, becoming more shabby.

Well at last we arrived about 8 at a little hamlet in a narrow little bay. It is called Tarsenah[32]. We landed and went to the *kafeneion* and drank coffee and questioned, and after wandering about a little and admiring the lovely view of snow mountains we started with 6 'boys' and 2 of the inhabitants in the big boat and rowed about an hour to a place called Karoupia (carob or locust tree), where there were rock-cut tombs like temples. The place we are in is a tangle of sea and land. Islands, islets, inlets, isthmuses and trees to the water's edge, and the sea like a glassy lake. We had stiff work to get up to these tombs, climbing round rocks, hanging by branches, and screwing ourselves up through bushes, but though we found all these splendid tombs open we had a delightful day's sightseeing. We got back to the ship about 4 and I took one or two photos with difficulty, and finally we dined on deck and watched the stars come out, and earnestly wished our friends could see us. And we were so glad to be still after our 48 hours' rolling.

I said to T, 'We have had Peace, Hope and Thankfulness to dine with us.' 'And Charity', he solemnly said, 'For you know we have given some quinine away!' A boat had come with a woman of fifty rowed by a boy. She came to beg some quinine saying she would bring 2 or 3 eggs, which however I begged her not to do. She had dressed herself thus. First a pair of long full trousers of coloured cotton, then a white shirt fastened at the neck only with a buckle, very like the Norwegian *söljes*, but only made of moulded lead.[33] There is a coat cut up to the waist at the sides and a handkerchief on her head. Also there came a boy bringing some milk to buy some rice, which M accordingly sold him.

Next morning, **March 17th** [presumably Mabel means **Friday, March 16th** here], was dead calm, so ordering the ship to follow we set off in the large boat with 5 of our men and M and a guide, and plenty of arms and also tools, and rowed over an hour, apparently in a lake, and landed at a little beach and then had first a fearful steep stony bit, with a path and then a sloping tract of smooth clover, then up and down a pretty good path and finally reached a paradise for

---

[32] The little island of Tersane across the bay from modern Fethiye. (The Greek word (from Turkish) *tarsanás* means boatyard or, even, arsenal.)
[33] The *solje* is a traditional Norwegian brooch most often associated with wedding costumes and other traditional folk attire. It is normally silver or gilt.

archaeologists and tortoises, a smooth carpet of clover with ruins sticking up and inscriptions and broken statues lying round.

We had a capital day, finding inscriptions constantly.[34] There are a great many mausoleums and from the inscriptions we find that the place was called 'the Lydais'[35] and it must have been a splendid place, looking down into 2 bays. We left off at 4.30, having to take squeezes[36] by the way. The upward side of the pass was very sunny and the weather this week has been quite summery.

Saturday [March 17th], St. Patrick's Day. We were badly in want of him, such a lot of venomous serpents and scorpions had to be killed.[37] It was a most happy time for us (truly, if the sorrows of archaeologists are keen, so are his joys). Inscriptions turned up faster than they could be squeezed.

T was to be seen flitting about in the distance with pail, brushes and paper, while I directed workmen in the morning and after luncheon we went up to 2 large mausoleums standing on a ridge over the sea. To my great joy I am spared the trudge back as a mule has been hired from a Yourouk[38] named Hassan to carry me up and down, or rather, over the pass. There are huts, or rather arbours, covered with goat's hair-felt, black with smoke, inhabited by nomads who have their camels browsing about. Naked camels of all ages look very pretty in a wood.

They seem quiet people but are armed, so we do too, and very formidable it looks to see all the guns stuck handy round the daggers and to see 6 inhabitants of Tarsenah who daily come by boats, arriving with guns as well as tools. 'Are many, perhaps, here,' said M in the most insinuating tones to a Greek-speaking Yourouk, 'sometimes a little bad?' 'Not at all!' said the Yourouk. 'Nevertheless,' said M, 'We being strangers, and not knowing, are armed'. 'You do well,' said the Yourouk, very quietly, 'to have one's weapons at hand, guards a man'.

The Yourouks are very funny to look at; all their hair is shaved but a lock in front which hangs back over the head. They wear waistcoats 6 or 8 inches deep and wide sashes, and their baggy drawers with wide hem at the top through which is a thin like an embroidered necktie which is tied so low and so loosely that it has a most precarious effect. They seem clean enough, though ragged.

---

[34] Canon E. L. Hicks was good enough to research Theodore's inscriptions from this expedition in an extremely interesting, and not always uncritical, paper (*JHS* 10, 1889, pp. 46–85). Not only does it contain the two detailed maps Theodore drew (reproduced here on p. 224), but also some rare extracts from his (lost?) notebooks.
[35] Ancient Lydae.
[36] For squeezing, see p. 78 note 23.
[37] Among other miracles, the patron saint of Ireland managed to rid the island of its snakes.
[38] *Yourouk* here means, not a tribe as such, but a generic for nomad or wandering herdsman, from the Turkish *yurumek*, to wander. Theodore presented a paper on them to the Royal Anthropological Institute of Great Britain and Ireland, subsequently published as 'The Yourouks of Asia Minor' in the *Journal of the Anthropological Institute,* (Vol. 22 (3), 1890–1891, p. 276).

Friday, the first day we dug, we had them all seated round as it is their day of rest.

Sunday [March] 18th. We spent the whole morning at home and after luncheon we walked up to the 2 big tombs with M and 4 'boys' and the armed archaeologist took squeezes while the armed photographer was about her business.

Monday and Tuesday the digging was chiefly at 2 large mausolea at the top. We found in one 2 sarcophagi, broken and very rough bad work, only interesting as having many busts, heads and figures and garlands all over them. In the other we found small fragments of a sarcophagus of very fine work and one not so good and bits of 2 reclining statues. We shipped a pretty bit of bas relief of the sarcophagus, Hercules and a ram, and a bit with a boar's head on it, and returning we announced that we were ready to leave that place in the morning.[39]

Though the way between these 2 mausolea was awfully difficult by reason of stones, there was also a very delightful dining room where we could be cool in the shade. It was like a little cottage. All this time has been like summer. Too hot.

Wednesday we set off to another part of our 'lake' but the wind being too slow for us we descended into the big boat and got long before the *Evangelistria* to a bay inhabited by Yourouks and filled with wood stacks. No beast being forthcoming for me I had to use that of the Apostles. First steep rocky path was cool and smooth through a pine forest and then down again.

We visited many tombs of all kinds: rock-cut, built and graves in the earth. Made out from coins we found and inscriptions that the name of the town had

---

[39] Many of these fragments are in the British Museum (1888, 1003.3–9). Some are said to be from the sarcophagus of one Coccias Sarponides. Some of Theodore's marbles are fairly bulky (one altar is 75 x 60cm) and indicate the strength of the team he had to employ to remove, pack, and stow them on his yacht. But Theodore would have liked more. On 20 April, from Istanbul, he writes to Arthur Smith at the British Museum, updating him on their expedition. 'Our noses are turned homewards again; our 50 days' cruise along the southern coast of Asia Minor has been productive of, I hope, several satisfactory discoveries. I think I have run to ground the home of our little marble figures and that cult and also hope to have found a town or two. Our stock of booty is not heavy owing to the fact that we never could stay more than 3 or 4 days in one place. Of new inscriptions I have between 30 or 40. Thanks for sending the map. It unfortunately arrived after our departure but I could not have done more at Capo Krio than I did, for we were driven away by force and nearly got into a scrape. I expect we shall be a few days in Constantinople but Hamdi is at his diggings now so I don't think we can get any nearer our permissions for Thasos just at present. It is something wonderful the system Hamdi has organized for protecting antiquities; the moudir at Capo Krio refunded the £10 baksheesh! And everywhere along the coast where there was anything in the shape a governor it was impossible to do anything. It would be far easier to turn brigand and rob the inhabitants than to play the part successfully of an archaeological pirate. We are well but attenuated, our privations on occasions having been excessive. What marbles we have we are despatching from Syra. We had a great fright there for the Greek government seized a lot of marbles dug up by a Frenchman on Amorgos, and the police were all alive, but luckily we had got our papers from Turkish waters and I hope they will be all right. We shall be at home on 15th of May. Yours sincerely, J. Theodore Bent'

been Lissa and found glass beads, copper and silver coins, a bronze disk, a silver salt-spoon, and a very nice earthen jug with a garland round it.[40]

We dug there 2 days. The 2nd I had the benefit of a horse to bestride. We dined on deck and as I was going below, T was holding a folded chair over the ladder that I might take it when I was down. This made me miscalculate the width of the ladder and I stepped into the air, but I was brought up by my jaw coming against the sliding lid of our cabin. T and Stavros picked me up. I felt rather stunned, but as I had broken neither my neck, by falling headlong down, nor my jaw, I felt very thankful.

On **Friday [March] 23rd,** we set sail early but were long in getting out of the 'lake'. Then after much calm we had great contrary winds and we changed our destination 8 times between Myra, Castelorizo, and Leviza.[41] Every time we changed to please the wind it changed too and there we stuck in the same hole in the sea and neither back nor forward could we get 2 days and nights.

By the time the first night came I did not feel so well as could be wished, so stayed in bed next day. There was no pleasure in being up and it was hard to dress and everything was banging about, so I read and had tea and arrowroot biscuits.

Next morning, **Sunday [March] 25th,** we had violent wind and reached Myra with great difficulty. We were all on deck holding on hard and getting ducked and wondering what was going on in the cabin, but it was impossible to look and see till we anchored in the wildly tossing water. Thus we found the table had not fallen, only turned round and shed all that was on it, but nothing was broken.

We soon landed on some rocks on the edge of a desert of some miles. First we sat and rested, then having brought our prayer books we pretended the rocks were a cathedral. Next we roasted chestnuts and afterwards walked over the desert. There were great things like railway embankments running in all directions and all carved into ribs down the sides by the wind, very hard to climb up if not down. There is a great shingly beach between this and the sea and under it a great city. In between this and the mountain is the present village of Myra. In the night, that anchorage not being safe, we voyaged some miles and found ourselves at the I. of Kakova, in a lake again but bare and rocky, not wooded like our last.

Monday [March] 26th. Off with M and all the 'boys' to go to Myra. We were in the big boat. We tried to land at another place where a dismal swamp which joins the desert runs down to a sandy beach. At each side of a pretty wide

---

[40] This whole region is widely enjoyed by yachtsmen and holidaymakers. The Bents are now in Sarsala/Sarsila, a pine-fringed bay and the starting point for the trail to ancient Lissa. This jug (15cm high) – '…decorated with garlands in relief' – is in the British Museum (1888, 1003.11).
[41] The area of Myra and Leviza is one of the main regions for classical antiquities and, above all, the famous Lycian rock tombs. The present-day island of Kastellórizo (Megísti) is the southernmost Greek island, although just a nautical mile off the Turkish coast, opposite Kaş.

bay close to the rocks ran down a small river with a sandy bar. We tried both sides and ran aground, got off, and at last clambered on to quite the outside of a mountain, where it was deep enough for the boat and had to scramble round it, over rocks and through bushes, up and down, as we could, then down on to the sand and finally struck into this path on the left bank of the left river which led us to Myra.

We did not know that a wider river was in the middle, over the bar of which we could have got the boat and had only about a mile or so to walk. But if we had we should have missed seeing a huge palace wanting only roof, windows and wallpapers to make it quite comfortable. It had an inscription about the Emperor Trajan. The whole swamp is crowded with ruins of fine buildings and great sarcophagi stick up in the water (oh! how the ship waggles!). This river smelt strongly of sulphur and indeed all the bay. When we left the swamp there was a great cracked plain and then Myra.

By the bye, a horse had been awaiting me at our first anchorage, so he was found and we lunched from our basket at his owner's house in a balcony, which serves as a kitchen, with the addition of some eggs and milk, at 10.30 and none too early for our appetites. Then, I bestriding my steed, which I can now do nearly as well as Jeanne d'Arc, we went first to the theatre, the best preserved I have seen, very nearly perfect, but a little earthquaked and much sunk.

I forgot to say that on our arrival at the village we met the *Egoúmenos* of a monastery of which he is the only monk. St. Nikolas was born here so it is considered a very holy spot.[42] The Russians therefore spent 4 years and £T 2000 on digging out the old church 18 or 20 feet full of earth. There are still some of the old vaults and domes with frescoes and pavements tessellated. Now it is re-roofed. It reminded us of S. Clemente in Rome. We were so hot we were thankful to have a shady seat and some coffee.

The women here all wear the dress of Kasteloriso: long full coloured cotton trousers, then the shirt fastened down the front with 5 large round silver buckles, and then married women wear a gown slit up to the waist at the side. The 2 front bits are often tied back as they become mere strings. Then a jacket with sleeves ending above the elbow and very long-waisted, and very low is wound a scarf. The girls do not wear the gown. They have a fez on the head and a turban round it or not.[43]

---

[42] Nicholas of Myra (AD c. 270–c. 350), was *the* bishop, Christian saint, and Santa Claus. His relics were removed from Myra in the 11th century and ended up in Bari, Italy. A tiny fragment of his finger has recently (2006) been donated to his eponymous church in Ermoúpoli, Sýros.

[43] An interesting observation. Mabel always takes a special interest in local costume. In the decades before the forced population exchanges of 1922, the Orthodox and Ottoman communities on the Turkish mainland had centuries of relatively peaceful coexistence behind them. As with their customs, music, and food, the regional costumes were the result of both 'Turkish' and 'Greek' influences.

But the strangest and most wonderful thing in Myra is the mass of rock-cut tombs, just like houses, one above the other on cliffs around. One stands quite free on a jutting point. Certainly things cut in the live rock are more awe-inspiring than anything built. They made quite a little door, then dug away inside as large as they like and made a slide for a slab of rock to slip along, and when the funeral was over drew this door shut and chiselled off the handle, so these doors only look like one panel of a large one. I had seen pictures of these but was perfectly delighted to see them actually. I never thought I should be in Lycia.

Before leaving we returned to the house where our basket was. A little girl of 6, fully dressed, ran out to see us. When we got into the sitting room she retired to a carpet with some pillows on it and a blanket, which she held up to her chin as she sat by a window down to the floor. Her mother complained that she had seen the doctor, who, as she has a fever, told them to keep her in bed. We said they should keep her covered and lying down and not in such a draught, with 2 windows and 2 doors open. The mother shrugged her shoulders and said, 'You see she does not like it'. All children are treated like this, also dogs.

We returned much better than we had come. How glad I was not to have to walk; it was bakingly hot. Not long after we had got among the rocks which skirt the plain we came to the river, where was our boat, which 2 'boys' had fetched. When we arrived at the bar, we alone stayed in; with much heaving and many fears of upsetting, we were lifted over into the sea. We brought an inhabitant with us as guide and interpreter who brought his bedclothes.

Tuesday [March] 27th. We went in the other direction, westwards, down a strait and landed at a mass of ruins (Kakova) where the Austrians spent 2 years, 4 years ago, with 2 ships taking anything they liked, lucky Austrians!, and they painted their flag very large on the rocks.[44] Here, of course, we found nothing to dig, but were very much interested with all we saw. This town had sunk in the sea a good deal and we could see foundations under water. There were high sarcophagi everywhere about and the remains of houses cut in the rocks. They evidently never put a loose stone in when they could cut a wall from rock and acted as if it were soapstone. There is a Turkish village and we persuaded a man for about a shilling to remove his wooden lock from his door for us. We lunched ashore and returned to the ship about 12 and we commenced a holiday, which for me is now at its 4th day.

---

[44] The Austrians were enthusiastic excavators in the Levant in the late 19th century. The site of Ephesus has been under the aegis of Austrian archaeologists since 1895. As well as finds from the region, the Ephesus Museum in Vienna also houses collections found (1873 and 1875) on Samothráki.

We now decided not to go to Cyprus, whither our papers were made out, as we have not enough things to make a great fuss about and transshipping would be difficult, but to go back to Syra. First to go to the island of Kasteloriso, where there is a Greek consul, and have a manifesto made that we came from Turkey so that the Greeks may not touch our things in Syra, and then who is to know where we call on the way.

Now all was preparation for this civilized place. T assured himself that his collar and tie were at hand. I hung out my best Ulster[45] and produced respectable gloves and shoes and M came to ask if the Kyria has not a pair of scissors to lend for the barber. Kostandinos cuts hair very well, that of others, not his own, and shaggy locks 2 inches long were cropped to the roots, beards shaved and trimmed. We really made a very tidy party when we reached our goal. They are a very clean set of men and most obliging and hard working. What the hold would have been like with 12 Bulgarians in it is awful to think. The 'boys' speak of it as '*to káto kósmos*', the lower world.

We had a very dreadfully calm voyage. An average time from Myra to Kasteloriso is 6 hours, though in our storm we did it in 2. We took about 26. We did not land in the regular harbour. The captain said questions would be asked as to why there were 18 people in such a boat. We landed about 8. It is a flourishing looking little town, divided by a point on which rise the ruins of a red castle. The name should be Castelrosso, but first the Greeks have made it 'orso' and then stuck in an 'i'. The Genoese or Venetians made it.

Kaptan Nikólas was greeted wherever he went by friends. He did not seem anxious to be questioned much and once when asked where he had come from gaily answered, '*Apo to pelago*!' (from the open sea). I was delighted at this answer and so, when some women, sitting spinning on rocks, called out, 'Welcome Kyria,' to which I answered, 'Well met!' and then asked, 'Whence have you troubled yourself?' '*Apo to pelago*!' I smilingly replied and swept on round a corner where we could laugh, and who more than Kaptan Nikóla. We went on board for luncheon and I stayed and T did not go on shore till evening. We lunched and now behold Mr. and Mrs. Theodore Bent kneeling at the washtub!!

I think if we had planned it beforehand the idea of so large an undertaking might have frightened us and we might have put off this evil day till a more evil day still fell on us. But it was not so very evil after all.

Stavros was amazed at seeing the india-rubber come up wrapped round the clothes. We made him fill it over and over again from the sea and we knelt and kneaded where a sail gave shade and had soap and soda in our basin and when

---

[45] Mabel's indispensable sleeveless coat.

we had washed enough we together and in unity wrung. Then T started off to the starboard side to hang them up. He soon came back asking, '*How* many towels did we wash?' and '*How* many have you there?' Well we counted and counted but there was no making the clothes come home right from this wash. T had gone down for pins and away a towel had flown to the fishes. They were very soon dry and folded and smoothed and stroked and fondly patted and proudly contemplated.

When night came we became rather anxious about the 'boys', they were *so* late. Not till half past 8 did they appear, gay enough, and usually by that time snores resound all over the ship. As we get up about 5 and always have a great hurry over our dressing, breakfasting and bed-making, it is not to be marvelled at.

Yesterday morning, **Good Friday [March 30th],** we had a very quiet voyage hither to Patara,[46] not too rapid by any means. We arrived at about 1.30 and before we were well anchored T and M and Vassili and a Boy, all armed, were over the side to go and survey the sites of the old towns; there have been 3 here. Going they took 2½, but coming back a shorter way 2 hours. They were late and very tired as they never rested.

Today I could not go as I had no beast. Really the place is only ½ an hour from the sea but no anchorage. Now I am expecting them from thence as T sent 2 'boys' to fetch the boat to that place. I have not been dull a minute, having plenty of books and work. At 9 I went, attended by Andreas and Grigorios, to a polygonal aqueduct about ½ an hour up and visible from the ship and took some photos and about 3 I set off with Stavros in search of a bathing place and was deposited in a delightful one where I much enjoyed myself and I now feel really rested. The weather is like summer.

April 1888 – The Turkish coast

Easter Sunday, April 1st. We rose filled with ideas of camping and planning what we should take with us. But thoughts of how we should sleep with one eye and 3 quarters open and might wish to leave suddenly and wild beasts, etc., made us change our minds and besides a cold wind rose up to determine us, which

---

[46] Located on the mouth of the Xanthos River, Patara was the major port of Lycia for around two hundred years either side of Christ's birth. St Nicholas was born there (see note 42 above). In common with many other river-mouth towns in the region, it lost its importance over time as the rivers silted up. Theodore's inscription notebook contains many 'squeezes' from Patara and there are still many impressive (mainly Roman) monuments to see there, including a triumphal arch, bath complex, amphitheatre, and 'Hadrian's Granary'. An impressive aqueduct leads to Patara, bringing water from the Tarus Mountains. For this and other sites visited by the Bents, there is this (summer 2006): http://www.lycianturkey.com/lycian_sites/patara.htm.

soon sank again. We never left the ship except to bathe. There is absolutely no place near to walk except the daily path.

Easter Monday saw us up extra early and off in the boat for Patara. We had about half an hour's walk along the sandy beach and up over sand-hills inland and through watery marshes which dry up in summer. Many ruins of Roman times were standing about and great palm trees, quite a wood of them.

We stopped at the tent of a Yorouk. T had on Saturday administered some brandy with good effect to his wife and they were very grateful. They seemed delightful people. They kept the tools at night and our oars and wraps by day. They asked us in and I nearly rushed out blinded by the smoke, but fortunately remembered I should be all right if I sat down. They gave us milk and then coffee.

We found nothing but inscriptions. Altogether 14 in Patara.

Tuesday it appeared too rough for the boat so they went overland and I had to stay behind and as before I got on very well and only landed to bathe, which was delicious. When they returned at dark they had brought the tools and done with Patara and now today, April 4th, we are off to Sirina, a small island called also Agios Ioannis, south of Astypalaia.[47] We are to go north of Rhodes, but are being becalmed I fear, a mixture of gentle contrary winds too.

April 5th, Thursday. Dreadfully quiet all yesterday. We worked at the inscriptions, 37 in all, copying out, sewing together, etc., and by evening had not passed the place we could reach by rowing 1½ hour.

It is now near 5 and we have got on gently today and passed the n. point of Rhodes, *Koum* (sand) *Bournou* (head) and close up along the town, very pretty in the evening light. These 2 days we are lunching and dining on deck, not proudly on our chairs, but on the ground where we shall not be in the sailors' way. I wonder what we shall have for dinner. We have no meat, as we could not obtain a kid from the Yourouks at Patara, our last chicken consumed yesterday. No milk. We have some eggs and bacon still. We had potted lobster and some arrowroot pudding for luncheon. We started with the largest piece of Gruyere I ever saw in a private family, or even in a grand hotel; a foot long, high and wide in proportion. It is less now.

The ship is kept very clean and there are no native fleas, but bugs abound. The captain however takes no more personal shame to himself at being their proprietor than to the hosts of mosquitoes or mice. They drop out of the deck and I always keep my mosquito curtain up (for we have them too sometimes) and that saves me a good deal.

---

[47] An uninhabited islet (also known as Ag. Ioánnis) south-east of Astypálea, due west of Tílos. See note 52 below.

April 6th, Friday. The wind got up in the night and in the morning became too strong for us, so here we are back rolling in Aplotheka[48] again. Our only consolation is that we now possess a kid, milk, eggs, a *mysethra*, and a salad of sorrel. The 'boys' and the sailors dine in a very simple way. First the biscuits are soaked, huge and many broken in big bits, then a bowl of lentils, beans and onions, or fish broth, is put in the middle and they all sit round on the deck and those who have no spoons scrape up with their knife on a bit of bread. The crew have a little table 6 inches high and tiny stools as high. They always sit near the steersman. Afterwards all crumbs are swept up and the place and the pots washed, and then they stroll to the water and drink. Indeed everyone is always drinking.

We are at all events halfway. On landing we walked to a *mandhra*, where, when we were last here, a wolf ate a goat's head off. We sat in the hut and they gave us each a little cup of milk and we bought a kid and a *mesythra* and some milk, welcome additions to our larder as potted lobster and bacon and eggs have been our staple commodities. While we were lunching in all security, before landing we were greatly startled by most of our things being cast into my hammock, including the coffee I was about to drink, the wine bottle being fortunately corked, and we being nearly hurled from our chairs. It appeared that a leak on the port side had to be mended and they moved the ballast and finally put the big boat over to starboard, and forgotten us. Great washing of my bedclothes and I had to make my bed a 2nd time.

Saturday, 7th April. As the captain assured that the wind outside was too high and also contrary, T took his merry men, all but 2, overland 1½ hour to Sigas to try and employ the time finding some inscriptions, which they did. I did not go. The 2 who stayed were invalids. Vassilis had cut a slice out of the sole of his foot and had to be doctored with Vaseline, and Gaïda had toothache and he had to be given quinine. He has tried several remedies, including the juice of spurge and a mouthful of seawater.

They all came back about 2.30, having perceived from the heights that the wind was excellent and so T proposed to start at once. At the first word the Kapitan Nikolas, who is very irascible, flew into a frightful fury and refused to go and said he was no *Indianos sklavos* from our country but a free Ellen and all the Ellenes are free, and so on, and fumed and raged and positively refused to go. T told him if he wasted time thus *he* should pay the men's wages, etc., but we had to stay all the same. I spent the rest of the afternoon making butter, about 2½ lbs.

---

[48] The winds have temporarily prevented the Bents from sailing back into Dodecanese waters and they land again on the Turkish mainland, at Aplotheka Bay (Kara Buran), the long spit of land just across the water from Rhodes.

Last time we were here we got some stuff, supposed to be eaten with honey but it seemed disappointing stuff. It struck me, though my dairy experiences are very limited, that I might make this into butter and great success crowned my labours. So this time I told M to take all we could get. It was like cream with all the buttermilk whipped up in it, but now it is pronounced excellent and indeed I hope I am not greedy, but even smelling it is a pleasure to me, and Thraki,[49] who likes it very much.

Sunday [April] 8th. Well, this morning we set sail, but not before dawn, for Sírina, as we thought and with the *scirocco* we should have sailed s. of Telos, which lay directly in our way. We were busy in the cabin but I peeped up and saw we were steering straight for Nisiros, north of Telos. So I told T and he proposed to go up and row the captain, but I said I would make less formal enquiries. I said to Grigorios, 'We are going n. of Telos it seems?' 'Yes,' he said, 'But *very* far n! We are going to Nisiros.'[50]

'We are keeping up to Kavo Kryos.'

'Well! I suppose we shall tack soon, for we shall no doubt pass Telos as close as we did Rhodes.'

The wind was quite fair for Telos.

He shrugged his shoulders as if to say *he* could not help it, and I said 'How soon shall we tack for the south?'

'We are going inside Nisiros.'

'But why?'

'To go to Kos!'

So T went up and there was a frightful, awful row. Now he said he did not wish to go to Sírina at all, and would not go there, and there was no water or harbours and many rocks and no lighthouse and he was always considered a most noble man, and honourable, and so on.

'Very well', said T. 'Go straight to Syra and we will go to the judge and the consul,' etc.

Later with M[51] as a go-between we said if we could not go south, we did not mind going to a small island called Levitha[52] on the way to Syra. This was agreed upon and we did not care a bit. It rained. I looked out again and saw that now we were going s. of Nisiros and close to Telos, past Kavos Kryos and Kos, where we had agreed to anchor for the night far to the dim north.

'Where are we going now, Andreas?'

---

[49] Mabel's pet tortoise.
[50] Níssyros and Tílos in the Dodecanese. The Bents dug on Tílos and toured the Dodecanese in 1885.
[51] Mabel's last mention of their friend Manthaios Símos in 1888. Presumably he would have remained with the Bents until Sýros, changing there for his home on the little Cycladic island of Anáfi.
[52] One of two islets falling between Léros and Amorgós, the other being Kinaro.

'To that place,' very sulkily.

'What place?'

'To Sirina!'

Of course we have lost hours by going so far north and are now fearing a calm.

Next morning about 10 we reached Sirina and landed after luncheon.

We walked across the island to the sea at the other side, where there is a deep bay. Here was a sort of farm, a very irregular enclosure of loose piled stones and very thick walls. The only thing with mortar was the oven. An old woman came out of the dark hut where she was shut in and brought us out little square blocks of wood to sit on and she directed T to where there were some old stones and so I returned to the ship with one man and the rest went off, but finding the earth all gone and only foundations on rocks they returned and we set off again in the afternoon.[53]

We appeared to get on very well and rushed up past Nisiros, Kos and Kalymnos, nearly up to Leros, and we also seemed to be getting on well during the night, but when morning dawned we were down at Astypalaia.

All day we tacked and got up to Amorgos and in the morning, instead of having got round west of Tenos, we found ourselves far too much n.e., at Nikaria, and soon the wind got so bad that we had to go for shelter to Patmos. We were not near the town but a place they call the Kambo. We landed with great difficulty and some very poor and kind people asked us into their cottage, which was very clean, and gave us coffee and I entrusted to them the photos I had done 2 years ago of the monks and the monastery to take to the *Egoúmenos*.[54]

We got very wet in returning to the ship, so I never landed again and T only to take some quinine and little gifts to our entertainers. By this time we were not on speaking terms with the captain, or rather he with us. We set sail again about

---

[53] The island is uninhabited now but for summer shepherds and yachtsmen. Theodore wrote a few words on his finds there for the *Classical Review*: 'The small island rock, anciently known as Sirina, now as Hagios Joannis, occupies a somewhat important position in the Aegean Sea, as one of the stepping-stones by which the earlier inhabitants of Karia must have travelled westwards; it has two good harbours, one to the north, and one to the south, and is placed midway in a long stretch of sea between Karpathos and Astypalaea, in both of which islands traces of this prehistoric race have been found. Having carefully examined Anaphi, an island lying to the west of this line of route, and having found there no traces whatsoever of this early population, and knowing that Astypalaea, Amorgos, Naxos and Paros are full of their tombs, I was considerably interested in discovering in the ruins of a square fortress on Sirina quantities of obsidian knives, which at once identified this rock with the grave in question, and proved to us that they made use of it as a halting-place on their way to and from the marble quarries of Paros; in fact Parian marble, objects of which are so frequently found in their tombs, would seem to have been their chief quest in these westward migrations.' *Classical Review* II, 1888, p. 329.

[54] The Bents were on Pátmos in 1886, see p. 143.

11.30 and had been gone about 20 minutes and were at luncheon when suddenly we found ourselves shut up, all down on one side. The captain had thrown the rug and books down on us and when T asked, '*vroché*' (rain), he replied '*bora*' (squall).

On looking out an awful scene presented itself. All the sails and sheets were flying wildly and all our men were helping the sailors to loosen them. Behind a black wall was advancing and just on the extreme stern heavy drops were falling. Waterspouts and spindrifts were rushing along and we were tearing back to the rocks. The sailors looking anxiously for the moment to cast anchor, and glad enough we were to hear it go down. Soon torrents of rain fell and there was no more hope of leaving Patmos that day nor the next and it was not till the morning of Sunday 15th that we started.

We had 7 of these squalls and had we not had so many men on board we should have fared like a rather smaller ship a little further out, which had all her sails torn to ribbons. This voyage was very quiet and a little slow and we had not very much to eat. We got near Syra at sunset but did not get to anchor till 2.30. They had to row in.

Tuesday 17th April. We were visited and counted by the health officer and looked at by the customhouse officer who came on board, and were most thankful to leave our blue ship to enjoy the blessings of the land.

We had a very wretched time in Syra. First we could only get a temporary bedroom till 8 pm. Then next morning we rose early and were ready for the French steamer, which never arrived till next day. Every meal we ate in haste and fear of having no time to finish it and finally undressed in a very *impromptu* way to sleep, and after all unpacked in the morning to dress, having been called up at 5. So we went on board before breakfast at 9.30, glad to pay extra for that meal for the pleasure of being settled for 3 days. But we enjoyed the Hôtel d'Angleterre food *very* much![55]

The *Volga*, on which we went on **Thursday 19th April,** is a fine large ship. There were a great many passengers. We recognized young Mr. Bell of the Asia Minor steamers and there were 3 student interpreters, Mssrs. Fontana, Monahan and Freeman, going out to Constantinople to learn eastern tongues and become consuls – a splendid thing which will deliver us from Levantines.

At Smyrna, Mr. Strauss, the American minister already known to T, came on with his wife and child, also Dr. Bliss and Miss Fensham of a school at Skutari, likewise Mrs. Mumford with her adopted Bulgarian daughter, who keep a school at Philippopolis. All these 4 call themselves missionaries. Every American who

---

[55] The Hôtel d'Angleterre, the Bents' favourite hotel on Sýros. At Istanbul, a few paragraphs down, it is the Hôtel de Byzance.

keeps a school does, though education and not religion is their object. There were also Sir Frederic and Lady Hughes.[56]

We had a very calm passage and just managed to be allowed to land, though we feared being kept on board till Sunday morning. We stayed at the Hôtel de Byzance till Wednesday. On Tuesday we lunched at the embassy and the company consisted of Sir W. and Lady White, Miss W. her German companion, Mr. de Graz, Mr. Finlay and Miss Gonne, a tall and handsome damsel dressed in white Broussa gauze, who says she means to go on the stage. They asked us to go to the reception in the evening, but we did not.[57]

We had wished to go to Nicea and go home by Adrianople and Soffia (this is how it is pronounced), but finding that our proposed companions would not be ready for another week, we left Constantinople by train on **Wednesday, April 25th** early, at 7 that is, and travelled 12 hours.

I forgot to say that on Tuesday we went over to Skutari, as Miss Fensham had asked us to visit the 'mission home', a large boarding school for Greeks, Bulgarians and Armenians, where they learn far too much and are made much too comfortable.

The line we travelled over is not interesting. It was made by Baron Hirsh.[58] The Turks refused to pay extra for tunnels, etc., and would only pay by the kilometre, so he waggled it about, sometimes quite in a zigzag with no cuttings or banks, and never near a village and they are all quarrelling over it still. Mrs. Mumford was in the train and asked us to visit her. We went to the Hôtel Gennik near the station, dirty and bad food. We had to drive about 2½ miles to the town.[59] It is a very picturesque town with 2 big rivers, Maritza and Toundja, and a good many fine old bridges. The Turks had their capital here after they left Broussa. The old palace, Eski Serai, is represented by a few ruins in a field. The old mosque is immense but only the outside is worth seeing, with its court and washing fountain. We had a letter for our consular agent, Mr. Cecil Hallward, a student interpreter; only here for a few weeks and going to Baghdad.

He was very kind in showing us about and we lunched together at the Roumeli Han in the town. Afterwards we took a walk near the Eski Serai and to my great sorrow I lost my dear little tortoise. I dropped him in some long green weeds and I can only hope he is happy. He is getting so intelligent and had been such an amusement on the ship that we miss him very much. One thing I have

---

[56] The Bents are *en route* for Istanbul, via Smyrna. As usual, Mabel enjoys listing her fellow travellers.
[57] A group photograph of Sir William White and his staff, including Mr de Graz (des Graz) and Mr Finlay (Findlay), can be seen on p. 344.
[58] This train line opened in 1873.
[59] The couple are in Adrianople (Edirne).

discovered is that tortoise babies are like others and do not begin to understand much till they are about a year old.[60]

We started on Friday at 7 with Mr. Hallward, who had been invited to stay some days at Philippopolis with Capt. Jones V. C., our Consul General.

The Turks had recognized at last the separation of Eastern Roumelia[61] and had set up a custom house at Moustapha Pasha on the previous Monday, so the very day we passed at 12 o'clock came a telegram from Sofia to make a custom house also, and at 1 o'clock they began upon us. They visited our carriage and took all our names down in pencil and threw away or took away some salad someone had for his luncheon for fear of phyloxera.[62]

At 3 we arrived, and as we had letters for Capt. Jones called on our way to the station. He is a perfectly delightful man who is covered with scars and was nearly buried alive after the Alma. He gave us some tea, sent his *kavass* to order our room at the Hotel of Bulgaria, invited us to dine and lunch while at Philippopolis, and then we returned to the hotel and cleaned ourselves and he and Mr. Hallward called in half an hour and took us a tremendous walk. The town once called Tremontium is situated on and round 3 hills at the edge of the plain of the Maritza. He took us up all these hills, very steep, and it was very windy and also for some time it poured and we had to shelter in a cottage. It is a very pretty place and we enjoyed our walk.

At 7 we got home and dinner was at 8. Mr. Richards, consul of Bourgas on the Black Sea, was also staying with Capt. Jones. We had the best and most civilized dinner since we left home. Excellent wines, hot plates and every sauce or pickle one could think of and most agreeable company. After dinner Mr. Dimetroff came in; we had a letter for him. He is Prefect and had been educated at Robert College.[63]

We went to see him in his *konak* and saw his garden, the public library, the tiny museum of marbles and the good collection of coins, and we lunched and dined with Capt. Jones and met at luncheon an adopted son of Lady Strangford's. Cap. Jones sent us a bottle of marsala and one of claret and half a seed cake for our journey, for which we blessed him much.

---

[60] This is the last we hear of little Thraki. Mabel and Theodore had no children.
[61] A much-disputed region, Eastern Rumelia was united with Bulgaria in 1885. A few paragraphs before, Mabel recounts their visit to 'Philippopolis' (Plovdiv), south-central Bulgaria, on the Maritsa River. Second city to Sofia, the Turks lost it to Russia in 1877. Its Roman theatre, ancient gates and walls still stand.
[62] Phyloxera = a parasitic louse that feeds on the roots of certain vines.
[63] Robert College was founded in Istanbul by Cyrus Hamlin (educator, inventor, technician, architect and builder) and Christopher Rheinlander Robert (a wealthy philanthropist merchant from New York). The college opened in 1863 and, as the nucleus of Bogazici University, still educates today.

May 1888 – Istanbul and Isnik

We reached Constantinople on Monday evening by the same way we came and the following **Wednesday, 2nd May** (St. Athanasios), at one, set off on our pilgrimage to Nice, or Nicea or Isnik or Nikaia. Mr. Pears and his son and Professor Albert Limerick Long L.L.D., head of Robert College, accompanied us, all glad of the opportunity as Isnik is not a place to go to alone.[64]

Dr. Long was the guest of the rest of us. He is about 55 and a very agreeable and very polyglot man – Turkish, Slavik, Bosniak, Bulgarian. We found it very useful and pleasant. We had a soldier and 2 Bosniaks. Mr. Pears caused us to travel free on the railway. In the first place I must say we were warned to say nothing of *our* plans that brigands might not make theirs. Our passports were made out for Ismid (Nicomedia) further along the line and not sent to the hotel but to Mr. Pears for secrecy.

We met at the bridge on the steamer and were soon at Haidar Pasha and reached Tavshandjil by dark. Here the railway *kaïque* was awaiting us to take us to the other side of the Bay of Ismid to Kara Moussa (Black Moses). It began to pour. We sat on the floor of this big canoe on carpets like wet bathing-dresses and endured this about an hour and a half and finally got to a poor, but clean, Turk's house. We had brought all our provisions with us, but as the Turks all sit round one bowl there were no plates forthcoming so we used bits of paper.

The trembling in my writing is caused by the good ship *Tchichatchaf* (ЧИХАЧОВЪ)[65] and the Black Sea. All lay on the floor that night, T and I in a harem room with a lattice, boards so far apart that we could see into the lower room.

We were all ready and anxious to start early, but Mr. Pears could not be got off before 10 to 8. We had also a Montenegrin called Bosco as a servant so we had 9 horses in all, 2 with baggage on which the Bosniaks rode. I have no doubt the 317 Holy Fathers who went to the Council and wrote the Nicene Creed must have gone by sea or some easier way. We saw stretches of a paved road for a hundred yards or so at a time soon lost or broken up. We also found our own way over the country or had to go out of some unpassable lane into cornfields.

---

[64] The travellers are headed for Nicea (Iznik). This city, famed in Christian theological history, was established around 300 BC. The original Council of Nicea was called by Constantine in June 325 AD and was the first ecumenical conference of bishops of the Christian Church. Mabel's later figure of 317 attendees is an unusual one. The figure of 318 is traditional, but other sources give 250 (Eusebius), 270 (Eustace of Antioch 270), 'around' 300 (Athanasius), and 'more than' 300 (Gelasius of Cyzicus). Theodore's inscription notebook of 1888 lists a few finds and he wrote up their visit in an article for the *Fortnightly Review* ('The City of the Creed', February 1890).

[65] Mabel is now practising her Cyrillic.

Sometimes we had a stretch of tracks 70 or more feet wide, sometimes sand, or rock and sometimes the narrowest footpath squeezing through wet trees: 2 on foot could not have passed without one climbing aside. We lunched at a village in a café with our own food and some hot eggs. The inhabitants, though Greek, cannot speak anything but Turkish and they are only just going to begin to have a boys school. I felt sorry and so did we all when the hour had fled and we must under fear of being benighted face the great difficulties of the way again.

Dr. Long's horse fell and he came off. T's fell and rose 3 times with him on his back and at last went over on his side but T was pulled out without damage. I was saved by Dr. Long seeing my girths quite loose; though I had been balancing the saddle some time I had not found out what was the matter and must soon have been over his head.

About 2 hours before we got to Nicea we reached the plain round Lake Askanias and saw our goal in the distance. Then we made our poor tired beasts go as quickly as we could and got to the walls by sunset. The great triple walls with towers all round now enclose large tracts of fields besides the poor village with its old church and ruined mosques. Here too the Greek inhabitants talk Turkish. The owners of the house we were in, opposite the church, however come from another place and speak Greek.

Oh! how tired and stiff we were. I was aching all over for the last 2 or 3 hours, but knowing it would not be long before we could have dinner, I at once made tea to the great refreshment of our bodies and support of our tempers. There were plenty of cakes, both seed and plum, and every day we had a regular sit down tea.

The 3 others had their beds laid on the floor of our dining room with holes between the boards that our feet would have gone down between if we had not been careful. There was a loose board, to be tripped over on the worse place and it was hard to manage the legs of a chair. They had no window glass. We had, in a room opposite, and our attendants abode in publicity [sic] and cooked on a brazier on a raised *daïs* in the passage.

We found the ringing of the bells in the night before the Greek Good Friday rather trying.

Mr. Pears had seen some inscriptions on large stones in a certain part of the wall some years before when he came with Hamdi Bey and these stones we daily sought and found not. As Mr. P. has not a good bump of locality, great doubt was thrown upon him. It was thought he had seen them in some other city walls and he became really uncomfortable, for inside and out, and above and below, and through bushes, swamps and ploughed fields we toiled in vain, till a happy idea struck someone; enquiries were made on the last day and it was elicited that Hamdi Bey had sent and carried them off and now they must be unticketed in the chaos of 'the Town'. However in the walls and other parts a few inscriptions were found and copied and I took a few photographs.

We attended the 'Second Resurrection' service and for the first time I did not hear the singing of '*Christos aneste ek nekron*', nor did I hear people greeting each other with '*Christos aneste*'. The church is very old and once was covered with mosaics but the dome fell in and little remains but a nice picture over the entrance. There are quantities of storks with their nests on the tops of mosques and one beautiful marble mosque with beautiful old pillars outside it. It is called the Yeshil Djammi (Green Mosque) from the glazed bricks of the minaret.

All the women wear trousers just like the men's bags and as they seem stuffed with clothes it is not a becoming dress.[66]

There are only foundations of where the Emperor Constantine's palace stood and where the Council was held.

On Tuesday Dr. Long, with great difficulty, got Mr. Pears up so we departed from the *Istambol Kapoussi*[67] at 10 to 7. We went back a somewhat different way and only took 9 hours over [it]. As in coming, we got to a village composed entirely of mud and with such a muddy road through it that we could hardly pass. At the worst a baggage horse fell and stopped us all, and while he had to be stripped of his saddle and all, there was sinking about. There was a causeway of stones and Bosko, the servant, tried to ride on these but they seemed to be floating on the mud and down went the horses' feet and the hoofs caught and for a moment it was very nasty; we were so close together that the plunging of one horse was likely to knock us all down like ninepins.

Getting to Kara Moussá so early we had time to stroll out and see it. There is a pretty little bazaar with vines trailed across it and a mosque at the end. Next morning we sailed across in the same *kaïque* in about an hour and in due course reached Constantinople at 10 o'clock, highly pleased with our pleasant week. We then had 24 hours for packing and preparation and having despatched all but absolute necessities by sea to England, we embarked with very little baggage on board the Russian steamer *Tchichatchaf.*

[Thursday] May 10th. We had a charming cabin, 10 by 12, with iron bedsteads in it and were quite sorry to leave it on Saturday 12th in the morning. N.B. though the Turks are particular, usually we did not have to go to the customhouse on leaving.

We only stayed at Odessa[68] the day, leaving at night, we found a Montenegrin porter at the hotel opposite the theatre who could talk Italian to us and was very kind. He advised us to take our tickets at an office in the town, and on

---

[66] Mabel's doodle is on p. 261 (top right).
[67] The Istanbul Gate.
[68] The Bents have opted for a different route home to London, overland via Odessa.

going there to enquire how much money we would need to change, we found among all the 30 clerks we were shown to, not one who could speak German, French, Italian, English or Greek, but at last someone pointed to a clock, and to half an hour later, and said 'Deutz', so we returned in half an hour and a man who could speak German answered our questions. When however we ultimately returned with the money we had to take the tickets in Russian! from the chief. Now we found those lessons on the steamer of use, for we could understand the numbers and say 'Yes' or 'No' as we thought fit.

At the frontier, Volochyska,[69] we had another linguistic difficulty and found ourselves tied up in so hard a knot with the waiter that we had to be marched all across the refreshment room to find a passenger who could disentangle us in German. All this very much upset our ideas as to the universality of polyglot powers among the Russians.

By the bye, the porter told us to go to the theatre, very large and new and splendid, and we understood all we saw quite as well as the natives as it was all in dumb-show. We also took a drive and were very much amused at the Istvoschiks. In their long gowns they look like immense women and they are all padded so that they look like melons.[70]

Odessa is a very ugly town, not 100 years old and very wide streets, and one-storeyed houses are not very impressive. The lovely green domes were not all copper as we thought, but we perceived many to be painted green. All the food we got was excellent and I think these are all the observations our limited stay permitted us to make.

We stopped 2 nights in Berlin at the Central Hotel. We had travelled from Saturday night to Monday night, the 14th, and nearly always through forests. We crossed from Flushing and on Thursday the 16th [Thursday was 17 May] we safely reached home.

All our marbles reached England soon after, and after spending some weeks here are housed in the British Museum.

---

[69] Woloczyska/Volochisk is a small town, on the eastern Ukraine border, located on the Zbruch River. It is noted for having a train station.
[70] Mabel's doodle is on the page opposite (lower).

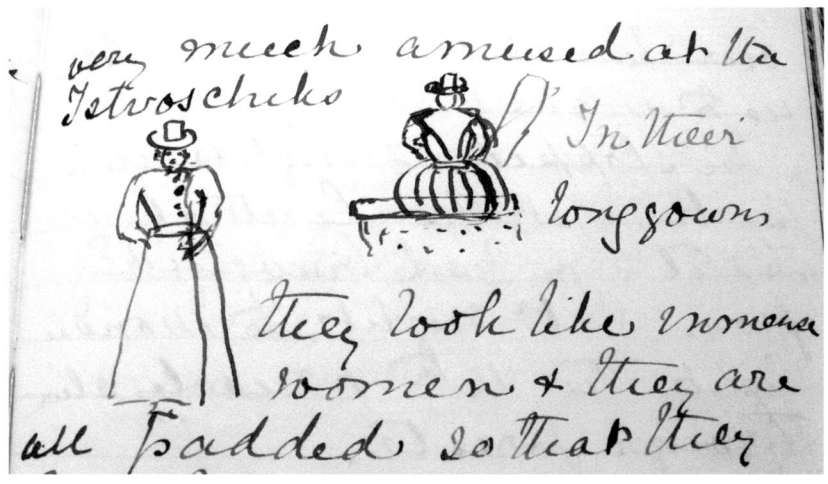

Three of Mabel's doodles: Top left: 'Our housemaid is something like this, with a bucket made of a paraffin can and bare legs.' (page 220, note 58); Top right: 'All the women wear trousers just like the men's bags…' (page 259, note 65); Lower: '…they are all padded so that they look like melons.' (opposite, note 70)

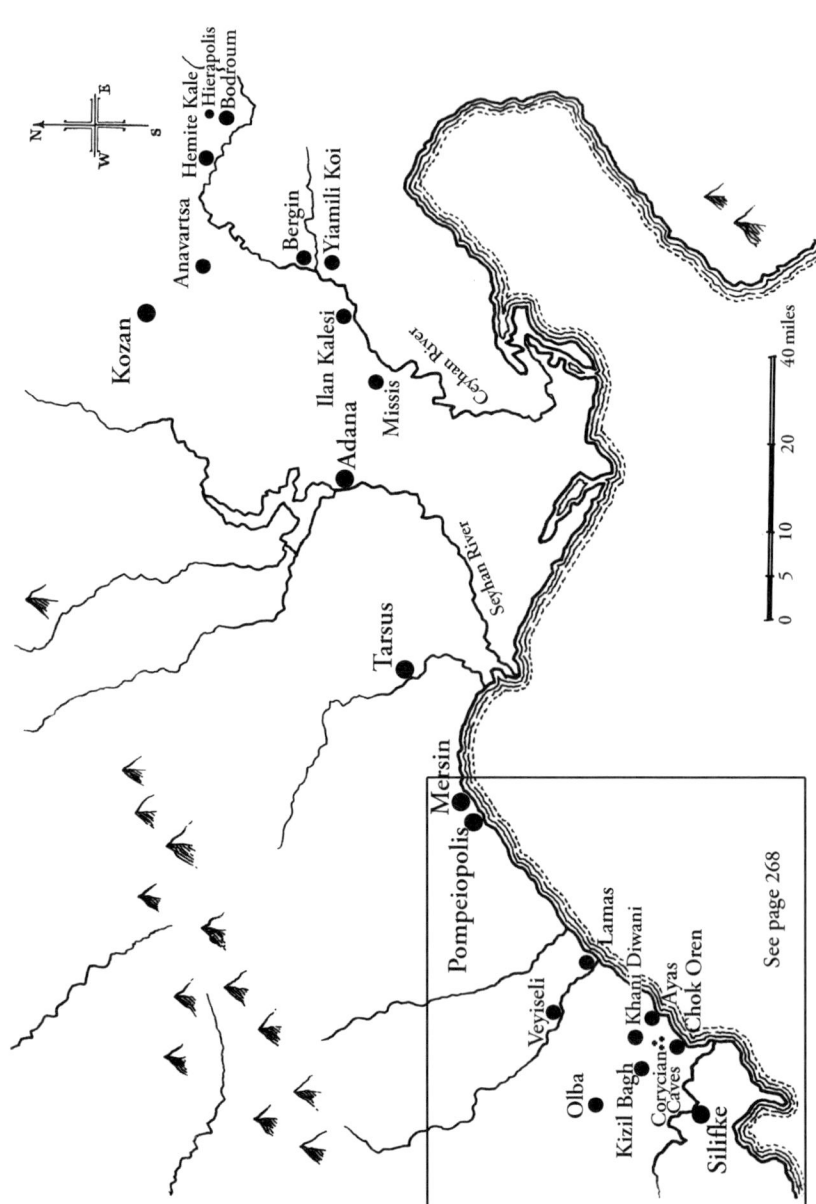

Map 6. 'Rough Cilicia'

Chronicle VII, January to May 1890:

'I looked round the room with an idea of settling but it was an idea to be banished, so I got out T's slippers, as a good wife does in books, and demanded tea, and determined as a feast we would eat some plum-pudding I had brought from home at dinner. It was *so* much better near Olba than at home... M[anthaios] retired to a tomb...'

To avoid the problems of excavating in Greece or Turkey without adequate documentation, Mabel and Theodore spent the 1889 season on an epic trek that takes them from a tour of Bahrein and then up through Persia, landing at Basra from Karachi. This gruelling trip takes up the three notebooks comprising Mabel's sixth *Chronicle* (which is to feature in her volume on Arabia and the Near East). Theodore is developing his personal theories on the origins and influence of the Phoenicians, en route, and publishes a short paper in the *Classical Review* in November 1889 ('The Ancient Home of the Phoenicians'). Two other articles, more topical, are published subsequently – 'The Bahrein Islands, in the Persian Gulf' (*Proceedings of the Royal Geographical Society*, 1890), and 'Under British Protection: Impressions of Muscat, Bunder Abbas & Bahrain' (for an 1893 issue of the *Fortnightly Review*).

It is this, the couple's first lengthy expedition in a region new to them, and the fact that they can freely excavate in lands where British interests are more favoured, that give Theodore and Mabel the appetite for exploring in a south-easterly arc, taking them far beyond Greece and Turkey, for the remainder of their travels together ...but one.

Mabel's seventh *Chronicle* finds the team (again joined by Manthaios Símos, who was offered, but declined, the extremely onerous Persian campaign) in the far south-east of Turkey, in ancient Cilicia (pronounced 'Kilikía'), about as far as Theodore can get from the suspicious eye of Hamdi Bey and his archaeological service officials. Even then, in this remote sweep of the Ottoman Empire, washed by the eastern Mediterranean as far as the shores of Crusader lands, Theodore runs into trouble with the local authorities as he negligently delves through Byzantine monuments in search of traces of the times of Alexander the Great.

The *Chronicle* even ends with Mabel copying a sharp, but polite, rebuke arriving from an official of the Adana consulate (9 April 1890) into the last page of her notebook:

'Dear Mr. Bent, The Governor General, having received information that you are revisiting the same places you had already visited some time ago on the road to Selefka, and that you are taking photos or plans of the various places, requests me to make you acquainted with the fact that the taking of photos or plans of the places is not allowed without the special permission of the government. His Excellency therefore requests me to invite you in a very polite manner to discontinue from taking photos, etc., as above mentioned. Complying with His Excellency's request, I ask leave to add that it would be better if you came back to Mersina in order to avoid any possible troubles with subaltern officials. The best way to continue your scientific investigations unmolested is, in my opinion, to request His Excellency, Sir William White, to obtain for you from the ministry at Constantinople the required permission. N. J. Christmann'

What drove the Bents to Turkey again in 1890 was the challenge of lost classical sites. The British pioneer of the region was Edwin John Davis, whose *Life in Asiatic Turkey* (London, 1879) remains in the bibliographies, and in Athens Mabel sees a 'circular from the Hellenic Society requesting us to subscribe to an Expedition of exploration in Cilicia, to be headed by Mr. Ramsay [the regional specialist, Sir William Mitchell Ramsay] to start in June. "It is most desirable that the site of *Olba* should be discovered and identified." So I declared that we would look for Olba too.' Certainly Theodore would have also been up for the challenge.

Olba was found in western Cilicia. This region, described so resonantly by Strabo, lies on the southern coast of modern-day

Turkey, and was divided in ancient times into two halves: to the west, Cilicia Trachea ('rough' or 'rugged'), a mountainous region bounded by Mount Taurus; and to the east, Cilicia Pedias ('flat'), with its rivers and fertile plans. Historically, the importance of Cilicia lay in its position on the great highway to the east that ran down from the Anatolian plateau to Tarsus and on through Syria into Asia. This highway passed through a narrow rocky gorge called the 'Cilician gate', and hence the strategic importance of Cilicia when invaded by Alexander and Darius.

The Bents and all their luggage arrive in the port of Mersin and make their way the short distance to Tarsus, the home of St Paul. Their explorations were divided into three phases: a reconnoitre along the coastal region, during which Theodore located the site of Hierapolis; a trip inland to see the Nestorian and Armenian churches around modern Kozan; and then up the Lamas valley, where they do, indeed, discover Olbian territory. Theodore's unscientific approach to excavating around the famous 'Caves of Heaven and Hell' has provided another occasion for critics to deplore his methods.

Be that as it may, he did return with much evidence of the region's historical past and his reports are to be found in several papers, including 'Recent discoveries in eastern Cilicia' for the *JHS* (Vol. 11, 1890) and 'A Journey in Cilicia Tracheia', also for the *JHS* (Vol. 12, 1891). The latter were scholarly reports but he also presented an entertaining and readable paper to the evening meeting of the Royal Geographical Society of 30 June 1890 entitled 'Explorations in Cilicia Tracheia'. It was subsequently published in the *Proceedings of the Royal Geographical Society* (London, 1890). Keen to tell academic London of his discovery of Olba, he writes to Arthur Smith (a future director of the British School at Athens) from Mersin. Smith is sceptical, and writes as much for a piece in the *Classical Review* of April 1890.

After his not inconsiderable discoveries in 'Rough Cilicia' Theodore never excavates in classical Greece or Turkey again – going off in search of the influences of the ancient Greeks and Phoenicians in more distant lands – but it was a typically bravura farewell to the region that had captivated the Bents for nearly a decade.

In Athens, the Bents spend time with Ernest Gardner and Charles Waldstein, directors of the British and American Schools respectively, and other archaeologists, including the great Heinrich Schliemann. They attend Court and renew acquaintance with old Greek friends, many now in positions of power. They have time, too, to take in a performance of Meyerbeer's *L'Africaine*. In this Athenian interlude, Mabel adds a throwaway remark, 'I need not say the Acropolis and Museums were not neglected', a line echoed in her last entry from Athens in just seven years, when, alone, she revisits the Greek capital and never begins another *Chronicle*.

Outward bound, Mabel celebrates her forty-fourth birthday, 28 January, on board the 'French M.M. steamer for Mersina'. Their itinerary for 1890 is as demanding as ever: London – Lucerne – Milan – Rimini – San Marino – Ancona – Corfu – Patras – Athens – Smyrna – Mersin – Tarsus and the entire region of ancient Cilicia – Smyrna – Thessaloníki – [Athens?] – Marseilles – Paris – London.

There are notes to this transcription on page xxv. Mabel again refers throughout to her husband as T, and their Greek assistant, Manthaios, as M. This *Chronicle* is written in a dark red leather book (185 x 120mm). The endpapers and edges are marbled. The paper is lined; there are 90 pages and Mabel has filled 89 of them. See Indices for people and places mentioned. Mabel's Cilician place names are written phonetically and occasionally vary in their spellings. They are not always easy to locate on modern Turkish maps, especially on the expedition the couple made to visit the Armenian churches around Sis/Kozan. Our chronicler has pinned a mandragora leaf to one of the pages (page 272). The 1890 volume has several references by Mabel to her photography and it is a great pity that so few of her photographs have survived. In the light of this it seems appropriate to reproduce one of the two very poor images (of Cilician monuments) that were inserted in the notebook (see page 281).

There is an odd departure in this *Chronicle*. Early on Mabel notes, 'Skip this page and the next. Theodore says I can keep the pages I have left out for meditations!' There is something playful in this: the hint of a joke between the couple. But she does not keep these 'meditations' up for long. In fact, they are rather out of character and appear nowhere else in this fifteen-year span of her writings.

At the end of January 1890, in the comfort of the Hôtel des Etrangers, Athens, Mabel decides to start her seventh *Chronicle* with a *résumé* of their journey thus far…

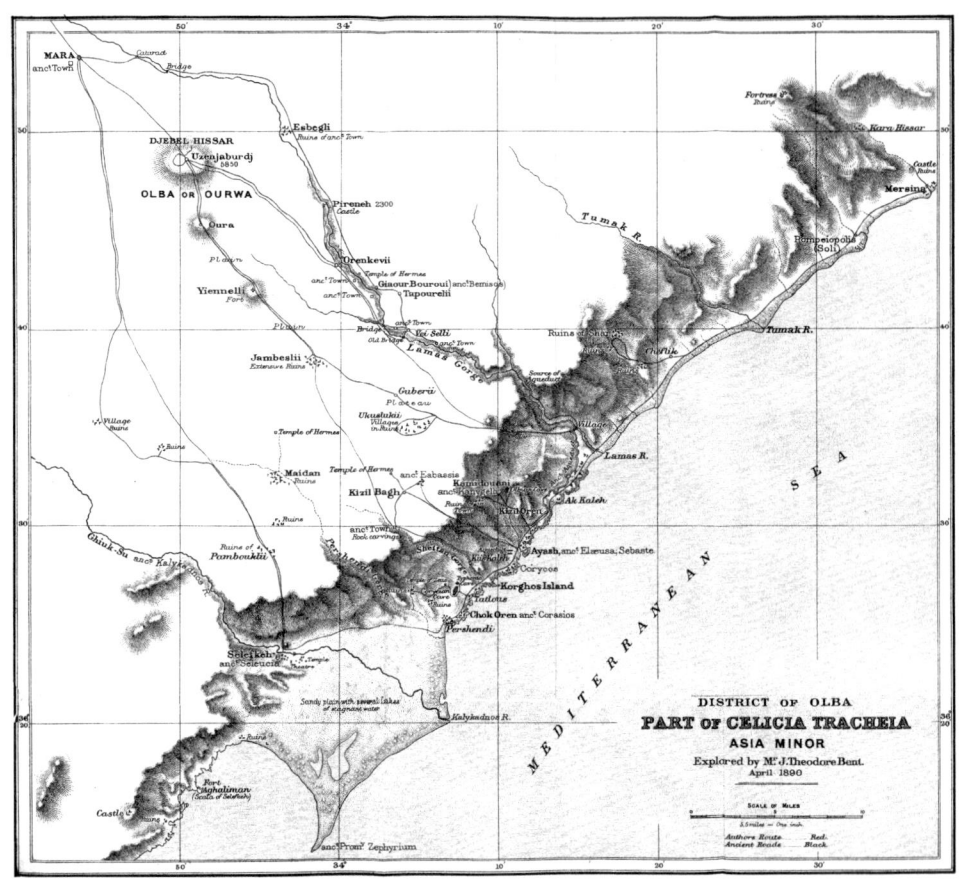

*Map 7. 'Part of Cilicia Tracheia',
Theodore Bent's own map of their routes in the area.*

My Seventh Chronicle
'Rugged Cilicia'
1890

January 1890 – Athens

We left England on **Saturday night, January 18th**, the waves dashing over the steamer from the other side of Dover pier, and neither stopped not stayed till we stopped for the night at Lucerne at the Hôtel St. Gothard, close to the station and very comfortable. And we got no further than Milan without something remarkable to record. Everyone who has been to Milan has seen the Cathedral – we did not, though we were inside it! There was such a fog. We stayed at the Hôtel Torino, not *very* near the station, and often wished we were at the Hôtel d'Europe in the Corso. However we sallied forth into the fog in the morning and thought at length we were near the Duomo. We struck out into the open and lost sight of the houses, then took arms for fear of losing each other, and finally met with a standing tram. 'Where is the Piazza del Duomo?' asked T. 'Here! Here!' said the man laughing. 'But where is the Duomo?' 'You will knock your nose against it if you go much further.' On we went and were within 40 feet of it when we first perceived something thick before us and on reaching the steps only saw a *vignette* round the door and neither height nor width could we see. We returned covered with little wet drops and icy cold and went on to Ancona, H. della Pau, or rather first to the Aquila d'oro at Rimini. I said to T just before we arrived, 'We expect really our warmest welcome at an inn here, though after all Pilade Casabianca may be dead as it is 11 years since we were here'.[1] When we asked after him the answer was 'He died this morning'.

Next morning, Wednesday 22nd, we went to San Marino and saw several improvements. A bad bit of road near the Borgo had been turned and in the Cittá new Palazzo Pubblico was nearly completed.

We ordered luncheon at the inn in the Borgo, whence our meals used to be daily sent to the Cittá, and went thither to the house of Checheko Casale where we used to abide. They seemed very much pleased to see us, especially old Checco, who constantly ejaculated that it was 'un vero carnavale' to have us

---

[1] Italy was Theodore's first field of study. He and Mabel spent several years there in the late 1870s and early 1880s. Pilade Cabianca was the proprietor of the popular Aquila d'Oro hostelry in corso d'Augusto, Rimini.

there again.² They *gave* us a drink and there we walked round and heard the news, and our friend told T many a time that 'if he wanted to have anything done *in republica* now was a favourable opportunity as his grandson-in-law, Ottavio, is the son of Domenico Fattore, the noble reigning captain'. We went on that evening, slept at Ancona and had eventually as much trouble at the steamer office as those passengers who had not Cook's tickets.³

We embarked at midnight on the *Florio Rubattino* S.S., neither large nor clean, and had a tempestuous voyage to Patras. At Corfu, which we reached at midday, we did not land and no one could have any idea of the beauty of the place as it was rainy and foggy. We had such a rough night. I was always out of bed saving things which jumped out of safe places. We kept well though and had even difficulty about getting to land. We had every article opened at the customhouse, which was unlocked for us and such curiosity did the officer display that I laughed at him well and made remarks to tease him, and at last said 'I should like to know this gentleman's name!' So out of the 8 people staring a good many shouted 'What is your name?' and most of the rest shouted 'Kostandinos Theodhoropoulos'. So T wrote it down and he looked much amazed.

At last I said, 'I will not allow these things to be opened except in a place with red light, such as you no doubt have to open photographic things in, like in all large European stations'. 'Red light!' was exclaimed by all, and they all departed still saying, 'Kokino phos!' and presently returned and the officer begged our pardon humbly. 'It was not *his* fault! Had he known *nothing* should have been opened! *That* man (one to whom we had been speaking English) should have said at once that T was an ambassador'. So we went off laughing and mystified. The English speaker explained, 'I said these are decent people!' He said 'Who are they?' 'I don't know but they appear to be very high.' 'Do you think he is an ambassador?' 'I dare say.' So the officer gave himself a jolly good fright. We had a slow, shaky, and pretty journey to Athens and arrived in the dark.⁴

Saturday [January] 25th. Manthaios met us so we could leave our luggage and go straight to the Hôtel des Etrangers, where we recognized the old head waiter and afterwards found the master had gone to the Grand Hotel opposite.

---

² Theodore's Preface to his short monograph, *A Freak of Freedom; or, The Republic of San Marino* (1879) provides a few clues here. The author made an exploratory visit in the spring of 1877, a few months before marrying Mabel. They returned together and Theodore wrote up his history in Florence in the winter of 1878. Signor Francesco Casali, 'old Checco', accommodated the couple in his pension next to the Franciscan Gate, 'most conveniently situated for the passing traveller'. Enlivened with his sketches (a hobby he enjoyed), the book is a much easier read than his lengthier study of Genoa and the Genoese. (His interest in the latter Italian city-state's activities in the eastern Aegean was one of the drivers for his early addiction to the region.)

³ Thomas Cook of course. See p. 176 note 67 and p. 222 note 63.

⁴ The direct railway line from Patras to Athens did not open until December 1897.

We met him one day and promised to go and see over the hotel and did and he took us even to the roof.

Theodore arrived with the influenza, so did not go out on the Sunday. I went to church and then drove to the British School of Archaeology to call on the Ernest Gardners. Some of the French School came in and stayed to tea. I was glad to have Mr. Bourchier to sit by me at dinner. He is writing for the Times. We stayed till Friday in Athens. Mr. Gardner and Dr. Schliemann, the Pericles Valaoriteses and Mme. Spiridion and the Kyriakouli Mavromichalises came to call, the latter several times, and one night took me to their box at the opera to see 'L'Africaine'. The savages with white hands and faces and ill-fitting black jerseys looked very funny.[5]

We dined with the Gardners. We made a party to drive up with Sir John Conway and Mr. Bourchier and there were 4 students. We also lunched with the Schliemanns. There were the Gardners and Mr. Kavadias of the Museum and old Mr. Rangabe, a great poet and authority on the language and literature. I was very glad to meet him and he ...

[Editor's note: On several occasions in this *Chronicle* (but no other in the 15-year series) Mabel has left a spread of blank pages 'for meditations'. Although subjective, there is to this editor a rare hint of intimacy, or even girlishness in this device. 1890 may have been one of Mabel's more happy travelling years, and the first few pages of her notebook have an appealing lightness of style. This first page spread has a 'mandragora' leaf pinned to it and these few lines.]

    Skip this page and the next. Theodore says I can keep the pages I have left out for meditations!

    This is said to be a leaf of mandragora or mandrake

    I have been given some roots and seen a good many which are certainly most extraordinary, but I cannot help thinking they are helped into their human form with a knife and then earthed over. Some say after being cut they are planted again to grow a little but as they grow very deep I do not think that likely. I shall believe in them better when I have seen one dug up –

---

[5] Giacomo Meyerbeer's opera *L'Africaine* was first performed in 1865.

Skip this page for + the next
Theodore says I can keep the pages
I have left out for meditations!

This is said
to be a leaf
of mandragora
or mandrake

I have been
given some
roots + seen
a good many
which are certainly
most extraordi-
nary, but I can-
not help
thinking
they are helped into their human
form with a knife + then earthed
over. Some say after being cut they
are planted again to grow a little

The mandragora leaf Mabel pinned into her 1890 Chronicle.

[Mabel leaves Montaigne here, returning to her Athenian luncheon party.]

... was delightfully surprised that I could speak Greek. Dr. Waldstein, the Rector of the American School, was there too and the daughter Andromache and little son Agamemmnon. Afterwards we went to the Pireaus to see the Consul and Mrs. de Puy. We knew them at Volo and liked them. They were not surprised to see us and only wondered at our not coming before as our coming has so long been announced in the papers. I need not say the Acropolis and Museums were not neglected.[6]

One afternoon I went to see Kyria K. Mavromichalis's new court dress. The Queen[7] used to wear this dress, adapted by her from the dress worn by the peasants at Elevsis, and no one else would. However she begged them to wear them for the coming of the Princess and so now they have all got them for what they call the *baise main*.

To begin with there are the shoes, cherry-pie coloured, velvet embroidered with gold. Then a white silk petticoat just to the ground. Over this a skirt with stripes round of fine silk gauze, every 2 inches a stripe of gold, 2 inches wide, woven in and the white stripe covered with gold lace, so the whole skirt is gold. Then a great heavy train is put on; it is of thick white woollen cloth with the velvet and gold round it. The bodice of white silk comes next, open in a V and trimmed with gold and gold open gauze sleeves to match the armholes of a great cloth coat to match the train. No use having a good figure with that dress! The coat has at the waist a huge gold clasp and on the head a lot of gold coins and a gauze veil with gold ends wound over the head and round the neck. Kyria M. told me they varied in colour and cost and hers cost, without the coins and clasp, 4,000 drachmas, £160.[8] The queen and royal family wear scarlet and the ladies of the court blue.

While in Athens there were a good many puzzling meetings in the streets with workmen and others we had known in the islands, likewise visits. Kyria Lorenziades of Nio we were very glad to see.[9]

We drove to the Pireaus in the middle of **Friday 31st January** and went on board the Egyptian ship *Chariä* and reached Smyrna next morning about

---

[6] The American School in Athens was established in 1881.
[7] The ruling dynasty in Greece at the time was Danish – George I (1845–1913), King of the Hellenes from 1863 to 1913, following the deposition of Otto. His claim was based on the fact that his ancestors, the Emperors of the Romans, had once controlled the region. In 1867 he married the Russian princess Olga Konstantinova. They had eight children, including Andrew (1882–1944), the father of Prince Philip, the Duke of Edinburgh. George was to be assassinated in Thessaloníki in 1912.
[8] A huge sum – approximately £8000 today.
[9] For this very kind and friendly Íos family, see p. 38.

11. We were in time to catch the French M.M. steamer for Mersina.[10] We must have stayed a fortnight in Smyrna if not. By this time T was better and I had influenza.

As we were dressed in the same clothes we had travelled 1st class from England, it must have been our behaviour which caused the maitre d'hôtel on the steamer to say 'second class?' to us. 'No, first' I said, 'Show us a cabin'. He gave us a very small one, but as it was amidships we did not complain. We then went ashore for our tickets, unpacked, and seated ourselves in the saloon. The maitre d'hôtel came and said, 'Come down. I'm going to change your cabin'. We said we had unpacked and did not care for so short a journey. 'But this is not the place for *you* to be sitting. This is the *first* class saloon.' 'Well we wish to stay here' said I. 'But you have taken a second class ticket'. 'Yes' said T. 'Well come along'. 'That was for our servant,' I explained. So he begged our pardon and left, but they evidently did not like English on that ship, for neither the captain nor anyone else spoke to us for 3 days and we were put like outcasts at a table alone. When we saw these places being laid we longed for them, to avoid being cross-questioned.

We were much entertained for a full hour before departure by all the addresses and bouquets brought to a nice old *pasha*, the new governor at Adana and the crowds who came and sat round him. There were all his family too, but they only once came up, well covered, to see the saloon. The *Niger* is a very huge ship with a well-illuminated saloon, having large windows on the deck and electric light, but poorly furnished, no carpet. I stayed 'in the house' all the voyage and was better by the time we arrived. We actually reached Mersina on Monday night at 7.30, but did not get *pratique*[11] till the morning so had plenty of time to think with dread of the customhouse to say it was no use landing too early, as one could not take the letter to Mr. Dillon or seek a home till a respectable time, and to wonder also if we should make any satisfactory discoveries.

In Athens we received a circular from the Hellenic Society requesting us to subscribe to an Expedition of exploration in Cilicia, to be headed by Mr. Ramsay and to start in June. 'It is most desirable that the site of *Olba* should be discovered and identified.' So I declared that we would look for Olba too.

---

[10] There were three or four main steamship companies controlling the Eastern Mediterranean at the time. The state-run Ottoman Egyptian line linked Turkey to its interests in north Africa. 'M.M' refers to the French operation Messageries Maritimes. The Bents are cruising down the Turkish coast to the port of Mersin. Strategically important in classical times, it declined (from silting up) in the early Middle Ages. Today however it is the busiest harbour on the south-west coast, being the terminus of the railway from Tarsus and Adana. It is still, for tourists, one of the most favoured bases for exploring 'Rough Cilicia'.

[11] The authority for a ship to berth and have dealings at port.

[Here follows the second of Mabel's interludes]

This is a meditation on Dogs.

It is difficult to understand how they are brought up. They never have a kind word said to them and are really terrified of their master or even any children of the camp. They are fed and I see no other reason why they should not like their own people more than strangers.

One alone is easily conquered or quelled, no matter how fierce. He flies if you brandish a stick at him and still more if he sees you stoop for a stone. Even if there is a rock that you cannot pick up, the act of stooping frightens him. It is a common precaution when people hear dogs bark to pick up each a stone or clod of earth and the dogs slink off when you are seen ready to throw it, but you *must* do something of this kind. The real danger is when there are 2 or more and then you must wait till one of his friends kicks, cuffs, screams and stands on his head.

We have sometimes made a dog friendly and wag his tail by giving him food, but never dared stroke him or he would have bitten for sheer fear.[12]

[Mabel continues]

February 1890 – Mersin

February 4th, Tuesday. Mersina. In the morning as I was slowly dressing T was called out and through the cabin walls I heard kind voices welcoming him, so I dressed fast and went up and found Mr. Dillon, the head of the railway, and Mr. Lykiardopoulos, our Vice Consul. It was delightful to be taken charge of. Mr. L. took our keys and he and M went to the customhouse. He said nothing should be opened and we waited with Mr. D. to his house, where he had invited us to stay. They had long expected us and actually our beds had been made since the very beginning of the year. I wish we had known it. Mrs. Dillon is a Bavarian but speaks English excellently and is very clever and charming. She has a nice little girl of about 13. They are R. Cs. We had a most pleasant welcome and while we sat waiting for the baggage we sat down to talk and very soon she asked if

---

[12] This aside must have been prompted by the fierce Yourouk dogs they encountered. Bent writes in his *RGS* article (1890, p. 454): 'Every tent has its formidable dog, great huge creatures accustomed to tackle the wild beasts of the mountains…They feed them on buttermilk poured into holes in the ground dug for this purpose, and it was impossible for us to stray alone far from the protection of the owners for fear of being attacked.'

we had read an article which had been reproduced in *Little's Living Age*.[13] It was *My Strange Mother-in-Law*. 'By me! do you mean?' said T. 'I don't think so' she said, 'it has no name and your articles which appear there are signed'. She was much surprised at having asked this question of the author. Curiously enough Mr. Dillon asked me the same in the evening. They really thought it was by an American woman.

It appears they had read several of his things and had been wondering with some friends who the 'we' could be and how strange it was that a man who knew so much about Turkey should never have been in the region and that they should never have met anyone who knew him. They said it was odd to have talked so much of T when the letters arrived in a day or two from Sir W. White to the consul and to Mr. Dillon from Mr. Collinson. The former put on his best clothes and gloves for every steamer, the latter examined the manifesto of the passengers when it came ashore. They disputed who should have us but Mr. Dillon won, as it was thought we might not be able to speak Greek and it was a merciful thing to be saved from Mr. L.

Very soon the porters bearing the 23 packages arrived. They were a wild looking lot of things, stove, table, chairs, beds, etc., and we had these to unpack and rearrange everything. I did not go out all day.

On **Wednesday [February] 5th** I photographed the drawing room and in the afternoon Mr. Dillon had a special train to take us to Tarsus. Mr. and Mrs. Lyk. came with us. She was a very dull Greek dressed and her dress, which was quite fit for an afternoon party in London, made me feel very plain and simple. We two sat in the harem carriage.

We reached Tarsus in 35 minutes and got a carriage and went to see the few sights of the place. What they call St. Paul's tomb was one;[14] the tomb of Sardanapalos, a great ruin, not the least like a tomb, the 2nd, and finally the pretty, rocky, tempting place where King Alexander took his fatal bath in the Kydnos. No one bathes now because they get fever.[15]

Afterwards we went to Mr. McLachlan's. He is an American 'Missionary,' a tall and handsome young widower. He has invited us to stay as long as we can and a week at least on our return from the expedition we mean to make to the westward. In the evening, 2 young American 'Missionary' ladies, Miss Joseph

---

[13] Eliakim Little (1797–1870), editor and publisher, founded *Littell's Living Age* (*Living Age*) in Boston in April 1844. It continued, weekly and then monthly, until 1941. Concerning itself primarily with reprintings of serious British non-fiction, it now and then included some of Theodore's articles.

[14] Of course, this is the ancient city of Tarsus, the setting for the romance of Antony and Cleopatra and birthplace of Saint Paul (AD 3–65).

[15] According to his chroniclers, Alexander bathed in the Cydnus after his descent from the Taurus Mountains in the summer of 333 BC and became very ill; the famous river ran through the centre of ancient Tarsus. He developed a severe infection and it was a near-fatal bath.

and Miss Dodds, came, and the following morning, Thursday, we set off on a voyage of discovery, 'to find Olba!' if possible.

Thursday [February] 6th. Mr. Lyk. has a farm house 4 or 5 hours away, which he says he will lend us for as long as we like. He came with us in a carriage which often had to be tied up with rotten ropes and with a 3rd horse, who was attached to the vehicle either in front or behind, by a rotten halter and he was often perceived far behind grazing, caused us many delays. M came with us, and 3 loaded horses followed with an Albanian very like Don Quixote, Ahmed Chaoush by name. This means Sergeant Ahmed. He is bristling with silver weapons and chains, speaks Greek and Turkish and knows the region we wish to explore, plus 3 men with the horses.

We did not stop at Pompeiopolis, the ancient Soli, meaning to do that on our return. The road goes to Selefka (Seleucea) and is very bad in places; we often had to leave it. We reached the *chiflik*[16] about 5 and the things did not arrive till after dark. It is a lonely house off the road forming one side of a yard. The rooms are upstairs opening on a gallery. We had a room with many unglazed windows, 10 chairs, a very high table, and a sofa and a nice clean board floor.

On Friday 7th we drove off in the carriage as it was remaining to take Mr. Lyk. back to Ayash.[17] Along the road we saw a great many ruins but nothing that was not Roman or Byzantine, though we climbed about a great deal. We got back by night and next day we rode round. There were quantities of sarcophagi hewn out of the rocks and some very nasty late bas reliefs, but the only really good thing we saw was a rock with ΠΟΥ (where?) very well cut in large letters. *Pou?* Where indeed is *What?* We came away none the wiser, and, as there were no more ruins in the neighbourhood, determined to depart on the morrow to Lamas.[18]

All this time we were rather wretched because a quantity of provisions had not yet arrived. We were advised to send all our belongings by sea so we did have 2 demijohns of wine, one of oil, a bag of bread and an immense sack of coarse rusk, which is eaten soaked in water, but our own things we would not part with. We had to leave the *chiflik* without them and reached a sort of café kept by an old retired Turkish soldier. The room here is not so luxurious: a very rough earth floor, some glazed windows, of which you lift the whole sash out when you open them, and a very open boarded partition between the next

---

[16] This is Mr Dillon's farmhouse, in the neighbourhood of which the Bents explore for a few days. A *chiflik* (*çiftlik*) is a fair-sized estate or manor.

[17] Ayaş, the ancient Elaiussa-Sebaste.

[18] Lamas/Lamos, the village at the head of the river of the same name. In antiquity the river marked the boundary between Cilicia Aspera and Cilicia Propria. The 100km walk north along the valley's precipitous walls is still unspoilt and connects the hamlets (now mostly deserted) that Mabel describes below. It is one of the region's many beautiful hiking trails.

room, where M made his kitchen, were the chief features. T went a fruitless walk after luncheon.

Monday, 10th February. In the morning one of the head legs of my hammock went through the floor and I went down all sideways, but the hammock did not break.

We rode off next morning early to visit the gorge of Lamas. The scenery was lovely and would be the object of many a picnic in England. We were guided by a man called Abdurrahman who had noticed more with his one than many with 2. Eyes, by the way, seem to be pretty scarce about here. The first part of the valley was full of trees with tremendous creepers hanging on them and with a banked up stream, but by degrees it became steep and very narrow between precipitous cliffs. High up we saw traces of an aqueduct cut. How they got up there we could not imagine and on a rock we saw a bas-relief which I tried to photograph with my little camera in the rain. Very luckily as it turned out it was too dull to take out the big one, and there was an inscription of which Theodore took a squeeze,[19] exalted on a tottery heap of stones.

We crossed the river, rather wide and deep, and lunched at the dwelling of some Yourouks or Wanderers.[20] It consisted of an open shelf in the rock. I saw 3 carpets spread as if for lying but no coverings, some cooking pots and milking pails, a lot of goats and a few children clad only in ragged shirts and girdles. They did not seem to mind the cold.

We went on to where the valley divided into a fork, riding through a ruined house of Roman times, which seemed to block the valley, some parts were hewn in the rock. First there was a lofty portal and then a lower door, lately broken open above by the Yourouks to let camels pass. We see tombs opened up in the same way. It seems a peculiarity of this region that so many doorways stand up alone.

If we had put on our waterproofs when it began to rain we might have been dry, but before we did they were wet on both sides, for M in crossing the river got the top of a fall a yard deep and his horse fell; he got off and it rolled over on its side. I was afraid it would be drowned. M however kept hold of his gun and the halter and dragged the horse with his head upstream; the saddlebags floated away and were caught some way down. The horses legs were entangled in a bunch of nosebags but at last he was got up with his knees badly cut.

We reached home early in the afternoon and spent the rest of the day drying our wet things by a brazier and preserving our dry from the drippings of the

---
[19] For 'squeezing', see p. 78 note 23.
[20] For the Bents' first encounters with the amiable Yourouks, see p. 243. The couple brought home quite a few souvenirs, now in the Pitt Rivers Museum, Oxford.

roof, which came in everywhere. Our hearts were gladdened by the arrival of the man who had been sent to fetch the missing provisions on a mule; everything wet.

We have to provide for Ahmet Chaoush, who has spent 22 years in prison at different times for being a robber he tells M, but now he has been Greek for 9 years, for Barb'Andon, who speaks Arabic, for Elias (pr. Eelyáss), orthodox Greek, speaks Turkish, and a Turk. Eelyáss is very intelligent and comes out on our daily rides. The others stay and mind the 2 horses left at home, fetch water and wood. We only take out 4. Mine is so pretty but shod horses are not the things for Rugged Cilicia, particularly shod with a plate all over the hoof.

We set off about 10, Tuesday 11th, and rode for about 4 hours to Kizil Oren Koi. First we went along the road some way, then a woman called to us that the Arnaout[21] Ahmed had told her to say he had gone up a path she guided us into. We soon found that though we might wrench ourselves through the bushes and rocks, the loaded horses could not possibly so, so we with the greatest difficulty turned round and got into the old road to Selefka, and after a bit got into a road which once cost a good deal of trouble in making, but was now most awful and the rocks very slippery after the rain. The same horse who had fallen in the river fell among the rocks, breaking a demijohn of wine, the *full* one, and had to be unloaded before he could get up.

At last, passing some horrid sarcophagi, we came to a hamlet of half a dozen houses inhabited by the Yourouks in winter only, just made up out of ruins; some live in old underground cisterns and tombs. Ahmed Chaoush was contentedly smoking out of his very long silver cigarette holder, proud of having induced the inhabitants of the very best house in the place to vacate for us.[22]

It is in fact the house of Hadji Abdurrahman Effendi, the *Hodja* or priest. Oh! my heart sank when I got in. It was so dark and still occupied by the family, but there was no other place so the baggage was brought in, and having only taken time to agree that it was no use opening things till the family had left, T set off with Ahmed Chaoush to a place said to be half an hour off and as I could not undertake at *least* an hour and a half's walk, and could not have my horse after the journey, I remained behind.

Black dismay was my only feeling with regard to our present home! If there were only anything worth seeing in the neighbourhood! Alas! I had forgotten to get the keys from Theodore. I sat in my chair, examined by the

---

[21] An Arnaout was a Turkish soldier, specifically an Albanian. (In the famous portrait of Byron by Thomas Phillips in the National Portrait Gallery, London, the legendary sitter is wearing Arnaout dress.)

[22] Mabel indicates later that this is the hamlet of 'Kizil Bagh', a little to the east of the cave of 'Khani Diwani'. Kizil Bagh means red garden, the earlier hamlet of Kizil Oren meaning red ruins; the distinctive red earth providing the epithet.

Yourouks and looked round. The room is about 20 feet x 17, so low and dark that you cannot see the whole of it. One side has a low door in the middle and 2 fireplaces. There were 2 tiny windows, or rather holes, and a good many accidental ones among the rough stones of the wall. The roof was supported by many posts, all blackened with smoke. As to the floor, it was partly earth with low ruined walls cropping up, and partly the living rock, which had a good many holes in it, all about 4 inches deep and the hole place was very uneven; still one could with care adjust the furniture. I felt sad as I became more and more sure there was no other bedroom for M. I felt dank and cold and could not get near the fire as M was sitting on his heels trying to prepare dinner, and as it was nasty outside the only comfort I had was seeing how very clean all the kitchen and pantry things were and how he arranged everything in rows on stones, gun-case etc. as neat as 9d.

At last T came home. I heard his voice. 'Welcome Home!' I cried, the first in real earnest and last in irony. But as soon as he had carefully stooped in and raised himself up he said:

'I've found Olba.'[23]
Up I jumped, warm and cheerful enough.
'Oh where? Oh how? Quite certainly?'
'Yes. Quite certainly.'

I looked round the room with an idea of settling but it was an idea to be banished, so I got out T's slippers, as a good wife does in books, and demanded tea, and determined as a feast we would eat some plum-pudding I had brought from home at dinner. It was *so* much better near Olba than at home.

We had made our beds first and levelled them as well as we could and pinned up a yard and a half of cotton print to 2 of the props, and having cast the shadow of another prop on this to avoid being a magic lantern, I undressed and M spread his bed at the other end of the room and we all slumbered as much as threats and mice would permit. In the dim dawn M got up, lit the fire, and went to fetch water and wood while I dressed. I did my hair in the dark in my hammock and so was quicker ready for breakfast. Then M and Ahmed Chaoush had theirs and so we abode for 4 days.

---

[23] Theodore thought he had discovered a long-lost temple there and seems to have initially confused the site for the 'city' of Olba. He certainly was within the Olbian 'state'. Cecil Harcourt-Smith (*Classical Review*, 4, 1890, pp. 185–186) encapsulates the argument: 'The occurrence therefore of the formulæ in Mr. Bent's inscription need not prove more than that this site was within the toparchia of Olba.' The Bents are exploring Khani Diwani (Kanytelis/Kanlidivane, literally 'bloody madness'). Mabel writes later that they thought this extraordinary limestone sinkhole was at first the famous Corycian Cave.

'A ladder was needed…and very cleverly it was managed.'
This paper print, taken by Mabel, was inserted in her 1890 Chronicle.

Wednesday, 12th February. We rode up after breakfast to Olba. Khani Diwani it is called now. There are quantities of ruins, Roman and Byzantine, and T said he never felt more disgusted in his life, when, at the edge of a most curious precipice, he espied a nice tower of polygonal masonry, which it would be profane to call rubble, with 2 good inscriptions on which he could read the name of Olba. They were very high up.

It stands on the edge of a most curious pit about ¼ mile across and 200 feet deep; 2/3rds of the sides are precipices. About 50 feet up there is a great bas relief of 6 figures, some sitting, some standing, and an inscription over it, and in another part a man holding a lance. His inscription is illegible.

A ladder was needed to read this, so one had to be built and very cleverly it was managed. Great plans had to be screamed, as no nails were forthcoming to make a joint, and at last a couple of trees were cut and notches cut in the back of them and then some large sticks just laced on with one loop which hitched into the notches. As one side was about a foot and a half longer than the other it had a queer and dangerous twist.

It rested against the legs of the carved people and its foot rested on a great built heap of stones like what Abraham had when he was going to sacrifice Isaac, which stood far out from the precipice. It took some climbing to get to the top of and the yielding rungs were about 2 feet apart. When T got up he had to bend backwards, standing on the top rung to get his hands on the bas relief, which overhung him, but could not take a squeeze, so determined to make a copy. He was up a long time and I sat below, very cold in the shade, picking out the exact place he might fall and praying for his safety. He came down twice to rest.

When the acrobatic work of the epigraphist was over, that of the photographer began. Only a goat could photograph comfortably. T leant hard against a tree, once he moved and it knocked me down. He supported my back as I made backward steps among rocks and bushes. The legs of the camera were held on little cairns and I positively ached when it was over. Another photo I did kneeling with my legs over the edge of a rock about 4 feet high, T facing me and holding on to my shoulders. The ladder had to be unlaced to carry it out of the pit to the tower and there T had such trouble with the wind that he told me to send him up only a narrow strip of paper for each line. These I sewed together afterwards.

We lunched behind the tower and then went to a great mausoleum much higher up. There was a very long inscription, which took long, and T was an hour sitting on his ladder facing it and copying it. There were other squeezes taken and photos and explorings and then we returned to our dark home. Really the rocky floor made it look like the cave of some robbers who had just plundered some wealthy traveller and had not had time to examine their spoils. We locked everything, even our brushes up, as our hosts though amiable were not too honest and several little things disappeared.

[Saturday] February 15th. We spent the same kind of days all the time we were there, and yesterday were preparing to start when it poured so we waited and waited and at last we packed our beds. It cleared somewhat and then looked very threatening. T consulted M. He said 'I don't know what to say. If we start we may get wet and if we stay it may clear'.

I was asked my opinion and it was thought a good one – namely to load the horses and then if necessary unload; it would be something to do. Well, when all was ready it did begin to drizzle but we started and by the time we got over an awful bit of road it poured, but we two and most of our things were waterproof, so very little got wet. We went down to the road by a more westerly way and went on some big ruins and then turned up again.

I had become very humble-minded by this time and whereas last time T had said he only hoped for a door, now I only hoped the family might not wish to live with us, for in rainy weather it is not easy to find a lodging for 7 men and 6 horses.

We went for about an hour and a half up a formerly well-made road and then seeing that the Chaoush had stuck 2 stones on others to the left and that his track went between, we waited till every one came up and turned into a little path. Many places were flooded and the walkers had great difficulty in getting along by rocks and bushes. I fortunately never had to dismount. I have the best horse and am light. My saddle is like those found convenient by ladies and gentlemen who want to jump through hoops in circuses. It is bound on by a girth once round, not 2 inches wide. Into this is looped a rope which I use to mount and by the time I am in the saddle it had slipped down, but a stirrup would be of no use. There is no kind of grip to hold on going up or down, but I have only been off twice, once when some one startled the horse and I came down on all fours, and once when I just forgot not to let the saddle turn and came down on my feet.

At last I arrived and T was very thankful in the distance to see me turn into the door of a cabin, the same door through which all my companions with 2 and 4 legs followed.

On the arrival of our messenger, the roof of our present room, which is used as a barn, was mended and the straw cleared out, 9 feet by 7, but rather larger up above. There is an outer room, also with a ruined wall in it, and there M and Ahmet Chaoush slept, the horses in a black room behind us, leading through that room, and the 3 other men had a black hole inside the stable where they made a fire, so with our own we had awful smoke. Our floor after 2½ days fire is like a sponge, but it is a fibrous earth which clogs on to our feet and shakes off. We have a doorway nearly 4 feet high and a partition which goes nearly up to the ceiling with many little holes among the rough blackened stones.

There is also a window with a shutter 18 by 5 inches and a good many holes in the outer wall so it is more light and more private. We drove some sticks among the stones and hung up one of the sheets of cotton print, of which we have 6 or 8. They are invaluable to the modest female Eastern traveller as they are light and pins will hold them on woodwork. We covered all the partition at Lamas with them.

With the furniture the room is pretty crowded and one has to move very slowly and cautiously not to knock anything's leg off the stones that prop it up. M and Ahmed Chaoush complain dreadfully of fleas and mice so the latter betook himself to a tent close by and there he and the other men now abide.

I stayed at home most of yesterday. It was so very wet and flooded and T went both morning and afternoon in different direction and found places, to one of which we went today and the other we go to tomorrow.

[Monday] February 17th. Today the road was not fit for horses so we only took a donkey to carry our luncheon, photography and inscription requisites. It was ¾ of an hour. First down hill to a river and then along it in and out and across and hopping from stone to stone and then we went up a very steep bank and finally reached the cliff, which is on both sides of every river valley we have seen here; below the cliff were many terraced platforms and the remains of a temple lying about, including the remains of a tympanum with 9 ugly Roman figures – 4½ of these were on their faces with only a small piece of the stone uncovered. But T found this out and very great was the amazement of the Yourouks on seeing the people turn up.

In the cliff are 3 storeys of caves, all filled in with polygonal masonry. There were 2 bas reliefs with inscriptions and the upper one was a matter of huge difficulty to secure, for it could not be read from below, but with ropes flung up and trees put up and great climbing with boots off, it was accomplished. I managed to stick on the little donkey for all the best bits on the way home.

Tuesday February 18th. We went more eastward this time, also down one valley and up another. I rode the little donkey nearly all the way. The place we went to was very pretty and filled with tombs, towers, temples of polygonal masonry. We found from a very tremendously large and puzzling inscription that the name of the place must have been Sabbatia. We were very busy with measurements, squeezes and photography and had a most pleasant day.

Wednesday February 19th. Rode our horses down one river and across another and when we got to the brow of the cliff we dismounted and began to wander. We saw some narrow ladder-like steps in the rock, dreadful to behold. We could from one place get a front view of them. It became clear to us that the bas-reliefs we came to see were down there, but all with one consent said that I could not go. I had almost given up, but I followed down the rocks and called to T, 'Do you think I *can* manage it?' He said, 'You have a good head. You might try'. So I determined to go as far as I could. The rock is rough so there are many little places for one's hands.

The sun was blazing on us, reflected off the rock. We crawled down sideways, sometimes sitting when a steep step came, and at last there was such a very deep step that I thought I was stopped. I could not very well let myself slide down on to such a very narrow step as the next, so I clung with my hands and T pulled hard at my leg till he dragged them down and held a heel into a little hole and so I got at last to some slopey grass and rocks. We were very careful not to step on anything but rock.

We had to get round an elbow of the cliff and there, high above a sloping ledge, we saw a quantity of large bas-reliefs, 13 people in all. There were several inscriptions to take. They were very high. T took off his boots, not to slip, and stood on tiptoe. M supported him like a buttress from behind and I made a

Yourouk hold M, for I was afraid they would both slip away. After that, Ahmed Chaoush made a table of his back and the Yourouk stood on it. It was most difficult.

'Now' said Theodore, 'I am so exhausted I can do nothing till I have my luncheon'.

'How can I eat till I have taken my photographs?' I responded. 'The sun will be off by the time we have done.' Of course, I cannot photograph unattended as I have to be held.

We lunched in a dirty little cave and I sewed up the inscriptions and then we set ourselves to the ascent again, assuring each other it would be easier than going down. There was great trouble over the big step. Everyone paused before it, and as I saw the place from below I thought a rope from above is my only hope. The first place I could get my toe in was about on a level with my waist. T held my heel and so I crawled up. It was so hot and the sun so in the steps we could hardly see them. I rushed to a little rock where I could curl myself up in the shade and had to oblige myself to get up and photograph. We had a good long ride home, the worst part being on a road which goes all the way to Kara Mousal on the Sea of Marmara. It once was scored with chisels but now is terribly slippery.

We passed the tents of several Yourouks, one in such a pretty situation in a wood. When we passed in the morning I took the portrait of a tiny camel, 24 hours old. It looked so funny tied up in a coat; a handkerchief was put over his nose, crossed under his chin and tied round his neck. The first question, 'Why?' only received the answer, 'It is the custom'. The second, to prevent the cold getting down its throat into its inside. We stopped and drank some milk and brought some home. We have now come to an end of eggs, wine, tobacco nearly, preserved milk (except that sacredly reserved for a case of illness), and we determined to leave Kizil Bagh on the morrow.

I slipped rather regretfully into my hammock, as the thought of my next dwelling did not appear charming, a tent of the Yourouks, for ours is not with us, a tomb or a cave. However next morning, **Thursday 19th [actually February 20th]** dawned for a long rainy day. No hope of moving, though T would not make his bed till I obliged him just before luncheon. You might as well be in a fog it was so dark. The fire was a help. Of course we cannot afford candles by daylight. It cleared up about 4. The dripping into the room was very like a shower at first, but we sent men up to roll the roof.

Friday the 20th [actually February 21st] was a day of great ignominy for us. We started about 9 and rode down to the road by the sea and proceeded westward and when we came to a *turbeh*, or tomb, there were a captain and 10 soldiers actually waiting to take us prisoners! though we did not know it at the time. The captain told Ahmet that the Mutesarrif, the Governor of Selefka, had gone on in his carriage and wished to see T. T said that we could not go to see him at present, then something was said about a letter. We thought T was to write it but he said there was nothing to write about. We continued our way and they all rode round us prancing. My horse began to dance and, though I can stand a gentle trot, with that saddle dancing is not safe. I said they must go on. They did not seem inclined so I jumped down and as it was 12 said we would lunch.

They rode on a good long way, all the men but 2 remained behind and 2 went in front. Every one on the road they spoke to and always told us the Chaoush was gone forward. At last T said we have gone much too far and we must have missed him and the baggage, so will return. We found out from some people the Chaoush had not passed. The soldiers made a great row but T led my horse by a halter and we returned about 2 miles. Presently we saw the Chaoush coming to meet us. He said he had duly left a man and could not think why we had gone on. The soldiers then came up and said we must go to the *Mutesarrif*. We said we would not and continued our backward way. One soldier galloped at us shouting and screaming. T quietly threaded his way backwards and forwards through their horses, there were now 14, and had nearly got through when they surrounded us, blocking the road and bawling most rudely.

We saw there was nothing left but to be shot at, so as Ahmet said the men had positive orders to fetch us and were determined to carry them out we sent M back to look after the baggage, and taking Elias to hold my horse and the Chaoush, as sad and furious prisoners we were led away, only half an hour off said they, but 2¼ we rode and thought we must be going to Selefka at last, which meant far from our beds and food.

I tried but failed to take comfort from the fact that prisoners are always provided with these. I was really feeling ill and had been longing to arrive. We told them this at first but it was no use. We came quite suddenly round the corner of a rock on a little hut, which is a public house, and as the foremost soldiers had announced us there was a little crowd.

'Well?' said T angrily, 'where is he who wants us?' in Greek.

A smartly dressed man in European clothes came smiling forward.

'Oh! I beg pardon. I did not know there was a lady.'

T said, 'You must have known it'.

'Oh no. I heard there was a gentleman and as I desired to make your acquaintance I sent to invite you to come here if it were possible.'

'Your men have made us prisoners and forced us to come here. They rode at us and surrounded us,' I said.

'I did not know.'
'They had your orders,' said T. 'What is your name that you dare to take English people prisoners?'
'Tell me yours first and I will tell you mine.'
'Here is my name on this card (handing mine) and if you wish to see our passports you can.'
'Oh no, thank you, there is no need.'
'What is your name?'
'Hassan Bey.'
'And who are you?'
'The governor.'
'Where of? Selefka?'
'Yes.'

[The third of Mabel's interludes follows]

The Chronicle continues over the next page.
A quotation from 'Tancred'[24] by B. Disraeli –

> He is taken prisoner and led to his
> captor who says
> 'Tell the prince that he mistook
> my message that I sent him this
> morning, which was an invitation
> to a feast, not to war.'
> 'Tell the Shaikh,' said Tancred,
> 'that I have no appetite for feasting
> and desire to be informed why he has
> taken me prisoner.'
> 'Tell the prince, brother of many
> queens, that he is not a prisoner
> but a guest.'
> 'Ask the Shaikh then whether we
> may depart at once.'

[Mabel continues]

---

[24] *Tancred, or the New Crusade* by Benjamin Disraeli, Earl of Beaconsfield (1804–1881), London 1862.

'Well, sir, you will suffer for this for I shall make a complaint through our ambassador at Constantinople.'[25]

'Will you not get down?'

'No!' from both.

'Will you not take a cup of coffee?'

'We want nothing; we are going to return at once,' said T.

'You are going to return?' said the governor with a voice of astonishment.

'Certainly,' I said. 'I am anxious to end my journey. I am tired and ill.'

'You will continue your journey, *madame*, when you have rested half an hour and drunk a cup of coffee.' He spoke French very well.

'I will rest where my bed is and my baggage.'

'But you are not going on?'

'No,' said T, 'we are going to Mersina. We never wished to come so far but have been brought here by force and by your order. And you will repent it.'

Again he said he did not know.

'Very well,' I said. 'You will inform yourself better before you take English prisoners next time'.

So I whisked round my horse and turned my back on him and without goodbye we rode off, visibly laughing at him. I took his photograph.

As soon as we got round the corner T gave up his horse to Elias and we were soon followed by the captain and a soldier. We found they were now on other business bent. I made Ahmet ride by him and he found out that the governor did know there was a lady and they had orders to ride up to Kizil Bagh and fetch us, only we saved them that trouble by coming down.

What did the man want us for if he did not keep us? He did nothing make [sic] excuses too. We heard him ask 'How long have you been here,' but we did not turn round to answer.

We were very tired when we got home. It was not very far up from the road. It was a dreadful abode; a ruin with a solid roof but no whole side. The gaps were filled partially for the occasion with loose stones and branches of locust tree. Outside a black tent was pitched as a kitchen. One part of our house had long, long been used as a stable or cow-house. We lit a fire on the floor, which being inflammable sent up a stifling smoke which reminded us of the *tezek* fires in Azerbeijan.[26] It never went out but smouldered and spread all night. We left nothing near enough to burn.

---

[25] This *longueur* is typical of the outrage felt by Mabel and Theodore whenever questioned by authorities. Embarrassing today, they illustrate the self-confidence of Victorians abroad. We get no clue as to whether the governor's hackles rose at Theodore's insistence on referring to Istanbul as Constantinople.

[26] Probably encountered by Mabel in their trek up through Persia in 1889, although not actually mentioned in her three-volume *Chronicle* for that year. *Tezek* is a Turkish word for dried animal dung fuel.

M retired to a tomb.

We put ourselves to bed in our airy ruin, tying up our heads and had put out the candle about 10 minutes when I heard 'Mabel!!' in such astonished tones that I quickly took my ears from under my bedclothes to enquire 'What?'

'*How* does the fire come *there*?'

I saw none but in the proper place.

'It is at your feet, near the legs of your hammock.' Still I could see nothing.

'Oh it is alive! It moves.'

'Perhaps you see something's eye,' I suggested.

'No, it is like a firey worm and it is coming here; light the candles, quick.'

So I did and T said it was my bonnet box on fire.

This is taken without bonnets in case we found some jug or pot and we could never hope for a box if we had not this. T had stood it on some wood ashes and on it a little *portemanteau* that comes that the squeezes may not be squeezed. As this last has 5 or 6 lbs of bacon in it we might, if T had not found out, have been awakened by a very bad conflagration. He had no idea there was any fire remaining there, nor had any of us. He had to put 4 cups of water over the box to put it out. One corner is so charred that I am sure it will break, so I have turned the cover round to protect it.

We did not enjoy our night, so this morning after breakfast M and T went off to find a suitable tomb while I remained to guard the property. M went on as a guide with his hands full. I went to protect things on arrival and T as rearguard and everything was carried to our present home which is certainly the lightest and best we have had for some time.

Our tomb is hewn in the living rock and the ground outside has risen much so we go down a hill sideways and get in at a hole about 3 ft 6 square. The floor is about 6 ft 6 square and T can stand comfortably. There are 6 beds in twos, like in a steamer. T has put his bedding in the top one opposite the door. My hammock stands on the floor to the right and there is room for the table, chairs and stove. The luggage is all in the shelves and berths. It is a little damp. We have hung a curtain at the door with sticks.

M has taken another similar tomb as a kitchen and Ahmet Chaoush has his tent close by and the horses are near. It has been very cold and raining a little and this is a horrid place, for the inscriptions are all worthless and we are going to start for Mersina tomorrow, sleeping at Mr. Lyk.'s *chiflik*.

March 1890 – Tarsus

Saturday, March 1st. Tarsus. We had a very wet ride along the sea with high wind and sea spray in our faces and lunched very damply and hastily at Lames.

We did as much trotting as we could and arrived at the *chiflik* about 3.30. We found some letters there. We had 30 miles to do next day and took 9 hours to do it. We arrived *very* wet, for we had dreadful hail storm. It was very pleasant to know that we had a very hospitable welcome before us. Mr. Stewart was there, the new director of the Ottoman Bank, moving to Adana from Beyrout.

It rained nearly all Wednesday 26th[27] but I got out with Mrs. Dillon to pay my visits to Mrs. Lykiardopoulo and the 2 American Missionary ladies. Mr. Lyk. was very furious to hear of the outrage of the *Mutesarrif* of Selefka. He says the French Embassy is now complaining of the similar conduct of that very Hassan Bey to a French family. The lady in that case fainted, so could go no further. A formal complaint was drawn up.

Thursday 27th. We and Mrs. Dillon and Sissy came down to Tarsus, to the American Missionary house. It is very large. Mr. McLachlan lives in one part and Mr. and Mrs. Jennanyan[28] in other rooms. Mrs. J. is a very pretty and charming American. Mr. McL. and Mr. J. came to meet us at the station and Mrs. J. said they had been so anxious to see us that they had deferred their departure to Adana a day and had asked Mr. McL. to leave us to them for one night. We were put into Mr. McL.'s bedroom that we might not have to move and Mr. McL. and the Dillons dined with them and we were given up to Mr. McLachlan after breakfast. We hope to see them again in Adana, where we go on Monday.

It rained all yesterday and we ladies stayed at home and fattened, for we were given immense quantities of excellent and mysterious food with strange names, and served in a new way: biscuits which were cakes; jelly which was jam; crackers which were biscuits and cookies and gems, etc.

I superintended the unpacking of a beautiful camera which for 2 years has been suffering from the ravages of mice and damp; great ruin was the result. I put it together, explained the various parts, and today there is to be a little practice.

From this window we can see a large low mound covered with tents and thousands of camels, which are always winding about in strings in a very picturesque way. There are very few traditions about this place and little to see. There are lots of trees and it is unhealthy and most of the inhabitants and all the missionaries are away in the mountains for 6 months.

Alas! I believe that all my photographs taken hitherto are spoilt. I gave them to be held in safety in the dark room by my pupil, but when I asked for them he had changed them to a safer place outside!

The cook's name in this establishment is Sennacherib, pronounced Sennekérim. We left Tarsus about 3 for Adana. Mr. McL. came to see us off

---

[27] Mabel is catching up with her *Chronicle* in Tarsus.
[28] In 1888 'St. Paul's Institute at Tarsus' begins its educational programme with eight students. Theodore enjoyed putting in an appearance at foreign schools and commentating on standards.

and meet Dr. Balfe, a missionary from Marash, and Mr. Mead and Mr. Cristman, our Vice Consul,[29] came to meet us. The latter is an Austrian Levantine. The former invited us to his house. Had he not we should have been in a very bad way as M got the last bed in the only hotel. There are 4 beds in a room and the sleeper pays 1/4 of a medjidié for one, but if he wishes the whole room he pays a whole medjidié.[30]

The Jennanyans are staying with Mr. and Mrs. Mead. She has very kindly lent me her saddle. We were at Adana 2 nights and T was very busy with the arrangements for our journey into the Interior, for, like Africa, Asia Minor has an Interior.

Mr. Christman undertook to settle everything. It had been thought well not to bring Ahmed Chaoush and many searchings took place and people were brought to us who could, so they said, speak French, but no one who could speak Greek. The French was not good enough and it would have been very inconvenient not to have had a language we could all 3 speak, so late in the afternoon a telegram was sent for Ahmed to come and 'take horse from Adana'. Mr. Cristman told us there was a good carriage road to Sis,[31] and he was in treaty for a carriage and therefore we sent off our packhorses early, that is the baggage was to start very early. When all was gone, hopelessly we heard there was no carriage, so very sad were we as of all our riding garments, my coat was all we had; very important to be sure. We were therefore very uncomfortable but promised ourselves to change our clothes at the first *khan*.[32]

I will not describe Adana, see books,[33] and will only say we were again very hospitably treated and having been lent whips, as ours were gone, we were seen 3 or 4 miles on our way by Mr. Jennanyan.

I never feel settled or really started till we are left to ourselves. We had much better horses so could go fast, but still after nine hours one is ready for a good night's rest. This however was denied us. We had to leave the road about a mile to reach a little village (Sarageshed) made chiefly of transparent walls of single reeds, protected from being knocked down by animals by a row of thorns set up as a hedge. We passed through a horrid cemetery. I thought there were a

[29] N. J. Christmann. See p. 320 for his letter to Theodore of 9 April 1890.
[30] A *medjidié* equated, roughly, to a Turkish pound (about 18 English shillings). This would have worked out at about £50 a night for a room, or £12.50 for four sharing. Quite a sum for the time, but high-season prices for today's tourists.
[31] The Bents are now venturing into the interior for this next phase of their trip. Ancient Sis is modern Kozan; the Bents don't in the end seemed to have reached it. The city played an eminent role in ecclesiastical history; St Gregory was enthroned there (AD 267) as the first leader of the Nestorian and Armenian churches.
[32] An inn in some Eastern countries with a large courtyard that provides accommodation.
[33] This is very typical of Mabel, who is quite happy to refer her readers to the guidebooks.

great many new graves. The new ones always have thorns laid on them and large stones to keep the wild beasts from unburying the bodies.

The *khan* was very low and contained a great many horses, men, women and children all mixed up, the latter on little platforms among the horses; of course this must be that they may watch their horses and keep them from being stolen. We were so fortunate as to be screened off from some of the other people: not more than about a dozen could see us. We had the residence of the owner. Having taken off our shoes we slept on a carpet and there was a fire so M could just screw in to cook some eggs and milk, which, with the remains of our luncheon, formed our dinner. Then I lay across the fire with my head on my saddle, T with the hold-all and M got on a box, and so we passed the night. I never closed an eye. I was the whole time trying to rival the activity of the fleas and, whenever I lit the candle, driving away the crickets. Our packhorses only arrived about 8.30, and as there was no room for bed and opening anything, could only admit various insects; we left the things as they were sewn up in 4 immense sacks, to be the more ready for the morning's start.

At 4 the men proposed to start with them, so we gave up the India-rubber rugs we had thrown over ourselves and let them go. We did not get away till 7. The place was lit up in the evening by chips of resinous pine wood and sometimes one and sometimes another lit up in the night. I was quite worn out and aching with fatigue. We had to ride 6 hours to Sis.

Thursday March 6th. The road today was very dull in long straight reaches and always the same dips down into riverbeds or morasses by reason of the state of the bridges, or places where they should have been. Sometimes a good bridge stood with no connection with the road; sometimes a new bridge stood unfinished and partly in ruins; sometimes a gap in a good road stood yawning for a bridge and sometimes a bridge was unsafe. These, and the meeting or overtaking of other caravans, and working our way through them, were the only break to the monotony and I was in continual danger of falling asleep.

About 10 we stopped at rather a pretty place where the road took a sharp turn past some rocks to go over a sound bridge and an otherwise impassable river, to rest the horses. I flung myself on the ground with my head on my little camera and was very nearly asleep when T's voice sounding very far off invited me to eat a bit of cake with some wine, all we had that we might not stop again to eat. When the horses were finally bitted I felt hardly able to rise, but of course one can't lie on wet earth.

Sis is one of those odious places which hide themselves behind mountains and round corners till the last minute and I felt an almost irresistible longing about ¾ of an hour before we arrived to jump off and lie down. The only cheer was that my bed had arrived and that with the letters of introduction we must have a house to ourselves.

We were led to the house of an Armenian, Kasarian by name, and found a nice large room was ready for us with a divan along one side where T could spread his bedding and save the unpacking. My bed was immediately set up by T and I was very soon undressed and in it. First it had to be made up though!

We reached Sis about 2.30. I only got up for dinner and tea and when T went to see the governor I desired M to lock my door and put the key in his pocket, for we have a door that flies open once the key is turned and no other fastening.

Nearby all the inhabitants are Armenians and fortunately for us do not know their own language, so we are spared attempting to understand it. Many are protestants converted by the Americans. This place has a large monastery and a Catholicos, who is the rival of him of Etchmiatzin,[34] each considering himself the head of the whole Armenian Church. It was very interesting to be able to compare the two places within 10 months.

Saturday [March] 8th. We went up to the monastery accompanied by a teacher or preacher who speaks some English, a great comfort to us as Ahmed had not come. His English was not always very clear. For instance I was much interested in some large wooden objects I saw in our yard, just the shape of an *enochoe*[35] (scan) and asked for what purpose they were used.

'To bring water but now they bring him in the gasoil's dish.' (petroleum can)

The town is laid against the foot of a rocky mountain which reminds us of S. Marino.[36] On the top is the very extensive ruin of a castle of the Armenian king, and midway is plastered the monastery in a triangular wall. It is very ruinous, poor and dirty. We went to see the Bishop, he having received the letter to Catholicos in his absence. He is a handsome and amiable looking old man. We sat for a long time in a room surrounded by divans and at last we asked to see the treasures.

We went into the church, which has once been lined with tiles from Persia, to which they attribute a fabulous antiquity. One of the Catholicos's thrones, a marble one in the body of the church, was that of the Kings of Armenia, with

---

[34] St Gregory the Illuminator was consecrated first head of the Armenian Apostolic Church in 302. Following the fall of the Arsacid dynasty he transferred his see to Echmiadzin (Ejmiatsin), in the province of Armavir. The town has three impressive churches and today is a UNESCO World Heritage Site. Mabel saw them ten months previously, in May 1889, on their way home, via Armenia, after their epic journey through Persia.
[35] Or *oinochoe*, a graceful domestic vessel usually used for wine.
[36] Mabel and Theodore were honorary citizens of the tiny Republic of San Marino following Theodore's researches there in the mid 1870s. See his short monograph *A Freak of Freedom* (1877).

his arms upon it. It did not look very old. The whole church looked dirty and neglected. In the sacristy, in a silver box, were 3 hands of various saints, 2 in silver cases, one gilt on the hand, and all roughly wrapped in dirty embroidered handkerchiefs. We did not see St. Gregory or Kirkor the Illuminator's hand. That is away with the Catholicos.

A little crowd had followed us but the Bishop shoved them out and then closed the door with pieces of wood and stones, looked to see all was safe, and then stooped down and made a whole cupboard swing out from before a concealed door and we entered a vaulted room with some rough wooden presses. There were a good many books with silver covers, crosiers, candlesticks and more hands and chalices, but nothing particularly rich and it all looked very poor indeed beside the beautifully arranged and well-exhibited rooms full of jewels at Etchmiadzin.

They showed us a picture of Etchmiadzin, a small white church standing alone, instead of a large red one in the midst of the college and monastery; also a picture of a wide and placid river with trees and a palace at the end of a bridge. This was in their minds a representation of Jerusalem.

After this we mounted a very steep and high flight of steps, each a foot high and with no banisters, rather dangerous for old Bishops. Here is another throne used at evening service. The Bishop was so tired he dropped down and sat on the steps of his own throne and when he had recovered he opened a gilt cupboard and we were shown a very large silver-gilt urn in bad taste, 90 years old, in which the holy oil is made by stirring with St. Gregory the Illuminator's hand. I said I should like to take a photo this afternoon and the Bishop said I might, but after we left he sent a man to demand 6 *medjidies*, more than £1, so I sent to say I should not care to buy so dear a privilege.

We visited the school of 24 orphans brought up at the expense of the Katholikos. Some are quite men and some about 12. They first sang a long song in Armenian and one of them made a speech in eulogy of T in French, pretty good, and said they were all the better for his unforgettable arrival and should continue permanently to be so. T was spared a response by their instantly striking up a lament over their banished kingdom. We saw one of their churches nearly dropping with neglect and after luncheon T climbed the castle.

Last night was our second of violent rain and we expect a 3rd. It cleared up in the morning and were off to visit a place called Kerk Kapou, or 40 doors, every window or hole counting as one. It is 2½ hours off. We had not been gone 20 minutes before it began to pour and though we put on our waterproofs we got a good deal of wet in consequence of the wind. My saddle had been put on T's horse and I had complained after we started of the looseness of the girth, but as there were no more holes it could not be tightened. In cantering it turned. I did not come off as I hoped someone would come and turn me straight and it was so muddy, but eventually I stepped cleanly down and the saddle was easily straightened, so I reached home in safety.

We took a walk in the afternoon.

I forgot to say Ahmed arrived yesterday at noon, having ridden from Adana in the wet night. He had taken on himself to bring 6 horses from Mersina and said he had ridden thence, though Mr. Dillon sent to say he had given him a free pass. We are keeping the 3 riding horses from Adana and have agreed to keep 3 Mersina ones for A and the baggage. For some very mysterious reason this arrangement is to be kept a great secret from the 3 that are sent back and those remaining are going to pretend they are going in other directions, but this is none of our business. I believe Elias has been brought and as he understands attending on the photography and squeezes I am glad.

Sunday [March] 9th. We went to Kerk Kaki, a Byzantine ruin, I mean Armenian, with many doors and windows. Near it was rather a good looking mausoleum of large stones, but no inscriptions. We lunched there and were home early.

We had a pleasant visit from the Greek Dr. Dimitri and later from Mr. Kasarian, the master of the house, and a protestant Armenian preacher and a female teacher who could speak a little English. The Family was very desirous of being photographed, so next morning I did a group of 11. Great were the preparations. Loose gowns were put off by the men and European trousers put on. Best gaudy clothes were put on by the ladies instead of their stockings, and more was thought of necklaces than of washing the legs.

Monday, March 10th. About 8, we set out for Anavartsa, the old Anasarba,[37] the Armenian capital, 4½ hours off. We now have a *zaptich*[38] from the governor. His name is also Ahmed Chaoush, but I will always leave that name for our old villain. We rode on but dismounted and waited till the rest of our caravan came up at a fat column, a yard out of the ground, where the roads divide to Kars Bazaar left and to Anavartsa right. Though I write road, I only mean a collection of muddy tracks across the plain, all pretence of a road stopping at Sis.

We stopped again about 12.30 at a well to lunch, but alas on drawing up a bucket with several halters tied together, the water smelled too bad to drink.

---

[37] There is a pleasant coincidence here. Anazarvos/Anazarbus is an ancient town, some 30km south of Kozan. In the 1st century a renowned doctor hailed from here, Pedanius Dioscorides, who wrote several medical reference works, including a herbal that went into some detail on the mandragora plant. Perhaps Mabel's leaf came from the area (see p. 272)? Lucky visitors to the National Library, Vienna, might be able to see Pedanius' original work.
[38] An armed guard.

Men drank from a leathern bottle, beasts a mile further on at a very pretty place called Hadjilar. There is a cane hamlet of Yourouks near, and a very picturesque long, double bridge and the ruins of an aqueduct leading straight to Anasarba. We had all to get down as the mud was too deep for the horses to get through to drink with us on their backs. We rode along the aqueduct about 2 miles, through swamps and floods as best we could find our way.

We had been horrified to find that one of the horses brought by Ahmed was the yellow one we had before and which used to tumble down. He had 2 tumbles today, on flat ground, necessitating unloading. We sent our soldier on to look for a lodging. The walls of Anasarba look very complete with their towers and have an inviting look to travellers arriving in the rain which was beginning. They lie at the foot of a steep rock crowned with castles.

We knew there was no town, only a winter encampment of Yourouks, but still we rode about a little before we could make out where the *zaptich* was. A Yourouk pointed out to us an almost undistinguishable little village of cane cottages, for there are reeds growing all around. The *zaptich* had caused a family to vacate its home for us and all their goods were lying in the mud – a saddle or two, a few pots, a few rough bits of goats' hair carpet, a churn and a few tools.

Our house is an immense basket about 30 feet by 15. There are 3 screens of reeds jutting from the sides, which, being parallel, don't meet. Two near the middle make a stall where we have accepted the charge of 4 young calves, and the other is on our side of the door and juts out a yard. The door is of very coarse and open osier wattle, just to keep animals out. The kitchen end is very damp; it is the cow house but a great many reeds have been laid down on the ground as a carpet: our end is pretty dry. We pinned up all the cotton curtains and so made ourselves quite private. There are places an inch wide between the reeds along one wall. The other 2 have loose leaves heaped against them. M's end is open all round. By an arrangement of saddlebags and saddlecloths we finished up our defences, but these last only can remain in place by day so within the house life is pretty public.

Of course it was very damp and we covered our beds with waterproof. It is a great comfort that we all three can have plenty to keep our beds warm and dry even in such an airy bower as this.

To our surprise, night did not bring rest or quiet. For quiet, if you want an exact idea of *all* night, fancy lying down and expecting to sleep in the height of the most noisy time of a cattle fair. Men, women, children and cattle made a row all night. The former only rest in turn that they may keep good watch and ward against cattle robbers, 2 and 4 legged. The dogs we heard not; they watch round at a distance. They were bawling at the cattle all night and we were made very uneasy by fear that our house would be torn down: the animals were eating at it. It dripped a good deal on T's bed and elsewhere.

Tuesday, 11th March. The noise went on till 9 and then all was quiet till 4. We have had a rainy day, all but a few hours in the afternoon. These Yourouks seem full of fun and most anxious to do all they can for us. We were impressively warned on our arrival not to stir by night outside the door for our lives, as the dogs would surely worry us and we cannot even move by day, so here we are, 10 people who each must have a guardian. It makes me laugh till I cry to see the soldier waiting to start till his guard comes with a big stick and some stone and then you see Ahmet hovering on a threshold and calling for help. Then M goes to the door with a milk jug and no one is in sight and he has to stay, not daring to go 6 steps into sight and then an awful barking and growling calls us to the door and 2 of our men, with a horse and a donkey and 2 huge sticks, are besieged by dogs and can go neither back nor forward till an old woman rushes to their rescue, bangs one dog, puts her foot on the head of another, and so they get off!

We are surrounded by filthy mire and all wearing boots; we pick our steps delicately while Yourouks stamp about barefooted, and to see the careful, anxious faces and the shrieking behind the guardians is most ridiculous. If one attempts to leave the house someone shouts to stop us and we might as well be prisoners, or trying to play Puss in the Corner.[39]

By way of knowing the cattle when stolen, 'ours' have one ear nearly cut in half and hanging off.

We went round the walls today to see if there was an inscription to be seen. The wall is Sarascenic, but there is also a ruined one outside of previously used stones from various sources. We went up to the castle, chiefly by the steps cut in the rocks, winding about. The wall is nearly complete and there are vaulted rooms quite so. We might have lived there but we should not have seen so much of Yourouk life as down below.

The women here have a large gold medal stamped out. This shape hung on both temples. One is such a real beauty and very tall. She often comes to see me. There is really no staring here. It is not like in Persia where every crack accommodated an eye and they even looked down the chimney at us.[40]

Our fires are lit on the ground and we have great difficulty about wood, there is so little here, and reeds do not make a good fire and, besides, one is always catching one's feet in the long ones. This is indeed a different place to

---

[39] A Victorian children's game. 'Puss' stands in the middle of the room, the 'mice' in the corners. The mice can only be caught when they leave the safety of their corners.
[40] A further reference to her 1889 journey.

what it was in Mr. Davis's time 15 years ago, when there was a Syrian colony with houses 2 storeys high and better than the generality of villages. He also mentions bushes.

We were wondering what had happened to the ruins of the town as the stones seem gone without being used for houses in these days. Even those few ruined buildings he mentions here seem to be reduced to about two. No town is known to have suffered more from earthquakes.

We are sometimes startled in the night by hearing as we think guns go off, but this is only the steam exploding damp reeds on the fires. They have no candles or lamps.

Wednesday [March] 12th. We were disturbed in our minds, as well as noses, while dining yesterday evening by mysteriously splashing sounds and an awful smell. To protect the house from the rain they were casting the filthy mire on the walls, but we stopped that.

T joyfully exclaimed at dinner, 'This has been a regular Gala day for us!'

'Yes indeed!' I rapturously responded. This will be Greek to you unless I tell you that we had been fasting on curds, fresh butter and milk and that the Greek for milk is *gala*.

I have been taking out the buttermilk, salting and packing it in a tin for future use, as these milk productions do not always fall in our way.

The house was much devoured and wrenched at and T tried to drive our enemy away by spearing at the walls with a long cane, but he could not very well go as he was one of our own animals, the donkey, secretly removed from the stable and tied there by the Yourouks, 10 men and 9 beasts being rather a tax on the accommodation.

Tomorrow we hope to get to Kars Bazaar. I said I could not leave till I had a day of sunshine. Now here this minute is the sun and T is off with the brushes after an inscription. He copied one yesterday; he had to be lowered on to a narrow ridge by the Yourouks and to take off his boots, to the damage of feet and stockings. There is a strong wind blowing through our cage.

Thursday 13th was a very fine morning. We started at 8 and were very glad to leave Anavartsa. The sun was beginning to draw up all sorts of unwholesome smells. In 6 weeks all these houses will be burnt. No one could remain in the summer. There are so many snakes and the vegetation prevents cattle from getting about.

We went round the rock, keeping to the right of the aqueduct and Hadjilar, and our road for 2 hours was a single path over the plain and through mud, partly beside the river Jehan. We had a real wild goose chase. We saw really 4 of these birds rise and great were the preparations with the horses in case of shooting. M was stalking carefully and everyone saw the wild goose sitting but I.

It was carefully pointed out to me. I who am so short-sighted said, 'Oh! Is that bird which sits like an eagle in the field the wild goose?' And I was told it was – but when it rose, lo!, it was an eagle.

After the 2 hours we joined the road from Sis to Kars Bazaar, whither we were bound. We had to dismount to lead our horses across a very much ruined bridge over the Sombass and thence forward our way was over grass plain and round swamps. We lunched on the bank of the Savroon, a very large river just past a very pretty cemetery, on a knoll with some large trees.

Our journey in all was about 5 hours. Kars Bazaar is a very small town situated quite on the edge of the plain. We had been travelling among beautiful bushes of blackthorn and with a great pointed snowy mountain in front of us to represent Fujiyama, it looked quite Japanese. We watched the snowy mountains sink behind a low ridge and having sent on our *zaptich* with a letter to a Greek, we followed him to the bank of the Savroon with pleasant anticipations of much instructive conversation with our host.

We were met by some riders to welcome us and show us the way across the river, which is very wide and deep. My horse got very frightened once we were fairly in and began to back upstream into deeper water. My reins being very long I was able to swing them to the nearest rider, a Turkoman, who gave them to the *zaptich*. Their length enabled the poor horse to bolt up the bank while I had only to sit with my hands before me and he danced so that he would let no one give me the reins for some time. All our baggage came dry, though I got my feet wet.

Alas! Hadji Andreas *Aga*[41] can only speak a few disjointed Greek words. He could read our Greek Testament but could not understand the last bit better than we when we read his Bible in Turkish with Greek letters. He was very kind and sat with us, often talking and smiling away. We could not understand much. He told us a most tremendous secret too and begged us not to tell it to anyone and particularly not at Stamboul. As well as we could we assured him we would not and this is one of the most private secrets I ever heard because I could not make it out, but I think it is that we are not to let out the Ismael Efendi has a Christian wife.

The bare room we had with only a wooden divan round 2 sides, on which baggage and T's bed were put, had access by the window to apparently a grass field, but really the roofs of every house in the block, ours being the only two-storeyed one, so we could look down into all the streets and admire the large stretches of Roman mosaic in some of them, over which all the traffic goes. There are a good many places where there is a mosaic. We went into 2 cabins

---

[41] 'Aga' is a term of respect or literally a captain, commander or chief officer.

made like big hampers and in one there was an inscription complete. We had it masked and returned in the afternoon and T copied it.

Of course the cottage filled with people and as they thoroughly examined me I did the same by them. All their hair is plaited in little light plaits and a few inches from the end it is plaited on to a bar, which holds a quantity of false plaits of silk with tassels at the end, so they look at first sight to have an immense quantity of hair. They all wore their faces uncovered but the newly married ones, not so very newly married either. These ladies had a thin red handkerchief all over the head and faces, and wait to unpack their heads till they have 2 or 3 children. I examined them all; some were pretty, some not. All had coins hung in their hair.

We visited the Kaïmakam, Hassan Bey,[42] a very nice young man who speaks French. He told us he has 40 brothers and sisters and is the son of Barbahan Pasha, a great chief of the Kourds. He has been educated at Constantinople and lived at Jerusalem, so having foreigners he suspected us of no evil design.

As our *zaptich* was to be changed I said 'Of course, we have nothing to do with his food or that of his horse?'

'Nothing,' he said. 'That is paid by the government.'

Ahmed Chaoush, who always wants us to pay much that he may share the spoil, had assured us we should pay this and wages besides. We told him we had never done it before but were weak enough to feed the *zaptich* but not the horse, and he was quite pleased with a *medjidié* on parting. The new man is Suleiman Chaoush.

I also went to see the wife of Ismael Bey, a very fat Greek in a dressing-gown of Persian cashmere with 8 different stripes about an inch wide. I enjoyed my visit. I sat cross-legged on a very high divan with one elbow on a cushion.

[Saturday, March] 15th. We felt that the joys of Kars Bazaar were exhausted, so this morning at 20 to 8 we rode off to Hemiteh Kaleh, which we reached about half past one. All the way was along low spurs of the mountain, sometimes covered with bad smelling asphodel (only in the infernal regions could anyone like it for a bed) sometimes thorny bushes or quagmires, but more interesting than the plain. One of the sights of the way was a quite naked woman crouching and doing her hair while a man was quite naked close by. They were in no way abashed by the passage of our party.

We lunched at a well near Bozkoi, a Turkman village. We went up to see it; it is all of wattles. The dogs were very fierce and so each one picked up a stone. Even if you pick up a clod of earth or are seen stooping it has a good effect on the dogs.

---

[42] A regional governor.

It was very odd to see the right nostril of the women pierced, merely to stick a clove in. I thought at first it was a nail.

Hemiteh Kaleh is on the other side of an island-like mountain, close to the Jehan. There is a ruined castle on a pointed rock and the little village is somewhat more scattered than Anavartsa. The riverbanks are low and reedy. We got a reed house, not as large as the other. All the cow-house ends of the houses are round like the apse of a church and being of single reeds set up are plastered with dirt, which still retains the marks of the fingers. The houses are falling to pieces a little as spring advances. The people seem very pleasant, but from Kars Bazaar we have found that they stare more. We could not keep them out, so as I'm the attraction I went out, all followed, then T shut the door and I slipped in again. We do not wish to be rude. It was merely very natural Anthropological Research on their part.

Do you not think the 'Nomads of Asia Minor Committee'[43] is being well served?

The women are so handsome, with beautiful complexions, sunburnt of course. The faces are very broad. They wear the false plaits too and a great many gold medals on their temples.

We had a very short journey on March 16th. We did not start till 8.20 and were at our present abode by 10.30, though we went out of our way, round the corner of Hemiteh hill and across the little valley to a cave called Direkli Mara, but the only *Direk* was a natural column.[44] We also saw an old man said to be 121 years old. There was a little reed hamlet.

We went along very near the Jehan, formerly Pyramus, and we saw Boudroum about a mile from it. The castle hill is very much the same as Hemiteh. One description will serve for both. The actual castle rock is divided from the hill by a deep cutting for a road to pass. All round the base are ruins of a city, which from inscriptions we find was Hieropolis. We established ourselves in a hamlet called Chumli Koi: a pasture village on a pine-covered knoll about half a mile from the castle.[45]

The name of this particular kind of people is Bozdan.[46] The house we are in seems more of a permanent dwelling than the others we have been in. There are little windows cut in the reeds in this but in no other. The walls have been daubed inside and once whitewashed and scribbled with patterns in henna, a

---

[43] This committee is untraced.
[44] Direk = column.
[45] Theodore studied the area carefully, proclaiming it the ancient Hieropolis. He drew a plan of the acropolis and considered the foundations he saw south of the colonnaded street to be the temple of Artemis Perasia.
[46] Theodore places the Bozdan/Bosdans among the Afshars, Kurds, Circassians…and other tribes which winter on the Cilician plain (*RGS* 1890, p. 453).

band midway up the wall. The house has no sort of door within or without. Our only protection is a cotton curtain. The arbour is divided into 2 unequal parts by a wide passage, into what might be called a yard or stable. It is partly roofed and has a hedge of thorns heaped round it; some of the horses lie there. On the right is a small room where we are and on the left is another room, separated by a fence from the passage. In this is the place for calves, kids and lambs.

I had been thinking how unfair it is that white lambs have such a good reputation. No one says 'As innocent as a kid'. However no one would wonder who saw the difference in their behaviour. The kids are always escaping and either invading our room and getting on beds, or being hunted for outside while the lambs are perfectly quiet.

After luncheon I mounted the donkey and we went about seeking places where we might dig up inscriptions. On the 17th March we took 5 men and with the full consent of our *zaptich* found a good many inscriptions. I occupied myself chiefly in taking squeezes while T went backwards and forwards and up and down and round and round, hunting. He found me in great despair over the first, which would not dry as there is a damp mist and no sun and he had a very good idea, that of a fire, so at every inscription throughout the day a fire of old stalks of asphodels and squills was kindled.

We were much bothered by the utter ignorance of the Bozdans as to what letters were, and being dragged about to see natural marks in stones and patterns. The *zaptich* became quite affected by Archaeological fever and began hewing away at the asphodels with his sword. He was also very anxious that T should read him the inscriptions, quite content with hearing, though he did not understand, and to aid T he pointed with his finger along the words from right to left.

A Bozdan, who evidently could not read or write, wishing to show us that there were many lines on a stone he wished to show us, made the motion of writing line after line from left to right, which looks as if ours were the more natural way. The ancient name of the place was Hieropolis.

We remained there 3 days. We escaped a shower by returning at 4 to our arbour, which was covered with a tent and had a rather quieter night than the …[a page has been torn out here – a rare occurrence in Mabel's *Chronicles*] …first when dogs, frogs, goats, sheep, cows, wolves, men, women, children, jackels, donkeys, camels, horse and cats combined in making a row all night. Nothing came within our curtain but they wandered in the passage and shook the walls.

There are no buffalos here as at Hemiteh Kala. They ran away there and the dogs after with a thundering row. The women here wear their clothes often open to the waist and all their skin is like brown wrinkled leather, but just round their throats where the handkerchief covers it it is quite smooth. They seem so thinly clad and not to mind the cold. They seem surprised at my thick clothes and very uneasy when they see my head bare.

Tuesday March 18th. We only worked half today, finishing up with photography and measurements and on Wednesday March 19th we set out on our return. First we went back to Hemiteh Kala and then kept along the river till we got near Anavartsa again, but not on the side where the village is. We kept along the Jehan for the most part; where there were bends we went straight across the grass with no path. We passed first a small hamlet and then a good-sized village, also of Bozdans, and near the village of Jehan Bekerli we crossed in a ferryboat.

It was rather hard to find out where the boat was, as it moves according to how the Jehan eats away its banks, and as the bank is a jungle of tall canes and brambles we rode about some time till we saw a train of camels emerging. There was plenty of traffic so we had to wait about an hour before we and our horses were across and then the latter were unloaded while we lunched and stayed another in a little cane arbour.

We went by a single little path till we came to a large Circassian village on the post road to Aleppo, which means that the track here becomes very wide. We passed several small Circassian villages and about half past four reached Bergin, a Turkish one, where we stayed in a house and were bitten all night. The family slept in an open gallery and were bathed in the awful mist which poured in when we opened the shutters in the morning. This mist did not rise till midday and we were so sorry as we had enjoyed the beauty of the mountains the day before.

Thursday, 20th March. In an hour we reached Yarsouat, otherwise Yiamili Koi from having a mosque. It is a little town. Ahmet tried to make us stop in a khan and wait for luncheon, saying the men and horses would wait. We said M won't wait; he will know we have not stopped at half past 9. We went on 2 hours and stopped near a village below Ilan Kalessi, but not on that side of the Jehan. There were trees and a small river so we waited for the packhorses.

At Yarsouat the *kerajees*[47] wanted to stay but M said that we had not stopped; he was sure so they came on. It was 2 hours to Missis, very hot, left the plain and crossed one or 2 little passes, the wide road becoming *very* narrow. It screws itself along the bank of the Jehan, one little slopey path along the steep side. It was very lovely scenery.

We passed *many* Circassian villages before Missis, after none. When we reached Missis, formerly Mopsuestia, Ahmet tried to prevail on us to go to an awful *khan*, or to lodge in black holes in coffee shops, but we rode to

[47] Grooms/animal handlers.

the *konak* and T went in and saw the Mudir and asked him to find a house, so immediately a *zaptich* was sent to a very nice place just opposite, within a garden and we were soon settled in an open gallery, while M had a kitchen below. The scullery was under the gallery. We hung up curtains and were very comfortable.

Friday, [March] 21st. Started at 7.15, 4 hours exactly to the bridge by a nearly straight road.[48] We found the Jenanyans still at the Meads, which we were glad of. We stayed a night and went next morning at 8 to Mersina, where for a third time we were kindly housed by the Dillons. We stayed till Monday. Of course a good time was spent in a thorough rearrangement of baggage. On Sunday afternoon we drove to Pompeiopolis, taking M to make tea for us. Mr. Schröder, the Austrian or Bavarian Consul at Beyrout, joined us. His steamer was in and Mr. Dillon had told him where to find us.

Monday [March] 24th found us on the old road to Selefka again. We took a carriage and drove all the way to Lamas to save ourselves that long hot ride. We had the same rooms and on Tuesday 25th set off with a guide for a village up in the mountains, 2½ hours off. We never got there for we lost our way. We went up the left side of the Lamas river, high above the valley, and we went up for about 2 hours, and after making a wide sweep came down and down, sometimes with and sometimes without a path, and got to a lot of ruins called Spiroli or Spiroglou, where there were 2 houses.

Into one of these it was hoped we might get but it was locked and the master away, so we sat down before it in all patience and have been sitting these 3 hours past. The horses were unloaded, chairs and tables set up, tea made and drunk, dinner prepared and the horses curry-combed and also vaselined where necessary, and it is getting a little chilly but the master is coming. He approached the door, which had a large slit in it like a letter-box, brandishing a huge object composed of iron and wood, introduced in the keyhole slit and admitted us to a house that has not been inhabited for a month, very dark, but not damp; one end was a stable.

We were much disturbed by the rats running in the roof, which is of grass-grown earth supported on rough, black beams and brushwood. They threw down earth by the pound and even little stones. I kept my head under my sheet.

The tablecloth which lay folded on the table was nearly quite covered with earth and so of course was everything else. However we were only there one night as there were only Christian remains,[49] and Wednesday 26th we rode off to Jambazli, about 4 hours in a north-westerly direction. This air seems much more healthy than the interior, but here at Jambazli we hear of an entomologist

---

[48] The Bents are back in Tarsus.
[49] Theodore at this time had very little interest in anything post Roman.

who, besides other insects, found 15 different species of mosquito.⁵⁰ They have not come yet and we found last night very cold.

About a mile we came to a very widely scattered village. Here a *mudir* lives. We had a very pretty journey among bushes but very up and down of course, over rocks, and not very pleasant for we had rain during fully half of it and hail, but there being no wind and having our waterproofs ready was an alleviation. We saw at last cliffs crowned with 2 high mausoleums and a village near, and had to go down very steeply into the valley and up the other side. We have tried very hard to get mules but it was impossible.

After luncheon I spent the rest of the rainy afternoon at home. We have a very dry house. Our room is not large; when the beds are up there is only a 3 ft passage from the door to the fire, but as there *is* a door and also 2 little windows and M is well housed, we should be well content to stay, but today's examinations with T's yesterday afternoon show nothing worth staying for, so we expect to start for Üzenjaburdj tomorrow.

As we did at Boudroum, we have sent a party of scouts out to report. There is a place 1½ hours away, which we shall pass and where we shall stay if we like.

Friday [March] 28th. First we came to a village called Yiyeni. We rode over the houses. There were several tombs and bits of polygonal masonry and here began a long flat narrow cultivated valley. On a rock above, about the middle of it, was a tower nearly complete of polygonal masonry with a wine press close under it and a very large cistern below it. I suppose there were vineyards there once.

Oura has an immense aqueduct with an inscription on it and many ruins and tombs. We wished to stay but no convenient tombs could be found and we soon gave up the idea, as indeed we should want a little village for 9 men and horses, beside such luxuries as milk, eggs, information and workmen would be denied us.

So after luncheon we went on to Üzenjaburdj.⁵¹ It is about 1½ hours off and all these places seem to have joined. We passed a tomb, a sarcophagus, perched

---

⁵⁰ For a theory that Alexander the Great eventually died of a malarial fever first contracted in Cilicia, see Donald Engels, *Classical Philosophy*,1978.

⁵¹ The couple are now at the heart of 'Olba', an extended Hellenistic and Roman administrative centre that included Oura and Diocaesarea (Üzenjaburdj/Uzuncaburç), some 20km inland (north-east) of Silifke. On the aqueduct Theodore spotted the inscription ΟΛΒΕΩΝΗΠΟΛΙΣ and writes… 'which was conclusive evidence that we had at last reached the central point of which we were in search' (*RGS* 1890, p.458). Theodore published 19 symbols copied from various Olbian sites in an article for *Classical Review* later in the year (Vol. 4, No. 7, pp. 321–322). For a contemporary monograph on some of the sites investigated by Theodore and Mabel, see *Provincial Cilicia and the Archaeology of Temple Conversion* by Richard Bayliss (Oxford, 2004). Interestingly, the work contains photographs taken by Gertrude Bell, who met Mabel in Jerusalem in the early 1900s.

on 2 columns. Üzenjaburdj is a most attractive looking place with nearly all the columns of a temple standing with some of their Corinthian capitals still on and several other columned ruins and, oh, such bushes of 'waitabit' thorns[52] and seas of stones to get over and through.

Our house has one wall, an ancient one of single large stones, airy for you can see between each. My hammock is against and fills this. T's bed at right angles is so close to the door that when it blows open it shakes him. The door wall is of sticks and daubed, but very open, and is now tapestried with Turkey red. The fireplace lets in more light than the windows and much smoke. The windows each side of the fire are little deep funnels which at night are stuffed with sacks and brushwood. The kitchen has 2 sides, so open and it is so impossible to protect our possessions from man and beast that M has to stay at home except when I or we are both in.

Saturday was occupied digging a little, squeezing, exploring, and a ladder was made and T with great difficulty took an inscription on a tower in 18 pieces of paper, as one would have blown away; a long job I had in sewing them together afterwards.

Sunday [March 30th]. I took some photos and some measurements were done, but we only dawdled about and were at home a good deal and greatly enjoyed a holiday. T alarmed me in the afternoon by getting feverish, but though 101, was better by the time he had eaten a good luncheon.

Monday [March] 31st. After copying an inscription which some man had concealed because he thought it contained gold, we rode down to Oura with 4 horses. At this moment we are sitting in a tower by a fire, lit to dry an inscription while a ladder is being made for another on the corner, high above the valley. All that we see here is late also, but as no one else has been here it is well to copy what there is.

We have attached to ourselves one Evthymios, a Greek, employed on the road; he is intelligent and saves us both trouble. He can hand T papers and hold the measure, which spares me many a scramble and he can go instead of T to see whether a stone has letters, or a pattern on it; also he knows the neighbourhood. Tomorrow we go to Oren Koi…So wrote one April Fool.

April 1890 – return to Mersin

[Tuesday] April 1st. We were the April Fools, who having waited till about 10.30 when it cleared, packed our beds and everything, and hardly was everything

---

[52] Mabel's first reference to a prickly customer the couple are to encounter on their future travels in Africa and elsewhere. It is the *Acacia brevispica*, the so called 'wait-a-bit thorn', so named because of the backward curving thorns which take time to remove.

finished when down the rain came again till night. We had had rain all night and dreadful dripping. I got up and dealt out waterproofs and well it was for me. T heard such thumping over my head, like handfuls being cast down and this was about as much earth from the roof as would fill a good flowerpot, which would have been on my face.

Well! We had to make our beds again but our already very limited space was so very much more so by reason of the drips that my bed had to stand over T's all day, which its greater length permits, well covered. At night this arrangement had to cease, and great difficulty had we to undress, and before breakfast could be admitted in the morning the beds had to be taken to pieces.

April 2nd. Wednesday was a fine morning so we sent on the 4 packhorses with Ahmed Chaoush and M to Oren Koi. We remained with Evthymios to take an impression of a band of curious hieroglyphs cut in relief over a doorway. (This has made a good cast but no fellow can understand it.)[53] It was a very difficult job. We had some stones put to stand on and I had to work almost on tiptoe on the shady side of the doorway with such a cold wind blowing through that it seemed quite warm to dabble one's fingers in the water with the paper. Then a fire was lighted, wet wood, and finally that tender and wet mould had to be anxiously packed on my horse.

We did not leave till past 9 and took just 3 hours. We went in a westerly direction and chiefly through woods and bushes. And almost everything that might be called wood was represented by burnt skeletons.

The others had lost their way and were not long in before us. We had quite a nice cottage. There was a small window with a shutter and a very rough wooden grating to keep out dogs; a coarse carpet on the floor and a key. We felt pleased at hearing that our landlord is a squinter, strabon, (Stravos) or Strabo; on such a journey we like to meet with such a person.[54] T also sometimes rides a squinting horse which is called To Stravó and we think it a good omen. Luncheon was soon ready and after it T departed and came back assured that we might go on tomorrow, as there was nothing worth staying for.

---

[53] Theodore presented a cast before the members of the Royal Geographical Society at the meeting of 30 June 1890.

[54] The classic *vade mecum* for travellers in the region was a set of the works of the great geographer, Strabo. The Bents and their fellow topographers and antiquarians in Cilicia would require his Volumes 12 (books 1 and 2) and 14 (book 5). Stabo was born in Roman Pontus around 60 BC and completed a 17-volume 'Geography' that, 2000 years later, provides today's scholars with an indespensible descriptive and historical 'gazetteer'. As well as exploring the then known world, the geographer spent some time in Rome, possibly in Trajan's time, dying about AD 20. 'As for Cilicia beyond the Taurus, one area is called Tracheia and the other Pedias. Tracheia is a narrow coastal strip and has no level ground, or scarcely any; and, in addition, lies below the Taurus and provides poor living...' So he famously begins in Volume 14.

April 3rd, Thursday. We all set off about the usual time but in about an hour came to some ruins which T went to inspect while I stayed reading on my horse. We sent all on but Elias and Evthymios and our 2 horses and followed later. In half an hour we came to more ruins, immense ones with a few cabins amongst them, but no living beings but 2 donkeys.

We hunted but saw neither inscriptions nor any fine work. There were numerous standing Stonehenge-like doorways; in one place the lintel of one was the threshold of another. The houses had been hewn out of the living rock as far as possible, and finished up with stones, one we measured was [illegible, possibly 7] feet by about 3, raised on to a wall of rock about 6 feet high.

We went on again, gradually sinking to the valley of a stream, very prettily wooded. Here against one of the rocky walls was a bas-relief, a common thing but there was an inscription to be taken. We lunched there and just as we had finished, who should appear from the other direction in which we had come but the same *yüzbashi*[55] who had taken us prisoners and 2 *zaptichs*.

I was packing the luncheon, T and Evthymios were up *in* the bas-relief and they all stopped and examined our actions with great curiosity. We did not mind for we knew they would not dare to harm us. They asked if we wished to have them as a protection for it was their duty to protect us if we wished.

'Much obliged!' was the answer. They need not trouble, we were not in the least afraid; we did not wish for them at all.

How many days did we intend to travel in this region? We must write to Selefkeh to say.

T said, 'Weeks, perhaps a month'; in any case it would be exactly as we chose; where we went and how long and he had no intention of writing.

Then they said they had orders to accompany us wherever we went and to '*phylax*' us. Now '*phylax*' may mean either *watch* or *guard*. They were told they might travel where they pleased. We should give them nothing. They went on. T went up with Evthymios to a great wall overhanging a cliff which protects the wonderful and amazing gorge of the Lamas river at a place of easy descent. We had to dismount and climb down a tremendous steep [sic] where the stream cut down between cliffs to join the river. We passed the *zaptichs* in a cave writing a letter.

At last we reached the river. All the rivers here have perfectly perpendicular cliffs with a small steep band of slope in some parts. These cliffs were immensely high and all honeycombed with caves, some had been used as tombs and some as hermitages, now quite inaccessible. Frescoes of saints can be seen in some

---

[55] Captain or other official.

places and particularly we had long heard of a 'box', a [word illegible, 'trassella'?] to be seen near an object white and shining like silver or glass, thought to be a lamp or a narghileh.

At the bottom there are four mills – old ones repaired. A Greek miller came out and told how our party had safely gone on and spoke excitedly of the aforesaid wonders. He offered to conduct us to the place whence they were visible. So we went on foot down the river half a mile, scrambling along up and down and at last in a lovely green meadow with huge plane trees by and in the water, and then up again. T made out the treasure box (with a field glass, through which Evthymios and the miller eagerly looked) to be a coffin and the shining silver lamp a wet stalagmite. The miller clung to his old notions.

On our return to the mill we mounted again. The *zaptichs* had gone on.

There was a good new bridge but that we did not cross. The road over it goes only downstream. We went up and crossed the open stream, and the men had to walk along stepping-stones at the top of the dam, and then we all crossed a really old big bridge and took to our feet again up a most awful ascent. When we reached the top of the cliff it took an hour to Veyiseli. In all I think our actual journey took 5 hours, but it was past 4 o'clock and our many divergences had taken about 4 hours more.

It was a very pleasant day, though there was rain at times and as soon as one's waterproof was buttoned on out came the sun.

'It is delightful to think', I said, 'that our fire will be lit!'

'Aren't you very hot?' said T. 'Yes, but I mean our house will be ready and most likely tea.' I did not say and never have mentioned it yet that I hoped M, having dinner well on the way and time to spare, would have set up the beds.

We arrived at the top of a village, one flat roof below another: no sign of inhabitants. At last, round a corner a miserable sight met our eyes. Five horses tied up, 6 men perched on walls, the baggage tied and still in sacks and bales lying round, and at the sight of us the men rose shouting. 'We have not been able to get the key of the house yet.'

The whole company seemed sad. They had been there 3 hours, had found 2 men, and sent one for wood, the other for the key of the best looking house.

We heard now they had had fried eggs and cakes at the mill and how M had slipped into the water in crossing the dam, grazed his legs and broken the bit of wood that rests on the hand of his gun, and how the horses had to be unladen and all the baggage carried up by the men.

There were only 2 houses open to our inspection, in ruins and full of mud, so we determined to wait till sun set and in the meantime have our tea. We chose a sort of open shed which, by chance, happened to be the entrance of the house taken by the *zaptichs*, so they had to walk over our fire and tried to bring in a horse, but that we did not permit. I stood in the way. After tea we wandered about and looked at the very strange view. We could trace how the river came up to meet us, took a bend to the right and then went off to the left by a smoke-like mist rising and creeping along.

At last we determined to make for any moderately dry shelters so the key having come and the house being found to be a muddy pond, we retired to a very dark place; indeed the chief light comes down the chimney and to write I have to put the table unpleasantly near the large fire that must be kept up because the floor sticks to our boots. We have not much room here. Our beds are both set up crookedly because certain rocks prevent their being level otherwise. T's touches mine and is partly under, so when I felt a shake and heard an awful groan last night I cried out but it was only T's bed creaking.

There are plenty of fleas and only a loose wall between us and the cow's bedroom, so you may fancy it is not a nice place for a rainy afternoon. M went off somewhere else, to sleep drier, so we fastened up the doors with sticks and a booby-trap of tin things.

Evthymios asked the *zaptichs* what they had heard of us and they said that in our first journey we had found inscriptions, telling us where treasure was to be found, and now we had returned that we might dig it up by night. He last night overheard one asking, 'What did you write in that letter?'

'That they only wish to see ruins and copy inscriptions.'

I think now they are awaiting an answer to that letter; we have not seen them today. We went out early about a mile to hideous bas-reliefs but found no letters. T then went down the river and found some curious boundary stones, etc. I hope the *zaptichs* will go for they increase the difficulty of finding oats and straw, etc., and take everything without paying. These houses will be badly repaired next winter and let to fall into ruins again in spring. There are very few inhabitants left; no milk and we have to send to the mill for eggs.

Evthymios we like very much; he has a wife and 3 little girls and as he seems poor I am very glad he has this little job. He has half a *medjidié* a day and his food with M and Ahmed.

Monday 7th April. We stayed 3 nights at Veyeseli, among darkness, fleas and damp, drawing all the neighbourhood – a complete blank as far as inscriptions went. The rides we went were picturesque enough. One day up to a castle situated on a cliff above the ruin. We went a long round to get there and from it we had exactly the reverse of the view I have tried to represent on the other side. Our village looked just a patch of red from the earthy stones of the houses with a few horizontal lines and that was all. We got a lot of butter from the shepherds up at this castle and I had plenty to do in making it up and packing it.

We left Veyseli yesterday morning about 7.30, and at 10.30 had reached Tapoureli. We had a beautiful journey southward and rising, and chiefly through a sort of gully or valley of rocks and always wooded and the path being narrow it is very hard for the packhorses to wrench their way along. We have a splendid room, rough and *full* of fleas, but there is a window with shutters and a couple of other holes so we have plenty of light. M has a comfortable kitchen and the stable is between, the last so very dirty I begged to have it at once cleaned. A travelling tinker was established here but he permitted himself to be turned out.

We had all our bed-making done before luncheon and that was over by ½ past 12, and being able to lock the doors, with our own padlocks, T and I and M, with a couple of the *kerajees* (the horses' men) and 3 Yourouks as guides, and my horse, went to see some ruins about a mile off. We found one inscription pretty good and had the most tremendous climbing and scrambling over stones and ruins, walls and rocks, always having to work our way through thorny bushes.

One large serpent was seen. There are quantities here. When we went to the castle the other day it was thought we might meet bears and leopards but I am glad to say we did not do so. The three guides spent their time sitting in a valley while we scrambled on both sides till I was tired and went and sat with them.

Today I have not been out at all. I had such a bad night with 24 fleas and was very tired, so as the day's work was in 2 directions I settled to stay in in the morning. Now I am still in for the day has been very unsuccessful and T has gone with Evthymios to the same ruined palace. If it had not been too late we should have gone to Mara today, but it is 4 or 5 hours and 2 hours to pack and load.

Tuesday, 8th April. It took us 6 hours to get to Mara, where Evthymios lives. First we went over hill and dale, always through bushes and thorns and then gradually round and down a valley full of fine trees, cedars, etc., all lopped by the Yourouks, and reached the Lamas river where we sat down to luncheon on the western right bank thereof, having crossed a bridge.

After luncheon we had a most tremendous climb to get to the top of the cliffs. I was glad not to be on a *palanko* (saddle), though I went up as steep places on one, but not on such an overhanging height. There were enormous cedars wherever there could be but in a hundred years there will be none. The Yourouks cut and burn the old and the goats prevent any young ones. There are no signs of any.

The scenery was, I need not say, magnificent. The other side was quite inaccessible and yet we saw where the mouths of caves had been walled up as tombs. We came to a place where 2 mills were wedged in and the river had hollowed a cave like a sea cave; soon after the cliffs sank down and we turned off to the left and gradually got down to Mara, a very flourishing little village, with a few Greek families on the high road from Selefka to Karamania. About an hour from Tapoureli we stopped about half an hour at a small hamlet called Erbeyli to take an inscription. It is a high, cold place and I saw children with coughs, and only one very ragged cotton coat on, sitting in the dew.

Mara is also very high and cold and the snow is only gone a week. There is still snow on the mountains and the journey to Karamania is 30 hours, only divided by a night in a cave. So, thinking of the hardships of that journey and the regrets at leaving the ruins unvisited that we are bound for, we did not regret giving up Karamania for this year.

We were splendidly lodged in a large boarded room with 2 glass windows. Those without glass had shutters tied on: as it had been built by a former *Mutessarif* of Selefka as a summer residence we had no fireplace and there was no charcoal; our brazier was always absurdly blazing in the street every time it was replenished.

Evthymios, who must be pretty well off, for he has a shop besides his employment on the road, wished to be paid so T gave him 7 medjidiés, saying that will be up to tomorrow night. Not till next morning did he let out that he did not mean to come further with us and T at the last minute did not care to fight over the half medjidié. We had too high an opinion of his honesty. As to Ahmed Chaoush, we have long not had any doubts of his veracity.

We never shall know what was the cause of our wanderings yesterday, i.e. **Wednesday, [April] 9th.** We started with the intention of going to Maïdan, where there were to be ruins, but no houses, only tombs or caves. 7 hours. However Ahmet, after we had set out, told us there was a fine square tower he had heard of with ruins of the same kind as at Kizil Oren Koi at Tchartuli, an hour less distant than Maïdan and not much off the road; the village was amongst the ruins – like idiots we said we would go.

We started on the Selefka road, most wild and dreary scenery, grey rocks and the wrecks of immense cedars, no sign of any young ones. Almost every tree besides, being fearfully hacked, had been used as a fireplace and we passed a fine one on fire. In about an hour and ½ we began to descend into a gorge, perfectly splendid. We went along the bottom. Anything more awful and melancholy as scenery could not be imagined. We were 2 hours passing and where the valley opened we waited for the packhorses and lunched.

About half a mile on we came to a well, or fountain, where our horses drank. Ahmet was ready first and T walked on as there was great thunder going on. I was following when shouts from behind called me to stop. T said Ahmed had gone he said to ask the way, but as a man who had been speaking to Ahmed said he had told him to lead us to Tchartuli, away we went into the bushes and in about ½ an hour came to a hamlet with no sign of ruins, so we went on to Tchartuli, 2 hours in pouring rain with thunder and lightning tearing through a narrow thorny way, up hill.

Ruins we saw none, so we wished to go on to Maïdan, one hour, but this the men, I am glad to say, resisted, so we stepped into a room which we shared with some cows. They did us no harm at all. There was a good deal of trouble in housing 8 men and 8 beasts, for we now have a donkey Ahmet has bought. We passed a peaceful night and T had to get out of bed to let the master come and feed the cows, bearing a torch, for candles and lamps are not known.

The door had been secured by a plant and a wooden spade. Ahmed had come in late, very angry that we had not waited for him and said he had gone to Maïdan, which we did not believe and he had a variety of stories which did not symphonize, so we have left off wondering and this morning, having vainly sought ruins, set out for Maïdan, an hour as was said.

Thursday [April] 10th. I am now writing in a black tent which belongs to the Yourouks.[56] We took 2½ hours getting here by a very dreadful road. We went along the bottom of another cliff-bound gorge but this looked gay in comparison to that traversed yesterday. The trees were leafy ones and there was ivy on some of the rocks. We had to dismount and lead our horses over an awful place, a long, steep, smooth, rounded rock, sloping on one side. How the packhorses got up, I wonder. I asked Ahmet if he had come this way last night, he said a different one, worse.

In 1½ hour we came to the ruins of a Byzantine church and some other modern buildings and at last got on to the Selefka road again, near a bridge which has its 2 arches exposed and can only be crossed by foot passengers. As the river is dry now this does not matter. Inquiries were now made of some passing Yourouks. They said there was only one cave but it was large enough for us all, men and beasts. How thankful we felt this was not all happening last night in the rain, for it poured till late.

At last some other people said there were tents higher up, so in about half an hour we reached a grassy little *plateau* with 4 or 5 tents and were soon in possession of one of them, the one we had brought being given up to the men. While our tent was being prepared I was sitting in another where the mistress made the greatest haste to get coffee for me. She took a basket to the fire in which she had all the implements. There were a bag of coffee-beans, a folding

---

[56] Mabel is in a tent, over-nighting on the way to 'Mara', via 'Tapoureli'.

pan in which she roasted them, a pretty wooden tray, with a spout in which she put them to cool,[57] and a carved wooden mortar, very thick and with little space inside. It was closed with a leather lid with a great blob of leather inside to keep dust out, an iron ornamented pestle, and one or two coffee pots with folding handles and a box which held the coffee cups and brass *zarfs*.[58] There was no sugar in the coffee but it was good and cleanly made.

Our tent is quite open at one end, the back, but the rock rises not far and there are stones and brushwood. All round inside are camel saddles, for it only comes within a yard of the ground where it is not hitched on growing bushes. In front it hangs down rather more. It is airy and far from shady, the cloth being so open. I have had to keep my hat on all day. We shall make curtains to our beds, for the tent is quite hopeless to shut. I have had several visitors but no peepers as in Persia[59] and many places.

Theodore and M went out to the ruins but found no inscription. Some man who can read is going to be sent round to look. There are so many wait-a-bit thorns, which they call 'the devil with many nails', that it is hard to get about.

Friday [April] 11th. We paid visits to our neighbours last evening but only sat down in one tent. I sat where invited but after some time was startled by the squalls of a young baby. The mistress of the tent, who had a swaddled baby about 5 months' old in her arms, swooped down, swept away the clothes, caught hold of a string that ran round a baby's chest and swung it up and into another woman's arms. This baby was not more than 6 weeks old and presented a very odd appearance. It had a stroke of charcoal across both eyebrows, joining them, a second across the eyelashes and bridge of the nose and 2 strokes from the bridge of the nose running down under its eyes. It had a fearful look.

There are 3 deformities here, which is many in so small a community where all the delicate die off. One is an idiot besides and seems very happy and kindly treated, but evidently cannot walk but only sit.

When evening came we lit a fire and T could keep it up all night as it was only a foot from the corner of his bed at the head. It was very cold as the tent

---

[57] Theodore presented a coffee cooler to the Pitt Rivers Museum, Oxford (1891.4.7) Perhaps it is this very item. The couple returned home with a few Yourouk souvenirs: a spindle (1891.4.6), three 'reaping gloves' with wooden finger caps (1891.4.4.1–3), a long-bladed sickle (1891.4.3), and a wooden mortar (1891.4.2). The prize exhibit, however, and reflecting the Bents' fascination with musical instruments, is a very fine wooden flute or '*nai*', complete with 'cleaning rod, hair covered at one end, and very elegant carved wood case with ornamental tassels and sling' (1891.4.1). We do not know how the couple paid for these artefacts, but in 1888 they gave 'a man about a shilling to remove his wooden lock from his door'. A shilling then would have been worth about £2.50 today.
[58] A *zarf* is a metal holder for a cup or glass.
[59] On their 1889 trek through Persia, the couple found themselves the centre of attention everywhere they went. Mabel eventually found it quite tiresome.

was by no means shut up. When we had put it all down there was a place quite high enough for a donkey to get in, but what was the good of fussing over this. Of course in a tent of ours we could not keep a fire. These people live in tents all the year round.

We had a quiet night, for though the dogs, which are not bad here, were evidently repelling some enemies, the human neighbours remained at peace till 5 when we all arose. Today we have promised 3 piastres, 6d,[60] to anyone who tells of 'letters', so a good many are off with pickaxes and hatchets. T is gone to copy one set.

Two ladies are now sitting on camel saddles watching me. I have given away some gilt beads which are being suspended to the babies' heads for the evil eye.

One woman has given us a large bowl of goats' beestings[61] and a good many sheets of bread and a man has just brought me a partridge. All will duly get return gifts. In consideration of the beads a very small round patchwork cap has been made for the black-faced baby. Its mother, a very handsome woman, came to show it. She clasped its legs between her knees and firmly worked and pressed the cap down on its wobbling head and bound a turban round it. It was too small and the head oozed out, so it had to be all done over again.

People took very little notice of our arrival; some did not even come out of their tents. I am so glad we have no *zaptichs* to make us unwelcome. They followed us to Tapoureli later in the day, but we are evidently abandoned.

At Mara the people said the *Mutessarif* had been called to Adona by the Vali[62] and they thought it was about our affair.

Saturday, April 12th. We started at 8 with the intention of going to [name blank] but as we came in about an hour to the ruins in the neighbourhood and they were all Christian, we settled to go to Pershendi. We ought to have turned back and gone through Maïdan again but instead of that we went on to within a mile of Selefka and then had 3 hours, or rather 4, along the road to Mersina. Most of the ride as far as Selefka was very pretty and wooded and the only bother was with caravans of camels, once forty to work our way through. Though tied one to the other in sixes and tens, sometimes they would be on both sides of the road and with the string you could not pass between.

We also passed nomad families going to Karamania. They are always interesting. We saw one where 2 beautiful children, about one and 2 years old, were standing in bags up to their arms, tied on to a donkey. A very old granny was walking along with her hair dyed red with henna.

---

[60] About £1.50 today.
[61] The first milk produced after an animal has given birth.
[62] The Wali/Vali was the senior regional leader.

We were so disgusted at finding ourselves once more on the old Mersina road that we decided we could not now go back to Selefka as we had intended, and to Mersina by Bell steamer,[63] but must go on and again spend a night at Mr. Lykiardopoulos' very uninteresting *cheflik*.

Pershendi is 20 minutes from the road, at the entrance of one of the gorges. It is very pretty and we found it hard to get along, there was so much that was good to eat and we had to go through a barley field and, of course, there was no keeping the packhorses out of that. Our men were eating the stalks of the yellow daisy[64] and very good they are and juicy. We got very good quarters; 2 houses near each other which could look the furthest up the valley. It seemed very warm after the mountains.

Sunday [April] 13th was the day that the Easter feast was kept by the majority of our party. All the kerajees were invited to dine and we had a magnificent meal with plenty of vegetables and salad. It is odd that out of seven Christians there should be 4 kinds – Anglican, Armenian, Maronite and Greek. In the afternoon we went with M, Ahmet and a Turk and a kerajee riding along the road to Chok Oren (many ruins) close to the café where we had been in such a furious rage with the Mutesarrif. There was one good inscription soon found and there I stuck, first to look after the drying squeeze and then we sat and stared at every variation of shadow as the sun came on, till T made out every word. Then everybody had tea and we came home.

Monday [April] 14th. We went 1½ hours on the road to Taklous and then turned up about half an hour to a place near Hassanbey Koi, which certainly is the Corycian cave.[65] We had thought the hole at Khani Diwani was it but this must be it. It is very like the other but larger and oblong and at one end a deep cavern, large and wide, with a small ruined Byzantine church within the mouth of it. A paved road winds right down into the cavern. Water drips from the roof and under the furthest part water runs with a sound like distant drums.

I managed to get to the very end alone. I went very, very slowly, to get accustomed to the light, or rather darkness, and I had a stick and at last I found a dry place to sit. T and M were brought by a guide with candles by a much more stony path and lights were not needed except just at the end. I was so angry at

---

[63] A famous name in steamship history, Henry Bell was a designer of paddle steamers in the early 1800s.
[64] There are a number of edible 'daisies'. This one may have been *Chrysanthemum coronarium*.
[65] At Bent's Hassanbey Koi, the famous cave complex, and legendary home of Typhon, of *Cennet ve Cehennem* (Heaven and Hell) above the ancient port of Corycus on the mouth of the river Calycadnus (Gȍksu). Formally it was an important harbour and commercial town and the Byzantines later built a fortress there. (Not to be confused with the eponymous location on Mount Parnassus which was named after the nymph Corycia.)

the waste as we are very poor in that respect and have to be very careful. We have not much more than a week now.

We found a brand-new inscription and had great trouble drying it with a fire. We settled to go there to stay and were sorry that having been misinformed we had thought Pershendi was the place to stay for this, and that we had not our baggage with us. Now dwellings had to be sought for. A very tiny hut was found for us but it was empty and it looks clean; some loose boards are lying near the door; there is no window. There is a small archway about 6 feet wide and 5 from side to side. M is going to hang things over this as his house, and the rest will have the tent.[66]

Tuesday [April] 15th. Great fuss this morning. We hear that T's horse, which belongs to Ahmed or Elias, is lost, saddle and all. They sleep in their saddles and packsaddles for fear of catching cold. We waited to start till after luncheon as a man hoping for 6d said there was a place as large as a door covered with writing, so high that it needed a ladder. Off went T with a *kerajee*, but all they saw were a few red paint words at a hermitage so came back after 3 hours' vain toil.

First Ahmet said no thief could have taken it as only one house was gone instead of all. He was found to be gone off in search with Elias, and T's horse and mine when we wanted to start. We were very angry at his never saying anything nor asking leave and could not know how long he would be away, so we determined to set off with the horses we had, leaving the donkey, and with only the 3 Adaniotises in attendance.

I went out at midday and saw a very strange sight, a woman sitting stark naked on the path by the stream, calmly pouring pails of water on herself and washing with great deliberation. Several people were about. When she had done she had about 10 yards to walk to her clothes.

Well, we started, I and the baggage on horses, T and M on foot, and had not gone far before we met Ahmed and Elias, so we went on and about a mile on the road who should we meet but one of the late set of *zaptichs*, who we had last seen at Veyseli, and a man riding beside him on the lost but now found horse. The thief had been discovered by a Yourouk who told the *zaptich* that was a stolen horse so they fired at the thief and he ran away leaving the horse, and the *zaptich* recognized whose it was.

We arrived without any adventures and took possession of the various dwellings we had fixed on yesterday.[67] Our house is an archway but one end is tightly filled in and quite safe from rain, the other end has loose stones and

---

[66] The couple spend the night in a hut near the caves, having sent their caravan on to Pershendi (in the area of modern-day Susanoğlu) having been told it was the base to use for their speleological studies.

[67] The couple are back at their dwelling near the cave.

branches. It is about 10 feet by 6.6 feet. It is light, that is when the door is open, and at night we leave a very small door of a few planks, much too small for the doorway, and hang up a curtain. Ahmet and co. have a tent and M has his arch stuffed with stones and a little eked out by a wall, roofed where the arch ceases, with branches, a sack and a threshing machine. We stuck a great many branches and sticks into our wall so we can hang our numerous small [things?]. Of course no work was done but settling and building; we went down into the hole again but not down into the cavern.

Wednesday [April] 16th. We had a very pleasant busy day after a much disturbed night – fleas that had come with us (now dead), mice (hole effectually stopped up), and ants, which got in the latter and are now circumvented. T, by some magic instinct, had a wall torn down as he discovered there were several yards of inscription behind.[68] It came down piece by piece that he might have a footing for one reach after another.

We had a dreadful threat of rain, though only a little fell and that not till midnight, but so bad did it seem to be going to be that we actually came home, roof our houses with waterproof rugs, the bath and an umbrella, to be put with its handle through a hole in our roof. There was such wind that the squeezing was very maddening. After tea we went to see the other hole called Purgatory.[69]

It is a truly awful place, quite terrifying in fact. It is quite inaccessible so no one has ever been down. It is surrounded by stalactites. I did not see the bottom. I was six feet from the edge. I mean to try and photograph it. You would never guess it as there, it is quite flush with the surrounding country, and the rocks near are torn and cracked in a most weird way. It is such a dreadful place that though I was quite near it this morning I did not go but let M, who had not seen it, go alone. I feel as if I should like to have my camera tied before I try to photograph it.

Theodore has gone off 'half an hour' away but more than 3 hours have fled. I shall go and see if it is ready (I mean the hole that is being dug for me to take any squeezes). How foolish! T has the brushes. He was away more than 4 hours. The first 'half hour' place was 1½ and a wretched little red paint Christian thing, but then he plodded on and found a really good and unexpected one, so was rewarded. In the afternoon we finished the inscriptions and so our work was

---

[68] This throwaway comment disguises an incident that dogged her husband ever afterwards. 'Outside the temple, quite accidentally,' Theodore is to read out to a meeting of the Royal Geographical Society in June 1890, 'by pulling down a wall, we came across a list of 162 names...' ('Explorations in Cilicia Tracheia', *RGS* 1890, p.448.) This oft-criticized destructive approach, employed by Theodore (from Thássos to Zimbabwe), has damaged his reputation as an archaeologist.
[69] The smaller of the two caves, 'Hell' or 'Purgatory' (Cehennem Deresi).

over and done and there was nothing to do but start home on the morrow to see whether all our work is worth anything or not.

Of course very little packing could be done till the morning as no needless things were out so we went down into the pit of the Corycian Cave again. We went into a large cavern at the other end, higher up, quite light and once divided off and shut in by a wall. It is used as a goats' place and probably has been so for thousands of years – two anyhow. In consequence, fleas abound. In about a minute I was in ubiquitous misery, so I hastened beneath a pomegranate tree, which grew like a weeping willow, undressed, and caught 20 or 30. We took our table and chairs outside our door and dined very like Job to be sure.

[Thursday April 17th] We lunched at Lamas, sitting on earth and just appearing barley, not a pleasant place, and got on very well as mercifully the day was cloudy, and no flies, and slept at Mr. Lykiardopoulos's *chiflik*, and rising at 4 found ourselves at Mr. Dillon's hospitable door about 11.30.[70]

I never left the house till Monday. 'Out of doors' had no charms for me and the rest was delightful. On Tuesday **[April 22nd]** we went to Tarsus, leaving our baggage nearly ready, to stay with the Jennanyans till Friday, where, without changing our bedroom, we became inmates of Mr. Maclachlan's dining and drawing rooms.

I tried to start Mrs. Jennanyan with photography and we had very bad luck with the weather so cloudy and even rainy. Once I had got the whole of the Jennanyan family placed, 8 grownups and a baby, it rained. I was nearly wild! But it was hard to get them all together, so I ventured and did 2 and both were good, but that in one the babe and mother were blurs, but all our efforts were successful.

On Friday there was such a crowd in the house. Mr., Mrs. and Miss Marden, missionaries going home, and came in the unexpected Meads. But the missionaries don't mind and are equal to the occasion. The 3 ladies slept together and Mr. Mead and Mr. Marden shared a bed and others were on sofas.

Mrs. Dillon and Sissy came to meet us and everyone went to Mersina on Saturday, and on Sunday afternoon **[April 27th]** we said farewell to our kind entertainers and embarked on this ship the Messageries *Senegal*, 3,667 tons,[71] so a very huge one. There are a party of 43 Gaze's,[72] 22 ministers among them of *all* kinds, and they are always all meeting and having prayer meetings in the salon and hymn singing everywhere and Bibles are all over the place. You sit

---

[70] Mabel and Theodore are back at Mersin/Mersina, staying with the Dillons.
[71] The Bents are passengers on *Le Sénégal*. There is an image of her (summer 2006) at http://www.es-conseil.fr/pramona/senegal/htm.
[72] See p. 222 note 63 for 'Gaze's Tours'.

on something hard and lo! it is a Bible. But they haven't one hymnbook among them, I heard. They were limited as to luggage and each thought someone would be sure to have a hymnbook. There are at least 50 other passengers. We hope to reach Smyrna tomorrow, Wednesday **[April 30th]**.

We duly reached Smyrna and went by train to Bournabat, a pretty Frankish village of villas, and lunched at Mr. Lawson's and enjoyed seeing his curiosities much. At Salonika, where we passed Thursday, we lunched at the Consulate with Mrs. Blunt, who took us a drive and gave us tea after a wander in the bazaar.

Now here we are on Tuesday, May 6th, in the Tyrrhene Sea and hope to reach Marseilles in time to catch the 8.20 train to Paris on Thursday morning. We want to stay there to see the things M. and Mme. Dieulafoy brought from Susa, as the Influenza prevented us in the spring, and we hope to be home on Saturday evening **[May 10th]**.[73]

And so my Chronicle might end, but I wish to tell about our imprisonment.[74]

When we were first in Adana I called on the Vali who said he was sorry about the mistake of the governor of Selefka. When we returned Mr. Crestman came to say the Vali was glad that T had agreed to overlook the matter, but T said it was in Mr. Lykiardopoulos's hands and he had written to Mr. Jago, our Consul General at Aleppo, so he could not do anything. Mr. Crestman said the Vali said we were free to go anywhere.

But on our return to Mersina we found a letter, which it had not been possible to forward to us, which would have done away with all the good of our leaving England.

Private – Adana, April 9, 1890.

Dear Mr. Bent,

The Governor General, having received information that you are revisiting the same places you had already visited some time ago on the road to Selefka, and that you are taking photos or plans of the various places, requests me to make you acquainted with the fact that the taking of photos or plans of the places is not allowed without the special permission of the government.

---

[73] Mabel is steaming somewhere off the western coast of Italy.
[74] Theodore and Mabel were outraged by their treatment at the hands of the local governor of Selefka (see p. 286). Great harbourers of grudges, and quite capable of getting questions 'asked in the House', this finale to the 1890 *Chronicle* has something of the personal *aide memoire* about it – to be filed away for future need. Christmann's letter (copied into the notebook; Mabel spells the consul 'Crestman') is something of a bombshell. Then, as now, taking photographs of sensitive areas in Greece and Turkey is ill advised.

His Excellency therefore requests me to invite you in a very polite manner to discontinue from taking photos, etc., as above mentioned. Complying with His Excellency's request, I ask leave to add that it would be better if you came back to Mersina in order to avoid any possible troubles with subaltern officials.

The best way to continue your scientific investigations unmolested is, in my opinion, to request His Excellency, Sir William White, to obtain for you from the ministry at Constantinople the required permission.

N. J. Christmann

Chronicle XIII, March to April 1896:
Athens revisited, and in time for the
first modern Olympic Games…

After their 1890 expedition to Cilicia, the Bents never undertook further researches in Greece or Turkey, preferring to concentrate on Africa and the Middle East in a series of extended, and often gruelling, treks. In 1891 Theodore became fascinated by the newly discovered ruins in Mashonaland (present-day Zimbabwe), and the couple spent the year travelling to and exploring the region. They were accompanied by their friend Robert Swan, from Andíparos, who provided cartographic services, but not Manthaios Símos. Theodore developed his own particular theories on the original settlers of the region, and similar ideas led the couple to Ethiopia the next year.

At the end of 1893, Theodore and Mabel began the series of explorations to little-known areas of the Arabian Gulf that were to occupy them until Theodore's death in 1897. These years were all chronicled by Mabel, except, perhaps, for their 1892 journey to Ethiopia. There is no *Chronicle* for this year in the archive; perhaps Theodore used it to help with the writing-up of his monograph *The Sacred City of the Ethiopians* (1893) and it was subsequently mislaid.

Two of these later *Chronicles* include short references to Greece, the Bents having included Athens on their itineraries back to London. On 2 December 1895, Mabel and Theodore set off to explore along the Sudanese coast, moving down through Egypt; they meet up with Manthaios in Port Said, and again he acts as cook and assistant for the length of the trip (he will have travelled from the tiny Cycladic island of Anáfi, via Sýros).

The Bents' five-month itinerary is London – Basle – Milan – Venice – Port Said – Cairo – the Sudan coast – Cairo – Alexandria – Athens – Milan – London.

By the end of March 1896, the couple are ready to return and leave Alexandria to spend a few days in Athens before the journey home. Their stay repeats the familiar pattern of visits to friends and archaeologists – Theodore is recruited to supervise a small dig below the Olympieion. They were endeavouring to locate the Kynosarges (the athletes' gymnasium), an apposite objective, as the Bents' visit coincided with the first staging of the modern Olympic Games (held between Monday 6 and Wednesday 15 April 1896). A very modest affair by the standards of the Athenian games of 2004, the events were limited to athletics, cycling, fencing, gymnastics, shooting, swimming, tennis, weight-lifting, and wrestling. It seems that the contests were more or less open to any gentleman amateur who happened to be in Athens – it is surprising that Theodore did not enter himself for something.

Mabel's thirteenth *Chronicle* is written in a lined, dark-red leather book (175 x 115mm), with marbled endpapers and edges. See selected Indices for people and places mentioned. For notes on this transcription the reader is referred to page xxv. As usual, Theodore is abbreviated to T and Manthaios Símos to M. Manthaios does not travel on to Pireaus and this is his last appearance in this set of *Chronicles*. There are 152 pages in the notebook, but the author completes only 62 of them, the last four devoted to this short stay in the Athens. The slim volume is unique in having a price pencilled in the front: one shilling, about £2.50 today…

we did + the latter, to go to lunch at the Eng. School on Monday. It was very pleasant seeing so many old friends. During our 9 days stay we dined and lunched twice at the School + dined twice besides the evening at the Legation + lunched with Mr Bourchier the Times Correspondent at the G^de Bretagne + we dined there one night too. We were to have dined at the Mavro michalis' but the King sent for Kyrios Kyriakoulis Mavro Michalis who is minister of the Interior + we could not go. The night they asked us to go instead Mr Smith being away I was asked to superintend some digging that must otherwise have been stopped but he did not find the site a good one so

An example of Mabel's handwriting from her 1896 Chronicle.

The Chronicle of my
Thirteenth Journey

13.

March 1896 – Athens

We remained in Cairo till **Friday 26th,** having had the pleasure of having Miss Booth and Miss Brocklehurst in the hotel with us, and then with Mr. Cholmley and M we went to Alexandria and embarked on the Khediveh steamer for the Pireas, Mr. C. going to Marseilles. The steamer was most crowded. T had a cabin with 5 Greeks and I was one of 5, for 2 nights.

We arrived at the Grand Hotel, Athens, **Sunday 28th March.** Iannis, the proprietor, Spiro and the other waiters were warm in their welcomes. The town was gayer than I have ever seen a town in Holy Week, as it was being all beflagged and illuminated for the Olympic Games, which were to take place on Easter Monday.

We went to see Miss Trikoupis in the afternoon, and called at the Legation and the English School and some other places, and Mr. Egerton and Mrs. Cecil Smith returned our visits, and the former asked us to go to the Legation that evening, which we did, and the latter to go to lunch at the English School on Monday.

It was very pleasant seeing so many old friends. During our 9 days' stay we dined once and lunched twice at the School, and dined twice besides the evening at the Legation and lunched with Mr. Bourchier, the Times correspondent, at the Grand Bretagne, and we dined there one night too. We were to have dined at the Mavromichalis's, but the King sent for Kyrios Kyriakoulis Mavro Michalis who is the Minister of the Interior, and we could not go the night they asked us to go instead.

Mr. Smith being away, T was asked to superintend some digging that must otherwise have been stopped but he did not find the site a good one so it was abandoned. It was by the Kephissos, below the Olympeion, and they thought it was the Kynosargos. We also lunched with Mme. Palli.

We left on April 7th via Corfou, having seen the first day of the Olympic Games.[1] We stopped in Milan 3 days and saw a good deal of Professor Conte

---

[1] Michael Llewellyn-Smith's *Olympics in Athens 1896: The Invention of the Modern Olympic Games* (London, 2004) provides the background to the Games and also an analysis of the political machinations in Athens at the time.

Giuseppe Ricchieri, who had stayed with us for the Geographical Congress, and we dined with him and his pretty wife and Signor Rossi was there also.

We went straight home from there with the help of a sleeping carriage and reached London on April 13th 1896.

Theodore and Mabel's grave and memorial (on the right) in the churchyard of St Mary's, Theydon Bois, Essex.

Theodore's epitaph reads: 'Here, after his many long journeys rests J. Theodore Bent, FRGS, FSA, husband of Mabel Virginia Anna Hall-Dare, son of James and Margaret Eleanor Bent of Baildon House, Yorks. "To be with Christ which is far better." '

Chronicle [unnumbered], February 1898: 'A lonely useless journey'

'To the great grief of his friends, Mr. Theodore Bent died last week in the prime of life…kind, genial, and unassuming, who never sought for selfish advantage…He and his accomplished wife made every winter an expedition to some out-of-the-way spot for archaeological research.'
(*The Athenaeum*, January–June 1897, p. 657)

The last few references to Greece in Mabel's *Chronicles* appear in her 1898 volume. She begins in melancholy mood, heading her notebook 'A lonely useless journey'. After nearly twenty years of travels with Theodore, she finds herself alone, but by now so used to spending her winters abroad, she signs up for a trip to Egypt without him. But it is not a success and prolonged travels lose their attraction for her. Apart from visits to Jerusalem in the early 1900s she stops her journeying, and her *Chronicles*, although she is to live another thirty years.

At the end of 1893, the Bents began visiting little-explored regions of the Arabian Gulf. It was a cycle of voyages that culminated in a celebrated monograph (*Southern Arabia*, 1900) and, on 5 May 1897, in Theodore's death. His obituary in the *The Athenaeum* prints the veritable gazetteer needed to tick off the places they saw, and adds, 'no doubt, in this way Mr. Bent unwittingly overtaxed his constitution…'

After a couple of seasons (1893–1895) trying to map and research the Hadhramaut lands on the Gulf of Aden, Theodore and Mabel set out, in November 1896, for their last trip together to southern Arabia and the small island of Socotra. The party, including Manthaios, suffered badly from malarial fevers and were admitted to hospital in Aden. They discharged themselves on 11 April and set sail as soon as they could for Marseilles. Theodore suffered a relapse soon after reaching home and was dead within a matter of days. He was forty-five.

In January 1898, Mabel decides on a solo winter cruise to the Egyptian tourist sights. Understandably, her notes are downbeat and she has little enthusiasm for sharing the monuments along the Nile with groups of happier visitors –'It was very strange the first day riding alone and unknown and unknowing in such a troop'. Her fifty-second birthday, on 28 January, goes uncelebrated and unmentioned. By Friday 11 February she has had enough and leaves Alexandria for Athens, and, for the moment, a peaceful Greece. (Her itinerary has been: London – Paris – Marseilles – Brindisi – Port Said –Karnak – Luxor – Abu Simbel – Luxor – Thebes – Alexandria – Athens.) After the loneliness of Egypt, Mabel enjoys seeing again their old friends at the British School. There is a visit to the fabulous Byzantine mosaics at Daphní. She is shown over the Acropolis by the famous German archaeologist Wilhelm Dörpfeld, and it is appropriate that the last words in her *Chronicles* reflect the Bents' fascination with the classical past – 'Of course I have not neglected the antiquities either'.

Mabel would have wanted to avoid a return to Greece twelve months before. War broke out with Turkey in April of that year (the so-called Thirty Days' War) as a result of continued Greek designs on Ottoman Crete. In January 1897 a Greek army landed in Crete with the aim of finally wresting control of the important island from Turkish control (after around 400 years of domination). The European powers, however, intervened, proclaiming Crete an international protectorate. The Greek army promptly retreated to the mainland, where it attempted to advance northwards into the then Turkish regions of Thessaly and Epirus. In early April the armies met: the Greeks were outnumbered, and retreated past Lárissa. In Epirus there was fierce fighting for Árta, with the Greek troops gaining early successes until they were forced to retreat. The international *status quo* prevented the Sultan from pressing home the Turkish advantage, and he ordered a ceasefire on 20 May. Peace was not signed until September, brokered by the international community: Turkey was remunerated and even gained a small strip of land on the Thessalian border, otherwise the territorial boundaries were to remain as they were for the time being. Crete eventually became part of the Greek nation in 1913, along with the northern regions.

The disastrous exchange of Greco-Turkish populations in 1920–2 resulted in the country's present-day borders. The Smyrna region (well known to the Bents) reverted to Turkey, but the offshore islands, including Sámos and Chíos (the target of Theodore's indignation in 1883), were Greek again. The Dodecanese, among them Kárpathos, from where Mabel and Theodore had spirited away the little female statue ('the most hideous thing ever made by human hands') in 1885, were handed to Greece only in 1947. Mabel had not been dead twenty years, and the beguiling Karpathiote figure smiles today in her case in Russell Square.

Mabel's last *Chronicle* (although unnumbered, it is her fifteenth) is written in a lined, dark-red leather book (175 x 115mm), with marbled endpapers and edges. See selected Indices for people and places mentioned. For notes on this transcription the reader is referred to page xxv. There are 109 pages in the notebook, but Mabel has only filled 17 of them over eight weeks. She clearly did not have the heart for it…no *kéfi* as the Greeks would say.

1898
A lonely useless journey

February 1898 – Athens

Friday 11th [February 1898]. I departed from Egypt and embarked at Alexandria on the Khedivial boat Tewfik Rabbana. It was pitching very much. I spent the afternoon and all next day in the saloon.

Sunday, 13 February. Arrived at Athens. Helped Lady Lovelace to land for a few hours. Hôtel de la Grande Bretagne. Sir Edwin Egerton walked home with me and asked me to dine next day. Paid visits.

[Monday, February] 14th. I lunched at the English School with the Hogarths. These are the 4th Rector's family I have seen installed; dined at the Legation.

Wednesday, 16 February. Mr. Hogarth took me to the Akropolis. The Parthenon is now being repaired and there is scaffolding up. Some stones are being withdrawn and replaced. This enables one to get up on a level with the frieze of the cella, only hitherto to be seen by straining one's neck and looking up from a short distance to a great height. Only favoured individuals are allowed access to the ladders. Dr. Dörpfeld thinks the whole frieze should be removed to a museum. If so there should be a marble copy put in its place. Casts have long ago been taken and I daresay show how fast the original is wearing away: little bits constantly drop.

The Kyriakoulis Mavromichalis's were most kind to me. I lunched there Thursday and Friday and am to lunch on Monday. Thursday I was taken to the sea-house at Phalerum, where there is a little islet. They have put rabbits in it. There is no water and they are seen coming down and drinking seawater. They have multiplied so much that they are to be exterminated. Friday I was taken to Daphne. I had not seen the mosaics since they were mended.[1]

---

[1] The Monastery of Daphní (founded 5th/6th century AD) has Byzantine mosaics that are paralleled at only a few other sites in all Greece. One such site is on Chíos, at Neá Moní, which the Bents visit in 1886 (p. 175). The Daphní mosaics underwent restoration in 1893, five years before this visit by Mabel; she does not report an earlier trip to see them in this series of her *Chronicles*, but perhaps she and Theodore wondered at them on their first visit to Greece in 1882/83.

We had tea, as it was raining, in the balcony of the caretaker. Saturday (?) I was taken out driving and home to tea and asked to dine, but this I refused, as also to a large party this Sunday evening. Mme. Palli has asked me to dine tomorrow. Besides this I have dined at the Corbetts. He is 2nd Secretary to the Legation.

Of course I have not neglected the antiquities either.

Bibliography and sources

Archive material

Twenty-five of Mabel Bent's personal travel notebooks (GB 1500 Bent) are held in the archives of the Joint Library of the Hellenic and Roman Societies, Senate House, Malet Street, London WC1E 7HU (http://www.aim25.ac.uk).

Mabel Bent's notebooks in the Archive are numbered as follows:

1.	1883/4	Greek Islands
2.	1885	Greece and Egypt
3.	1886	Istanbul and Greek Islands
4.	1887	Greece
5.	1888	Greek Inscriptions (this is Theodore's notebook of inscriptions from the Asia Minor littoral)
6.	1888	Turkey, Russia
7.	1889	India (this covers the couple's trip to Bahrein)
8.	1889	Persia
9.	1889	Persia
10.	1890	Cilicia
11.	1891	Central Africa (Mashonaland/Zimbabwe)
12.	1891	Central Africa (Mashonaland/Zimbabwe)
13.	1893	Hadramout (this is Theodore's notebook)
14.	1893/4	Hadramout
15.	1894	Hadramout
16.	1894	Arabia
17.	1894	Muscat (this is Theodore's notebook)
18.	1894/5	Hadramout
19.	1895	Suez (this is Theordore's notebook)
20.	1895/6	Suez. Kourbat, Athens
21.	1896	Socotra
22.	1896/7	Socotra

23.   1898   Egypt, Athens (this is Mabel's last notebook)
24/25.   1896/7   Theodore's Socotran notebook

(The 1892/3 *Chronicle* for the couple's trip to Ethiopia appears to be missing. Mabel did keep one and Theodore quotes from it twice in his monograph *The Sacred City of the Ethiopians*.)

Correspondence

Letters from Theodore Bent are in several museums, libraries and Institutions, including the Royal Geographical Society and the Victoria and Albert Museum; however the Department of Greek and Roman Antiquities at the British Museum has the most relevant (but small) archive for this volume.

Biographical sources

The Dictionary of National Biography; *The Illustrated London News*, 15 May 1897; *The Times*, 6 July 1929 and 7 May 1897 and 6 July 1929; *Who Was Who*, Vol. 3, 29–40, 1941; La Page, J., *The Story of Baildon* (published privately, 1951); *The Athenaeum* (January–June 1897, p. 657); *The Geographical Journal* 9 (6) (1897, pp. 670-671, 674); *Journal of the Anthropological Institute of Great Britain and Ireland* 27 (1898, pp. 546–565); *The Geographical Journal* 74 (4) (1929, p. 416).

Selected works of Theodore (J. T.) and Mabel Bent (M. V. A.)

1877 – *A Freak of Freedom* (J. T.)
1881 – *A Life of Garibaldi* (J. T.)
1881 – *Genoa, how the Republic Rose and Fell* (J. T.)
1885 – *The Cyclades, or Life Among the Insular Greeks* (J. T.)
1892 – *The Ruined Cities of Mashonaland* (J. T.)
1893 – *Early Voyages and Travels in the Levant* (edited by J. T.)
1893 – *The Sacred City of the Ethiopians* (J. T.)
1900 – *Southern Arabia* (J. T. B., completed by M. V. A.)
1903 – *A Patience Pocket-book* (M. V. A.)
1908 – *Anglo-Saxons from Palestine* (M. V. A.)
1925? – *Jerusalem. The Garden Tomb of Golgotha* (by A. W. Crawley-Bovey, revised and enlarged by M. V. A. and Miss Hussey; undated, but around 1925)

Selected list of reprinted editions

A Freak of Freedom (Port Washington, 1970)
The Cyclades, or Life Among the Insular Greeks (Oxford, 2002)
The Cyclades, or Life Among the Insular Greeks (Chicago, 1965)
The Ruined Cities of Mashonaland (Bulawayo, 1969)
Southern Arabia (Reading, 1994)

Articles and papers

Theodore wrote many tens of articles and papers over a period of twenty years of scholarship and research. The following selected list, which also includes related articles by Theodore's colleagues contains only those of reference to this selection of Mabel's *Chronicles* on Greece and Turkey.

1880	'Where did Edward II die?', *Notes and Queries*
1883	'Games Played by Modern Greeks', *The Athenaeum*
1883	'Two Turkish Islands Today' [Sámos/Chíos], *Macmillan's Magazine*
1884	'Games played by modern Greeks', *The Folk-Lore Journal* and *The Athenaeum*
1884	'Researches among the Cyclades' (with J. G. Garson), *Journal of Hellenic Studies*
1885	(Book review) 'The Cyclades, or Life Among the Insular Greeks', *The Folk-Lore Journal*
1885	'Notes on Prehistoric Remains in Antiparos', *Journal of the Anthropological Institute of Great Britain and Ireland*
1885	'On the Gold and Silver Mines of Siphnos', *Journal of Hellenic Studies*
1885	'Rock-cut tombs of Carpathos', *The Athenaeum*
1885	'The Islands of Telos and Karpathos', *Journal of Hellenic Studies*
1886	'An Archaeological Visit to Samos' (with P. Gardner), *Journal of Hellenic Studies*
1886	'King Theodore of Corsica', *English Historical Review*
1886	'On Insular Greek Customs', *Journal of the Anthropological Institute of Great Britain and Ireland*
1886	'The Aqueduct of Samos', *The Athenaeum*
1887	'A Thasian Decree' (by E. L. Hicks), *Journal of Hellenic Studies*
1887	'Byzantine Palaces', *English Historical Review*
1887	'Discoveries in Thasos', *The Athenaeum*
1887	'Inscriptions from Thasos' (with E. L. Hicks), *Journal of Hellenic Studies*

1888	'Discoveries in Asia Minor', *Journal of Hellenic Studies*
1888	'What John saw on Patmos', *The Nineteenth Century*
1889	'Habits and Customs and Physical Characteristics of the Nomad Tribes of Asia Minor', *Report of the Fifty-Ninth Meeting of the British Association for the Advancement of Science* (John Murray)
1889	'Inscriptions found by Mr. Bent at Casarea, Lydae, Patara, Myra', (by E. L. Hicks, based on the notebooks of J. T. Bent), *Journal of Hellenic Studies*
1889	'The Lords of Chios', *English Historical Review*
1890	'Cilician Symbols', *Classical Review*
1890	'Explorations in Cilicia Tracheia', *Proceedings of the Royal Geographical Society*
1890	'Notes of Cilicia, Mersina', *The Athenaeum*
1890	'Notes on the Armenians in Asia Minor', *Journal of the Geographical Society*
1890	'Recent Discoveries in Eastern Cilicia', *Journal of Hellenic Studies*
1890	'The City of the Creed', *The Fortnightly Review*
1890	'The English in the Levant', *English Historical Review*
1890	'The Site of Hieropolis-Castabala', *The Athenaeum*
1890	'The Site of Olba in Cilicia' (by C. Smith), *Classical Review*
1891	'A Journey in Cilicia Tracheia', *Journal of Hellenic Studies*
1891	'Inscriptions from western Cilicia' (by E. L. Hicks), *Journal of Hellenic Studies*
1891	'Cilicia Aspera', *Blackwood's Magazine*
1891	'Modern life and thought amongst the Greeks', *National life and thought of the various nations throughout the world: a series of addresses* (E. Magnússon (ed.), Unwin)
1891	'The Ansairee of Asia Minor', *Journal of the Anthropological Institute of Great Britain and Ireland*
1891	'The Yourouks of Asia Minor', *Journal of the Anthropological Institute of Great Britain and Ireland*
1892	'The Two Capitals of Armenia (Sis and Etchmiad-zin)', *Eastern and Western Review*
1896	'Travels amongst Armenians', *Contemporary Review*

Other related works of interest for this volume

Travel writers and guides

Ayliffe, R. et al., *Rough Guide to Turkey* (2003)
Baedeker, K., *Greece: Handbook for Travellers* (1905)
Barber, R., *Greece, Blue Guide* (1995)
Berger, F. K., *A winter in the city of pleasure; or, Life on the lower Danube* (1877)

Blunt, F. J., *The people of Turkey, by a consul's daughter and wife* (1878)
Blunt (Blount), H., *A voyage into the Levant* (1636)
Brisch, G., 'To Anáfi for a name', in *Mondo Greco* (Spring, 2003)
Cochran, W., *Pen and Pencil in Asia Minor: or, Notes from the Levant* (1887)
Davis, E. J., *Life in Asiatic Turkey* (1879)
Dolan, B., *Ladies of the Grand Tour* (2001)
Dubin, M.,*Trekking in Greece* (1993)
Durrell, L., *The Greek Islands* (1978)
Ellingham, M. et al., *Rough Guide to the Greek Islands* (1995)
Hogarth, D. G., *A Wandering Scholar* (1896)
Jinkinson, R., *Tales from a Greek Island* [Kárpathos] (2005)
Knox, J., *Robert Byron* (2003)
Leigh Fermor, P., *Mani* (1958)
Leigh Fermor, P., *Roumeli* (1966)
Liddell, R., *Aegean Greece* (1954)
Mahaffy, J. P., *Greek Pictures* (1890)
Mahaffy, J. P., *Rambles and Studies in Greece* (1878)
McDonagh, B., *Blue Guide: Turkey* (2001)
Murray's Handbook for travellers in Greece: including the Ionian Islands, continental Greece, the Peloponnese, the islands of the Aegean, Crete, Albania, Thessaly, & Macedonia (1884)
Murray's Handbook for travellers in Turkey in Asia: including Constantinople, the Bosphorus, Dardenelles, Brousa and Plain of Troy (1878)
O'Connor, Scott, V. C., *Isles of the Aegean* (1929)
Ramona, P., *Les paquebots vers l'Orient* (2001)
Ramsay, W. M., *Historical Geography of Asia Minor* (1890)
Ross, Ludwig (ed.), *An Account of the Travels of King Otto and Queen Amalie* (1851)
Ross, Ludwig, *Inselreisen*, Tübingen (1840–1843)
Searight, S. and Wagstaff, M. (eds.), *Travellers in the Levant* (2001)
Strabo *Geography* (Books 12 and 14) (Loeb Classical Library, trans. H. L. Jones)
Tennent, J. E., *Letters from the Aegean* (1829)
Theakstone, J., 'An alphabetical bibliography of books by Victorian and Edwardian women travellers published between 1837 and 1910', http://victorianresearch.org/wtravelbib2003.pdf (September 2006)
Tomkinson, J. L., *Travellers' Greece: Memories of an Enchanted Land* (2002)
Tournefort, de, J. P., *Travels in the East, Voyage into the Levant* (tr. John Ozell, 1741)
Tozer, H. F., *The Islands of the Aegean* (1890)

History and archaeology
Barber, R., *The Cyclades in the Bronze Age* (1987)

Bayliss, R., *Provincial Cilicia and the Archaeology of Temple Conversion* (2004)
Braudel, F., *The Mediterranean* (1992)
Braudel, F., *The Mediterranean in the Ancient World* (1998)
Droop, J. P., *Archaeological Excavation* (1915)
Fitton, J. L. *Cycladic Art* (1999)
Gardner, E. A., *Greece and the Aegean* (1933)
Llewellyn-Smith, Michael, *Olympics in Athens 1896: The Invention of the Modern Olympic Games* (2004)
MacKendrick, P. L., The Greek stones speak: the story of archaeology in Greek lands (1962)
Manolakakes, E., *Karpathiaká* (1896)
Mazower, M., *Salonika: City of Ghosts* (2004)
Mendel, G., *Catalogue des sculptures greques, romaines et byzantines* (1912)
Mendoni, L. G. (ed.), *Archaiologia tes nesou Keas, syntachtheisa upo tou Konstantinou Manthou* (1991)
Morris, J., *The Venetian Empire* (1980)
Paradissis, A., *Fortresses and Castles of Greece* (1975)
Petrie, W. M. F., *Methods and Aims in Archaeology* (1904)
Renfrew, C., *The Cycladic Spirit* (1991)
Smith, C. L., *The Embassy of Sir William White at Constantinople 1886–1891* (1957)
Stoneman, R., *Land of Lost Gods* (1987)
Wood, M., *In Search of the Trojan War* (1985)
Zarinebaf, F. et al., *A Historical and Economic Geography of Ottoman Greece. The Southwestern Morea in the 18th Century* (2006)

Natural history and geography
Polunin, O., *Flowers of Greece and the Balkans* (1987)
Rackham, O. and Moody, J., *The Making of the Cretan Landscape* (1996)

Mythology and folklore
Lawson, J. C., *Modern Greek folklore and ancient Greek religion: a study in survivals* (1910)
Graves, R., *Greek Myths* (1955)

19th-century travel equipment
Opie, R., *Rule Britannia: trading on the British image* (1985)
Opie, R., *The Victorian Scrapbook* (1999)
Victorian Shopping: Harrods 1895 Catalogue (1972)
Yesterday's Shopping: The Army and Navy Stores Catalogue, 1907 (1969)

Sidetrack

A tale of two dragomans: George Phaedros and Manthaios Símos

Long before the Bents took to the Eastern Mediterranean, travellers knew the importance of good, local help when far from the security of consul or friendly flag. Jules Verne, very likely packed among Theodore's books, with Rider Haggard, had published *Around the World in Eighty Days* only ten years before the couple embarked for Smyrna in 1882, and they soon turned to their embassy in that busy port in search of their own Passepartout.

Having benefited from the services of one Konstandinos Verviziotes for their mainland tour of the classic sites (see page 186), Theodore and Mabel engaged, on the recommendation of Mr Dennis at the Smyrna consulate, one George Phaedros for their brief cruise around the Aegean isles. That he was only a moderate success may be inferred by Mabel's initial lack of enthusiasm when he joins them again, at Ermoúpolis, Sýros, the following winter. Apparently he enjoyed his drink, but he was also a grumbler and a terrible sailor – a distinct disadvantage when island-hopping, out of season, on small fishing boats.

By Náxos the Bents had had enough of him, and one day, high up in a mountain village, they find themselves sitting in a warm room, and, 'When Mr. Konstantinides our host came home he found 10 people drying their clothes, us two and P, Mr. Swan, and a man called Mantheos, a native of Anaphi who is to show Mr. Swan mines there…'

Within a few days Phaedros has been abandoned, a whiskery Ariadne, on Náxos, and Mantheos (Mabel spells him a multitude of ways over the next fifteen years, but Manthaios seems to predominate) begins a partnership with Theodore and Mabel that continues until 1897. Missing only two or three seasons, Theodore (using the English telegraph station at Ermoúpolis) wires Manthaios from London to be, on such and such a date, at Sýros, or Rhodes, or Chíos, or Alexandria, or Port Said, or wherever, to act as their translator, guide, cook, lodgings officer, victualler, foreman and general factotum.

It is interesting to see how their relationship develops in print. In his book *The Cyclades*, this is Theodore in 1885: 'My first experiences [of the islands] were made with the assistance of a dragoman; but, on better acquaintance with the language, I learnt to despise his services, and took as servant a native of one of the islands, who became invaluable in assisting me to discover points of folklore which without him it would have been impossible to arrive at.'

In the Community offices of Anáfi, two hours' ferry ride away, a little southeast of Santoríni, the early registers of births (men only) record the arrival of Manthaios in 1846, son of a subsistence farmer, like nearly every other child.

Mabel took this photograph in Socotra in 1897. Theodore is seated on the left. The figure standing on the right is thought to be the Bents' long-serving dragoman, Manthaios Símos from Anáfi in the Cyclades.

The chance that led him to Náxos and a meeting with the Bents in 1884, aged nearly forty, alters his life. In Mabel's 1897 *Chronicle*, the year of her husband's death, there is a list of amounts payable, in Theodore's hand. Manthaios' wages for the trip are £50, about £3000 today, and a huge sum for a Cycladic farmer at the turn of the 19th century. He is able to retire to Anáfi, marry, have a family (his descendants are now in Athens and no Símoses remain on the island) and tell of his adventures in foreign lands as dragoman and friend to an extraordinary English couple. He died in the mid-1930s, five years after Mabel.

Did Mabel take his photograph? We cannot be sure, but there is a figure captured in Bent's last camp, on Socotra in 1897…Theodore sits on the left, taking down notes for his dictionary of Socotran. An unmistakable Englishman sits to the right in his topee. And between the two, just in the background, and by no means clear, stands a middle-aged man in his working clothes. Not an Arab, certainly...A Greek? Manthaios Símos? Almost a certainty; no other photograph of him remains in Mabel's works.

There was another serendipitous meeting for Manthaios Símos. The writer Vincent Scott O'Connor travelled in the Cyclades in the 1920s and found his way to Anáfi. O'Connor had a copy of Bent's book on the islands and jumped at the chance of an interview with Theodore's famous (at least on Anáfi) dragoman. He records him one evening, up in Chóra, 'The story-teller relaxed from his labours; a fine little old man with a curved nose and clean-cut features...' Manthaios tells of how he 'saved' the Bents from the pirates on Sámos in 1886:

'"At Samos," he said, "there were pirates, who had made up their minds to kidnap the English travellers, and for that reason my master was unable to leave the island. It was I who circumnavigated their wiles... But it was not in these isles that we had our greatest adventures, it was in Arabia... Mrs. Bent was always eager to press on. One night we slept in a damp spot, and while there I had a dream in which I saw two horses and a chariot in Anaphe; but there was no driver, and one of the horses fell down and died. The chariot was overturned. My interpretation of the dream was that this portended a disaster to our party. But Bent only laughed at my fears. He said dreams were nothing but dreams. Nevertheless, as I expected, Mrs. Bent fell seriously ill of a fever which each day grew worse. She could ride no more, and the Arabs refused to carry a Christian, especially a woman. But the Sheikh put his shoulder to one end of the litter, as I did to the other; and so we carried her till the rest of them became ashamed and each took his turn. We arrived at the sea and the Sheikh sent out some milk for the lady, but she was so ill that she could not retain it and daily she became worse; yet she went on, saying that it was only a little fever, and she would not hear of our abandoning the journey... I decided then to act upon my own initiative, and a Dhow having come into the harbour, I spoke to the Captain and contracted with him to take us to Aden. Then, for I knew how obstinate are these English, I went to Bent and said, 'Kyrios, why not take ship to Aden?' 'Nonsense,' he replied, 'you know very well that there is no ship.' 'Maybe, Kyrios, but suppose that there were one, would you take it?' 'Well! Yes,' he said, 'I would, for she is very ill.' I took him to the top of a hill and showed him the Dhow at anchor! So we started; but on arriving at Aden, there was a 'quarantine' and Madame was not allowed to land. The Governor however intervened in her favour and a doctor came at once to see her. He was only just in time, but her life was saved. It was after this that Bent himself began the illness that ended in his death."

…All were agreed that here was a great traveller, one like unto Odysseus himself.' (V. C. Scott O'Connor, *Isles of the Aegean*)

And what of poor George Phaedros? In Mabel's 1883/4 *Chronicle* there is the following letter, written in a thin hand:

C/O British Consulate
Smyrna
1st February /84

Dear Mr Bent

I am happy to learn from your favours of 20th January which I received on the 30th of the same, that both you and Mrs Bent are quite well.

I have been always thinking of you how you managed with the continuation of your excursion, and how you got on with the unusual rough winter of this year exposing yourselves so, to the mercy and providence I dare say of God.

As regards my passage to Smyrna after we departed, you will please learn that your hopes did not prove as expected for I did not escape of what I was fearing.

The wretched steamer 'Eptanisos' which took you from Naxos on Monday the 7th of January 1884, did not come back to that island to pick me up for Syra until Wednesday the 9th January, (and about noon) and subsequently she kept going so slow, that I missed the Messageries steamer for Smyrna which was leaving Syra (bound for that town) on the same day.

I have been waiting consequently six days in Syra and was obliged to spend almost all the money you gave me at Naxos, (viz: the 100 francs) that is to say in expenses for the Hotel in Syra, in changing my broken and shabby hat, and in paying for my passage or fare ticket to Smyrna which brought me home almost penniless. And my wife had already spent also, what I had sent her from Syra in buying some necessary things for the house, with the cause of the holidays etc. So my friends who expected me to return quite a rich man, contemplating, in their idea and opinion that I was getting £$_T$5 [Turkish pounds] per day in consideration of the winter season travelling, were quite disappointed to find that I was obliged and in need to borrow money off them. Mr Dennis also told me that he did not think it was right for me to pay out of my pocket my passage to Syra and back and the expenses for the delay in waiting you in Syra etc., etc.

As regards the salary I do not exactly appreciate the opinion of my friends, but I think it is fair that you should make a little allowance for the winter season, that is to say if you do not find it so inconvenient, so as to make it worth my while, as I am a fellow with a family as you know.

I left Syra on the evening of Monday 14th January. I don't know where you have spent that fearful evening and night but it was in my destiny to find myself in a most violent gale, but fortunately in a brave Arab steamer with Greek captains which was fighting with the elements of the nature that night and stand up like a giant against them. All the plates and glaces [sic] are broken and the water found its way in to the cabins. We overtook a steamer called Simiotis and saw her bow deeped into the water and we thought she was going to be lost but we learnt that she turned back to Tinos.

We kept up but we suffered until we faced the Bay of Smyrna. The impression of that night is still very brisk in my memory. But the necessity of a man is superior to the impression of fear. Although I foresee steel [sic] bad weather going to be, I made up my mind to come and accompany you again and to be at Syra on the 16th February with the hopes that we shall avoy [sic] the caïques and you will pay for my passage, etc.

Please send through Mr. Binney some money for my travelling expenses, etc., enabling me thus to make my start.

    With my best regards to Mrs. Bent and Mr. Swan.

    I remain yours sincerely

        George Phaedros

His letter fell on deaf ears, or blind eyes; Manthaios Símos got the job.

Mr. Findlay. Mr. Bax Ironside. Mr. Tower. Mr. Stronge. Mr. des Graz.
Mr. R. Kennedy. Colonel Trotter. Sir William White. Mr. Edmund Fane. Mr. Gerard Lowther.

Sir William White, H. B. M. Ambassador, and his staff in Istanbul during the Bents' travels in Turkey.

Index of principal characters

An Index, with very brief biographical backgrounds, of most of the characters mentioned by Mabel Bent in these pages of her *Chronicles*. The list, sadly, cannot include the thousands of anonymous personalities Mabel encounters along the paths of Greece and Turkey, and on the seas in between, but they are, nevertheless, acknowledged and remembered.

Afentákis (Family); 16
 Well-to-do Melian family. The name still occurs on the island.

Anson (Family); 59, 60, 61
 The Ansons were neighbours of the Hall-Dares in Wexford.

Aristarchis, Miltiadis Stavraki (1809–1893); 69-72, 111
 Governor of Sámos between 1859 and 1866.

Baring, Evelyn, Sir (1841–1917); 68 n.2, 181, 183, 197 n.28, 204 n.36, 215, 216
 First earl of Cromer, distinguished diplomat. From 1883 he was consular-general in Cairo, and, as such, the most powerful Commonwealth official after the Viceroy of India.

Bent, James Theodore (1852–1897); *passim*
 Mabel Bent's husband and mentioned throughout by her as T.

Billiotti, Alfred (1833–1915); 64, 70
 Career diplomat and enthusiastic excavator. During a posting as a (British) consular official on Rhodes in 1858, he discovered tombs material at Kamiros and Ialyssos.

Binney, William Pryor (1839–1888); 8, 21, 32, 54, 111, 227-28, 233 n.16, 343
 In charge of British consular business on Sýros and the Bents' particular friend. His fine memorial is in Ermoúpoli's Frankish cemetery.

Blunt, John Elijah, Sir (1832–1916); 194-95, 197, 320
 British consul at Salonika, having served in the Crimean War. He fought at Alma, Balaclava and Inkerman.

Blunt (Blount), Henry, Sir (1602–1682); 194
 Traveller and author of *A voyage into the Levant* (London 1636).

Boothby, Brooke, Sir (1856–1913); 7
 10th Baronet Boothby, of Broadlow Ash, Derbyshire.

Bothamley, Grafton; 59
 Mabel's cousin.

Bourchier, James (1850–1920); 271, 325
 English journalist and political activist, specializing in Bulgaria and the Balkans. He worked for *The Times* as the newspaper's Balkan correspondent, based in Sofia from 1892 to 1915.

Brest, M.; 17, 20
Vice-consul on Mélos and son of consul Louis Brest (1789–1862), instrumental in securing the Melian 'Venus' for the Louvre, after 1821. The Brest family had long associations with Mílos, and there is a memorial in the Catholic church in Pláka.

Calvert, Frank (1828–1908); 64, 69, 70
British resident who served as American vice-consul in the Dardanelles. He was a keen part-time archaeologist. His strong hunch, followed by spadework, that the site of Hissarlik might be Homer's Troy, gave Heinrich Schliemann the encouragement in the 1870s to excavate there. (*In Search of the Trojan War* by Michael Wood (1985) contains a short background to the story.)

Charcutsis, Mr; 8
Friend of Theodore's and editor of a newspaper on Sýros.

Cook, Thomas (1808–1892); 176-77, 222-23, 270
Founder of the travel company (and the 'package tour') in 1841. The Bents occasionally encountered the company's clients and representatives.

Crowder, George (1852–1885); 160
Long-term travelling companion of Henry Tozer. The Bents meet him on Sámos; like Theodore, he was a graduate of Wadham College, Oxford.

Curtis (Curteis), Canon; 133
Of the Memorial Chapel, Istanbul, antiquarian and collector.

Da Corogna (Family); 35, 38
In the 14th century an Antonio da Corogna proclaimed himself master of Sífnos (Cyclades), controlling the island from Kástro. Traces of the buildings he had erected may still be seen.

Damales, Mrs; 7
Mother-in-law of Sara Bernhardt. Sara married a Greek-born actor Aristides Damala, scion of a Chiot family, in London in 1882. He died in 1889. There is still a Dámala Street in Chíos town.

Davis, Edwin John; 264, 298
Early English pioneer of southern Turkey region. His *Life in Asiatic Turkey* (London, 1879) remains in the bibliographies.

De Branteghem, van, Alphonse; 135
A Belgian collector resident in Istanbul.

De Graz (des Graz), Mr; 255
Consular official, Istanbul.

Dennis, George (1879–1888); 132, 339
British Consul at Smyrna and elsewhere and author of *The Cities and Cemeteries of Etruria* (London, 1848).

Dieulafoy, Marcel and Jeanne (1844–1920); 320
With his wife, Jeanne, the Dieulafoys were accomplished French archaeologists who dug the palaces of Persian kings (Darius I and Artaxerxes II) at

Susa in 1885. A number of their finds are in the Louvre. There is no record of the Bents meeting them. There is a sense that Mabel was rather envious of Mrs Dieulafoy (and her finds), who wrote an acclaimed monograph *At Susa*, published in 1890.

Dillon, Mr; 274-77, 290, 295, 304, 319
Head of railway service in Mersin.

Disraeli, Benjamin (1804–1881); 287
British Prime Minister and Earl of Beaconsfield. Mabel quotes from his 1862 poem, *Tancred, or the New Crusade*.

Dörpfeld, Wilhelm (1853–1940); 328, 330
German architect who achieved celebrity as a classical archaeolgist. He is very much credited for the development of the modern 'science' of archaeology. He excavated at Olympia before joining Schliemann at Troy (1882) and Tiryns (1884). By 1898, when showing Mabel around the Parthenon, he was co-directing the latest excavations on the Acropolis as head of the German Archaeological Institute in Athens, a post he retained until 1912. Gertrude Bell (letter, 11 April 1899) thought him 'a most agreeable person, extremely good looking'.

Egerton, Edwin, Sir (b. 1841); 7, 325, 330
British Ambassador in Athens. Gertrude Bell describes him (letter, 7 April 1899) as 'extremely friendly, but with a funny brusque manner'.

Finlay (Findlay), Mr; 255
Consular official, Istanbul.

Gardner, Ernest (1862–1939); 183, 186, 266, 271
Archaeologist, classical art historian, and editor of the *Journal of Hellenic Studies*. In 1887 he was appointed director of the British School at Athens, before moving back to London to teach; his students included Mortimer Wheeler.

Gardner, Percy (1846–1937); 127, 160 n.44
Brother of Ernest, Percy was Disney Professor of Archaeology at Cambridge (1880–87) before his appointment as Professor of Classical Archaeology at Oxford.

Gaze, Henry; 222-23, 319
Founder of a tour company in the 1850s, and a competitor of Thomas Cook.

George I, King (1845–1913); 59 n.88, 186, 273 n.6
From the Germano-Danish House of Oldenburg, King of the Hellenes between 1863 and 1913. He and his consort, Olga Konstantinova of Russia, had eight children. Their eldest son and Heir Apparent was Constantine (1868–1923), who succeeded his father as king. George was assassinated in Thessaloníki in 1912. The Bents were friends of various courtiers.

Gonne, Edith Maud (1865–1953); 226, 255

'…A tall and handsome damsel dressed in white Broussa gauze, who says she means to go on the stage.' This 'damsel' is, of course, the charismatic Irishwoman and great beauty who is later to become the famous actress, nationalist, and muse of W. B. Yeats. In her autobiography, *A servant of the Queen* (London, 1938), she writes that, after a 'haemorrhage of the lungs', she sails in 1886 from Marseilles to Istanbul, via Sýros and Smyrna, 'going to Constantinople on a visit to Lillian White, the daughter of the British Ambassador'. On Sýros she avoids abduction by a party of Greek fisherman: 'He only laughed and the men rowed quicker. Suddenly I stood up, with my revolver pointed straight at him and said: "Obey, or I fire."'

Gordon, Charles George (1833–1885); 64, 97

Mabel reads of his death at the siege of Khartoum, on or around 26 January 1885.

Graham (Family); 59, 131-33, 186, 193

Friends and fellow travellers with the Bents. It is Mary Graham who pleads with Mabel to publish her first two Chronicles: 'I must just write you a line to say that I carried off your Chronicle…And that I never enjoyed these hours more than when reading it in the train coming down here yesterday – as soon as I have finished it I will send it you back – but why oh why don't you publish it? It simply bristles with epigrams and I am certain would be a great success! You ought to blend the 2 Chronicles into one and I am sure everyone would buy it…[we] send you and Theodore all good wishes of the season.'

Hall-Dare (Family); 7, 48, 173

Mabel's large Anglo-Irish family, with properties in England (Essex) and Ireland (Wexford). Iva was her sister Olivia, who married the Rev. Johnstone in July 1883. Another sister, Frances (Faneen) married the Rev. E. Hobson in 1891. Mabel's niece Elizabeth (Ella) married J. O. Adair in 1886. See family tree p. 357.

Hallward, Cecil; 255-56

Consular agent and a student interpreter.

Hamdi Bey, Osman (1842–1910); 130, 134, 183, 201, 225-26, 228-230, 233, 244, 258, 264

Artist, diplomat, archaeologist, museologist, he was eldest son of the Grand Vizier, Ibrahim Edhem Pasha. He studied in Istanbul, Vienna and Paris, and was (1871) appointed Director of the Empire Museum (Müze-i Humayun). With his appointment began modern Turkish museum services and the protection of antiquities. From 1881 he supervised the creation of the Istanbul Archaeology Museum, which houses his own great find from Sidon, the 'Alexander Sarcophagus'.

Harcourt-Smith, Cecil (1859–1944); 280 n.23, 325

Archaeologist and Director of the British School at Athens between 1895 and 1897.

Hirsh, Maurice, Baron (1831–1896); 255

German born financier of the Turkish railway network which opened in 1873.

Hogarth, David George (1897–1900); 330

One of the early Directors of the British School at Athens.

Hore-Ruthven, Walter James (b. 1838); 41

Of Harperstown, County Wexford, a near neighbour of the Hall-Dares.

Ibelligeka, Georgios Hadgi Nikolaos; 13

One of the Bents' many sailing-boat skippers in the Cyclades.

Jenanyan, Hartune; 304

One of the two founders (with Alexander MacLachlan), in 1888, of 'St. Paul's Institute at Tarsus'. The school started with eight students and still operates (as the Tarsus American School) today.

Jones, Henry Mitchell (1831–1916); 226, 256

Gained the Victoria Cross for his actions at Sebastopol in the Crimea on 7 June 1855. Some months before he was wounded at the battle of 'the Alma Heights' (20 September 1854), when British, French and Turkish troops were victorious against the Imperial Russian Army.

Kavadias, Panagiotis (1849–1928); 271

Archaeologist and academic. He was instrumental in founding the leading Greek museums, including the National Archeological Museum, Athens.

Kennedy, Robert John (later Sir) 1851–1936; 7, 134

Chargé d'Affaires in Bulgaria between 1882 and 1884. He held the office of Secretary at Constantinople between 1877 and 1879.

Khamel Bey (Namik Kemal) (1840–1888); 70-72

Pasha at Rhodes and Híos. He was an influential and successful poet and author as well as politician/diplomat. His celebrated work is *Fatherland* (1872). Theodore writes elsewhere of his son, Khem, '…he is not a pleasant youth to look upon, being fat and pasty, and as he talks to you he cracks his knuckle joints in a most irritating fashion'.

Konstantinos, Manthos (c. 1826–c. 1890); 31, 57

Autodidact and local historian. Inspired by the researches on Kéa of the Danish archaeologist Peter Olaf Brøndsted (1780-1842),

Konstantinos became an expert on the antiquities of his island. In the 1870s he compiled catalogues of his finds, now published as *Archaiologia tes nesou Keas: Syntachtheisa hypo tou K. Manthou, Keiou kai Historika tina tes Archaiotates Epoches*, edited by Lina Mendone (Athens, 1991).

Koronaios, General; 122
He took part in the Cretan revolution 1866-1869, commanding the troops around Réthymnon.

Lambros, Nikólaos; 234
Captain of the schooner *Evangelistria*, hired by the Bents in 1888.

Little, Eliakim (1797–1870); 276
Editor and publisher, founded *Littell's Living Age* (*Living Age*) in Boston in April 1844. It continued, until 1941, concerning itself primarily with reprintings of serious British non-fiction; it now and then included some of Theodore's articles.

Logothetis (Family); 73, 154-56
A prominent family from the islands around Chíos. Lykourgos Logothetis (1772–1850) led an uprising against the Turks in 1821. The remains of his 'tower' are still to be seen at Pythagório, Sámos.

Longworth, John; 60-61, 195
British Consul first in Bitola (Macedonia) and then Vólos.

Lorenziades (Family); 38, 41, 186, 273
From Íos. The Bents were particularly fond of the children.

One of them met the English traveller Vincent O'Connor in the late 1920s and he writes of them (and the Bents) in his book *Isles of the Aegean* (London, 1929).

Lovelace, Lady (d. 1941); 330
Mary Caroline Wortley married Ralph Gordon Noel King, 2nd Earl of Lovelace in 1880.

Mahaffy, John Pentland, Sir (1839–1919); 59
Fellow of Trinity College, Dublin; Hon. Fellow of Queen's College, Oxford, Professor of Ancient History. He was an influence on Oscar Wilde and took him along on trips to Italy and Greece (1877). 'Few men,' he wrote, '… who having once visited Greece do not contrive to visit it again… Excepting Southern Italy, there is no country which can compare with Greece in beauty and interest to the intelligent traveller.' He was the author of a number of books on Greek history and literature, including *Rambles and Studies in Greece* (London, 1878).

Malatya, 'Prince Bishop' of; 132, 157
From the former Armenian region of Malatya/Melitene, on the upper Euphrates. The town is now in modern (central eastern) Turkey.

Manolakakis (Family); 82, 84-87, 90-91, 100-101, 125
From Kárpathos. Emmanuel Manolakakis published *Karpathiaká* (1896), a valued

monograph on the history and
culture of the island.
Marigó, Kýria; 84-85,105
Karpathian eccentric.
Mavris (Family); 120
An important local family. A
Nichólas Mavrís (1899-1978)
was later the first governor of the
Dodecanese.
Mavromichalis (Family); 177-78,
271, 273, 325, 330
A family with an involvement in
Greek political interests since
Independence times. The Bents
knew the Minister of the Interior.
**Mavroyenis (Mavrojeni/
Mavrogyanni) (Family)**; 24, 26, 32,
38, 43-44
A prosperous Cycladic family.
Moscopolides, Mr; 197
Banker and host to the Bents in
Kaválla.
Murray, John (1745–1793); 69, 235
Founded the eponymous
publishing house. His son was
Byron's publisher. They produced
a very popular series of travel
guides. Murray's *Handbook for the
Ionian Islands, Greece, Turkey,
Asia Minor, and Constantinople*
was first published in 1840. Mabel
travelled with it and often quoted
snippets.
Myrianthos, Jeronomos; 145
Chief Archimandrite in London.

**Newton, Charles Thomas (1816–
1894)**; 123, 197
Diplomat, antiquary and
archaeologist. He specialized
in the Levantine coastal areas
in the 1850s, and Theodore,
of course, knew him and his
great finds – especially the
sensational discoveries made
at Halicarnassus. Many of
his marbles are in the British
Museum, of which he was
Keeper of the Greek and Roman
department until 1885.
**Nicholas, of Myra (AD c. 270–c.
350)**; 246, 249
Bishop, Christian saint, and Santa
Claus. His relics were removed
from Myra in the 11th century and
ended up in Bari, Italy. In 2006
a tiny fragment of his finger was
donated to his eponymous church
in Ermoúpoli, Sýros.
Nomikos (Family); 35
A well-known Cycladic family. The
collections of Petros Nomikos,
seen by the Bents, are housed in
the Monastery of Ayio Elías above
Pírgos, Santoríni.

**Obrenović, Milan, King (1854–
1901)**; 222
The Serbian king from 1882 to
1889. His grandfather was Jevrem
Teodorović Obrenović.
Olympítis, Iríni (Mrs W. Paton);152
From Kálymnos, the first wife of
William Paton.
Oman, Djem, Sultan (1459–1495);
231
Colourful younger son of Sultan
Mehmed III and claimant to the
Ottoman Imperial throne. After
feuding with his brother, Djem

fled to Egypt and then to Rhodes, seeking the protection of the Knights of St John there. His house is still pointed out in the Old Town.

Otto I, King (1815–1867); 44, 56-57, 273 n.7

Appointed King of Greece by the European powers following the Greek Independence Wars. His consort was Amelie of Oldenburg. He was deposed in 1862.

Palli, Philippe, Madame; 325, 331

Founder member of the 'Union of Greek Women' and in the so-called 'Thirty Days' War' with Turkey (1897) ran the nursing services. She helped set up a hospital at Vólos (with the help of four English volunteer nurses). The US journal *The Nursing Record and Hospital World* of 3 July 1897 ran a 4-page feature on the role of Greek women in the war; interested readers will find a photograph of Madame Palli on page 8 of the issue.

Paton, William Roger (1857–1921); 130, 152-54

Of Grandhome, Aberdeenshire, Paton became a leading Greek scholar of his generation. A scion of Scottish aristocracy, he travelled far from his baronial home in the Highlands. Opting to work in the fields of Greek literature and arcane inscriptions; his publications are many. An obituary (*Aberdeen Daily Journal*, 14 May 1921) recalls him as

'a man of charming manners and a delightful companion of the most finished culture'. Passionate about the Aegean, he spent several years on Sámos, returning to die there in May 1921. Mabel and Theodore meet his first wife, Iríni Olympítis from Kálymnos. He was to remarry later (Clío Nomíkos), and he had in all five children.

Penrose, Francis Cranmer (1817–1903); 183, 186

Studied architecture in Rome and in Athens and in 1886 was selected as the first Director of the British School at Athens.

Phaedros, George; 3, 8, 24ff., 100, 161, 339ff.

From Smyrna, the Bents' dragoman, replaced in 1884 by Manthaios Símos. Most often referred to as P.

Philemon, Consul; 69-70, 72, 100

Had a successful career along the Ottoman littoral, serving on Sámos, Rhodes and Cyprus, where, in May 1899, he was something of an *agent provocateur*.

Photiades, Ioannis; 134

Pasha. Governor of Crete under the Turks between 1879 and 1885.

Ralli, Pandeli (d. 1928); 71

Liberal MP, a British subject born in Marseilles whose family had come to England from Híos in the early 1800s.

Ramsay, William Mitchell, Sir (1851–1939); 264, 274

The foremost authority at this time on the topography, antiquities, and history of Asia Minor in ancient times. At Smyrna he met C. W. Wilson, then British consul for Anatolia, who encouraged him to begin a long series of expeditions in Turkey and elsewhere that continued (with one short break) until 1914. (He, in turn, motivated Theodore Bent to search for the site of Olba.) His major work was *Historical Geography of Asia Minor* (London, 1890), but he later produced a shorter paper for the Royal Geographical Society, 'Cilicia, Tarsus, and the Great Taurus Pass' (*RGS*, 1903).

Rangabe, Alexandros Rizos (1810–1892); 271

Distinguished and long-serving Greek academic. In 1844 he became professor of archaeology at the University of Athens but he was also a leading figure in contemporary literature, being particularly successful as a dramatist.

Ricchieri, Giuseppe (b. 1861); 325

Italian academic.

Sampson, Thornton Rogers (1852–1915); 194-95, 218

Served as a missionary in Greece until 1897 before returning to the United States, where he died in a climbing accident in 1915.

Schliemann, Heinrich (1822–1890); 182, 233, 266, 271

The leading archaeologist of his day and celebrated excavator of Mycenae and Troy. This great figure died in somewhat tragic circumstances in Naples at the end of 1890.

Schuyler, Eugene (1840–1890); 7, 60

An experienced diplomat and traveller, he was the US Minister to Romania when he met the Bents. He died of malaria in Venice and is buried there.

Schwartz, Baroness, von (1818–1899); 7

Marie Esperance Brandt was a close friend of many influential figures. A resident of Crete, she was the mistress of Garibaldi, editing and publishing a translation of his memoirs in 1861 (*Garibaldi's Memoirs from his Manuscript, Personal Notes, and Authentic Sources Assembled and Published by Elpis Melena*). From the Villa d'Este, Franz Liszt sent gossipy letters to her at her neoclassical villa outside Chaniá; built in 1860 it still stands.

Símos, Manthaios (*c.* 1845–*c.* 1935); *passim*

Anáfi-born dragoman to the Bents for 15 years. Referred to as M in the *Chronicles*.

Smith, Arthur Hamilton (1860–1941); 130, 133 n.4, 135 n.7, 197 n.28, 204 n.36, 225 n.1, 229 n.8, 233 n.16, 244 n.39, 265

Archaeologist, Keeper of Greek and Roman Antiquities at the British Museum from 1886 until 1925, and then appointed Director at the British School at Rome in 1928.

Spiridion (Family); 271

Leading Athenian family and acquaintances of the Bents.

Sponti, Mr; 196-99

Agent of the Austrian Lloyd Company and consular agent at Kaválla.

Stangen, Louis (1828–1876) and Carl (1833–1911); 176

German package-tour operators.

Strangford, Emily Anne (d. 1887); 256

Viscountess Strangford, widow of the 8th Viscount Strangford, was a celebrated traveller who trained as a nurse after her husband's death. She was champion of nursing reform, superintending a hospital for Turkish soldiers at Adrianople. She had died a year before Mabel's visit there.

Strauss, Oscar; 254

Subsequently US ambassador in Istanbul.

Swan, John; 6, 45

Scottish mine owner, with his brother Robert, resident of Andíparos.

Swan, Robert, M. W. (1858–1903); 6, 21-23, 31-35, 41-46, 59, 234, 322, 338, 343

The Swan bothers became close friends and future travelling companions of the Bents. Robert accompanied the Bents to Mashonaland (Zimbabwe) in 1891 and wrote a chapter in Bent's monograph (*The Ruined Cities of Mashonaland*, London, 1892). A Fellow of the Royal Geographical, Geological, and Chemical Societies, he became a respected scientist and traveller in his own right. He died in Malacca. The *Geographical Journal* of May 1904 includes a short obituary (p. 694).

Tauchnitz, Christian, Bernhard (1816–1895); 177

A friend of Charles Dickens, the publisher of a highly successful series of classics under the imprint 'The Collection of British and American Authors'. His Leipzig firm remained in business until 1943, at which time his list exceeded 5000 titles.

Tozer, Henry Fanshawe, Rev. (1829–1916); 130, 160

Historian, Fellow and Tutor of Exeter College, Oxford. He wrote several books on Greece, notably *The Islands of the Aegean* (Oxford, 1890), in which he recalls that 'We were lodged in a large disused warehouse belonging to Mr. Marc; and here we had the pleasure of meeting Mr. and Mrs. Theodore Bent, who occupied other rooms in the same building; they were engaged in excavating some of the tombs that lie outside the city walls.' This was the second of three extended trips (1874, 1886, 1889) that he was to make in the region;

his dragoman was the capable and admired Alexandros Anemoyannes.

Trikoupis (Family); 7, 177, 323
Charilaos Trikoupis (1832–1896) served as Greek prime minister on a number of occasions from 1875 to 1895. Mabel enjoyed the company of his family.

Tzerlendi (Tcherlendi, Tseylendi), Mr; 9, 21, 23-24, 45
Businessman and friend from Sýros.

Valaoritis (Family); 177, 271
The Bents knew several family members, including the poet and politician Aristotelis (1824–1879), as well as Pericles.

Venier (Family); 44
An old Venetian family, they were granted the island of Kíthera by Marco Sanudo a few years after the fall of Constantinople in 1204.

Venning, Rosamund, Miss; 186
Archaeologist. In the early lists of members of the Hellenic Society she gives her address as 'care of R. S. Poole Esq., British Museum, W. C.'

Verne, Jules (1828–1905); 103, 339
French novelist, whose story *The English at the North Pole* causes the Bents some confusion on Kárpathos.

Verviziotes, Kostandinos; 3, 186, 339
The Bents' dragoman on their first trip to Greece in 1882/3.

Villiers, Frederic (1851–1922); 130, 178
'Villiers of *The Graphic*', one of the great early war correspondents/illustrators. He was decorated twelve times and witnessed campaigns in Afghanistan, Tel-el-Kebir, and China. He was with Lord Kitchener at Omdurman. His many exploits are detailed in his autobiography, *Villiers: His Five Decades of Adventure* (London, 1921). *The Graphic* (founded 1869) was a highly successful British magazine in the same style as *The Sphere* and *The Illustrated London News*. It ceased publication in 1933.

Waldstein, Charles (1856–1927); 266, 273
Anglo-American archaeologist. He took British nationality in 1899 after six years as director of the Fitzwilliam Museum, Cambridge. In 1889 he moved to Athens as director of the American School of Classical Studies (until 1893). While in Athens he conducted several excavations, among them Plataea, Eretria, and the Heraeum near Argos.

White, William Arthur, Sir (1824–1891); 130, 134 n.4, 183, 225-26, 229 n.8, 255, 264, 276, 321
Born in Poland, a graduate of Trinity College, Cambridge, he was desended on his father's side from an Irish Catholic family. An immensely able diplomat, he served extensively in the Balkans, making himself

an expert on the region's complicated affairs. He was still ambassador at Istanbul when he died of influenza on a visit to Berlin. Theodore had occasion to petition him frequently regarding his business in Turkey and he seems to have been rather less than sympathetic to the archaeologist's cause. In 1867 he married Katherine Kendzior and the couple had a daughter, Lillian (later Lady Abinger), friend of Maud Gonne. See photograph on page 344.

Wilkie, Hales (b. 1837); 124
Major General and host of the Bents on Malta, Commander of the Infantry Brigade, he resided at Auberge D'Aragon, Strada Vescovo, Valletta, with his wife and daughter.

Wrench, Mr; 228, 229 n.8
Consular official, Istanbul.

GEORGE MILDMAY OF CORBETTS STYE ESSEX.

Elizabeth Mildmay M.
1. John Dare of Bentry Heath Essex d 1779
2. John Marmaduke Grafton of Cranbroke Ilford (he added the name of Dare in 1805)
3. Elizabeth Grafton Dare married Robert Westley Hall of Wyefield Essex (the added name of Dare in 1823).

John Hobkins died 1805

Henry — Francis — Mary — Agnes — Robert Westley M. Francis Lambart in 1839. — Emma married T.H. Bothamley — Elizabeth married Rev. T. Fussell

Henry Grafton — Dorothy married F. Whitwell

Olivia M. Rev. R. Johnson — Faneen M. Rev. Hobson — Ethel M Beauchamp Bagenal of Benekerry — Robert Westley M Caroline Newton of Mt. Leinster 1863.

Mabel M. Theodore Bent

Walter M Marion Seymour — Charles M Ethel Natalie — Violet M. Colonel Ffolliot — Prudence M W. Blackett.

Henry M Agatha Kekwick — Blanche M John Lee Warner.

William M K. Williams Wynne.

Henry d 1886. — Granville M. Audrey Lee-Warner — Maude — Ruth — Agatha married L. Gurney — 3 Children

Gillian married Cowan.

John — Robert — Mary

The early branches of the Hall-Dare family tree.

Grand Hôtel d'Angleterre à Syra   Ξενοδοχεῖον τῆς Ἀγγλίας ἐν Σύρῳ.

The Grand Hôtel D'Angleterre, Ermoúpoli (1905). Mabel's hotel of choice on Sýros.

Index of place names

A selected Index of place names and locations mentioned by Mabel Bent in these pages of her *Chronicles*. Apart from a few exceptions, this list is restricted to larger sites and centres, for example, names of Cycladic islands and not the villages within them.

As a rule, Mabel's spellings are given, but she was prone to vary (also in her use of accents) and the alternatives are not, generally, included here. Numbers in italics indicate a page reference to a map.

The Bents very much enjoyed the comforts of hotels after months under canvas or in humble shelters. A list of some of them is placed at the end of this Index.

Adalia; 156
Adana; 264, 274, 290ff., 320
Adrianople (Edirne); 51 n.69, 205, 227, 255, 353, 360
Agathonisi; 143, 158
Alexandria; 63, 65, 67, 79, 81, 322-23, 325, 328, 330, 339
Alexandroúpolis (Dedéaghatch); 205
Amorgos; 224 n.39, 252ff.
Anafi; 3, 68 n.2, 70, 129, 136 n.11, 169 n.55, 185 n.4, 226, 252 n.51, 322, 340-41
Anavartsa (Anasarba); 295ff., 303
Ancona; 3, 61, 266, 269-70
Andros; 3, 48, 52, 54
Ante Kythera (Cerigotto); 122
Antiparos; 2, 21-22, 34, 41ff., 115, 123 n.74, 153, 234
Aplotheka, Bay; 240ff.
Aráchova; 186
Argos; 186
Arkassa; 88-89
Astypalaia; 130, 150ff., 237, 250ff.

Athens; 3, 6ff., 15, 19 n.23, 39, 47 n.61, 58ff., 100, 129, 130, 175ff., 183, 185ff., 194, 264, 266-67 322ff., 340
Athos, Mount; 90, 182, 207
Avignon; 178
Azerbeijan; 288

Baghdad; 255
Basle; 3, 61, 322
Bebek; 135
Belgrade (Beograd); 184, 222
Benyza; 60
Berlin; 227, 260, 355
Beyrout; 290, 304
Black Sea, The; 256-57
Bologna; 3, 61
Bosphorus, The; 135, 228
Boudroum; 301, 305
Brindisi; 3, 61, 130, 177-78, 328
Broussa; 51, 226-27, 230ff., 255

Cairo; 59, 65, 67, 133, 322, 325
Calais; 3, 7, 65, 130, 178

Castelorizo (Kastellórizo); 245ff., 226-27
Cephalonia (Kephalenìa); 60
Chalki; 28-29, 72
Chalkis; 186
Chesmé (Çeşme); 8, 130, 174 n.63
Chios (Scio); 2, 8ff., 63ff., 100, 102, 127, 129-30, 132 n.3, 134, 136, 152, 170, 174-75, 329, 330 n.1, 339
Cilicia; 263ff., 322
Constantinople (see Istanbul);
Corfu (Kerkera); 3, 60, 81, 122, 195
Corinth; 3, 60 n. 88, 129, 177 n.68, 186
Corycian, Caves, The; 280 n. 23, 316, 319
Crete (Krete) (Kalé Liminas or the Fair Havens (Lasea); 7, 20, 65, 72, 117ff.
Cyprus; 112, 134, 248

Dacha; 237ff.
Damankoor; 67
Dardanelles, The; 136, 233, 346
Daphne; 330
Delphi; 182, 186
Despotico (Island); 46
Dover; 65, 269
Drama; 197, 218

Ermoupolis; 8, 14 n.15, 246 n.42, 339, 345, 351, 358
Etchmiatzin; 293-94
Euboea; 129, 177 n.68, 187

Flushing; 260
Folègandros (Pholegandros); 20, 41ff.
Fourni (Phourni/Phournoi); 46 n. 57, 148ff., 165ff., 171 n.58, 172, 199

Fujiyama, Mount; 299

Gaidáronisi; 144
Gibraltar; 124

Heybeli; 134 n.5
Hieropolis (Kastabala); 301ff.

Ialé (Yialí); 73
Ikaria (Nikaria); 130, 147ff., 157, 166, 171, 174
Ios (Nio); 38, 40ff., 86 n.38
Istanbul (Constantinople); 63, 130ff., 153, 177, 183, 201 n.33, 225ff., 244 n.39, 254ff., 300, 321
Isternia; 48

Jambazli; 304ff.
Jehan, River; 298ff.
Jerusalem; 9, 222 n.63, 294, 300, 305 n.51, 327

Kakova (Island); 245, 247
Kalamaka; 187ff.
Kalymnos (Kalimnos); 72 n.12, 130, 144ff., 235, 253
Kanapitza, Cape; 158
Karpathos; 63ff., 79ff., 136, 139, 154, 230, 253 n.53, 329
Kastaniá; 163-64
Kèa (Kèos, or Zeà); 36 n.46, 55ff., 177
Kenchrae; 60
Kerke, Mount (Sámos); 140, 166-67
Keuprülü; 219
Kimolos; 15ff.
Kizil Bagh; 279 n.22, 285, 288
Kizil Oren Koi; 279, 312
Knydos; 236
Komiakì; 30-31

Kondeïka; 162
Kos; 73, 75, 151, 235, 238, 252-53
Krakatoa; 6, 43 n.53
Krios, Cape; 233, 241, 244
Kythera (Cerigo); 65, 121ff.
Kythnos or Thermià; 54ff., 69

Lamas, River; 265, 277ff., 304, 308, 311, 319
Lemnos; 209
Leros; 67, 252 n.52, 253
Leviza; 245
Lipsós; 143-44
Lissa; 224, 245
London; 2, 3, 7, 65, 79 n.26, 87, 124, 130, 145, 183-84, 225-27, 259 n.68, 266, 276, 322, 326, 328
Loreto; 3, 61
Loryma; 224, 226, 241
Lucerne; 266, 269
Lycia; 68 n.2, 245 n.41, 247, 249 n.46, 224, 243
Lydais; 224, 243

Maïdan; 312-13, 315
Makri; 68 n.2, 70, 241
Malattiah; 132
Malea, Cape; 121, 129, 177 n.68
Malta; 9, 65, 123-24
Mara; 311ff.
Marash; 291
Marathrokambos; 163ff., 172
Marmara, Sea of; 230, 285
Marseilles; 65, 123 n.74, 130, 132, 177-78, 183, 185, 227-28, 266, 320, 325, 328
Matapan, Cape; 228
Mecca; 135
Mersina (Mersin); 264ff., 274ff., 288-89, 295, 304, 306, 315ff.

Messina; 123
Metéora; 181ff.
Milan; 266, 269, 322, 325
Milos (Melos); 15ff., 36 n.46, 73 n.14
Missis (Mopsuestia); 303
Modaniá; 230-31
Mykene (Mycenae); 1, 2, 52, 182, 186
Mykonos; 1, 46ff.
Myndos; 235
Myra; 226, 245ff.
Mytelene (Mytilene); 71-72, 102, 132, 136, 138, 159, 166 n.50, 175 n.66, 193 n.17

Nauplia; 186
Naxos; 3, 21ff., 32, 40 n.50, 45, 50, 253 n.53, 339, 340, 342
Nicea (Isnik, Nikaia); 227, 255, 257ff.
Niloufer, River; 232
Nish; 222
Nisiros (Níssyros); 65, 72ff., 73 n.13 & n.15, 76 n.18, 155, 252 n.50, 253

Odessa; 125, 259, 260
Olba (Khani Diwani); 261, 264-65, 274, 277, 280-81, 305 n.51
Ólymbos/Elymbos (Kárpathos); 82ff., 90ff., 108ff.
Olympos, Mount; 182, 194, 219
Ossa, Mount; 182, 194
Othíos; 84
Oura; 305-06

Paris; 7, 44, 124 n.76, 183-85, 222, 229, 266, 320, 328
Paros; 22 n.28, 23 n.29, 26, 43, 45, 47 n.64, 253 n.53
Patara; 249ff.
Patmos; 130, 143ff., 160, 166 n.50, 167, 170, 227, 253-54

Patras; 60, 266, 270
Perissa; 35-36
Pershendi; 315ff.
Persia; 133, 209, 263, 288 n.26, 293, 297-98, 300, 314
Phalerum; 330
Philippi; 184-85, 196ff.
Pireaus; 186, 273, 323, 325
Plovdiv (Philippopolis); 227, 254ff.
Pompeiopolis (Soli); 277, 304
Prinkips (Island); 134
Pyramus, River; 301

Rhodes; 63ff., 83, 85 n.35, 100, 102, 111, 154, 171, 225-26, 241 n.29, 250ff., 339
Rimini; 266, 269

Sabbatia; 284
Salonika (see Thessaloniki);
Samos; 2, 10, 39, 68 n.4, 69, 71, 98, 102, 127, 129-30, 133 n.44, 136ff., 166ff., 200 n.31, 329
Samothraki; 182, 184, 199 n. 30, 203, 205, 206 n.40, 209-10, 212, 214, 247 n.44
San Marino; 1, 7 n.3, 266, 269
Santorini; 23, 32, 34, 36 n.45, 129, 146 n.25, 177, 226
Sarageshed; 291
Saría (Island); 81, 90, 99, 110ff., 118
Savroon, River; 299
Scutari; 134, 217 n.55, 227, 254-55
Selefka (Seleucea); 264, 277, 279, 286
Serífos; 9ff.
Sigás; 241, 251
Sikies; 241
Sikinos; 16 n.20, 20, 41-42, 45, 85 n.34

Silakka; 55, 58
Simi (Symi); 72, 79, 111, 154, 236, 238, 240, 242
Siphnos; 10, 13, 14 n.15, 17-18, 148
Sírina (Island); 237 n.25, 250ff.
Sis (Kozan); 266, 291ff., 299
Skiathos; 184, 193
Skopelos; 193
Smyrna; 3, 67-68, 71, 100, 123, 130ff., 152, 172, 227ff., 254-55, 266, 273ff., 320, 329, 339, 342-43
Sombass, River; 299
Susa; 320
Syra (Syros); 3, 7ff., 20-21, 32, 46, 48, 50-51, 54, 65, 68n.2, 72, 90, 100, 102, 110, 111, 119ff., 123 n.74, 129-30, 132, 166ff., 176-77, 183, 185ff., 226-28, 233, 235 n.21, 244 n.39, 246 n.42, 248, 252, 254, 322, 339, 342-43

Tarsus; 265-66, 274 n.10, 276, 289ff., 304 n.48, 319
Tatoë; 59
Telos (Télos); 65, 72ff., 93, 102, 123 n.74, 153, 166 n.50, 237 n.25, 250 n.47, 252
Tenos (Ténos); 47ff., 54, 253, 343
Thasos; 181ff., 196ff., 206, 209ff., 216-17, 225, 228, 229 n.8, 230 n.10, 232, 233 n.16, 235 n.22, 244 n.39
Themina (Island); 171
Thera (see Santorini);
Therasia; 32, 35, 37
Thessaloniki; 90, 134 n.5, 182, 184, 187 n.9, 193ff., 212, 218, 220, 266, 273 n.7, 320
Thessaly; 60, 185, 187, 192 n.14, 193, 328
Trieste; 130, 133, 177

Trikkala; 187
Tyrins; 182, 347

Üsküb (Skopje); 184, 218ff.
Üzenjaburdj; 305-06

Venice; 130, 132, 177, 322, 353
Volos; 60, 182ff., 193 n.16

Volochyska; 260
Vostitza; 60
Vranya (Sophia); 184, 218ff.

Xeropotamos; 207

Zante; 60

Hotels patronized by the Bents in these *Chronicles*. The star indicates a particular favourite. The photograph on p. 356 is of the Hôtel d'Angleterre in Ermoúpolis, Sýros. The wonderful building still stands on Platía Miaoúli, however only the *magaziá* below are occupied.

Adrianople: Hôtel Gennik ('dirty and bad food'); 255
Athens: Hôtel des Etrangers*; 67, 176, 186, 267, 270
Athens: Hôtel de la Grande Bretagne; 330
Bologna: Hotel Brun; 61
Broussa: Hôtel d'Anatolie; 230
Corfu: Hotel St. George; 60
Istanbul: Hôtel de Byzance*; 130-32, 228, 229 n.8, 254 n.55, 255
Loreto: Albergo delle Panegemelli ('they charged enormously'); 61
Lucerne: Hôtel St. Gothard ('close to the station and very comfortable'); 269

Malta: Grand Hotel; 123
Milan: Hôtel d'Europe (in the Corso); 269
Milan: Hôtel Torino; 269
Plovdiv: Hotel Bulgaria; 256
Samos: Hotel Samos (not as good as the Kerketeos apparently); 159
Samos: Kerketeos Inn; 159
Smyrna: Hôtel d'Égypte; 136
Syros: Hotel Aigyptos; 233
Syros: Hôtel d'Angleterre*; 8, 54, 123, 233, 254, 356
Thessaloniki: Hotel Trikále; 194
Volos: Hôtel de France ('pretty'); 187
Vrania: Hôtel d'Europe ('an...untidy sort of place'); 222

Illustration credits

Frontispiece, page ii. Mabel Virginia Anna Bent. Reproduced from *Hearth and Home*, 2 November 1893. From the studio of H. S. Mendelssohn, South Kensington.

1, page v. Four of Mabel Bent's *Chronicle* covers, reproduced with the permission of The Hellenic Society and the Joint Library of the Hellenic and Roman Societies.

2, page xxii. James Theodore Bent. Photograph from the *Illustrated London News* 15th May 1897. Reference (shelfmark) N. 2288 b.6, reproduced by permission of Bodleian Library, University of Oxford.

3, page 66. Limestone female figure from Kárpathos in the Dodecanese. Neolithic, c. 4500–3200 BC. © Copyright the Trustees of The British Museum.

4, page 126. Theodore Bent's *samboúna* acquired in the Dodecanese in 1885 and now in the Pitt Rivers Museum, Oxford (acquisition number 1903.130.23.PR342Q). Photograph © Pitt Rivers Museum, University of Oxford.

5, page 128. Theodore Bent's *lýra* acquired in the Dodecanese in 1885 and now in the Pitt Rivers Museum, Oxford (acquisition number 1903.131.18.F151). Photograph © Pitt Rivers Museum, University of Oxford.

6, page 201. From Thássos, northern Greece, the Bents' 1887 find of Fl. Vibia Sabina (2nd century AD). After Gustave Mendel, *Catalogue des Sculptures Grecques, Romaines et Byzantines* (Constantinople, 1912, pp. 347–348, no.137. Istanbul Museum inventory number 375).

7, page 261. Three of Mabel's doodles. Reproduced with the permission of the Hellenic Society and the Joint Library of the Hellenic and Roman Societies.

8, page 272. Mandragora leaf in Mabel's 1890 *Chronicle*. Reproduced with the permission of the Hellenic Society and the Joint Library of the Hellenic and Roman Societies.

9, page 281. Paper print taken by Mabel and inserted in her 1890 *Chronicle*. Reproduced with the permission of the Hellenic Society and the Joint Library of the Hellenic and Roman Societies. Photograph © the Hellenic Society.

10, page 324. An example of Mabel's handwriting. Photograph from Mabel Bent's *Chronicle* of 1896. Reproduced with the permission of the Hellenic Society and the Joint Library of the Hellenic and Roman Societies.

11, page 326 Theodore and Mabel's grave and memorial (on the right) in the churchyard of St Mary's, Theydon Bois, Essex.

12, page 340. Around the camp in Socotra, 1897. Photograph from *Southern Arabia* by J. T. and M. V. A. Bent (1900). Reference (shelfmark) 20608 d.10, reproduced by permission of Bodleian Library, University of Oxford.

13, page 344. Sir William White, H. B. M. Ambassador, Istanbul. Reference (shelfmark) 2489 d.4, reproduced by permission of Bodleian Library, University of Oxford.

14. The Hall-Dare family tree. Kindly provided by a descendant of Mabel's sister, Ethel.

15, page 356. The Grand Hôtel D'Angleterre, Ermoúpoli, a reproduction based on a postcard of the time.

Images 1, 6, 7, 8, 10, 11, 14 and Frontispiece © Gerald Brisch, 2006.

Back cover. Mabel Bent. Taken from *The Ruined Cities of Mashonaland* by J. Theodore Bent, 1892.

Map credits

1. The Eastern Mediterranean. Drawn by Glyn Griffiths.
2. The Cyclades. Reproduced from J. Theodore Bent, *The Cyclades, or Life Among the Insular Greeks*, 1885.
3. The Dodecanese and Eastern Aegean. Drawn by Glyn Griffiths.
4. The Northern Aegean. Drawn by Glyn Griffiths.
5. 'Loryma', 'Lissae', and 'Lydae'. Theodore Bent's own details from a contemporary Admiralty Chart. Originally published in 'Inscriptions from Casarea, Lydae, Patara, Myra', *Journal of Hellenic Studies*, Vol. 10 (1889), pp. 46–85. Reproduced with the permission of the Hellenic Society.
6. 'Rough Cilicia'. Drawn by Glyn Griffiths.
7. 'Part of Cilicia Tracheia'. Theodore Bent's own map of their routes in the area. Originally published in *Proceedings of the Royal Geographical Society*, New Series, Vol. 12, No. 8, August 1890.

Maps 1, 3, 4, 6 © Gerald Brisch, 2006.

Quotations

The preliminary quotations are from *Aegean Greece* by Robert Liddell, published by Jonathan Cape in 1954, and *Zorba the Greek* by Nikos Kazantzakis, translated by Carl Wildman and published by Faber & Faber in 1961.

Extracts from letters of J. Theodore Bent

Unless otherwise stated, all extracts from the letters of J. Theodore Bent are from the Letter Books of the Department of Greek and Roman Antiquities at the British Museum, and are reproduced with the kind permission of the Trustees.